T0342089

The
DUTCH EAST
INDIA COMPANY
and the
ECONOMY OF BENGAL,
1630-1720

Om Prakash

Princeton University Press
Princeton, New Jersey

Publication of this book has been aided by a grant from
The Andrew W. Mellon Fund of Princeton University Press

This book has been composed in Linotron Goudy
Clothbound editions of Princeton University Press books
are printed on acid-free paper, and binding materials are
chosen for strength and durability. Paperbacks, while satisfactory
for personal collections, are not usually suitable for library rebinding

Printed in the United States of America
by Princeton University Press
Princeton, New Jersey

CONTENTS

CONTENTS

LIST OF TABLES

LIST OF FIGURES

ACKNOWLEDGMENTS

It is impossible to acknowledge all the kindness and help I have received while writing this book. Fellowships awarded by the University of Delhi, the Government of the Netherlands, and the British Council enabled me to collect the necessary materials at the *Algemeen Rijksarchief* in The Hague, and the India Office Records in London. Thanks are due to the staff of both these institutions. In particular, Mrs. M.A.P. Meilink-Roelofsz., whose knowledge of the archives of the Dutch Company is unique, provided much-needed help in reading and translating the Dutch documents.

Tapan Raychaudhuri initiated me into the fascinating world of intercontinental trade in the early modern period. Others who have generously helped through discussions and comments on earlier drafts include Dharma Kumar, Holden Furber, K. N. Chaudhuri, K. Sundaram, John F. Richards, Henry Rosovsky, and J. Krishnamurty.

The award of a fellowship by the Netherlands Institute of Advanced Study, Wassenaar, during 1982-1983 enabled me to put the manuscript into its present form. My thanks are due to the Director and the staff of the Institute for making my stay in Wassenaar extremely pleasant. Mrs. Pilar van Breda-Burgueño typed the manuscript for the press with great competence and patience.

Jan Heesterman and Henk Wesseling have contributed to the completion of this book in a variety of ways. I also gratefully acknowledge the assistance provided by Leonard Blussé, F. S. Gaastra, George Winius, and other members of the Centre for the History of European Expansion at Leiden University.

My wife, Santosh, has borne with this book with great patience and understanding for many years. I gratefully dedicate it to her.

July 1983

ABBREVIATIONS

B.	The Batavia Council of the Dutch Company
B.M.	British Museum
F.R.	Factory Records
G.M.	Generale Missive (General letter from the Batavia Council to the Board of Directors of the Dutch Company)
H.	The Hugli Council of the Dutch Company
K.	The Kasimbazar Council of the Dutch Company
K.A.	Koloniaal Archief
L.B.	Letter Book
N.A.	Not available
O.C.	Original Correspondence
P.	The Pipli Council of the Dutch Company
XVII	The Board of Directors of the Dutch Company
f. 20v	means folio 20 verso
f. 20-v	means folios 20 and 20 verso
P.B., etc.	means communication from the Pipli Council to the Batavia Council, etc.

THE DUTCH EAST INDIA COMPANY
AND THE ECONOMY OF BENGAL, 1630-1720

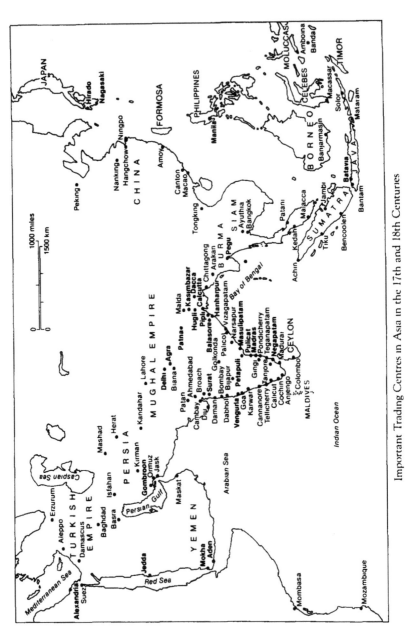

Important Trading Centres in Asia in the 17th and 18th Centuries

INTRODUCTION

The discovery of the Cape route to the East Indies and the growing import of American silver into Spain are generally recognized as the two major forces behind the rise of a premodern world economy in the sixteenth century. The implications of these developments for the economic history of Europe have long been recognized. But these were evidently of crucial importance for the economic history of Asia as well. Until the late eighteenth century, when much of Asia was brought under effective European domination, the growing involvement of a number of Asian countries in world trade had profound—and, with some exceptions, generally favourable—effects on their economies and societies. During the seventeenth and the eighteenth centuries, the principal agencies that engaged in large-scale trade from Asia were the so-called chartered monopoly companies operating from a number of countries in northwestern Europe. The most important among these were the Dutch and the English East India companies established in 1602 and 1600, respectively. The present study deals with the trading operations of the Dutch East India Company in Mughal Bengal between 1630 and 1720. A particular concern of the study is an analysis of the implications of the Company's trade for the economy of the region.

The Indian economy of the seventeenth century was predominantly agrarian in character. Though the absence of data for the period makes it impossible to assign precise values to the sectoral origin of output and the occupational distribution of the work force, there can be very little doubt that the agricultural sector accounted for an overwhelming proportion of both the total output and the total employment in the economy. By the same token, the bulk of the state revenue was provided by this very sector in the form of land revenue. Each of the other two sectors, the nonagricultural sector producing manufactured goods and the services sector (including the trade sector), was much smaller, though obviously no precise estimate of their respective sizes is possible. But although this conventional form of analyzing the structure of an economy has its uses, it would be misleading to measure the contribution of a particular sector to the efficient functioning of the economy by its size so defined. This was particularly so in the case of the Indian subcontinent with respect to both manufacturing and trade.

The most important constituent of the manufacturing sector in the

Indian economy was that producing textiles. These ranged from painted or printed coarse cottons to the most exquisite Dacca muslins and the celebrated gold embroideries of Gujarat. The production for the market was organised mainly on the basis of contracts between merchants and weavers, specifying the quantity to be supplied, the price, and the date of delivery. The contract system was a variant of the standard European putting-out system insofar as in the Indian system, raw materials were provided by the merchants only rarely. A highly developed and sophisticated credit organization contributed to the efficient working of this system. Merchants could raise short-term loans at remarkably low rates of interest and could transfer money from one place to another by using the *hundi*. The *sarrafs* who ran the credit and the banking structure were also indispensable to the working of the currency and the monetary system. The Mughal coinage system, with its uniform imperial standards of weights and measures, was imposed throughout the empire over dozens of local monetary systems. Centrally appointed functionaries of the imperial mints accepted bullion or coin from local *sarrafs* or other private individuals. The system of free minting ensured that the Mughal coins retained their high degree of fineness without any known debasement for nearly two centuries.

The organization of commercial manufacturing was also closely linked to the network of trade in and from the subcontinent. The pattern and extent of specialization achieved in manufacturing production was contingent upon the movement of large quantities of raw materials and intermediate goods as well as finished products, often over long distances. A well-known example of large-scale interregional trade in raw materials is that between the east and the west coasts. During the seventeenth century, the bulk of the raw silk needed for the flourishing silk textile industry of Gujarat was obtained from Bengal in exchange for, among other things, cotton needed by the extensive cotton textile industry in the latter region. Cotton was, of course, a relatively low-value bulk item, and a part of it was carried by the land and river route via Agra. Ordinarily, this would not have been done unless the cost of movement, including that by land where *rahdari* duties might be payable at a number of points, had been kept within reasonable limits. Indigo, also used in textile manufacturing, was another raw material extensively traded. The two major areas of production of this item in northern India were Biana near Agra and Sarkhej near Ahmedabad.

There was also a flourishing interregional trade in finished textiles as well as other consumption goods. The textiles that entered trade included both the superior varieties and the relatively coarse and inexpensive cotton ones. Foodgrains and other agricultural goods figured in this trade, as well.

The trade in foodgrains was occasioned by the existence of clear-cut food surplus and deficit areas. For example, Bengal was perennially a surplus area, whereas Gujarat often needed grains brought from outside the region. *Banjaras* moved foodgrains by land on pack oxen, and a substantial volume of trade in food was also carried on by river and by sea.

Partly because of its location at midpoint, but more because of its capacity to put on the market large quantities of relatively inexpensive and highly competitive manufactured goods, the Indian subcontinent played a central role in the structure of Asian trade. Equatorial Asia, rich in different types of vegetation, spices, and drugs, had traditionally been a major buyer of coarse cotton textiles manufactured in India, among other goods. Malacca, the most important port in the region, also handled a substantial amount of reexport trade from the area to countries such as China. In the south, the trading partners of India were Ceylon and the Maldive islands. The exports to these areas consisted primarily of coarse cotton cloth, foodgrains, and other provisions. In the west, a large amount of trade was carried on between the Indian ports, particularly those on the western coast, and the ports in the Red Sea and the Persian Gulf. Although foodgrains and other goods, including expensive silk and fine cotton textiles, did enter this trade, an overwhelming part of the total Indian exports to the region was accounted for by coarse cotton textiles intended for mass consumption. The principal goods imported from the Malay peninsula and the Indonesian archipelago were spices and drugs, elephants, and nonprecious metals such as tin. Ceylon supplied a variety of items such as cinnamon, areca nuts, conch shells, and elephants, but the only item imported from the Maldive islands were small seashells known as *cauris*. The Red Sea and the Persian Gulf paid for imports from India mainly in precious metals, and only to a small extent in goods such as rose water, dates, and horses. It might be noted that this pattern of trade would seem to establish the standing of India at this time as among the most advanced and cost-competitive "industrialized" countries in Asia. At the same time, it puts in grave doubt the validity of Jacob van Leur's characterization of Asian trade as consisting mainly of trade in luxury goods.

The composition of the Indian import bill held significant implications for the economy. For one thing, in view of the negligible domestic production of precious metals, the coinage systems in the subcontinent overwhelmingly depended for their supplies of these metals on the imports from the Red Sea and the Persian Gulf. The crucial importance of this particular dimension of foreign trade was fully appreciated by the Mughals, as is evident from the lower import duties imposed on these metals than on ordinary trade goods in Mughal ports such as Surat. Copper, the third coinage metal, was also imported in important quantities. Finally, the *cauris* imported from the Maldive islands traditionally constituted an important medium of exchange for small transactions in Bengal and other areas.

The silver imported into Surat and other ports on the west coast of India from Mocha and Gombroon was partly of European origin, and had travelled to these ports via the Levant in payment of Asian spices and other luxury goods. The Euro-Asian trade via the Levant was of great antiquity and substantial value. Goods of Chinese, Japanese, Malay, Indonesian, Indian, Ceylonese, and Middle Eastern origin were assembled through a series of commercial transactions involving a host of mercantile groups and communities. They were then carried either via the Red Sea to the Levantine port of Alexandria or via the Persian Gulf to Aleppo and Tripoli in Syria. The caravans carrying these goods across Egypt or across Iraq and the Syrian desert were obliged to pay a protection cost to the authorities controlling the particular route taken.

The discovery of the Cape route at the end of the fifteenth century provided a major potential institutional change in the structure of Euro-Asian trade. The import of goods into Europe via the Levant was now supplemented by direct shipments calling at Lisbon. Europe at this time was not in a position to offer price-competitive goods to Asia. The Asian spices and other luxury goods it wanted, therefore, had necessarily to be paid for mainly in precious metals. The funds provided by the Casa da India to the Estado da India initially consisted of West Indies and West African gold.[1] By the middle of the sixteenth century, however, official shipments of treasure from Lisbon were an important conduit for the New World silver pouring into India. The Portuguese also participated in intra-Asian trade and, beginning in 1560, supplemented the supplies of American and European silver with large amounts of Japanese silver. It must nevertheless be emphasized that the Portuguese kept the exploitation of opportunities opened up by the Cape route to a minimum. They concentrated their energies largely on the redistributive potential of their armed presence in the Eastern waters. Hence their attempts at redirecting Asian shipping and the continued prosperity of the trade via the Levant.

A proper integration of the Indian economy into the premodern world economy with its economic centre in northwestern Europe had to wait until the seventeenth century. It was only with the growing use of the Cape route that a multilateral trading pattern on a world scale became important, and the full implications of the American silver mines for the

---

[1] The Casa da India could broadly be defined as the department of the state in Lisbon in charge of foreign trade with Asia. The Estado da India (State of India) was governed from Goa by a royally appointed viceroy and his council and comprised all Portuguese possessions in Asia and the East Coast of Africa.

Indian and other Asian economies began to be realized. The agencies that carried this out were the chartered monopoly companies. The most important among these were the Dutch East India Company, chartered in 1602 (which for a number of decades was the largest trading company in the world), and the English East India Company, which had been founded two years earlier. The companies represented a major institutional innovation over their predecessors, the Portuguese, and concentrated on exploiting the Cape route. They successfully integrated the functions of a sovereign power with those of a business partnership: the new joint stock company represented a fusion of public and private interests within a technically superior organization. By adopting specific policies in relation to stocks, pricing, and the mode of the disposal of their goods, the companies, to use the terminology of Steensgaard, made impressive gains in the transparency and the predictability of the markets in which they operated.

Both the Dutch and the English companies started out in Asia looking mainly for pepper and other spices. But soon enough, India acquired a key role in the trading strategy of each of the two companies, though for different reasons. In the case of the Dutch Company, this role derived from its growing participation in intra-Asian trade. It has been estimated that by the mid-seventeenth century, nearly half of the Company's ships that left Europe remained in Asia to be used in intra-Asian trade. The principal goods the Company procured in India included finished manufacturing goods such as textiles of all varieties, intermediate goods such as reeled raw silk, and, to a smaller extent, raw materials such as saltpetre and indigo. Like other foreign traders, the Company adapted itself quite well to the requirements of the well-organized and reasonably efficient structure of production and procurement that it discovered in the areas of its operation in the subcontinent.

The purchasing power the Company brought to India consisted partly of goods of both European and Asian origin, but an overwhelming proportion consisted of silver and gold bullion and coins that were converted into the local currencies. This fact conditioned to a significant extent the nature and the magnitude of the impact of European trade on the Indian economy and society. Since it would seem that the companies' trade was not instrumental in depriving the Indian producers of alternative markets for their output, an increase in their own demand for textiles and other goods evidently involved a substantial expansion in domestic output. In the absence of labour-saving technological change, this, in turn, led to a rise in total employment. At a more general level, of course, the companies' trade had much wider ramifications for the economy and the society of the subcontinent.

Within the subcontinent, there were substantive regional variations in regard to the intensity of the European companies' involvement in trade and economic activity. From the last quarter of the seventeenth century on, when the "invasion" of the European market by the Indian textiles inaugurated a new phase in the history of Indo-European trade, Bengal was by far the most important theatre of company activity not only in the subcontinent but in the whole of Asia. At the turn of the eighteenth century, the Bengal region—roughly defined to include the territory now covered by Bangladesh and the Indian states of West Bengal, Bihar, and Orissa—provided nearly 40 percent of the average annual value in Asian goods the Dutch Company sent to Holland. More than half of the total value in textiles the Company exported from Asia was in the form of Bengal textiles. The picture was not too different in the case of the English East India Company. Indeed, writing in 1730, Alexander Hume, the chief of the Ostend Company, described the Dutch and the English as the greatest foreign traders in Bengal.

Long before the Bengal textiles and silks had become important for the European market, the Dutch Company had carried on an extensive trade in Bengal goods all over Asia. Among the northwestern Europeans, only the Dutch engaged in intra-Asian trade on a large scale. In addition to bringing in substantial profits, this trade supplemented the supplies of precious metals obtained from home by supplies obtained within Asia. And by the middle of the seventeenth century, Bengal had become the single most important supplier of cargo shipped from Batavia to Japan, which was by far the most important Asian source of precious metals.

The period over which the Dutch Company's trade in Bengal is discussed in the present study extends from the early 1630s, when a trading post was first established in the region, to about 1720. At the close of the period, the Company was still ahead of its English rival in terms of the total volume of trade carried on in the region, but if we consider only the value of the trade carried on with Europe, the English had surpassed the Dutch. Since the English Company's trade was among the most vital factors affecting the Dutch Company's fortunes as well as its trading strategy, the broad outlines of the English trade in the region have also been indicated. The scheme of chapters adopted in the study reflects its dual concern. While on the one hand it attempts an analysis of the Dutch Company's trade in the Bengal region in the wider framework of its trading strategy in Asia and Europe, on the other it examines the implications of the integration of Bengal's economy into the premodern world economy with special reference to the inflow of precious metals into the region. The reader will thus find himself shuffled back and forth between the Company and the economy of Bengal.

· 1 ·

THE COMPANY IN ASIAN TRADE

The Dutch East India Company was founded in 1602 by a charter granted by the States-General, the national administrative body of the Dutch Republic.[1] During the last quarter of the sixteenth century—and particularly since the closure, in 1585, of Seville and Lisbon to vessels from Holland—the Dutch had been actively engaged in trying to reach the Asian sources of spices and other luxury goods and contest the Portuguese monopoly of the Cape route.[2] In April 1595, the Amsterdam-based "Company of Far Lands" (Compagnie van Verre), which was the first among the so-called "precompanies' (voorcompagnieën) and which had managed to raise a capital of f. 290,000, sent out four ships to the East Indies under the command of Cornelis de Houtman. One of the ships was lost, but the remaining three came back in August 1597 with a cargo of pepper, nutmeg, and mace. Another voyage was scheduled for the spring of the following year, even though the Company lamented that it had suffered a net loss on the first voyage. In the meantime, a number of new companies had been organized for trade with the East Indies. One of these was in Amsterdam, two in Zeeland, and another two in Rotterdam. The two Amsterdam companies were merged in 1598 and came to be known as the "Old Company." It was on the account of this company that eight vessels were sent out to the East in the spring of 1598. The profit of the voyage was estimated at around 400 percent.[3] By 1600, yet another four companies had been formed in the various provinces of the Netherlands. The inevitable result was an increase in the cost price of the pepper and other spices and a decline in their sale prices. To all those who realised the enormous potential of the East India trade, it was imperative that some-

---

[1] The Company was called "De Verenigde Oost-Indische Compagnie" (The United East India Company). In the literature, it is often referred to as the V.O.C.

[2] The Dutch actually devised a number of ways to circumvent the ban on the trade with Seville and Lisbon. The notaries in Amsterdam were adept at counterfeiting for Dutch skippers the passports issued by the port authorities of Hamburg, Lübeck, and Danzig. Dutch goods were also transported in ships flying foreign colours. Nevertheless, the volume of trade did suffer considerably, and for the merchants whose ships and/or goods were confiscated, the losses were catastrophic. J. H. Kernkamp, De Handel op den Vijand, 1572-1609, I (Utrecht, 1931), 201-202; Violet Barbour, Capitalism in Amsterdam in the Seventeenth Century (Baltimore, 1950), p. 15; G. Masselman, The Cradle of Colonialism (New Haven, 1963), p. 38.

[3] C. R. Boxer, The Dutch Seaborne Empire (New York, 1965), p. 23.

thing be done to curb the cutthroat competition among the various companies.

The initiative was taken by the Old Company which, on the strength of being the pioneer in the East India trade and the most important participant in it, petitioned the States of Holland in 1601 for a monopoly of all trade east of the Cape of Good Hope for a period of twenty-five years. The request was turned down, but it was instrumental in setting in motion other moves to eliminate competition among the various companies. The States-General was interested in having the various companies come together, not only because a financially strong United Company would be equipped to conduct the East India trade more profitably but also because it would be in a stronger position to face the combined opposition of the Portuguese and the Spaniards in the East Indies. Indeed, the East India Company could then be used as an instrument in the war against Spain and Portugal. Mainly through the mediatory efforts of Johan van Oldenbarnevelt, the various units agreed to come together, and the United East India Company was chartered on March 20, 1602. The Company was given the sole right for a period of twenty-one years to sail east of the Cape of Good Hope and west through the Strait of Magellan.[4]

Earlier, on December 31, 1600, the English East India Company had received a charter from the Crown. The two national monopoly companies introduced far-reaching changes in the organisation and structure of the seaborne trade between Europe and Asia. For the first time, trade with Asia was regarded as a purely economic enterprise with profit and loss as the ultimate measure of success or failure—and not, as in the case of the Portuguese, simply an activity engaged in by a "department of the State" without obligation to earn a profit. Although the Dutch East India Company was not as independent of the political authorities at home as was its English counterpart, and although there was often extensive cooperation between the Company and the Admiralty in the matter of ships and so on, nevertheless "there was never at any time a question of confusing the Company's and the Republic's separate economies."[5]

Although the organisational structure of the Dutch East India Company is well known, one or two key features bear repetition.[6] For one thing, even though the individual chambers of the Company enjoyed a certain

---

[4] Oldenbarnevelt was the Pensionary (chief advocate or representative) of the State of Holland. Masselman, *Cradle of Colonialism*, p. 149.

[5] Niels Steensgaard, *The Asian Trade Revolution of the Seventeenth Century* (Chicago, 1974), p. 136.

[6] See for example Kristof Glamann, *Dutch-Asiatic Trade 1620-1740* (Copenhagen/The Hague, 1958); Steensgaard, *Asian Trade Revolution*; and F. S. Gaastra, *De Geschiedenis van de VOC* (Bussum, 1982).

measure of autonomy insofar as they equipped—and received—their respective ships on their individual accounts, the real decision-making authority in all respects was centralised in the Board of Directors, known as the *Heeren XVII* (seventeen Gentlemen). Again, though the charter provided that a stockholder might withdraw his stock at the close of each decade, this clause was withdrawn even before the first decade had closed. Shares could be sold but no longer withdrawn, so that a permanent joint stock was guaranteed. Further, the procedure of election of the Directors ensured that they were not responsible to the stockholders. As Steensgaard has put it, "In relation to VOC the stockholder was like the owner of a government bond: he could dispose of his claim at whatever price he could obtain, but he could no more influence the Company's policy than the owner of the bond can influence the State's policy."[7] It might also be noted that, given the high price of the limited amount of land available and the heavy rate of land taxation, the favoured forms of investment in the Netherlands were shares in ships or mills and in fishing or trading voyages. It was, therefore, not very difficult to raise capital even under relatively adverse stockholding conditions.

THE ROLE OF BULLION

During the seventeenth and eighteenth centuries, Euro-Asian trade was characterized by a chronically and significantly unfavourable balance of trade for Europe. This necessitated the movement of large quantities of precious metals to Asia to settle the accounts. Thus, of the total value of cargo sent out by the Dutch Company to the East Indies in 1615, goods accounted for only 6 percent, the remainder being in the form of precious metals. Eight years earlier, the only merchandise exported by the Company was some iron and lead, the value of which was too small to be mentioned in the relevant resolution of the Directors.[8] Even in the mid-seventeenth century, when significant amounts of precious metals were already being obtained within Asia, the proportion of bullion in the total export bill to the East Indies continued to be larger than that of goods. Thus, over the seven years 1651 to 1657, goods accounted for only 45 percent of the total of bullion and commercial goods received at Batavia.[9] Again, be-

---

[7] Steensgaard, *Asian Trade Revolution*, p. 129.

[8] M.A.P. Meilink-Roelofsz., *Asian Trade and European Influence in the Indonesian Archipelago between 1500 and about 1630* (The Hague, 1962), pp. 377-378 n. 149.

[9] Victuals and equipment have not been included in this calculation. Calculated from W. Ph. Coolhaas, ed., *Generale Missiven van Gouverneurs-Generaal en Raden aan Heren XVII der Verenigde Oost-Indische Compagnie* (The Hague, 1964, 1968), II, 481, 586, 744, 817; III, 78, 145, 208.

tween 1700 and 1750, commercial goods, together with provisions, equipment, ammunition, and so on accounted for only about a third of the
total exports from Holland to Batavia.[10] The picture was not very different
in the case of the English East India Company.[11] It should be obvious
that if Europe had not been able to send out increasing quantities of
bullion to Asia through this period, the trade between the two continents
would not have attained such significant proportions.

The crucial role of bullion in the Euro-Asian trade of the seventeenth
and the eighteenth century has sometimes been ascribed to the rigidity
of consumer tastes in the East, which rendered the Asian markets for
European goods extremely small and static. Alternatively, it has been
suggested that the absorption of precious metals by India or China reflected
the hoarding habits in these societies.[12] But perhaps a more convincing
explanation of this phenomenon is the inability of Europe to supply Western products at prices that would generate a large enough demand for
them to provide the necessary revenue for the purchase of the Asian goods.
Europe at this time had an undoubted overall superiority over Asia in the
field of scientific and technological knowledge, but as yet did not have
the cost advantage that came with the Industrial Revolution in the nineteenth century. This put the Indian producers, with their considerably
lower labour costs and a much longer history of sophisticated skills in
handicrafts of various kinds, in a position of advantage over their European
counterparts in the production of a variety of manufactured goods. This
is reflected in a wide disparity in the price level in the two continents,
commented upon by several Europeans in the eighteenth century. The
only major item Europe was in a position to provide to Asia was precious
metals. This dimension of Euro-Asian trade conditioned to a large extent
the nature of the impact of this trade on the Asian economies.

Since Europe imported a large quantity of silver from the New World
during the sixteenth and early seventeenth centuries, it possessed a stock
of precious metals necessary for a steady growth in trade with Asia. And
within Europe, Holland was in a particularly happy position in this regard.
It is remarkable that even though the Dutch were not permitted to trade
in Spanish ports from 1585 onward and, in any case, there was a general

[10] Ivo Schöffer and F. S. Gaastra, "The Import of Bullion and Coin into Asia by the
Dutch East India Company in the Seventeenth and Eighteenth Centuries" in Maurice
Aymard, ed., *Dutch Capitalism and World Capitalism* (Cambridge, 1982), pp. 222-223.

[11] K. N. Chaudhuri's figures show that over the period 1660 to 1760, the average proportion
of treasure to total English exports to the East Indies was 74.8 percent. Calculated from *The
Trading World of Asia and the English East India Company, 1660-1760* (Cambridge, 1978),
Appendix 5, Table C.4, p. 512.

[12] For example, see Rudolph C. Blitz, "Mercantilist Policies and the Pattern of World
Trade, 1500-1750," *Journal of Economic History*, 27 (1967), 39-55.

prohibition on the export of precious metals from Spain, a substantial proportion of the South American silver coming to Spain did eventually find its way to Amsterdam, mainly via Hamburg. This made the Dutch the undoubted masters of the European bullion trade and Amsterdam the leading world centre of the trade in precious metals.[13] It is an indication of the international standing of this city as a market for precious metals that the English East India Company obtained a large part of its requirements of these metals in Amsterdam.

Easy access to precious metals was a necessary but not a sufficient condition for their export to the East, for active mercantilist prejudice against the export of these metals could be a source of anxiety to the companies. Given the leading position of Amsterdam as a centre for trade in precious metals, however, this prejudice was far less vocal in Holland than it was in England. The only restriction that the Dutch Company had to contend with in the early stages of its trade was the prohibition against exporting precious metals in the form of bullion. In 1647, the States-General withdrew even this restriction, provided one-third of the amount exported was surrendered to one of the state mints or the Amsterdam Exchange Bank. In any case, practically throughout our period the export of foreign coins and of Dutch coins specifically intended for export—the so-called *negotie-penningen*—was freely allowed.[14]

THE SPICE MONOPOLY

The Dutch realised from the very beginning that if the spice trade was to continue to be highly profitable, they must strive to gain control of both the total amount reaching Europe and the cost price in the Indies.[15] The 1602 merger of the precompanies into the United Company was only the

[13] J. G. van Dillen, "Amsterdam als Wereldmarkt der Edele Metalen in de 17de en 18de Eeuw," *De Economist*, 72 (1923), 541-550.

[14] It is, of course, true that in November 1701, when in the context of the impending War of Spanish Succession it was feared that the flow of American bullion would be cut off, the export of both bullion and the *negotie-penningen* was banned. However, in June 1702, the College of Admiralty was authorized to permit individual companies and merchants to export the *negotie-penningen* after examining the merits of each case. In this milder form, the restriction continued for several years, but had effectively lapsed long before the War of Spanish Succession came to an end in 1713 (van Dillen, "Amsterdam als Wereldmarkt," pp. 588-590, 594-596).

[15] The region producing the spices was designated as the "spice islands." These were Amboina, off the southern coast of Ceram; the Banda group in the Banda sea, south of Ceram; and Ternate and Tidore much farther to the north, off the coast of the large island of Halmahera. Amboina was the chief source of cloves; the others were the chief source of nutmeg and its derivative, mace. The Dutch Company's policy was to confine the production of cloves, nutmeg, and mace to Amboina and the Banda group, where local authority was weakest. Pepper, another major spice, was grown over a much wider area in the archipelago.

first step in this direction. The ultimate aim was to eliminate the rivals in this trade—the Portuguese, the English, and the Asian merchants. Between 1605 and 1609, the Company managed to wrest from the authorities in Amboina and Ternate agreements obliging the natives to supply their cloves exclusively to the Dutch. A similar agreement was concluded in 1605 with the Banda group of islands regarding the procurement of nutmeg and mace. The latter agreement was renewed after the conquest of the islands by the Company in 1621.[16] Although the agreement with the English East India Company in 1619 obliged the Dutch to permit the former to buy one-third of the total amount of spices available in the archipelago, the English found the accompanying obligation to bear one-third of the cost of Dutch garrisons in the area to be crippling, and as early as 1622, they were planning to withdraw from the spice trade.[17]

By the early 1620s then, the Dutch had acquired effective monopsony rights in nutmeg and mace. The case of cloves was somewhat more complex. There was a large-scale smuggling trade carried on between the producing areas and Macassar, enabling the English, among others, to obtain large quantities of this spice. Though from 1643 onward the Company had managed to reduce such smuggling, it was only after the conquest of Macassar in 1667 that the Dutch fully controlled the trade in cloves.[18] As for pepper—which was a substantially more important item of investment in the Indies than all the other spices put together—in spite of the availability of formal monopsony rights in a number of states in the region, the Company never acquired effective monopsony rights.[19] Pepper was,

---

[16] See the relevant contracts in J. E. Heeres, ed., *Corpus Diplomaticum Neerlando-Indicum*, I (The Hague, 1907), 31-33, 36-41, 50-53, 66-69, 160-161.

[17] D. K. Basset, "The Amboyna Massacre of 1623," *Journal of Southeast Asian History*, 1:2 (1960), 4-5.

[18] Ibid., pp. 8-12. The Dutch had in 1663 driven the Spaniards out of Ternate, which was the only other important source of cloves.

[19] In the mid-seventeenth century, pepper accounted for 50 percent of the total Dutch investment in the East, as against a mere 18 percent for the other spices. Even at the end of the century, the investment in pepper nearly equalled that in other spices. The ruler of Palembang conferred monopsony rights in pepper on the Company in 1642 and renewed them in 1662. The Achinese dominions of Tiku, Priaman, and Indrapoera in western Sumatra did so in 1649. The ruler of Indragiri signed a similar agreement in October 1664, but the Company had to wait until August 1681 before it succeeded in wresting monopsonistic rights in pepper from the ruler of Jambi, one of the major pepper-growing districts of Sumatra. The July 1643 agreement with Jambi had conferred exclusive buying rights in pepper jointly on the Dutch and the English, providing to the latter legal access to a major source of this spice. The English continued trading at Jambi until 1679, when their factory was destroyed in a Malay attack. The English also obtained substantial quantities of pepper at Benkulen, where it was smuggled in by native traders from Jambi and Palembang. In 1736, the *Heeren* XVII recorded that the English were importing as much pepper into Europe annually as was brought into Batavia from all the Dutch-controlled pepper districts in the archipelago.

it is true, more abundant and the cost price probably lower for the Dutch than for the English East India Company. But the Dutch Company had to incur substantial costs in maintaining the forts and the garrisons necessary to enforce its privileges in buying spices. It is, therefore, important that the limitations of the term "spice monopoly/monopsony" used in this study be realised.

The control exercised by the Company on the spice islands enabled it to procure spices at unusually low prices. This ensured a very high rate of gross profit, often exceeding 1,000 percent.[20] Before the advent of the Dutch, the spice growers had been used to exchanging their wares for Indian cloth, rice, and other necessities brought to them by Indian and other Asian merchants as well as the Portuguese. The Company could have obtained the Indian textiles—by far the most important medium of exchange in the spice islands—at Achin and other places in the archipelago, but its acute business instinct drove it to their source, the Coromandel coast, where a factory was established at Petapuli in 1606, and Gujarat, where regular trade was started around 1618 at the port of Surat. Thus began the Company's participation in intra-Asian trade, which in course of time assumed important proportions and became an object of as much concern as the Euro-Asian trade itself. The involvement of the Company in intra-Asian trade was facilitated by the spice monopsony available to it. Spices were in demand all over Asia, and provided the Company with an important source of purchasing power in areas where it sought trade, particularly because with its monopoly power, the Company was able to keep the selling prices at a fairly high level.[21]

THE INTRA-ASIAN TRADE

The high profitability and the crucial importance of the intra-Asian trade was evident to the Company soon after it first became involved in it. As

---

Glamann, *Dutch-Asiatic Trade*, pp. 13, 89-90; *Corpus-Diplomaticum*, I, 380-386, 407-412, 528-531; II, 209-212, 280-285, 285-287, 291-297.

[20] Ordinarily, the purchase price was specified in the contracts themselves, and was invariably kept at a very low level. Even when this was not the case, the price paid was lower than the one that obtained during the Portuguese period. Thus, in Ceram, the price paid for cloves was 50 to 60 rials per *bahar*, whereas earlier the price had been between 70 to 80 rials per *bahar* (Meilink Roelofsz., *Asian Trade*, p. 214). See also Glamann, *Dutch-Asiatic Trade*, p. 93.

[21] Spices almost invariably constituted an important item sold by the Company in its various Asian factories. According to Meilink-Roelofsz., the "sales of spices formed the basis of Company expansion in other spheres of trade in Asia and were usually decisive when it was a question of continuing with a certain line of business or dropping it." In 1667, the gross profit on spices sold in Bengal was: cloves 710%, broken nutmeg 1,443%, and mace 903% (Meilink-Roelofsz., *Asian Trade*, p. 227; H. XVII.5.9.1667, K.A. 1156, f. 871).

early as 1612, Hendrik Brouwer, a future governor-general of the East Indies, described the Coromandel coast as the "left arm of the Moluccas and the surrounding islands because without textiles that come from there [the Coromandel coast], the trade in the Moluccas will be dead."[22] In his discourse dated January 1, 1614, Director-General Coen emphasized the strategic significance of the intra-Asian trade.[23] Four years later, Coen— now Governor-General—visualised a situation in which the entire Euro-Asian trade of the Company could eventually be financed out of the profits of its intra-Asian trade.[24] In 1619, Coen sent to the Directors a blueprint of the Company's intra-Asian trade: cloth from Gujarat (obtained against spices, other goods, and rials) to be exchanged against pepper and gold on the coast of Sumatra; cloth from Coromandel (obtained against spices, Chinese goods and gold, and rials) to be exchanged against pepper at Bantam; sandalwood, pepper, and rials to be exchanged against Chinese gold and goods, the latter also being used in exchange for silver from Japan. Finally, rials of eight could be obtained at Arabia against spices and other sundry items. Since the Company already had spices available to it, all that was needed to turn this blueprint into reality was an adequate number of ships and enough capital for some time to establish the intra-Asian trade—"a little water to prime the pump."[25] The Company already had a permanently circulating capital of between f. 2.5 and f. 3.5 million in the East Indies at this time, but Coen wanted more.

The Directors, however, would not have found it easy to meet Coen's demands. Though there were no serious problems with regard to the export of precious metals from Holland, there was a limit to the capital that the Directors were in a position to send to the East Indies. Whereas the total share capital of the Company was less than f. 6.5 million, its total debts in 1623 stood at f. 8 million. Although merchants of good standing could obtain credit in Amsterdam at between 3 and 4.5 percent, the Dutch East India Company in its early years had to pay as much as 6.25 percent.[26]

---

[22] *Corpus-Diplomaticum*, I, 154. The term Moluccas usually applied only to the spice islands to the north of Amboina but was sometimes used to describe the islands as a whole.

[23] H. T. Colenbrander, ed., *Jan Pietersz. Coen, Bescheiden Omtrent Zijn Bedrijf in Indie*, vol. 6 (The Hague, 1934), 451.

[24] "I am of the opinion that matters can be brought to a point that you will not be obliged to send any money whatever from Holland" (letter from Governor-General Coen to the Directors dated June 24, 1618. *Jan Pietersz. Coen*, I [The Hague, 1919], 348).

[25] Letter from Coen to the Directors, August 5, 1619, ibid., pp. 485-486.

[26] In their letter of August 9, 1624, to Pieter van den Broecke at Surat, Governor-General Pieter Carpentier and the Batavia Council wrote that of the total debt of f. 8 million, the Directors were trying to repay f. 4.5 million. Therefore, no more than two ships were sent by them to Batavia that year "with not a single rëal in cash" (K.A. 994, f. 297vo; Glamann, *Dutch-Asiatic Trade*, p. 34); Barbour, *Capitalism in Amsterdam*, p. 86.

Resources for the development of intra-Asian trade, therefore, had to be found partly within Asia.

In addition to pepper and other spices, the key commodity in Coen's blueprint was Indian textiles, which had to be paid for in Coromandel mainly in gold and in Surat mainly in silver. It was, therefore, imperative to establish trade relations with Asian sources of precious metals—whether they be themselves producers of these metals or obtain them through trade. Such places were China and, to a smaller extent, the west coast of Sumatra for gold, and Japan and Arabia for silver. The small quantity of gold available at Sumatra was of local produce, and the Company was already entrenched there. Arabia received its supply of silver mainly from Europe via the Levant. As early as 1616, attempts were made to establish trade relations with Mocha. Among other goods, Indonesian spices were sent there even at the risk of their being smuggled into Europe via the Levant, compromising the Company's European monopoly.[27] But the Company withdrew from Mocha in 1624, following problems arising out of the seizure of two ships belonging to the port of Dabhol on the west coast of India. The other major Asian sources of precious metals (besides the Philippines, which obtained South American silver from Acapulco but which was under the control of the Spaniards and, therefore, out of the Company's reach) were Japan and China.

A factory was established at Hirado in southwestern Japan in 1609. Although items such as fine quality cotton textiles, spices, sugar, lead, quicksilver, and musk could be sold in Japan, the principal items in demand there during the early period of Dutch trade were Chinese silk, silk textiles, and other Chinese goods.[28] The Dutch initially tried to obtain Chinese wares from ports in the China sea and the Malay peninsula where Chinese junks came in large numbers to trade. The establishment of trade relations with Patani and Siam, and later with Cambodia, Annam, and Tonkin was partly in the quest of Chinese goods. But success was limited, and attempts were made almost from the very beginning of trading relations with Japan to establish a trading post, by force if necessary, on the coast of China or its immediate vicinity. The efforts to blockade Chinese trade with Manila were followed by an attack on Macao in 1622 and the subsequent occupation of the Pescadores. But soon thereafter, in 1624, the Dutch were persuaded to move to Taiwan in return for an informal agreement that Chinese merchants would be allowed to go there to trade with

[27] Meilink-Roelofsz., Asian Trade, p. 224.

[28] Oskar Nachod, Die Beziehungen der Niederländischen Ostindischen Kompagnie zu Japan im Siebzehnten Jahrhundert (Leipzig, 1897), p. 130.

them.[29] The importance that the Company attached to the potential trade with China at this time is evident from the fact that large stocks of ready money were kept at Batavia "for the China trade," while important factories such as the ones on the Coromandel coast faced acute shortages of funds.[30] The principal commodities procured by the Company in Taiwan were, of course, Chinese silk and silk textiles for the Japanese market. A part of the silver obtained from Japan was then invested not only in getting the next round of silk in Taiwan but also gold. As indicated earlier, the yellow metal was needed for the crucial Coromandel trade. Until its capture in 1662 by the forces of Cheng Cheng-kung ("Coxinga" of the European accounts), Taiwan remained an important source of gold for the Company. All through this period, the Company obtained gold in Taiwan in exchange for Japanese silver, rather than procuring it directly in Japan. This was because until 1637, given the different gold/silver parity in the two countries, it was more profitable to buy gold in Taiwan. And from 1641 onward, the export of gold from Japan was banned.[31] However, when Japan's "era of seclusion" began in 1639, the Dutch were the only Europeans permitted to continue trading in the country.

The Company obtained trading rights in Persia in 1623. Initially, the most important item procured there was raw silk, but from the middle of the seventeenth century, the Company engaged in a thriving smuggling trade in Persian silver coins called *abbasies* and in "Moorish" ducats.[32] In Ceylon—the source of cinnamon—the Company obtained important commercial privileges practically amounting to a monopoly of the island's trade in return for a promise of armed assistance against the Portuguese.[33] The Company's quest for pepper took it to Malabar on the southwest coast of India. The first contacts were made as early as 1604, though a regular factory was not established there until 1647.[34]

Thus in the first few decades of its existence, the Dutch East India

---

[29] John E. Wills, Jr., *Pepper, Guns and Parleys: The Dutch East India Company and China, 1662-1681* (Cambridge, Mass., 1974), pp. 21-22.

[30] See, for example, letters from Governor-General Carpentier to van Uffelen at Masulipatam dated August 18, 1623, K.A. 992, ff. 131-vo; September 21, 1623, K.A. 992, ff. 137-vo; and March 16, 1624, K.A. 994, f. 208.

[31] The parity in Japan was 1:12, and in China 1:8 in the 1620s, 1:10 in 1635, and about 1:13 from 1637 onward. A. Kobata, "The Production and Uses of Gold and Silver in 16th and 17th century Japan," *Economic History Review*, second series, 18 (1965), 254; Nachod, *Niederländischen Ostindischen Kompagnie*, pp. 136-137, 357, and appendix 63D, p. cci.

[32] Glamann, *Dutch-Asiatic Trade*, p. 120.

[33] *Corpus-Diplomaticum*, I, 95-99; K. W. Goonewardena, *The Foundation of Dutch Power in Ceylon, 1638-1658* (Amsterdam, 1958), pp. 7-8.

[34] *Corpus-Diplomaticum*, I, 30-31; J. van Lohuizen, *The Dutch East India Company and Mysore* (The Hague, 1961), p. 11.

Company had succeeded in carving out a significant role for itself in both the intra-Asian and the Euro-Asian trade. Its intra-Asian trading network stretched from Arabia at one end to Japan at the other. At the risk of oversimplification, the most important links in this complex multilateral pattern of trade in the early 1630s might be summarized as follows. The European precious metals, the Japanese silver obtained against Chinese silk and other goods, and the gold obtained at Taiwan mainly against Japanese silver and Indonesian pepper were invested primarily in Indian textiles. These textiles were exchanged largely for Indonesian pepper and other spices, but also sent to Europe and various Asian factories. The bulk of the pepper and other spices was exported to Europe, but a certain amount was used for investment in India, Persia, Taiwan, and Japan. Raw silk from Persia—obtained against pepper, other spices, sugar, and Indian textiles—and from China also found its way to Europe. Needless to say, this multilateral pattern of trade involved forging new links among the various Asian markets and between the markets of Asia and Europe.[35]

This rapid survey of the growth of Dutch trade in Asia in the early part of the seventeenth century suggests that the two key factors that enabled the Dutch to achieve their enviable position were the near-monopsony privileges in spices, and, more importantly, the exclusive trade with Japan. These two factors explain at least partly the marked edge that the Dutch East India Company had over its English rival in intra-Asian trade (and to a smaller extent in the Euro-Asian trade) through the greater part of the seventeenth century. By the same token, the decline in the crucial role of these two factors in the last two decades or so of the seventeenth century helps to explain the decline in the Dutch intra-Asian trade and the increasing loss of ground in India to the English in the Euro-Asian trade.

The spice monopsony—notwithstanding the limitations it was subject to—entailed an extraordinarily high rate of return on spices sold in Europe, besides providing the Company with a highly remunerative staple item of trade that considerably facilitated the expansion of its intra-Asian trade. But with the steep decline in the relative significance of spices in the

[35] To take only one example of new links among the various Asian markets, Bengal raw silk and silk textiles appear to have been introduced in the Japanese market for the first time by the Dutch in the 1630s and the 1640s. There is no evidence that these items formed part of the Portuguese cargoes to Japan. An examination of the cargo list of the annual great ship of Amacon and of the list of goods imported by the Portuguese into Macao from India did not reveal the presence of these items. (See C. R. Boxer, *The Great Ship of Amacon, Annals of Macao and the Old Japan Trade, 1555-1640* [Lisbon, 1959], pp. 179-183.) Similarly, there is no evidence to suggest that the Japanese and other Asian merchants operating between Japan and the Indonesian archipelago dealt in these items.

exports to Europe in the latter part of the seventeenth century, the effect of the spice monopsony on Euro-Asian trade was correspondingly reduced.[36]

The pattern of Dutch participation in intra-Asian trade was determined in part by the requirements of the trade with Japan, which was by far the most important Asian source of precious metals for the Company during the seventeenth century.[37] Table 1.1 illustrates the magnitudes involved. As Glamann has pointed out, in certain years the precious metals procured in Japan were of greater value than those received at Batavia from Holland. In 1651, presumably in view of the great success achieved in the Japan trade, the Directors even entertained hopes of getting, at a future date, supplies of precious metals from the East Indies in addition, of course, to the spices and other goods for which they would have to send out no

TABLE 1.1

The Dutch East India Company's Exports of Silver and
Gold from Japan, 1621-1699
(annual average in florins)

Period	Silver	Gold
1621-1624	157,924	—
1628-1632	—	—
1633-1636	921,044	—
1637	3,029,550	—
1640-1649	1,518,871	—
1650-1659	1,315,121	—
1660-1669	1,048,821	406,092
1670-1679	—	1,154,148
1680-1689	—	298,383
1690-1699	—	228,952

Source. The figures are available only from 1621 onward with a gap for the years 1625 to 1627 and 1638 to 1639. Until 1637, they are based on Oskar Nachod, *Niederlandischen Ostindischen Kompagnie*, Appendix, Table E, pp. ccvii-ccviii. The figures for 1621-1624 are given in Nachod directly in florins but those after 1624 are in *taels*. The rate of conversion used here is the same as that used by the company: 62.5 stuivers to a *tael* until 1636 and 57 stuivers to a *tael* for 1637.

The figures for 1640-1699 are based on Kristof Glamann, *Dutch-Asiatic Trade*, Table 11, p. 58, who based himself on Nachod and other sources.

[36] Glamann, *Dutch-Asiatic Trade*, p. 13.

[37] A large number of new gold and silver mines had been opened in Japan during the last half of the sixteenth and in the early seventeenth century; A. Kobata, "Production and Uses of Gold and Silver," p. 245.

bullion from Holland.[38] Although these extravagant hopes were never realised, the crucial significance of the exclusive Japan trade cannot be overemphasized. In the first place, the substantial amounts of precious metals obtained in Japan were exchanged for commodities that were themselves sold at a good profit.[39] Second, the cost per unit of silver seems to have been lower in Japan than it was in Holland. If one assumed that the value that the factors in Batavia assigned to a *tael* of Japanese *schuit* silver in their books correctly represented its cost price, the cost of the Japanese silver works out to be 24.75 percent lower than in Holland until 1636 and 35.58 percent thereafter.[40] But this profitable source of silver suddenly dried up in 1668, when the Japanese banned the export of this metal, probably in response to a decline in domestic output.[41] Fortunately for the Company, however, the ban on the export of gold imposed in 1641 had been withdrawn in 1664. This had served to absorb partially the shock

[38] Glamann, *Dutch-Asiatic Trade*, p. 58; Letter from the Directors to the Governor-General and Council at Batavia dated October 14, 1651, Pieter van Dam, *Beschrijvinge van de Oost-Indische Compagnie*, edited by F. W. Stapel, Book I, Part II (The Hague, 1929), p. 61 note 6.

[39] For example, in 1623, it was estimated that in one voyage, goods worth 600,000 rials sent to Japan could be sold for 1,050,000 rials, giving a profit of seventy-five percent (Advice by Outgoing Governor-General Coen to the Council of the Indies, January 31, 1623, K.A. 989, f. 51).

[40] This assumption is necessary because the Dutch factors were paid for their goods in silver, and they had no occasion to record the cost price per unit of silver in terms of the Japanese currency. The authorities at Batavia reckoned a *tael*—which was both a measure of weight equivalent to 37.565 grams and also a unit of account, though it was not a coin— as equivalent of 62.5 stuivers until 1636, 57 stuivers until 1666, and 70 "light" stuivers thereafter. The 1666 adjustment did not represent a change in the real valuation of the *tael*. At these rates, the price per ounce avoirdupois (= 28.4375 grams) of Japanese silver works out at 47.31 stuivers until 1636 and 43.15 stuivers thereafter. Regarding the price of silver in Holland, van Dam gives the figure of 60 stuivers per ounce around the middle of the seventeenth century. K. N. Chaudhuri's figures suggest a price of 58⅓ stuivers per ounce in the last half of the seventeenth century (the English rate of 5s. 3d. per ounce being converted into stuivers at 4s. 6d. to a rijksdaalder of 50 stuivers). We have assumed an average cost price of 59 stuivers per ounce of European silver. See Nachod, *Niederländischen Ostindischen Kompagnie*, pp. 134-136 and note 1 p. 136, and Appendix 63, p. cxcv; van Dam, *Beschrijvinge*, I, ii, 88, "Memorie van de waardije van't navolgende goud en silver." The ounce in van Dam was equivalent to 2 *loot*, which apparently is the same as the old German *lot*. According to the *Encyclopaedia Britannica*, this *lot* used to be about one-half ounce avoirdupois, so that van Dam's ounce is broadly comparable to the ounce avoirdupois; *Beschrijvinge* I, ii, 834-835. K. N. Chaudhuri, *The East India Company* (London, 1965), p. 116, Table IV; idem, "Treasure and Trade Balances: The East India Company's Export Trade, 1660-1720," *Economic History Review*, Second Series, 21 (1968), 499.

[41] J. A. van der Chijs, ed., *Dagh-Register gehouden in 't Casteel Batavia, 1668-1671* (Batavia/ The Hague, 1897), pp. 203-204; Nachod, *Niederländischen Ostindischen Kompagnie*, p. 356; Kobata, "Production and Uses of Gold and Silver," pp. 245, 256.

following the loss of Taiwan in 1662. Following the ban on the export of silver in 1668, the Company exported increasing quantities of gold *koban* from Japan.[42] The price per *koban*, which stood at 6.8 *taels* in 1664, was reduced to 5.6 *taels* in 1668, raised to 5.8 *taels* in 1670, and raised further to the 1664 level of 6.8 *taels* in 1672.[43] The Dutch procurement of these coins continued to be large until 1696, when the gold content of the *koban* was reduced from 85.69 to 56.41 percent, while its silver price continued to be 6.8 *taels*.[44] It is true that without a major alternative Asian source of gold the Company did continue to procure *koban* in Japan until the middle of the eighteenth century.[45] But the crucial role of the Japan trade in the framework of Dutch intra-Asian and Euro-Asian trade appears to have been compromised significantly after 1696.

How did the Company's trade with Bengal fit into the Dutch network of intra-Asian and Euro-Asian trade? In the initial decades, Bengal was viewed as a source of textiles, provisions such as rice and sugar, and saltpetre, besides slaves needed to provide the labour force in Coen's scheme of developing and securing Dutch colonies in Indonesia.[46] But the trade with the region was not considered important enough to form a part of Coen's blueprint of intra-Asian trade sent to the Directors in August 1619. However, in their letter to the Directors dated March 7, 1631, the Governor-General and Council at Batavia indicated that a considerable amount of inexpensive raw silk could be obtained in the region.[47] This would potentially tie the Bengal trade to the crucial Japan trade. This indeed happened rapidly, and by the middle of the seventeenth century Bengal was probably the single most important supplier of cargo shipped to Japan. In the second half of the century, Bengal became an important source of goods sent to various other parts of Asia, as well. The most

[42] The *koban* was an oval-shaped gold coin that until 1695 weighed 4.73 momme (= 17.768 grams) and contained 85.69% gold, 14.25% silver, and 0.06% alloy; Nachod, *Niederländischen Ostindischen Kompagnie*, p. 135; J. T. Kussaka, *Das Japanische Geldwezen* (Jena, 1890), p. 22.

[43] Nachod, *Niederländischen Ostindischen Kompagnie*, Appendix 63 D, p. ccvii.

[44] Kussaka, *Das Japanische Geldwezen*, p. 22; Nachod, *Niederlandischen Ostindischen Kompagnie*, p. ccvii.

[45] Glamann, *Dutch-Asiatic Trade*, pp. 68-69.

[46] See, for example, *Generale Missiven*, 1, 121, 204-205; *Jan Pietersz. Coen*, III, 75, 177, 180, 209.

[47] "We have received from Agra a sample of Bengal raw silk. It costs at Agra 4 rupees or 2 rials of eight per 1¼ ponds. According to the advice from Vapour, a large amount of this silk is brought from Bengal to Agra and in a year about 1,000 bales can be bought at Agra. With the *Deventer*, we are sending you a sample of this silk and will wait for your assessment of it. Apparently, if this silk is bought at first hand at the source, it would be available cheaper." General letter from the Governor-General to the Directors dated March 7, 1631, K.A. 1011, f. 19.

notable example of this was the export of high-profit-yielding opium to the Indonesian archipelago almost exclusively from Bengal.

From the eighties of the seventeenth century, as the relative importance of intra-Asian trade declined, Bengal emerged as a major source of raw silk and fine cotton and silk textiles exported to Holland. Since these items now dominated the exports to Europe, the trade with Bengal assumed a new importance. Indeed, around the time this study comes to a close, the Bengal factory was probably the single largest provider of goods sent to Europe.

· 2 ·

THE COMPANY IN BENGAL: THE POLITICS
OF TRADE

THE STRUCTURE OF BENGAL'S TRADE

The Afghan sultanate of Bengal was incorporated into the Mughal empire in 1576, though it was not until the early part of the seventeenth century that the conquest was consolidated. The administration of the province (*subah*) was organised along the standard Mughal model. All senior positions in the administration were held by the *mansabdars*—a class of officials who' constituted a central pool and were eligible to occupy both civil and military offices. To prevent these officials from cultivating local sources of power and influence, they were transferred at frequent intervals from one province to another. The central government also enforced a system of checks and balances in the provincial administration by dividing authority between the *subahdar* and the imperial *diwan*. The former was responsible for the maintenance of law and order, the command of the armed forces, and the administration of criminal justice. The *diwan* controlled finance and taxation, besides administering civil justice.[1] In the second decade of the eighteenth century, however, Murshid Quli Khan was allowed to hold both offices: this coincided with the beginning of an era of near autonomy for the province.

During the seventeenth century and the first half of the eighteenth, the geographical limits of the *subah* of Bengal often exceeded the area presently covered by Bangladesh and the Indian state of West Bengal.[2] Thus until 1607 and again intermittently after 1697, the province of Bihar formed part of the Bengal *subah*. So did parts of the province of Orissa at different times. To the European trading companies, the provinces of Bengal, Bihar, and Orissa together constituted a natural unit of operation denoted by the term "Bengal." The word is thus used in the present study except when it specifically refers to the province alone.

An important distinguishing feature of the province of Bengal was the high level of productivity achieved in the various sectors of the economy. The early years of Mughal rule in the province coincided with an important

---

[1] The system of checks and balances also incorporated the independent office of the *bakshi* who was in charge of military finance. Another important official, the *wakianavis*, kept the central government informed of provincial developments.

[2] The district of Chittagong was conquered by the Mughals only in 1666. For a detailed description of the geographical limits of the Bengal *subah*, see Anjali Chatterjee, *Bengal in the Reign of Aurangzib, 1658-1707* (Calcutta, 1967).

shift in the course of the rivers of the Delta and in the distribution of alluvial soil. This permitted the settlement of eastern Bengal, and there the peasants increasingly took to the cultivation of rice and cash crops. In the 1660s, the French traveller, François Bernier, wrote: "In a word, *Bengale* abounds with every necessary of life; and it is this abundance that has induced so many *Portuguese, Half-castes* and other *Christians* to seek an asylum in this fertile kingdom."[3] The high level of productivity embraced both food production and commercial crops. The latter, including such items as mulberry, cotton, and sugarcane, were highly market-oriented, and the acreage and output responded quickly to changes in market demand. To take an example, while urging the imperial authorities to settle their dispute with the Dutch in Bengal, Murshid Quli Khan, the imperial *diwan* in the province, wrote in 1706 that following the closure of the Dutch factory at Kasimbazar two years earlier, the Hollanders' demand for raw silk had registered a considerable decline, leading to a substantial shift of land away from mulberry into rice and pulses. This had had an injurious effect on the income from land revenue, inasmuch as mulberry lands were assessed at Rs. 3 per *bigha*, whereas the corresponding rates for rice and pulses—being lower-value crops—were only Rs. 0.75 and Rs. 0.37 per *bigha*, respectively. This could be reversed only if the Company were persuaded to reopen its factory at Kasimbazar.[4]

The production of manufactured goods was similarly characterized by both high quality and competitive pricing. The premier industry in the region was the textile industry, comprising manufacture from cotton, silk, and mixed yarns. The availability of artisans skilled in their respective crafts over generations, together with abundant and cheap raw materials and intermediate goods, contributed to the growth of this industry. Writing in 1620, the factors of the English East India Company noted that at Maxudabad (later renamed Murshidabad), raw silk "may be provided in infinite quantetyes at least twenty percent cheaper than in anye other place of India, and of the choysest stufe, wounde off into what condition you shall require it, as it comes from the worme: where are also innumerable of silk wynderes, experte workmen and labour cheaper by a third than else where."[5]

It should be stressed that although the province of Bengal specialised

---

[3] François Bernier, *Travels in the Mogul Empire, A.D. 1656-1668*, ed. A. Constable (Oxford, 1934), pp. 438-439. Writing at the beginning of the sixteenth century, the Italian traveller Verthema had commented, "This country [the province of Bengal] abounds more in grain, flesh of every kind, in great quantity of sugar, also of ginger, and of great abundance of cotton, than any country in the world" (quoted in L.S.S. O'Malley and M. Chakravarti, *District Gazetteer Hooghly* [Calcutta, 1912], p. 44).

[4] Enclosure to H.B. 9.10.1706, K.A. 1622, ff. 63-68.

[5] W. Foster, ed., *The English Factories in India, 1618-1621* (Oxford, 1906), p. 153.

in the production of high-value textiles such as the world-renowned Dacca muslins, a large proportion of the total output of the textile industry intended for the market consisted of coarse cottons. The capacity of the province to put large quantities of goods on the market helped promote substantial trade relations with other parts of the subcontinent as well as with countries across the seas. Although luxury goods such as high-value textiles and raw silk certainly figured in this trade, a large part of the exports from Bengal consisted of foodstuffs such as rice, sugar, clarified butter and oil, and coarse cotton textiles.[6]

The trade in bulk goods was facilitated by the extensive and rather inexpensive network of transportation. Within the subcontinent, the trade from Bengal was carried on both along land and river routes as well as along the coast. A major route connecting centres of manufacturing production such as Malda, Hugli, and Dacca with the important north Indian distribution centre of Agra involved the use of the tributaries of the river Ganga to Rajmahal, the Ganga itself until Allahabad via Patna and Banaras, and finally the river Yamuna from Allahabad to Agra. An important land route from Agra to Gujarat passed through western Rajasthan, while another more easterly route passed through Malwa and Khandesh. In addition to foodstuffs, a substantial quantity of Bengal raw silk was carried to Agra, a part of which eventually found its way to Persia and Turkey via the land route passing through Kandahar.[7] Among the major items of import into Bengal along these routes were cotton from Gujarat and salt from Rajasthan, besides some varieties of textiles from Burhanpur.

The greater part of Bengal's trade with the rest of the subcontinent as well as with other countries, however, was carried on by sea. Until the middle of the sixteenth century, the principal port in the province of Bengal was Satgaon. Its successor, Hugli, remained the premier port of the region until the early eighteenth century, when Calcutta overshadowed it, though at first the use of the port of Calcutta was confined largely to the English East India Company and the private English traders. The other ports in the region were Pipli and Balasore in Orissa, but the former ceased operation around 1670 when the river on which it was situated silted up.

In the absence of such source materials as the account books of merchants engaged in coastal and overseas trade, customs house records, and the like, a detailed analysis of the composition, direction, and organisa-

---

[6] Some idea of the magnitude of the trade in these items can be formed from the following statement of Manrique: "So extensive is the trade that over one hundred vessels are yearly loaded up in the ports of Bengala with only rice, sugar, fats, oils, wax and other similar articles." *Travels of Fray Sebastien Manrique* (Oxford, 1927), I, 56. See also Bernier, *Travels in the Mogul Empire*, pp. 437-439.

[7] Statement in K.A. 1025, ff. 112-vo.

tional structure of the seaborne trade of Bengal on the eve of the arrival of the Dutch and the English East India companies is extremely difficult. A description of the barest essentials of the structure can, however, be based on the "shipping lists" for the ports of Hugli and Balasore available in the Dutch documents. The Company liked to keep an eye on the volume of indigenous trade handled at the Bengal ports, and compiled these lists from information obtained from the officials of the imperial customs house. The lists contain, for each ship, the name of the merchant who owned the ship, the port of destination/origin, the cargo carried, and occasionally, the place of domicile of the merchant, the name of the *nakhuda* (captain of the ship), the name of the agent, if any, who had organised the work of equipping the ship, and the name and type of the ship. Unfortunately, these lists are available only from the last quarter of the seventeenth century on, and even then are not available on a regular basis.[8] But the broad structure of trade that these lists portray seems to be valid for the earlier part of the century as well. Table 2.1 sets out the direction and the composition of the trade from the Bengal ports.

In addition to a substantial coastal trade, a large amount of trade was carried on with Siam and the Indonesian archipelago. The volume of trade with the Persian Gulf and the Red Sea, however, was quite small. The exports from Bengal included raw silk, opium, sugar, and saltpetre in addition to foodstuffs and textiles, a large part of which were manufactured from coarse cotton. The major import goods were pepper, nonprecious metals, elephants, *cauris*, areca nuts, and tobacco. The balance of trade was usually favourable to Bengal, and settlement was made by the inflow of a certain amount of specie from such regions as Sumatra, the Coromandel coast, Malabar, Gujarat, and the Persian Gulf. The greater part of this specie was in the form of silver coins, and the largest single contributor to the stream was Gujarat, which itself received large quantities of coins through its trading links with the Persian Gulf and Mocha in the Red Sea, sometimes described as the "treasure chest" of the Mughal empire. Broadly speaking, the trade with the Persian Gulf and the Red Sea, Gujarat, Malabar, and the Coromandel coast was carried on primarily from the port of Hugli, whereas that with Ceylon was largely the preserve of Balasore.[9] Both ports participated in the trade with Southeast Asia and

---

[8] Some of the problems in the use of these lists for analysing trends in the volume of trade are discussed in Chapter 8.

[9] All ten ships that are known to have gone from Bengal to the Persian Gulf and the Red Sea between 1680 and 1718 started their voyage at Hugli. Of the 102 ships that went to Surat over the same period, 94 started out from this port. The corresponding figures for the Coromandel coast were 138 and 129, respectively. No ships are recorded as having left Balasore for the Malabar coast during this period. Of the total of 18 ships that are recorded

TABLE 2.1

Direction and Composition of the Trade from Bengal

South-east Asia (Arakan, Pegu, Tenasserim, Achin, Kedah, Junk-Ceylon, Malacca, Manila)		Coromandel Coast (Masulipatam, Madras, Porto Novo)		Ceylon		Maldive Islands	
Exports	Imports	Exports	Imports	Exports	Imports	Exports	Imports
Textiles, rice, opium, butter, oil, saltpetre, raw silk	Tin, specie, pepper, spelter, copper, bell-metal, elephants, ivory	Raw silk, rice, textiles, sugar, saltpetre, butter	Textiles, spelter, tin, conch-shells, pepper, areca nuts, salt, ivory, sandalwood	Rice, textiles, oil, raw silk, opium, sugar	Elephants, areca nuts, conch shells, ivory, pepper, salt	Rice, textiles, butter, oil, raw silk, opium, sugar	Cauris, conch shells, tin

Malabar Coast (Cannanore, Calicut, Cochin, Narsapur)		Gujarat (Surat, Cambay)		Persian Gulf and the Red Sea (Bandar Abbas, Ormuz, Jeddah)	
Exports	Imports	Exports	Imports	Exports	Imports
Opium, textiles, raw silk, rice, saltpetre, iron	Specie, pepper, cauris, cotton, cotton yarn, areca nuts, salt	Raw silk, textiles, sugar, iron, opium, saltpetre, rice, oil, butter	Specie, cotton, textiles, Persian tobacco, Persian rosewater, pepper, tin, spelter, cotton yarn, areca nuts, conch shells, ivory, copper	Sugar, textiles, iron, raw silk, opium, saltpetre, rice	Persian abassis, tobacco, rosewater, tin, spelter, textiles, salt

Source Bengal shipping lists in the Dutch records. The individual references are too numerous to be mentioned here.

Note The export and the import items have been arranged in a descending order of importance.

the Maldive islands, though Balasore had an edge over Hugli in this respect.[10] An analysis of the shipping lists also suggests that the trade between Bengal and the ports of Gujarat, the Malabar coast, and the Coromandel coast was carried on overwhelmingly by merchants based at these ports.[11] On the other hand, the trade with Southeast Asia, Ceylon, and the Maldive islands was overwhelmingly in the hands of Bengal merchants.[12]

We noted earlier that the merchants mentioned in the shipping lists are only the shipowning merchants. A larger group who did not own a ship and hired freight space on vessels owned by fellow merchants did not figure in the lists. These merchants ordinarily travelled with their goods and, indeed, were the true pedlars of the Indian Ocean. Without information about this group, it is impossible to give a true picture of the composition of the mercantile community engaged in the coastal and the intra-Asian trade from the Bengal ports; this can be done only for the shipowning merchants.

It will be seen from Table 2.2 that only 41 percent (accounting for 46 percent of the outgoing and 39 percent of the incoming vessels) of the merchants operating at the Bengal ports belonged to Bengal.[13] About a third of these merchants were Mughal state officials, both those at a junior

---

as having left for Ceylon during 1680-1718, as many as 17 started out from Balasore (Bengal shipping lists in the Dutch records).

[10] Of the 53 ships that are known to have gone to Southeast Asia from Bengal during 1680-1718, 21 were from Hugli and 32 from Balasore. Of the 91 departures for the Maldive islands over the same period, 27 were from Hugli and the remaining 64 from Balasore (Bengal shipping lists).

[11] For the period 1680-1718, information regarding the ownership and operation of vessels departing from Bengal for Gujarat is available for 26 vessels. As many as 23 of these vessels were on the account of Surat merchants, one on that of the king of Siam, whereas only two were on the account of merchants based at Hugli. Of the 45 vessels departing for Coromandel for which information regarding ownership and operation is available, only three are known to have been owned by merchants based in Bengal. For Malabar, information regarding the place of domicile of the merchants is available only for the three vessels that left Hugli for this coast in 1713-1714. All these vessels were on the account of the Malabari merchant Ali Raza (Bengal shipping lists).

[12] Thus of the 17 vessels that left Balasore for Ceylon between 1680 and 1684, as many as 15 were on the account of Bengal merchants. As for the Maldive islands, information regarding the place of domicile of the merchants is available for 65 vessels that left Balasore and Hugli for these islands between 1680 and 1718. Of these vessels 60 were on the account of merchants based in Bengal (Bengal shipping lists). For the information available for Southeast Asia or the eastward trade, see Chapter 8.

[13] Information about domicile is available for only one-third of the total number of merchants listed in the Bengal shipping lists. But since the selection of the merchants for whom this information is provided seems to have been purely random, this should not affect the validity of conclusions drawn from the table.

TABLE 2.2

Composition of the Shipowning Merchants Engaged in Coastal
and Intra-Asian Trade from Bengal Ports, 1670-1718

	Number of merchants	Number of outgoing vessels accounted for by these merchants	Number of incoming vessels accounted for by these merchants
A. Total number of merchants listed in the Dutch shipping lists	366	413	420
Of the 366 merchants, information regarding place of domicile available for	121	228	188
Of the 121 merchants, number of Bengal merchants	50	106	73
B. Composition of the 50 Bengal merchants (by status)			
Ordinary merchants	34	69	49
State officials engaged in trade	16	37	24

C. Composition of the 34 ordinary merchants (by religion)

Muslims	21	37	25
Hindus	12	30	24
Armenians	1	2	0

D. Composition of the 16 state officials engaged in trade (by religion)

Muslims	15	37	23
Hindus	1	0	1
Armenians	0	0	0

Source: Bengal shipping lists in the Dutch records.

Note: The discrepancy between the number of outgoing and incoming vessels handled by the merchants is partly explained by the fact that the lists of the outgoing and the incoming vessels do not always pertain to the same seasons.

level and important *mansabdars*. An overwhelming proportion of these officials were Muslims.[14] State officials generally found participation in foreign trade a lucrative form of investment for their funds. Although they engaged in trade purely in their private capacity, and the use of their official position to further their trading interests was frowned upon, they often did exactly that to enhance their margin of profit from trade.[15] The provisions of *sauda-i-khas* and *farmaish* authorising the administration to requisition goods for official use at a reasonable price were invoked to procure goods for private trade at prices below the market.[16] On other occasions, trade in particular commodities was monopolised by an official in the area under his jurisdiction.[17] The extent of this phenomenon and

[14] *Mansabdars* held a dual numerical rank—*zat* (personal) and *sawar* (cavalry). The *zat* rank determined the official's status in the hierarchy as well as his personal salary, and those with a *zat* rank over 1,000 constituted the Mughal nobility. *Sawar* rank specified the extent of an official's military obligations, as well as the annual sum of money to be reimbursed to him against this obligation.

Important members of this group of merchant-officials included Subahdar Shaista Khan and his sons Buzurg Ummed Khan, *subahdar* of Bihar, and Abu Nassar Khan, nawab of Orissa. Some other names one comes across frequently are Muhammad Sadiq, sometime *diwan* of Orissa; Malik Qasim, *faujdar* of Hugli; Haji Beg, ex-*faujdar* of Hugli; Nasib Khan, *shahbandar* of Balasore; his son Shuja Khan; and Nawab Nurullah Khan.

[15] In 1672, the English factors at Kasimbazar wrote to their counterparts at Hugli, "Trade all over Bengall (by reason of almost all governors, greate and small turning merchants and most unreasonably abusing those they deale with) is at present very dead" (letter dated 9.8.1672, India Office Records, London, F.R. Misc. Vol. 3, f. 173).

[16] A number of instances of this practice are available. In 1660, Subahdar Mir Jumla forced a number of merchants in Kasimbazar to supply him raw silk at half the market price. Four years later when the new *subahdar*, Shaista Khan, sent his representative to Kasimbazar with orders to buy raw silk worth Rs. 300,000, a number of silk merchants, fearing a repetition of the events of 1660, declared themselves bankrupt and went out of business. Others told the local *faujdar* that they would much rather leave Bengal than subject themselves to such high-handed treatment. The *subahdar*'s representative nevertheless managed to procure one hundred bales against a provisional payment of 50 percent of the market price. He told the merchants that once he had collected two hundred bales, he would announce the final price he would pay for the silk. The actual amount collected by him and the price finally paid for it is not recorded (H.B. 6.3.1660, K.A. 1123, ff. 637-vo; H.B. 31.10.1664, K.A. 1139, ff. 2975-2977; H.B. 27.11.1664, K.A. 1140, f. 94). The situation was equally bad with respect to other commodities such as saltpetre and opium. In 1664, for example, Job Charnock, the English factor at Patna, wrote that the *daroga* (the agent who actually carried out the procurement) of Subahdar Shaista Khan "hath so abused the merchants [of saltpetre] that they are almost all runne away. He pretends that all the peeter he buys is for the King. It was never known he had occasion for more than mds. 1,000 or 1,500 yearely for all his warrs." It might be noted that at the then prevailing market price, the value of 1,500 maunds of saltpetre would have been about Rs. 2,500, whereas the amount actually asked for was worth Rs. 20,000. (W. Foster, ed., *The English Factories in India, 1661-1664* [Oxford, 1923], pp. 395-396; H.B. 31.10.1664, K.A. 1139, ff. 2966-2968.)

[17] Thus trade in saltpetre was monopolized by the *subahdar* of Bengal in 1636, by the

of its benefits to the merchant/official can, however, be exaggerated. By the same token, it is important to be careful while analysing the negative implications of this phenomenon for the producers and the suppliers of trade goods.

Among the ordinary shipowning merchants engaged in trade and based in Bengal were Muslims, Hindus, and Armenians. The only merchant of note among the last-mentioned group was Khoja Sarhad Israeli. The Muslim merchants, though more numerous than the Hindus in our sample, were only marginally ahead in terms of the number of ships handled. The Hindu merchants operated mainly from the port of Balasore, and the dominant group among them was that of the immigrant Gujarati Shahs.[18] The two most celebrated members of this group were the well-known Khem Chand Shah and Chintamani Shah, who had extensive trade connections with Ceylon, the Maldives, Pegu, Siam, and Sumatra. Hindu merchants with typical Bengali names such as Kalyan Ray and Jadu Ray handled only a small proportion of the total trade handled by the Hindu community.

Although most ships were operated by the merchants on their individual accounts, there were frequent cases of ships being sent out and received in the name of two merchants jointly.[19] Such ventures were evidently on the account of partnership firms. But curiously enough, partners who sent out ships in joint names also sent out ships on their individual accounts.[20] State officials engaged in trade often used the services of an agent to organise a given venture on their behalf.[21] Although many of the merchants chose to travel on their ships, and organised the sales and the

---

subahdar of Bihar in 1653, by the imperial diwan at Patna in 1660, by the provincial diwan at Patna in 1675, and by the subahdar of Bengal in 1699. (Batavia Dagh-Register, 1637, p. 102; P.B. 10.11.1653, K.A. 1091, ff. 456-457vo; H.B. 7.1.1661, K.A. 1126, ff. 96-97; H.B. 15.1.1676, K.A. 1209, ff. 502vo-503; H.B. 7.9.1699, K.A. 1516, ff. 157-159.) Important attempts to monopolize trade in opium included the one made in 1681 by the subahdar of Bihar and in 1699 by the subahdar of Bengal (H.B. 25.9.1683, K.A. 1276, f. 1209vo; H.B. 7.9.1699, K.A. 1516, ff. 159-160).

[18] This group accounted for 22 of the 28 outgoing and 17 of the 22 incoming vesels at Balasore on the account of Hindu merchants for whom we have detailed information.

[19] To take only a few examples, merchants Beni Das and Bhawani Das jointly sent a vessel from Hugli to Calicut in 1696-1697 (shipping list, Hugli, 1696-1697, K.A. 1484, ff. 69-72). In 1704-1705, Mohammad Sharif and Ghulam Mohammad are recorded as having sent a vessel from Hugli to the Maldives (shipping list, Hugli, 1704-1705, K.A. 1604, ff. 81-85, I Section). In 1708, a ship arrived at Hugli from Goa on the account of Armenian merchants Saraad and Capreel (shipping list, Hugli, 1708, K.A. 1653, ff. 153-156, II Section).

[20] This was done, for example, by Khem Chand Shah and Chintamani Shah.

[21] To take an example, the Salamat Roo belonging to Nawab Nasib Khan was despatched in 1682-1683 from Balasore to the Maldives by the nawab's agent, Rahimdad Khan (shipping list, Balasore, 1682-1683, K.A. 1276, ff. 1175vo-1180vo).

procurement of the return cargo at the ports of call themselves (probably with the assistance of local agents), others left the job to the *nakhuda*, who acted on their behalf on a commission basis.[22] The state officials/ merchants almost invariably followed the latter course. The *nakhuda* was often a merchant in his own right and simultaneously carried on trade on his own account as well.[23] Occasionally, individual merchants also chartered ships from fellow merchants for particular voyages.[24]

Many of the merchants carrying on trade at the Bengal ports but based outside Bengal themselves travelled with their cargo. Others, however, operated through local agents, who usually were themselves merchants of standing and engaged in trade on their own.[25] It is not clear whether these agents were paid by a commission or by a reciprocal service at the other end. Another category of agents, known as *gomashtas*, worked on a full-time basis for their clients. The, most notable example in this category was one Zulfiqar Khan, who looked after the extensive trading interests of the king of Siam.[26]

THE COMPANY IN BENGAL

The rich potential of the Bengal trade attracted the Dutch to the region. The trade goods that caught their fancy at first were textiles for Holland

[22] To take the list of ships that left Hugli during 1698-1699 as a sample, we find that of the total of 17 ships, 7 were under the overall charge of a *nakhuda* (shipping list, Hugli, 1698-1699, K.A. 1516, ff. 122-125, 1 Section).

[23] Thus of the three vessels that Nakhuda Faizi commanded from Hugli to Coromandel in 1698-1699, one was on the account of merchant Mohiuddin, whereas the other two were on Faizi's own account (shipping list, Hugli, 1698-1699, K.A. 1516, ff. 122-125, I Section). In the following season, Faizı was in charge of two vessels that left Hugli for Coromandel. One of these belonged to merchant Mır Husaın; the other was on Faizi's own account (shipping list, Hugli, 1699-1700, K.A. 1530, ff. 89-93).

[24] For example, a vessel that arrived at Hugli from the Maldives in 1701 on the account of merchant Jaas Mohammed Tabki had been chartered by him from an Armenian merchant, Khoja Ghatjek (shipping list, Hugli, 1701, K.A. 1537, ff. 54-56).

[25] Among the important Bengal merchants also operating as agents were Khoja Sarhad Israeli and Haji Nasir. In 1699-1700, the former despatched from Hugli two ships on the account of Surat merchant Aka Beyrie and another on that of Surat merchant Koursie. One of Aka Beyrie's ships was destined for Coromandel, while the other went to Surat. Koursie's ship also went to Surat. In the same season, he sent a ship each to Surat and Ormuz on his own account. Haji Nasir is recorded as having sent two ships from Hugli to Surat in 1704-1705 on the account of Surat merchant Haji Mohammad Nakki. In 1711-1712, the same agent despatched three ships to Surat, two of which belonged to Sheikh Fazil and the third to Mırza Jahed. In 1713-1714, Haji Nasir is recorded as having sent two ships to Surat on his own account (shipping list, Hugli, 1699-1700, K.A. 1530, ff. 89-92; shipping list, Hugli, 1704-1705, K.A. 1604, ff. 81-85, II Section; shipping list, Hugli, 1711-1712, K.A. 1720, ff. 233-236; shipping list, Hugli, 1713-1714, K.A. 1741, ff. 172-175).

[26] In 1681-1682, for example, Zulfiqar Khan despatched from Balasore the *Roepareel* to

34

and to a smaller extent the Indonesian archipelago, sugar for Holland and Persia, and saltpetre for Holland. Besides, Bengal rice and clarified butter could be used in the Company's establishment at Batavia, while Bengali slaves were to provide the work force in Coen's scheme of developing and securing Dutch colonies in Indonesia.[27] At this stage, the Company bought the Bengal goods on the Coromandel coast, where these had been brought by the Indian merchants. But this naturally involved both a higher cost price and a less certain availability than if the Company were to procure these goods at their source.[28] Since it was the responsibility of the factors at Coromandel to extend the Company's trade into Bengal, Chief Factor Jan Gaeff was sent in May 1615 from Masulipatam to Arakan and Bengal to ascertain the prospects of trade and, if possible, to obtain formal permission to trade there.[29] But the *Duive*, the yacht with which Gaeff had travelled, could not leave Arakan until January 10, 1616, and was then driven off course by strong winds, thus missing Bengal.[30] Over the following decade or so, the Company was unable to take a firm decision as to whether or not to establish a factory in Bengal. In 1623, for example, Governor-General Carpentier wrote to Governor van Uffelen at Masulipatam, saying that pending the receipt of a report from Commander Kunst, who had been sent to Bengal the previous year with three vessels to investigate the prospects of trade there, the decision had been further postponed.[31] Political uncertainty following Shahjahan's rebellion, and

---

Surat and the *Tawakali* to Tenasserim on behalf of the king of Siam (shipping list, Balasore, 1681-1682, K.A. 1267, ff. 1337vo-1342vo).

[27] *Generale Missiven*, I, 121, 204-205.

[28] Masulipatam-Bantam, 30.8.1613, K.A. 968, ff. 146-166; Masulipatam-Bantam, 16.8.1614, K.A. 969, ff. 127-140; Masulipatam-Directors, 10.5.1616, K.A. 973, ff. 159-160.

[29] Instructions to Jan Gaeff, 5.5.1615, K.A. 971, f. 57vo. In the period prior to this, several abortive attempts had been made to reach Bengal. According to Valentijn, all the three ships sent to the East Indies in March 1602 under the command of Vice-Admiral Sebald de Weert as part of the first fleet on the account of the United Dutch East India Company were scheduled to go to both the Coromandel coast and Bengal. He suggests that notwithstanding the slaughter of De Weert and a number of his associates at the hands of the king of Kandi, one ship each did go to the Coromandel coast and Bengal in July 1603 (François Valentijn, *Oud en Nieuwe Oost-Indien* [Dordrecht/Amsterdam, 1726], V, 172). This account, however, is not corroborated by other evidence. Again, the set of instructions issued in December 1603 to Steven van der Hagen, the commander of the second fleet, contained a clause stipulating that on arrival at Achin, van der Hagen would make enquiries regarding the possibilities of trade in Bengal and would despatch two of his ships to the Coromandel coast and Bengal for the procurement of cotton textiles, rice, and other provisions (N. Macleod, *De Oost-Indische Compagnie als Zeemogenheid in Azië, 1602-1605* [Rijswijk, 1927], I, 19).

[30] Jan Gaeff-Bimilipatam, 27.4.1616, K.A. 973, f. 171vo; Masulipatam-Directors, 27.4.1616, K.A. 973, ff. 168-169.

[31] Batavia-Masulipatam, 27.4.1623, K.A. 992, ff. 84vo-89vo.

temporary occupation of the province in 1624 led to a further delay in the matter. In March 1626, Masulipatam reported to the Directors that the factors sent to Bengal with the *Schiedam* and the *Medenblick* were of the opinion that no profitable trade appeared possible in the region.[32] The disturbed conditions in Bengal also led to a decline in the volume of trade carried on by the Coromandel merchants with Bengal. This, in turn, brought about an increase in the cost of Bengal textiles procured by the Company in Coromandel. In 1628, for example, Governor-General Coen wrote to the factors at Pulicat that these textiles were selling at no more than their cost price.[33]

The next major effort by the Company to penetrate the Bengal trade was made in July 1629, when two yachts, the *Duive* and the *David*, were despatched to the region under the charge of Hendrik de Witt. The *Duive* arrived at Balasore on August 9 and was soon followed by the *David*. Hendrik de Witt and his assistants stayed in Balasore and Pipli until the end of January 1630. During this period, the factors realised that if trade was to be carried on in the region, the principal item of import would have to be specie. Hugli, which was described as "the most suitable place for trade in the whole of Bengal," was at this time dominated by the Portuguese and, therefore, out of the reach of the Dutch. But the factors managed to obtain a *kaul* from the *faujdar* of Pipli acting in the name of the nawab of Orissa. This document permitted the Company to engage in trade in the area under the jurisdiction of the nawab subject to the payment of a once-over toll of 3 percent on goods procured in the area.[34] In 1630, the hope of procuring a considerable amount of inexpensive raw silk in the region led the Company to intensify its efforts to open up the Bengal trade on a regular basis.[35] Fortunately for the Dutch, the Mughal forces drove the Portuguese out of Hugli in 1632, clearing the way for the Company to establish regular trade relations with this port.

As trade along the river Hugli—a tributary of the river Ganga—seemed within the grasp of the Company, new advantages were seen in establishing commercial relations with Bengal. The governor-general, for example,

---

[32] Masulipatam-Directors, 8.3.1626, K.A. 999, ff. 1-5.

[33] Batavia-Pulicat, 18.7.1628, K.A. 1007, ff. 338-340. In 1628, Governor Ysbrantsz. wrote to Coen and the Batavia Council: "Believe us, Gentlemen, that if any profit was to be made in Bengal, these Masulipatam merchants would have gone there in their small vessels as they used to do earlier and not leave that trade to us" (Masulipatam-Batavia, 24.9.1628, K.A. 1007, ff. 11-18).

[34] The journal kept by Hendrik de Witt, K.A. 1012, ff. 111vo-129; see especially 29 October 1629, f. 121; 24 October 1629, f. 120; 31 August 1629, ff. 113vo-114. A *kaul* is a lease or grant in writing, a safe conduct, amnesty, or any written engagement.

[35] Letter from the Governor-General to the Directors (general letter) dated March 7, 1631, K.A. 1011, f. 19.

argued in 1634 that the Company's trade with northern India, which had hitherto been conducted overland from Surat, could be carried on far more inexpensively from Bengal, which was connected by river transportation with Agra and other parts of upper India. It was even believed that the river Ganga connected Bengal to the "world-famous emporium of Cathay (China)." Instructions were, therefore, issued in July 1634 for a ship to be sent to Hugli.[36] The Coromandel factors had already done that in May, when the yacht *Westzanen* was despatched with goods and cash of a total value of *f.* 18,000 to Hariharpur in Orissa with instructions to go on to Hugli. On arrival at Hariharpur, the factors found trade rather slack, and after leaving some spices, textiles, and cash at the local factory, which had been established in 1633, they continued their voyage to Hugli.[37] It was around this time that the Dutch succeeded in obtaining from Subahdar Azam Khan of Bengal formal permission to establish a factory at Hugli and trade anywhere in the province.[38] The rate of customs duty payable by them was to be determined by Mir Kamaluddin Haji Jamal in consultation with other merchants.[39] On arrival at Hugli, however, the *Westzanen* was seized, ostensibly because a number of free Dutch merchants had recently left Hugli without paying the customs duty. The yacht was released soon after, but without its goods. It started back for Masulipatam in March 1635 but, because of problems on the way, did not arrive there until October.[40]

In the meantime, on 21 September, the *Santvoort* had been sent from Masulipatam to Hugli, where it arrived on October 23, 1635. Subahdar Azam Khan had since been succeeded by Islam Khan, and under the Mughal administrative procedure, it was necessary to obtain permission to trade afresh from the new *subahdar*. Islam Khan granted the necessary permission, allowed the Company to construct a small factory at Hugli, and ordered the restitution of the goods seized from the *Westzanen*. Shahjahan's *farman* of August 1, 1635, permitting the Dutch to trade in Bengal, arrived at Hugli soon after.[41] The local officials at Hugli were distinctly unfriendly; in 1636, the chief of the Hugli factory, Jacob Mahuizen, was

---

[36] *Batavia Dagh-Register*, 1631-1634, pp. 352-353.

[37] Ibid., p. 415; *Generale Missiven*, I, 523.

[38] In the "contract-book" in the Company's archives, the undated *kaul* is found placed between documents relating to 1631 and those to 1632. But as J. E. Heeres has pointed out, it was probably only in 1634 that the *kaul* was granted (*Corpus-Diplomaticum*, I, 266, 267). The factor who secured this *kaul* was probably one Gerrit Pietersen Hollaer, who informed Coromandel about it on August 30, 1634 (MacLeod, *Zeemogenheid*, II, 16-17).

[39] This certainly was a most unusual procedure. The exact role of Mir Kamaluddin Haji Jamal is not clear.

[40] Macleod, *Zeemogenheid*, II, 17.

[41] *Batavia Dagh-Register*, 1636, pp. 122-123, 244; *Corpus-Diplomaticum*, I, 268-269.

arrested along with the other factors, and the factory plundered. But the *subahdar* granted a *kaul* in September 1636 permitting the factors to export all goods except saltpetre and slaves. The customs duty the factors were obliged to pay was Rs. 3,000 per large ship, Rs. 2,000 per medium-sized ship, and Rs. 1,200 per small ship.[42]

The factors at Surat, who had experience in dealing at the Mughal court, managed to obtain from Emperor Shahjahan two *farmans* in 1636 and another in 1638 concerning the Company's trade in Bengal. The *farmans* allowed the Company to trade freely in the region, though the rate of customs duty payable by it was left vague.[43] But Jacob Mahuizen continued to be dissatisfied with the prospect of trade at Hugli.[44] At his suggestion, the Hugli factory was abandoned in December 1636 and the factors went over to Pipli in Orissa, where a *kaul* was obtained permitting the Company to trade, subject to the payment of customs duty at the rate of Rs. 450 per ship. The transit duty on goods brought into Pipli from other parts of the province and on those so carried out of Pipli was fixed at 3.5 percent.[45] In January 1641, the customs duty at Pipli was reduced to Rs. 300 per ship and the transit duty to 3 percent.[46] An imperial *farman* issued in November 1642 was the first document to exempt the Company from the payment of transit duty on the Pipli-Agra route, which passed through Bengal, Bihar, and a part of northern India.[47]

By this time, the Company had firmly established itself in Pipli. Soon after, a small factory was opened at neighbouring Balasore. The Hariharpur factory established in 1633, on the other hand, had since been abandoned because of inadequate opportunities of trade there. A factory had also been set up at Patna in 1638 but closed the same year for reasons of

---

[42] *Batavia Dagh-Register*, 1637, pp. 97-100; *Corpus-Diplomaticum*, I, 282-284.

[43] See *Corpus-Diplomaticum*, I, 280-281. The 1638 *farman* specifically permitted the Company to trade in saltpetre, negating the ban imposed by Subahdar Islam Khan in September 1636 (ibid., pp. 327-332). The second *farman* of 1636 and the one of 1638 simply stated that the rates indicated on the back of the document (which were those prevalent at Surat) would be applicable to Bengal. But in a postscript to the document, Wazir Afzal Khan added that if the prevalent rates at the Bengal ports happened to be higher than the Surat rates (which, indeed, was the case at least at Hugli, where the rate was 4 percent), the local rates should continue to be enforced (ibid., pp. 285-289, 327-332; *Batavia Dagh-Register*, 1637, p. 102).

[44] *Batavia Dagh-Register*, 1637, p. 102.

[45] MacLeod, *Zeemogenheid*, II, 197-198.

[46] *Corpus-Diplomaticum*, I, 339-342. Among other things, the document recognized the right of the Company to use its own devices to recover debts, subject to the provision that the individual concerned could not be carried away on the Company ships. In the event of an employee committing a crime other than murder or robbery, the Company was free to decide the nature and the extent of the punishment. But if it failed to inflict any punishment, the authorities would take the matter into their own hands.

[47] *Corpus-Diplomaticum*, I, 390-391.

economy.[48] On assuming the office of *subahdar* of Bengal in 1639, Prince Shah Shuja had written to the Dutch governor at Pulicat suggesting a reopening of the Hugli factory. This suggestion had been ignored, however, and it was not until sometime between 1645 and 1647 that the Company reestablished the factory at Hugli.[49] The chief factory of the Bengal region continued to be at Pipli. Sometime between 1645 and 1651, the Patna factory was also reestablished and a new factory opened at Kasimbazar.[50]

In February 1648, Nawab Fidai Khan, who had replaced Shah Shuja as the *subahdar* of Bengal, exempted the Company from the payment of transit duties in the province.[51] Shah Shuja returned to the office of the provincial *subahdar* later that year, and in 1650 granted to the Dutch a *nishan* instructing officials on the Pipli-Patna route to exempt the Company's goods from transit and other duties in accordance with the imperial *farman* of November 1642. Between 1653 and 1656, Shuja issued at least four more *nishans* along similar lines.[52]

In light of the growing importance of the Bengal trade, the Batavia Council appointed Johan Verpoorten as special commissioner in 1653 to suggest measures for improvements in the Company's arrangements in the region.[53] Verpoorten recommended reorganisation of the Bengal factories into a directorate independent of the "government" at Pulicat.[54] The other suggestion Verpoorten made was recognition of the Hugli factory as the chief factory of the Bengal region.[55] Both suggestions were received fa-

---

[48] MacLeod, *Zeemogenheid*, II, 198; *Generale Missiven*, II, 61.

[49] In 1645, Upper-merchant Thomas Kuick was planning to visit Hugli on his way back from Kasimbazar to Pipli and discuss the question of the duties payable there with the local authorities (*Batavia Dagh-Register*, 1644-1645, p. 359). The general letter from Batavia to Amsterdam dated December 31, 1647, implies the existence of a Dutch factory at Hugli (*Generale Missiven*, II, 327).

[50] In 1645, the factors were reported to be contemplating the establishment of factories at Patna and Kasimbazar (*Batavia Dagh-Register*, 1644-1645, p. 324). The general letter from Batavia to Amsterdam dated January 24, 1652, shows that at that time factories existed at Pipli, Balasore, Patna, Kasimbazar, and Hugli (*Generale Missiven*, II, 564). Besides the factory at Patna, the Company had two saltpetre collection agencies nearby. One was at Chuprah, near the village of Daulatganj northwest of Patna; the other was at Singia, north of Patna.

[51] *Corpus-Diplomaticum*, I, 505-506. The officials to whom this document was addressed included those at Patna.

[52] A *nishan* was the letters-patent ordinarily issued by provincial govenors. "Firmans granted to the Dutch East India Company, 17th and 18th Century," Warren Hastings Papers, B.M. Addl. Ms. 29095, ff. 46-50; *Generale Missiven*, II, 411-412.

[53] The total value of goods the Company exported from the region had increased from *f.* 150,000 in 1648-1649 to *f.* 685,000 in 1652-1653 (calculated from the invoices of goods the Company exported from the Bengal region).

[54] Letter from Johan Verpoorten to Batavia, 12.6.1653, K.A. 1091, ff. 436-vo.

[55] The immediate provocation behind this suggestion was the fact that following a clash earlier in the year between some Dutch factors and a number of Muslims at Pipli carrying out the Muharram procession in which one Dutchman and several Muslims were killed, the

vourably at Batavia. A resolution adopted by the Batavia Council in August 1655 noted the considerably increased importance of the Bengal trade, necessitating on-the-spot decisions, as the main factor behind the creation of the independent directorate of Bengal.[56] Pieter Sterthemius was appointed the first director of the Bengal factories and authorized to choose between Kasimbazar and Hugli for his headquarters.[57] In April 1656, Sterthemius provisionally chose Kasimbazar, but later in the year moved over to Hugli, which continued to be the seat of the Dutch directorate of Bengal for nearly a century and a half. The Company leased the villages of Chinsura, Baranagar, and Bazar Mirzapur for an annual ground rent of Rs. 1,574.[58] The factory was moved from its earlier site to the village of Chinsura (though it continued to be referred to as the Hugli factory), which was also used to house a number of Indian merchants and weavers associated with the Company.

As the trade at Hugli grew, the factory at Pipli became progressively less important, until it was abandoned altogether in 1675. The personnel at the factory at Balasore was also decreased bit by bit until the factory was reduced to the position of an agency attending to the requirements of ships calling there before entering the Bay of Bengal.[59] As far as new factories were concerned, one was established at Dacca sometime in the

out the Muharram procession in which one Dutchman and several Muslims were killed, the local Dutch factory had been attacked and burned down. The Company estimated the loss from this outrage at ƒ 40,058 (P.B. 2.4.1653, K.A. 1091, ff. 415-vo; P.B. 10.11.1653, K.A. 1091, f. 448vo; P.B. 15.12.1653, K.A. 1094, ff. 612-613; B.P. 28.8.1654, K.A. 781, ff. 359-363; letter from Johan Verpoorten to Nawab Shamshudaulla of Orissa, enclosure to P.B. 15.11.1654, K.A. 1094, ff. 675-677vo; H.B. 6.3.1660, K.A. 1123, f. 736vo; *Generale Missiven*, II, 762-763).

[56] Commission given to the first director-designate of Bengal, Pieter Sterthemius, dated 23.8.1655, K.A. 782, ff. 558-559.

[57] P.B. 27.1.1656, K.A. 1104, ff. 428-431; B.P. 7.9.1656, K.A. 783, ff. 348-349.

[58] The annual ground rent was Rs. 582 for Chinsura, Rs. 793 for Baranagar, and Rs. 199 for Bazar Mirzapur. Secret letter from Commissioner van Rheede at Hugli to the Batavia Council dated 6.11.1686, K.A. 1318, f. 1004; instructions by van Rheede to the Bengal factors dated 21.2.1687, K.A. 1324; H.B. 18.9.1689, K.A. 1352, f. 65vo.

[59] B.H. 17.8.1666, K.A. 793, f. 446; B.H. 20.8.1669, K.A. 796, ff. 605-606; H.B. 3.8.1671, K.A. 1174, ff. 1861vo-1862; B.H. 13.11.1671, K.A. 798, f. 814; H.B. 28.2. 1672, K.A. 1178, ff. 22vo-23; H.B. 10.5.1673, K.A. 1185, f. 96vo; B.H. 3.8.1674, K.A. 801, f. 400; H.B. 19.11.1674, K.A. 1193, ff. 206-vo; H.XVII. 10.12.1674, K.A. 1189, f. 601vo; instructions to van den Hemel, the newly appointed chief of Balasore, dated 1.2.1675, K.A. 1202, ff. 77vo-78vo; H.B. 26.8.1675, K.A. 1202, f. 130; H.B. 29.8.1676, K.A. 1209, f. 606vo; instructions by van Rheede to Bengal factors dated 21.2.1687, K.A. 1324, ff. 196-vo; A.K.A. Gijsberti Hodenpijl, "De Handhavig der Neutraliteyt van de Nederlandsche Loge te Houghly, by de Overrompeling van de Engelsche Kolonie Calcutta in Juni, 1756," *Bijdragen tot de Taal-Land- en Volkenkunde van Nederlandsch Indie*, 76 (1920), 259.

early 1650s and another at Udaiganj in 1651.[60] Following an attack on the latter in 1658 by the forces of the local raja, the Company had no choice but to abandon it.[61] When the attempts to reestablish this unit proved abortive, a factory was opened in 1669 in neighbouring Khanakul, but this too was closed soon after. In 1676 a factory was opened at Malda in north Bengal primarily for the procurement of textiles. But it was closed in 1687 in persuance of Commissioner van Rheede's directive to make do with as few establishments as possible.[62]

Commercial and other matters at the chief factory at Hugli were looked after by a council consisting of the director, a senior factor (*opperkoopman*) in charge of the Company's trade books, a law-enforcement officer called the *fiscaal*, the person in charge of the warehouses, the person in charge of the loading and unloading of the ships, and six junior factors, one of whom acted as secretary to the council.[63] Each of the subordinate factories also had a council. The chief of the Kasimbazar factory, who held the rank of a senior factor, was treated as number two in the directorate, and in the event of the death or incapacitation of the director took over the latter's functions pending the appointment of a regular incumbent to the position.

With the accession of Aurangzeb to the Mughal throne in 1658, the concessions his father, Shahjahan, had accorded the Company automatically lapsed. The van Adrichem embassy was, therefore, sent to Delhi in 1662 to try and obtain identical concessions from the new emperor. One of the *farmans* obtained by the embassy related to Bengal, Bihar, and Orissa; the Company was thereby exempted from transit and similar duties throughout the three provinces. As for the custom duties, the *farman* instructed the relevant officials to go on charging from the Company at the "formerly established" rate (which was 4 percent at Hugil and 3 percent

---

[60] Udaiganj seems to be the most likely equivalent of "Oedagins" one comes across in Dutch records. In van den Broecke's map, this place is shown between Bardha and Khanakul in Midnapur district.

[61] Although all that the Company had lost in the attack was goods worth Rs. 8,301, a claim of Rs. 43,789 was filed with the *subahdar* of Bengal. By 1662, this had been increased to Rs. 105,452. When Subahdar Mir Jumla ordered the raja to appear before him at Dacca, the latter offered to negotiate with the Company. The negotiations, however, did not succeed. In the meantime, Mir Jumla died and the Company failed to recover anything. Memorandum by the outgoing director of the Bengal factories, van den Broecke, for his successor, van Hyningen, dated 14.2.1664, K.A. 1137, ff. 438-443.

[62] H.B. 4.4.1670, K.A. 1167, f. 1404vo; H.B. 28.2.1671, K.A. 1174, f. 1835; H.B. 15.1.1676, K.A. 1209, ff. 510vo-511; B.H. 17.6.1676, K.A. 803, f. 198; H.B. 29.8.1676, K.A. 1209, f. 603; XVII.B. 31.8.1678, K.A. 458; XVII.B. 6.10.1688, K.A. 460, f. 495.

[63] Pieter van Dam, *Beschrijvinge van de Oost-Indische Compagnie*, II, II, 34-41. The salaries of the director, a senior factor, a factor, and a junior factor were *f*. 160-180, *f*. 80, *f*. 60, and *f*. 36 per month, respectively.

at Pipli and Balasore).[64] But when a copy of the *farman* was taken to Subahdar Mir Jumla, he misinterpreted it to imply that the Company was obliged to pay transit and similar duties like everyone else. Even as the factors were deliberating upon the means to persuade the *subahdar* to change his mind, the latter died. The new *subahdar* readily confirmed the Company's interpretation of the *farman*.[65]

The next major *farman* available to us is the one Emperor Shah Alam issued on January 30, 1709. According to this document, the rate of the customs duty payable by the Dutch at Surat and Hugli was reduced from 3.5 to 2.5 percent. According to information in the Company's archives, as late as April 1670, the rate of the customs duty payable by the Dutch at Hugli was 4 percent.[66] The *nishan* granted by Prince Muhammad Azam in December 1678 had confirmed this arrangement. This, taken together with the *farman* of January 1709, leads us to infer that the rate of the customs duty payable by the Company at Hugli was changed to 3.5 percent in 1679 or later. This might have been done to ensure uniformity with the rate at Surat, where it was 2.5 percent prior to 1679, but was later increased to 3.5 percent to include 1 percent in lieu of the *jazia*. The 1709 rates were confirmed in August 1712, according to a *farman* by Shah Alam's successor, Jahandar Shah. By a separate *farman* granted at the same

---

[64] *Farman* dated October 29, 1662, *Corpus-Diplomaticum*, II, 217-220. After the designation of the Hugli factory as the chief factory of the Bengal region, the ports of Pipli and Balasore had hardly been used for loading or unloading ships to and from a port outside the region. For all practical purposes, therefore, all that the Company was now supposed to pay by way of customs duty was a 4 percent charge at Hugli. The *farman* instructed the officials in the three provinces to be helpful to the Company in the recovery of debts from merchants and others. The officials were also ordered not to detain the Company's ships under any pretext. *Batavia Dagh Register*, 1637, p. 102; *Generale Missiven*, II, 718; H.B. 4.4.1670, K.A. 1167, f. 1405; B.M. Addl. Ms. 29095, pp. 78-79.

[65] H.B. 4.3.1663, K.A. 1133, ff. 311-312. The provisions of the *farman* were reaffirmed in two *parwanas* issued in January 1678 under the seal of Wazir Asad Khan. In December 1678, Prince Muhammad Azam, who earlier in the year had been appointed *subahdar* of Bengal and Orissa, granted a *nishan* instructing officials in the two provinces to implement the 1662 imperial *farman* faithfully. In June 1682, the Company obtained a *parwana* on the lines of the royal *farman* of 1662 from Haji Sufi Khan, the imperial *diwan* at Dacca. *Corpus-Diplomaticum*, III, 116-119, 170-172, 295-296; B.M. Addl. Ms. 29095, f. 52.

At the request of the Company, Shaista Khan often agreed to issue *parwanas* instructing officials who insisted on asking for transit duties to desist from making such demands. Particular mention might be made of the *parwanas* issued in 1669 to officials at Balasore (B.M. Addl. Ms. 29095, f. 59), in 1671 to officials at Sripur, Hariaal, and the neighbouring places (H.B. 1.4.1671, K.A. 1174, f. 1848), in 1682 to officials at Hugli and Satgaon (B.M. Addl. Ms. 29095, ff. 58-59), and in 1684 to all the officials in Bengal and Orissa (B.M. Addl. Ms. 29095, ff. 57-58).

[66] *Corpus-Diplomaticum*, IV, 314-317; H.B. 4.4.1670, K.A. 1167, f. 1405.

42

time, the new emperor also confirmed the Company's exemption from transit and similar duties throughout the Mughal empire.[67]

The exemption from transit duties was an important concession. In principle, it enabled the Company to buy in the cheapest market in the region and sell in the dearest. In the case of many of the export goods, the difference between the price at Hugli and that at the places where they were produced was substantial and considerably in excess of the physical cost of transportation.[68] Why did the imperial authorities make this concession to the Dutch and other Europeans? Because the imperial government regarded an expansion in trade with favour, particularly because it brought about an increase in the revenue from customs duties. Under the Mughal fiscal structure, this revenue accrued to the imperial treasury and could be farmed or assigned at the discretion of the emperor. The income from the transit and similar duties, on the other hand, ordinarily went to the local administration or the local assignee.[69] An expansion in the trade by the Europeans was particularly welcome because of the large import of precious metals that it entailed.[70] From the point

[67] *Corpus-Diplomaticum*, IV, 424-428, 432-434. Between 1704 and 1712, the Company obtained, among other documents, a *nishan* (September 1708) and a *hasb-ul-omar* (February 1709; comparable to the *hasb-ul-hukm*) by Prince Farrukhsiyar, the son and representative of Prince Azim-us-Shan, the *subahdar* of Bengal (Farrukhsiyar himself acceded to the Mughal throne in January 1713); *parwanas* by Murshid Quli Khan (November 1704, June 1711, and February 1712) and Ziaullah Khan (February 1708, March 1708, August 1708, September 1708, and February-March 1709), by the imperial *diwan* at Patna, Imtiad Khan (April 1708), by the *diwan* of Prince Azim-us-Shan, Sarbulund Khan (September 1708), by the imperial *diwan* at Patna, Mohammad Ali Khan (February 1709), and by the *subahdar* of Bihar, Hasan Ali Khan (April 1709). In one form or another, most of these documents confirmed that the Company was to be exempt from the transit duties. *Corpus-Diplomaticum*, IV, 225-226, 275-276, 293-305, 318-321, 327-328, 387-388; H.B. 21.10.1704, K.A. 1584, ff. 160-162; enclosure to H.B. 15.10.1708, K.A. 1653, ff. 150-151; enclosure to H.B. 16.10.1709, K.A. 1669, ff. 207-210; enclosure to H.B. 31.10.1711, K.A. 1720, ff. 71-72; B.M. Addl. Ms. 29095, ff. 54, 65, 67-69, 73-76.

[68] For example, in 1703, Patna opium and saltpetre cost 43 percent and 16 percent more, respectively, when bought at Hugli. The corresponding figure in the case of Kasimbazar silk *alachas* and plain ginghams was 28 percent and 22 percent, respectively. The cost of transport worked out at only a fraction of these differences. Enclosure to H.B. 8.4.1703, K.A. 1570, ff. 143-144.

[69] For exceptions to this pattern, see W. H. Moreland, *From Akbar to Aurangzeb: A Study in Indian Economic History* (London, 1923), p. 282.

[70] The importance attached by the Mughals to the importation of precious metals is illustrated by the following incident. In 1657, following refusal to pay the local toll, the captain of one of Prince Shuja's ships on its way back from Kedah had been forced by the Dutch factors at Malacca to part with tin worth Rs. 1,631. On top of this affront had come the Hugli factors' refusal to provide naval assistance for the proposed campaign against Arakan. These two episodes together so infuriated the *subahdar* that he threatened to raise the rate of the customs duty payable by the Dutch at Hugli from the usual 4 percent to 20

of view of the imperial government, a practically costless means of encouraging this trade was to exempt it from transit duties. The Company's goods carrying a permit (*dastak*) issued by the chief of the Dutch factory where the journey originated were, in principle, exempt from the *rahdari* duties on the way. To facilitate this, the toll authorities at the point of origin issued a document called the *rawana* formally clearing the goods.

The Company's exemption from transit duties was not looked upon with favour by the local authorities and the assignees whose income was adversely affected as a result. In practice, therefore, the concession was often not actually made available to the Company. These authorities were fully aware that a violation of the provisions of the royal *farman* in this respect was unlikely to attract punishment.[71] Indeed, whenever such violations were brought to the attention of the imperial or the provincial authorities, the response consisted at most in the issue of a supplementary order directing the relevant authorities to honour the exemption made available to the Company.[72]

The Company faced the most exasperating situations in the procurement of the *rawana* papers at Patna and Kasimbazar.[73] Indeed, as of 1690, the

---

percent. But he was careful to exempt precious metals from this threatened increase (B.H. 19.7.1657, K.A. 784, f. 311; H.XVII. 4.12.1657, K.A. 1111, ff. 760-761; B.XVII. 17.12.1657, K.A. 1110, ff. 108vo-110).

[71] See Moreland, *From Akbar to Aurangzeb*, pp. 283-286. This was particularly so in the case of the tributary rajas and chiefs. Though these chiefs were usually formally covered by the *farmans* (thus Shahjahan's *farman* of November 1642 was addressed, among others, to "Hindu rajas" and Aurangzeb's of October 1662 addressed to officials at Agra, Oudh, and Allahabad was also applicable to the "rajas"), they were the group from whom the imperial administration was least likely to demand compliance. These chiefs, therefore, asked for the *rahdari* duty from the Company with absolute impunity. In 1654, for example, the rajas of Sripur, Udaiganj, and Chandrakona were reported to be levying tolls on goods the Company had procured in or transported through their territories. Memorandum by Commissioner Verpoorten for Director-Designate Pieter Sterthemius dated 28.10.1655, K.A. 1102, ff. 201-225vo; P.B. 10.3.1655, K.A. 1100, ff. 368vo-370. In the course of time, the Company had to give in to the payment of duties in these tracts on a regular basis, as is borne out by the order issued in April 1708 by Raja Dhir—whose territory included Chuprah, where the Company had a saltpetre collection agency—instructing his officials not to charge the Dutch anything in excess of the "usual duties." *Corpus-Diplomaticum*, I, 295-296.

[72] The authorities issuing these orders rarely took steps to ensure compliance. One such occasion was a *sanad* sent in 1709 by Sarbulund Khan, *diwan* of Prince Azim-us-Shan, to Director Willem de Roo informing him that in persuance of instructions he had received from the prince, he (the *diwan*) would ensure that the Dutch did not have to pay the *rahdari* duties from which they had been exempted. He asked the director to report to him immediately any cases in which the Company had been charged this duty, promising that he would make sure that the amount was refunded. B.M. Addl. Ms. 29095, ff. 71-72.

[73] In 1653, Prince Shuja's *diwan* instructed the *faujdar* of Maxudabad to allow the Dutch to send out of Kasimbazar duty-free each year a maximum of 1,000 bales of raw silk. An appeal to the prince secured a withdrawal of this order, but the matter did not end there. In 1661, at the instigation of Mir Jumla, who had taken over as *subahdar* in 1660 and whose

44

Company was obliged to pay a 3.5 percent toll on all goods leaving Patna.[74] Even after the goods had left the point of origin, there were frequently problems on the way. To take an extreme case, a number of Dutch saltpetre boats on their way from Patna to Hugli in 1703 were detained at Rajmahal and toll was demanded. The boats were released only after they had been under detention for 47 days, and 7 tons of saltpetre together with a sum of Rs. 600 paid as tolls. A few days later, the boats were detained again at Balaghat north of Kasimbazar, necessitating the payment of tolls once again.[75]

But there was another side of the coin, too. The Company extensively misused the concession of carrying goods duty-free from one point in the region to another by including under its protection goods that did not belong to it. Indian merchants who had bought goods from the Company at Hugli and who intended to transport them to other parts of the region, as well as those who had undertaken to supply goods to the Company at Hugli but had procured them elsewhere, were provided with Dutch *dastaks* almost as a matter of course. Even instances of *dastaks* being sold to merchants who had had no business dealings whatever with the Company were not altogether unknown. As a countermeasure, the authorities often obliged the merchants to sign bonds (*muchalkas*) that if found transporting their own goods against *dastaks* issued by any of the European companies,

---

jagir included Kasimbazar, a number of Indian silk merchants operating at Kasimbazar and Saidabad sent a petition to the imperial court at Delhi urging at least a partial withdrawal of the Company's *rahdari* exemption on the ground that it made it impossible for them to compete with the Dutch. The petition was referred for advice to Mir Jumla, who naturally supported the merchants' contention. Early in 1662, therefore, an order issued from Delhi imposed a limit of 1,000 bales on the amount of raw silk the Dutch could carry out of Kasimbazar per annum duty-free. As a countermove, the Company persuaded a number of merchants with whom it did business to issue a statement to the effect that the *rahdari* exemption enjoyed by the Company was in no way detrimental to the interests of the Indian merchants. A copy of the statement was sent to Delhi with the van Adrichem embassy that procured the *farmans* of October 1662. The *farman* relating to Bengal, Bihar, and Orissa, which superseded all earlier *farmans* pertaining to the region, imposed no limit on the amount of any commodity the Company carried from one part of the three provinces to another duty-free. The toll authorities at Kasimbazar were inclined to disregard the *farman*, but were dissuaded from doing so on the strength of regular gifts to Faujdar Bal Chand. In 1703, at the instigation of Murshid Quli Khan, a Hindu farmer of the Kasimbazar tolls tried to revive the limit of 1,000 bales on the amount of raw silk the Company could carry out of the town duty-free, but the attempt was not successful. H.XVII. 12.5.1659, K.A. 1119, f. 889vo; H.XVII. 8.12.1661, K.A. 1124, f. 182; H.B. 7.8.1662, K.A. 1130, f. 1125; H.B. 4.3.1663, K.A. 1133, ff. 303-304; H.B. 10.5.1673, K.A. 1185, f. 223; H.B. 30.9.1703, K.A. 1570, ff. 32-38.

[74] "Memorandum of tolls paid . . . at Patna since 1690, when they were first instituted," enclosure to H.B. 30.9.1703, K.A. 1570, ff. 79-80.

[75] H.B. 30.9.1703, K.A. 1570, ff. 32-38.

they would be subject to severe punishment besides forfeiting the goods so apprehended.[76] It is not known how effective this measure was.

In addition to misusing the concession of *dastaks*, the Company often evaded part of the customs duty payable at Hugli. The duty was charged on the basis of *talikas*—statements containing details of the physical quantities and the value of the goods imported and exported—supplied by the Company. The customs duty being *ad valorem*, all that an evasion of part of the duty required was an undervaluation of the cargo.[77] In an estimate prepared in 1671, it was noted that over the preceding sixteen years, on an average, the Company had evaded customs duties to the extent of a little over 14 percent of the amount actually due. In a particularly "good" year such as 1670-1671, this figure could go up to as much as 50 percent.[78] In 1672, the director and council at Hugli wrote to Batavia that subject to their approval, they could safely raise the average rate of evasion to 25 percent. The approval came forth readily not only from Batavia but also from the Board of Directors in Amsterdam. But even as the factors were writing this letter to Batavia, the provincial authorities detected the evasion and imposed a fine of Rs. 300,000 (later reduced to Rs. 150,000) on the Company. Pending the payment of the fine, the Company was ordered to suspend all its trading activities in the province of Bengal. It was only after the sum of Rs. 150,000 had actually been collected that the embargo on Dutch trade was withdrawn. For nearly two years after this, the Company refrained from evading the customs duties. At that point, however, Batavia, after stressing the necessity of extreme caution in the matter, authorized the factors at Hugli to resume the practice.[79]

---

[76] Report by Hofmeester to the director at Hugli regarding his mission to Dacca, 26.8.1672, K.A. 1178, ff. 74-79. For a copy of a *muchalka* taken from the merchants at Kasimbazar in 1707, see enclosure to H.B. 31.12.1707, K.A. 1653, f. 68.

[77] To take an example, saltpetre bought at Patna in 1672 at Rs. 3 per maund was declared in the relevant *talika* to have been purchased at Rs. 1.25 per maund. (H.B. 9.6.1672, K.A. 1078, ff. 43vo-45.)

[78] Against Rs. 48,714 the Company ought to have paid as customs duty that year, the actual amount paid was only Rs. 24,407. H.XVII. 6.11.1671, K.A. 1169, ff. 613vo-614.

[79] H.B. 28.2.1672, K.A. 1178, ff. 30-31; B.H. 14.6.1672, K.A. 799, ff. 438-439; B.H. 4.8.1673, K.A. 860, ff. 680-681; H.B. 19.9.1673, K.A. 1185, ff. 38-vo; B.H. 2.4.1674, K.A. 801, f. 109; H.B. 28.2.1672, K.A. 1178, ff. 30-31vo; H.B. 22.3.1672, K.A. 1178, f. 41vo; Nawab Shaista Khan's order imposing an embargo on the Dutch trade in Bengal, 11.5.1672, K.A. 1194, ff. 429-430; H.B. 9.6.1672, K.A. 1178, ff. 43vo-45; B.H. 14.6.1672, K.A. 799, f. 441; report by Pieter Hofmeester, 26.8.1672, K.A. 1178, f. 76vo; H.B. 8.9.1672, K.A. 1178, ff. 49vo-51, 54-55, 66vo; H.XVII. 14.11.1672, K.A. 1178, f. 116vo; H.B. 19.9.1673, K.A. 1185, ff. 33vo-34vo, 35, 66vo; statement signed by Rameshwar and Gauri Kant, enclosure to H.B. 19.4.1674, K.A. 1192, ff. 352-353vo; resolution dated 28.8.1674, K.A. 1193, ff. 178-179; B.H. 17.6.1676, K.A. 803, f. 227; H.B. 28.9.1676, K.A. 1269, f. 606; H.B. 1.3.1677, K.A. 1217, ff. 483-vo; instructions given to Factor

In order to ensure the smooth functioning of its trading apparatus in the region, the Company found it necessary to keep officials at various levels in good humour by presenting them gifts on a regular basis. The list of such officials could often be quite long.[80] On particular occasions, of course, the "gifts" might have to be given under duress.[81] Even more annoying and commercially more injurious was the occasional monopolization of trade in particular commodities by these officials. This might result in inadequate availability or higher prices for the Company.[82]

The Company had no choice but to live with these problems. Indeed, the only weapon it could use against the high-handedness of the provincial and the local authorities was the threat to attack Indian shipping on the high seas. Indian mercantile ships did carry an impressively large number of cannon, but they were so heavily overloaded that the guns could not be brought into action when there was need for them. This was true even

Bacherus in 1677, K.A. 1213, ff. 512-514; secret letter from Batavia to Director Volger dated 2.8.1677, K.A. 804, ff. 434-435; Corpus-Diplomaticum, III, 114-116; Nawab Muhammad Azam's reply to Wazir Asad Khan, 8.4.1678, K.A. 1228, ff. 863vo-864; parwana by Subahdar Muhammad Azam to Director Volger received in Hugli on 21.4.1678, K.A. 1228, f. 864; XVII.B. 8.6.1682, K.A. 459, f. 61.

[80] For example, between September 1, 1696, and August 31, 1697, gifts worth a total of f. 9,147 were given at various places in Bengal. At Dacca, the list included the subahdar, the bakshi, the imperial and the provincial diwans, confidential advisors to the two diwans, the priest of the provincial diwan, the qazi, the daroga of Aliganj, and lesser officials. The Patna list included the subahdar-designate of Bengal (Prince Azim-us-Shan, who was on his way to Dacca), the deputy and the bakshi of the prince, the subahdar of Bihar, the imperial and the provincial diwans, the wakianavis, the qazi, officials of the weighing house, the karori and his staff, several faujdars, officials of the mint, the chief bailiff, and a number of other officials. Gifts were also given to officials at Hugli, Kasimbazar, Rajmahal, and Balasore. Enclosure to H.B. 23.12.1697, K.A. 1500, ff. 6-25.

[81] A case in point was the occasion of the elevation of the imperial diwan, Murshid Quli Khan, to the higher and additional rank of the provincial subahdar in 1716. The Company agreed to the presentation of the gifts mentioned in a list handed over by the deputy to the subahdar to the Company's attorney (vakil) at the court, provided the two elephants asked for were excused. Without the elephants, the total value of the gift would have worked out at approximately Rs. 7,500. But when Murshid Quli came to know of it, he felt offended and insisted that a body of the standing of the Dutch Company could afford a gift of a value of Rs. 40,000. The Company offered to go up to Rs. 10,500, at which stage the subahdar declared that even a gift of Rs. 40,000 would no longer be acceptable. At the same time, he asked for an assurance that, like the English, the Company would soon send an embassy to the imperial court, and even asked for details of the gifts that would be sent along. This was more than the Company had bargained for, and negotiations were resumed. The final settlement was for a gift of the value of Rs. 40,000 to the subahdar and of Rs. 3,000 to his deputy. H.B. 31.10.1716, K.A. 1769, ff. 75-106vo.

[82] For example, the 1681 monopolization of opium by Buzurg Ummed Khan led to a rise in the market price from Rs. 74-75 to Rs. 85-86 per maund. H.B. 25.9.1683, K.A. 1276, f. 1209vo.

of the imperial ships. The result was that in the event of an attack by a European vessel, the outcome could always be safely predicted.[83] The Mughals did not have a navy worth the name, and were in no position to provide protection to their shipping against attacks by the Europeans.[84] The flotilla at Dacca and the fleet maintained by the Sidis at Janjira near Bombay were clearly inadequate for an offensive against the European ships.

Not surprisingly, considering that the Mughal state officials at various levels owned a part of the shipping operating from the Bengal ports, the threat of an attack on the high seas was at times quite effective. For example, in the face of grave provocation at the hands of Muhammad Yusuf, the *faujdar* of Pipli and Balasore, the Company wrote in 1663 to Khan Dauran, the *subahdar* of Orissa, asking for an immediate dismissal of Yusuf from both his positions. Pending the *subahdar*'s decision, the Company closed its factories at both Pipli and Balasore and put out a threat that Indian ships leaving these ports would be seized on the high seas. Before the Company had occasion to put the threat into effect, Muhammad Yusuf was removed from his position at Pipli and an assurance given to the Company that he would soon be relieved of his position at Balasore as well. A shaken Muhammad Yusuf put out an offer for con-ciliation, which the Company accepted. Soon after, the *faujdar* was rein-stated to his Pipli post and the Company reopened both factories.[85]

The naval superiority of the Company, however, often brought in its

[83] As Ashin Das Gupta has pointed out, for naval guns to be effective it was essential that enough space be left behind them to allow the ammunition trolleys to pass freely. This the merchants were reluctant to do, since the cargo space in question was precious (Ashin Das Gupta, *Indian Merchants and the Decline of Surat c. 1700-1750* [Weisbaden, 1979], p. 97). Partly as a result of the intense rivalry and hostility among the European nations engaged in the Eastern trade, the vessels used by Europeans were heavily and properly armed. The same was true of vessels used by European pirates.

[84] The so-called *katchan* fleet at Surat could be effective only against local pirates like the Sanganias (Das Gupta, *Indian Merchants*, p. 97). The following incident is instructive in this regard. Fearing an attempt by the English and the Dutch to take over the islands, the king of the Maldive islands sent an emissary in 1662 to the *faujdar* of Balasore, which had extensive trade relations with the islands. The *faujdar* was requested to use his good offices to persuade Emperor Aurangzeb to impose a ban on English and Dutch shipping to the Maldives. The *faujdar*'s response was that even if the emperor wanted to oblige the king, he was in no position to do so, since he was "master only of land and not of the sea." H.B. 26.10.1662, K.A. 1130, f. 1380vo.

[85] Instructions to Herman Voorburg, 21.11.1663, K.A. 1137, ff. 928-929vo; instructions to van Leenen, 27.11.1663, K.A. 1135, ff. 2645-2648; H.XVII. 19.1.1664, K.A. 1132, ff. 1065-1068; H.B. 5.4.1664, K.A. 1137, f. 1269; H.B. 31.10.1664, K.A. 1139, f. 2982; H.B. 27.11.1664, K.A. 1140, ff. 98-100; H.B. 22.6.1665, K.A. 1145, f. 1800; H.B. 9.1.1666, K.A. 1149, ff. 2230-2231; H.B. 1.4.1666, K.A. 1149, f. 2247; H.B. 14.5.1667, K.A. 1156, f. 855.

wake more problems than it helped solve. The administration called upon the Company to provide naval and other assistance in organising campaigns against neighbouring states, in crushing local rebellions, or in containing the depredations of the European pirates. The general policy of the Company was to avoid becoming involved in these matters as far as possible. When there was no alternative, the Company tried to fulfil its obligations with as little investment in men and materials as possible.

The first such major involvement of the Company was in the Mughal campaign against Chittagong in 1665-1666. The attempt to conquer Chittagong and, if possible, Arakan was intended to contain the Magh pirates who had rendered impossible any profitable trade along the river Meghna, which was one of the two estuaries serving Bengal. These pirates had joined hands with Portuguese renegades and operated from Chittagong with the active connivance of the king of Arakan, who shared in the spoils. Between 1656 and 1664, campaigns were planned twice but not executed for various reasons.[86] Matters came to a head in 1664, when sixty to seventy pirate vessels were reported to have captured as many as 160 boats of the imperial flotilla.[87] The provincial authorities were ordered to reorganise the flotilla and execute the campaign. Subahdar Shaista Khan asked the Portuguese, the English, and the Dutch for assistance in the form of armed vessels. The Dutch were requested to provide ten to twenty vessels against the promise of a reimbursement of the costs incurred, the grant of one-fourth of the territory that might be conquered (with the Company having the option to demand a cash payment in lieu thereof), and an exemption in perpetuity from the payment of customs duties throughout the Mughal empire.[88] The Batavia Council agreed to provide two small ships, the *Landsmeer* and the *Purmerland*, for the campaign. But the vessels arrived at Chittagong only on October 11, 1666, long after the forts at both Chittagong and Rambu—midway between Chittagong and Arakan—had been captured by the Mughal forces under the command of Buzurg Ummed Khan, the son of Subahdar Shaista Khan. Due to the shortage of supplies and other factors, the campaign had been suspended

[86] B.H. 19.7.1657, K.A. 784, f. 311; H.XVII. 4.12.1657, K.A. 1111, ff. 760-761; B.XVII. 17.12.1657, K.A. 1110, ff. 108vo-110; H.XVII. 19.9.1660, K.A. 1122, f. 411vo; H.XVII. 9.12.1660, K.A. 1122, f. 659.

[87] Later the same year, the pirates were reported to have captured in one raid 2,700-2,800 Bengalis from Bhushna to be sold as slaves. (H.B. 31.10.1664, K.A. 1139, ff. 2936-2938; H.B. 27.11.1664, K.A. 1140, f. 10; *Batavia Dagh-Register*, 1664, pp. 554, 593.)

[88] H.B. 31.10.1664, K.A. 1139, ff. 2936-2938; *Batavia Dagh-Register*, 1664, p. 554; H.B. 6.1.1665, K.A. 1143, ff. 47-50; resolution adopted by the Batavia Council, 27.7.1665, K.A. 580, ff. 194-204, *Batavia Dagh-Register*, 1666-1667, p. 40. Even if one assumed that not all the promises would have been kept, the very fact that such extravagant terms were offered underscores the pathetic state of naval capability in Mughal India.

at this stage. Commander van Leenen, therefore, proceeded with the vessels for Dacca, where they were placed at the disposal of the local factors for commercial use. The planned campaign against Arakan did not materialize, and the Mughal forces returned to Dacca.[89]

Naval assistance by the Dutch actually prevented the possible annihilation of Mughal authority in the Bengal *subah* during the revolt by Zamindar Sobha Singh of Chatwa-Barda in Midnapore district, which kept the province in a state of serious disorder for nearly two and a half years between the middle of 1695 and the close of 1697. Initially, the factors turned down the request by the provincial administration for assistance in crushing the revolt. But in August 1696, the rebels succeeded in capturing the fort at Hugli, exposing the local Dutch factory to grave danger. It was then decided to disregard the standing instructions by Batavia to maintain strict neutrality in situations of this sort, and steps were taken to restore the control of the fort to the Mughal authorities. A contingent of Dutch soldiers was deployed to surround the fort, and the *Berkensteyn* was stationed in the Hugli river at a point from which its guns could cover the fort. The known superiority of European weaponry persuaded the rebels not to put up a fight. The fort was promptly vacated, and the Dutch restored Bakshi Mirza Hasan Ali's control over it.[90] The Dutch action was, of course, in response to compelling local circumstances and did not represent a shift away from the basic policy of neutrality. This is borne out by the Company's reluctance to take advantage of the permission given by Subahdar Ibrahim Khan to all the European companies to strengthen their defences and even have a fortified settlement. In fact, once the revolt had been crushed, the temporary measures taken to strengthen the defences of the Hugli factory were undone. It was only in 1743 that the factory at Hugli (Chinsura) was fortified and given the name of Fort Gustavus.[91]

Another possible area of conflict between the Mughal authorities and the Company was the demand made on the Company to provide protection to Indian shipping against the depredations of European pirates operating from their bases in Madagascar. Although the Dutch factory at Surat was most affected by the sudden increase of such piracy in the closing years of the seventeenth century, there was also some impact on Bengal.[92] The

[89] Resolution adopted by the Batavia Council, 27.7.1666, K.A. 581, ff. 151-156; report of van Leenen, 2.7.1667, K.A. 1155, ff. 328-329; H.B. 7.4.1668, K.A. 1158, f. 907.

[90] H.B. 2.9.1696, K.A. 1471, ff. 126-134; B.H. 9.8.1698, K.A. 835, ff. 547-550.

[91] B.H. 9.8.1698, K.A. 835, ff. 545-550; Hodenpijl, "De Handhavig der Neutraliteyt van de Nederlandsche Loge te Houghly," p. 259.

[92] A detailed account of the developments at Surat is available in Das Gupta, *Indian Merchants*, ch. II.

1692 plunder of four Surat vessels, two of which were owned by Mulla Abdul Ghafur, brought forth a demand on all three European companies to equip a warship each for the purpose of apprehending the pirate ships. The failure to comply with this demand led to a ban on the Dutch trade throughout the Mughal empire in February 1693—although bribes to officials at the local and the provincial level in Bengal persuaded them to allow the Company to continue trading on a clandestine basis. The ban was formally withdrawn in February 1694.[93]

The plunder of the *Ganj-i-Sawai* in 1695 was instrumental in the introduction of the system of Dutch and English convoys to the Red Sea. A large ship of 1,000 *khandies* was paid a fee of Rs. 20,000 for a round trip; a smaller vessel qualified for Rs. 15,000.[94] Half the sum was found by the *mutasaddi* of Surat from the customs duties, while the rest was jointly subscribed by the merchants whose ships were to make the trip. The Company was free to carry its own cargo or freight goods on the escort vessels it made available.[95] This arrangement worked well until 1698, when Surat merchant Hasan Hamadani lost a richly laden ship. The ship had not formed part of the convoy, but each of the three companies was nevertheless obliged in February 1699 to give a bond (*muchalka*) accepting responsibility for any losses that vessels from Surat might in future sustain at the hands of the pirates. The English were made responsible for the vessels going to the southwest coast of India, the Malay peninsula, and the Indonesian archipelago, the French for those going to the Persian Gulf, the Dutch for vessels going to the Red Sea.[96] Abdul Ghafur and other merchants interpreted the *muchalkas* to imply the companies' responsibility for losses whether or not a particular ship that might be captured formed part of the convoy, an interpretation that the Dutch contested.

An occasion for testing the enforceability of the *muchalkas* arose in September 1701, when news reached Surat that one of Abdul Ghafur's ships from the Red Sea, the *Husaini*, had been plundered. The Dutch

[93] *Corpus-Diplomaticum*, IV, 22-23; H.B. 6.4.1693, K.A. 1435, ff. 83-84vo; enclosure to H.B. 6.4.1693, K.A. 1427, ff. 60vo-61; B.H. 1.7.1693, K.A. 825, ff. 1080-1085; H.B. 6.4.1693, K.A. 1435, ff. 83-84vo; B.H. 1.7.1693, K.A. 825, ff. 1080-1085; Patna-Hugli 29.3.1693, K.A. 1427, ff. 60-vo; B.H. 19.8.1693, K.A. 825, ff. 1521-1523; H.XVII. 15.1.1694, K.A. 1435, ff. 11-16vo; B.H. 26.8.1694, K.A. 826, ff. 936-937; H.B. 5.9. 1693, K.A. 1435, ff. 90-92; H.B. 26.3.1694, K.A. 1435, ff. 936-937; *Corpus-Diplomaticum*, IV, 23 note 6; H.B. 20.9.1694, K.A. 1435, ff. 317-320vo.

[94] Three *khandies* made one deadweight ton.

[95] *Corpus-Diplomaticum*, IV, 124-127; Das Gupta, *Indian Merchants*, p. 99.

[96] *Corpus-Diplomaticum*, IV, 144-146, 150-152; H.B. 10.3.1699, K.A. 1516, ff. 39-40; enclosure to H.B. 6.4.1699, K.A. 1516, ff. 142-143; Edward Littleton and Council to the Directors of the New English Company, 6.3.1702, O.C. 7892, ff. 21-28, vol. 57 (III).

refused to pay compensation, claiming that this was one of the ships that had broken convoy. Ghafur organised his fellow merchants, who decided that until the Dutch paid the compensation, no one would fit out a ship. They also demanded suspension of the Company's trade until a settlement was reached. The imperial court decreed in favour of the merchants, and ordered the Dutch to pay the compensation claimed. Pending this, their trade was banned throughout the Mughal empire.[97] As was usual in such situations, however, the ban was only partially enforced.[98] The demand for compensation was met but it was only in November 1702 that the ban on trade was withdrawn.[99]

In August 1703, yet another of Abdul Ghafur's ships was attacked and captured while it was anchored at the Surat bar. The Dutch refused to pay compensation, as the piracy had not occurred on the high seas. In Bengal, the resulting tension led to a temporary closure of the factories at Patna and Kasimbazar in 1704. A strong Dutch naval force made its appearance off Surat in September 1703 and again a year later. At the suggestion of the new governor of Surat, Najabat Khan, the emperor agreed to relieve the Dutch of the 1699 muchalka, thereby restoring the status quo ante of 1696 stipulating only the provision of convoy to the Surat ships. This was in January 1705, but the Dutch blockade of Surat was lifted only in 1707.[100] The factories at Patna and Kasimbazar also remained closed during this period. The authorities of the Company in Batavia and Amsterdam regarded situations such as these as irritants that they had no option but to deal with as best they could. Fortunately for them, the resulting addition to the overall costs of the operations in Bengal was only marginal and did not cut significantly into the profitability of the trade from the region.

[97] H.B. 22.3.1702, K.A. 1556, ff. 156-158; Edward Littleton and Council at Calcutta to the Directors of the New English Company, 6.3.1702, O.C. 7892, ff. 21-28, vol. 57 (III).

[98] Thus, in the case of Bengal, the Dutch were prevented from carrying on their trade at Patna and some other places but allowed to do so clandestinely at Hugli. H.B. 10.4.1702, K.A. 1556, ff. 182-191; H.B. 30.9.1702, K.A. 1548, ff. 1218-1225vo; secret letter from Murshid Quli Khan to his son-in-law, the faujdar of Balasore, which accidentally fell into Dutch hands, H.B. 30.9.1702, K.A. 1548, ff. 1200vo-1201.

[99] The relevant hasb-ul-hukm reached Bengal in January 1703, but was not implemented until March. Over the intervening period, Murshid Quli had been trying to extract something from the companies in consideration of implementing the hukm. Only a clever move on the part of the Dutch in arranging to have the demand inserted in the wakia persuaded Murshid Quli to withdraw it. H.B. 12.3.1703, K.A. 1570, ff. 3, 12-23; H.B. 8.4.1703, K.A. 1570, ff. 79-80, 97-101.

[100] Corpus-Diplomaticum, IV, 221; H.B. 15.12.1703, K.A. 1570, ff. 100-103; H.B. 22.3.1704, K.A. 1584, ff. 10-15; Das Gupta, Indian Merchants, pp. 122, 133-134.

· 3 ·

THE BENGAL TRADE: LONG-TERM TRENDS

The Dutch East India Company established trade relations with Bengal only after it had been operating elsewhere in the subcontinent for a period of nearly three decades. But once a beginning had been made, the growth of the Company's trade in the region was remarkably rapid. During the latter half of the seventeenth century, the Bengal trade played a crucial role in the Company's intra-Asian trade. Thus in the 1660s, Bengal goods accounted, on an average, for 48 percent of the cargo sent to Japan.[1] Similarly, at a slightly later date, opium procured in Bihar accounted for a substantial proportion of the total Dutch imports into the Indonesian archipelago. Toward the close of the seventeenth century, as the composition of the exports to Europe underwent a drastic change in favour of textiles and silks manufactured in Bengal and elsewhere, the trade from this region assumed an altogether new significance. In the early years of the eighteenth century, approximately two-fifths of the total export to Europe were procured in Bengal.

The Import Trade: Precious Metals and Goods

The raison d'être of the Company's operations in Bengal (and elsewhere in the subcontinent) was the procurement of export goods for other parts of Asia as well as for Europe. The role of the precious metals and goods imported into the region from Europe and other parts of Asia was chiefly to provide purchasing power needed to buy the export goods. Most of these imports were precious metals because, given the structure of relative prices, the local demand for imported goods was comparatively small. This was more true of goods of European origin than of goods obtained by the Company in other parts of Asia, but even in the latter case the extent of the market was fairly limited. The determining consideration with the Council of the Indies at Batavia when it worked out the mix of the goods to be sent to Bengal in a given year was not the rate of profit to be earned on a particular item but the total amount of purchasing power that the

---

[1] This figure is based on an average for three years, 1661, 1669, and 1672. For the value of Bengal goods exported to Japan, see Table 3.5. The total value of goods the Company exported to Nagasaki during these years is based, except for 1672, on Nachod, *Niederländischen Ostindischen Kompagnie*, pp. ccii-cciv, Table A. For 1672, the information contained in the *Batavia Dagh-Register* has been preferred because Nachod's figure for that year falls short of the actual by the value of the cargo of a ship that was lost on the way.

sale of that item was likely to generate over the year. In the case of many of the goods, the Bengal factors were authorized to sell even at cost price. Nevertheless, the sale of goods was limited, and an overwhelming proportion of the imports was of necessity in the form of precious metals.

Silver imported from Europe included coins such as Mexican, Seville, and Spanish rials, rials of eight, rix-, provincial-, crown-, lion-, and cross-dollars as well as *dukatons*. A substantial proportion of the total precious metals imported into Bengal used to be obtained within Asia. This included silver and gold from Japan (the latter being in the form of an oval-shaped coin, the *koban*), and silver from Pegu, Arakan, and Persia. Small quantities of gold bullion were also imported from Timor and the west coast of Sumatra.

The goods the Company imported into Bengal were practically all of Asian origin. An important constituent was pepper and other spices. Pepper was obtained mainly in the interior of Sumatra and the hinterland of Patani on the Malay peninsula. The other spices were obtained in the so-called spice islands in the eastern part of the Indonesian archipelago. Amboina was the chief source of cloves, whereas the other islands provided nutmeg and its derivative, mace. Nonprecious metals such as copper, tin, lead, and spelter were also important items of import. Copper was procured mainly in Japan, whereas the other metals were obtained in several parts of the Malay peninsula. Comparatively minor items included cinnamon, areca nuts, elephants, and conch shells from Ceylon and sandalwood from Timor.

The Export Trade: The Items of Export

The principal items procured by the Company in the region were raw silk, textiles, opium, and saltpetre. Comparatively minor items (constituting the miscellaneous category) included provisions such as sugar, rice, wheat, clarified butter and mustard oil, wax, borax, sea shells (*cauris*), and gunny bags. Of the four principal items of export, raw silk played a crucial role first in the Company's intra-Asian trade and subsequently in the trade with Europe. Trade in opium and saltpetre was confined to the intra-Asian and the Euro-Asian branches of trade, respectively. Some varieties of textiles figured in the intra-Asian trade, but the bulk of the procurement was for the European market.

Raw Silk

The Company procured raw silk mainly for the Japanese and the Dutch markets. The three important raw silk-exporting areas in Asia were China,

54

Persia, and Bengal. The principal attraction of Bengal silk was that al-though it cost substantially less than both the Chinese and the Persian varieties, it usually sold in Holland at a price only marginally lower than that fetched by the former and about the same as that fetched by the latter.[2] Prior to the arrival of the Europeans on the scene, there was a substantial interregional and international trade in raw silk from Bengal. The principal merchant groups involved in this trade were those from Agra, Gujarat, and Central Asia. The raw silk procured by the Europeans was produced almost exclusively in the area around Kasimbazar in Mur-shidabad district in north Bengal. There were three harvests (called *bands*) in a year—in November, February-March, and June-July. The lot produced in the November *band* was by far the best in quality because the dry and cold weather helped the stuff produced by the chrysalis coagulate rapidly. The lot produced in February-March came next, followed by that of June-July.[3]

The processes involved in the production of raw silk were first, drawing the filaments from the cocoons, and second, reeling these filaments into recognizable grades of raw silk, differentiated by fineness and length. Fil-aments drawn from the better-grade cocoons were known as *pattani*, the others as *potti*. The raw silk reeled from the *pattani* filaments was of two distinct varieties: *tanna-banna* and *tanny*. The latter was a considerably superior variety that used a larger number of cocoons per unit of output. This variety had reportedly been introduced only in 1669, at the initiative of silk merchants from Agra who were among the principal groups of buyers of raw silk in Bengal. In the case of both *tanna-banna* and *tanny*, a given quantity of *pattani* filaments generated several distinct subqualities of reeled raw silk in well-defined proportions. Thus in *tanna-banna*, there were three distinct subqualities: *cabessa*, *bariga*, and *pee* (corresponding to the *head*, *belly*, and *foot*, of the English documents). The first two qualities accounted for 93.75 percent of the total output (the proportion between *cabessa* and *bariga* varied between 12:8 and 11:9). The remaining 6.25 percent was equally divided between the third variety and the waste ma-terial. The quality differentiation was even more marked in the *tanny* variety. The seven subqualities (the first five of which corresponded to the Arabic numerals 1 to 5) were *cora* 25 percent, *duam* 37.5 percent,

---

[2] In 1631, Chinese and Persian raw silk were estimated to have cost *f.* 3.5 and *f.* 4.00 per pond, respectively. The cost of Bengal silk in this particular year is not known, but eleven years later the Directors estimated its cost at *f.* 2.25 per pond. In September 1636, the sale price of the Chinese, Persian, and Bengal varieties was reported to be *f.* 10.2, *f.* 9.0 and *f.* 9.3 per pond, respectively. Glamann, *Dutch-Asiatic Trade*, pp. 116-121; resolution adopted by the Directors dated 18.9.1636, K.A. 250.

[3] Van Dam, *Beschrijvinge*, II, ɪɪ, 68.

ceem 18.75 percent, *charum*, 6.25 percent, *panjam* 3.12 percent, *fayn* 3.12 percent, and *ketser* 3.12 percent. The remaining 3.12 percent was waste material.[4] These proportions are important because the merchants insisted that the Company accept the subqualities within each of the two major varieties broadly in the proportion in which they were produced. Yet another variety of raw silk procured by the Company in Bengal, though in comparatively small quantities, was the so-called *mochta* silk, which the Europeans described as florette yarn.[5] This was an unreeled silk-based thread produced from cocoons that had been pierced by the moth, which had escaped death while it was still a chrysalis. Finally, the Company also procured in Bengal negligible amounts of the knitting and sewing silk.

According to Pieter van Dam, one seer of *tanna-banna* raw silk cost Rs. 2.40 and of *tanny* raw silk, Rs. 3.27.[6] An analysis of these amounts is presented in Table 3.1. The real wage bill works out at 17.5 percent of the total cost in the case of the *tanna-banna* variety and 23.5 percent for the *tanny*. Raw silk reeled from the *potti* filaments was also known as *tanna-banna*, but was of a distinctly inferior quality. The average cost of production of a seer of *potti tanna-banna* silk was estimated at Rs. 2.25. As

TABLE 3.1
Cost of Production of One Seer of *Tanna-banna*
and *Tanny* Raw Silk

Item of Cost	Tanna-banna (in rupees)	Tanny (in rupees)
Cocoons at 6¾ seers per rupee	1.90 (12¾ seers)	2.37 (16 seers)
Wages of the drawers of the *pattani* filaments	0.19	0.31
Food provided to the *pattani* drawers	0.04	0.09
Wood used as fuel	0.08	0.13
Wages of the reelers	0.19	0.37
Total cost	2.40	3.27

Source. Pieter van Dam, *Beschrijvinge*, II, II, pp. 69-70.

[4] Ibid., 70; P.B. 27.10.1654, K.A. 1094, f. 665.

[5] This presumably was the *matka* silk, so named because the pierced cocoon from which it was produced was called *mukhkata*. J. C. Ray, "Textile Industry in Ancient India," *Journal of the Bihar and Orissa Research Society*, 3 (1917), 219.

[6] One seer was equal to 2.057 lbs. avoirdupois. The figures from van Dam's account have been converted from rupees and annas into rupees and paise.

far as possible, the Company tried to procure raw silk reeled from *pattani* filaments alone.

Information regarding the average annual output of raw silk in Bengal in the seventeenth century is extremely difficult to obtain. The French traveller, Jean Baptiste Tavernier, has suggested that the annual output in the 1660s-1670s was around 22,000 bales of 100 lbs. each. But given that Tavernier's figure of 6,000-7,000 bales as the volume of annual Dutch trade in this item at this time is a gross exaggeration, one wonders what degree of credence to attach to his figure of annual output of raw silk.[7] Unfortunately, one cannot indicate even broadly the proportion the Dutch procurement of raw silk formed to the total output.

Opium

Besides raw silk, the only Bengal item that figured in the Company's intra-Asian trade in a significant manner was opium. The two major centres of production of this drug in seventeenth-century India were Bihar and Malwa. Until about 1670, the main area to which Bihar opium was sent was the Malabar coast, but thereafter the Indonesian archipelago became the principal market for this item. Indeed, Bihar soon became the sole supplier of opium to the archipelago. Opium was obtained from the immature fruits of the opium poppy *Papaver somniferum*. When incised, the fruit exuded a thick juice that was later dried and cut into cakes. The quality of the dried opium was judged by its colour. The best grade was brown, whereas the worst would have turned nearly red. There was an extensive range in between. Fresh opium could easily be adulterated with sand or other impurities without risk of immediate detection.

A Dutch account pertaining to the year 1688 estimated the annual output of opium in Bihar in a normal year at 8,700 maunds.[8] This amount was produced in forty-eight parganas, half of which were held in *jagir* by Wazir Asad Khan, Nawab Shaista Khan, and his son Buzurg Ummed Khan, among others. The remaining parganas, accounting for nearly 61 percent of the total output were administered by revenue officials on behalf of the king as *khalisa* lands.[9] Of the total output, 62 percent was of very

---

[7] J. B. Tavernier, *Travels in India* (London, 1889), II, 2. This figure of total procurement in a year was not achieved by the Company even at the close of our period. The maximum amount procured in the 1660s was under 300,000 ponds.

[8] Instructions by Adriaan van Ommen and van Heck, representatives of Commissioner van Rheede, to the Patna factors dated June 30, 1688. Enclosure to H.B. 22.9.1688, K.A. 1343, ff. 764vo-768vo. 1 Bengal maund = 68 Dutch ponds = 75 lbs. avoirdupois = 34.05 Kg.

[9] In the Mughal land revenue structure, a part of the total land revenue used to be alienated

good quality. The remaining 38 percent was distributed among various grades in a descending order of quality as follows: Grade II, 8.04 percent; grade III, 9.19 percent; grades IV and V, 8.62 percent each, and grade VI, 3.44 percent. The account went on to suggest further that of the total output, only about 0.6 percent was consumed within Bihar. Another about 10 to 12 percent was sent to other parts of the Bengal region. The exports to Agra and Allahabad reportedly accounted for yet another 34.5 to 46 percent of the total output. The remaining 41 to 55 percent was exported to other national and international markets. The average amount procured annually by the Dutch Company around this time was approximately 1,000 maunds, accounting for about 11.5 percent of the total output. This, of course, does not take into account the illegal private trade carried on by the Company's servants in this item, which often matched the trade carried on by the Company.

Saltpetre

Whereas opium was an item exclusive to the intra-Asian trade of the Company, saltpetre figured exclusively in the trade with Europe. This item was not only a high profit-yielding commercial good like any other handled by the Company; it had the added advantage that it could be used to ballast the homebound ships. Saltpetre was an essential ingredient in the manufacture of gunpowder, and its indigenous production in Europe had not been keeping pace with the rise in demand. During periods of conflict (of which the seventeenth century had more than its share), the demand for imported saltpetre increased considerably. Of course, the war potential of this item occasionally created problems in procurement for the Company. Thus although the trade in textiles and raw silk in Bengal had begun on a regular basis in 1636, that in saltpetre had to wait another two years because the agreement concluded with Subahdar Islam Khan in 1636 explicitly banned the Company from procuring this item—a restriction that was removed only by the royal *farman* of 1638.[10] More than half a century later, in 1692, Wazir Asad Khan issued a *hasb-ul-hukm* banning the export of saltpetre from Bihar by the European companies. According to the information of the Dutch, Aurangzeb had been urged by the sultan of Turkey to take this step, claiming that the saltpetre reaching Europe

---

to the state officials, the so-called *mansabdars-jagirdars* in settlement of their claims on account of personal salary and reimbursement for military expenses. The remaining land area was designated *khalisa*, the income from which went directly into the imperial treasury.

[10] *Corpus-Diplomaticum*, I, 282-284, 327-332.

through the companies was designed to be used against him. The ban was withdrawn only in 1694.[11]

Saltpetre was produced in the Indian subcontinent mainly in Gujarat, the Coromandel coast, and Bihar. From about the middle of the seventeenth century onward, Bihar became virtually the only supplier of saltpetre for the European market. This reflected the distinct advantage that Bihar saltpetre had over its rivals in the form of a lower price and the proximity to the river Ganga for a quick and relatively inexpensive transportation to the port of Hugli. Saltpetre was produced in Bihar mainly in the districts of Bihar, Champaran, Hajipur, Saran, and Tirhut. The producers belonged to a particular caste called the *luniahs*, and the period of production was between November and the middle of June. The first step in the process was the collection of saline earth by scraping the surface of old mud heaps and waste grounds where saltpetre had developed in a thin white efflorescence resembling frost rind. This earth was then dissolved and filtered through bamboos and grass mats. Next the saltpetre liquor was evaporated to a crystallizing state, which was done in earthen pots fixed in two rows over an oblong cavity dug in the ground, the interstices between the pots being filled up with clay. The product at this stage was known as *dobara* saltpetre, and contained 80 to 85 percent pure nitre. In order to produce refined saltpetre called *dobara-cabessa* or *kalmi*— whose nitre content was about 95 percent—the *dobara* saltpetre was redissolved and crystallized.[12]

According to a Dutch account of 1688, the annual output of saltpetre in Bihar was estimated at 226,000 maunds, which, when refined, came down to 127,238 maunds (56.25 percent). The production was spread over about twenty-eight parganas. Eleven of these parganas, accounting for about 22 percent of the output of unrefined saltpetre, were administered as *khalisa* lands on behalf of the king, while the remaining ones were held as *jagirs* by, among others, Wazir Asad Khan, Nawab Shaista Khan, and Nawab Ikram Khan of Orissa. Of the refined saltpetre, 5.5 percent was reportedly consumed within Bihar, while another 11.75 percent was sent to other parts of the Bengal region. That left about 82.75 percent of the

[11] Letter from Patna to Hugli, 8.12.1692, K.A. 1397, ff. 183vo-184; Hugli to Patna, 20.12.1692, K.A. 1397, ff. 185-186vo; enclosure to H.B. 30.1.1693, K.A. 1427, f. 21vo; secret letter from Batavia to Director Muykens at Hugli, 10.5.1693, K.A. 824, ff. 763-766; resolution adopted by the Hugli Council, 11.1.1694, K.A. 1435, ff. 247-249.

[12] Instructions by Adriaan van Ommen and van Heck, representatives of Commissioner van Rheede to Patna factors dated June 30, 1688. Enclosure to H.B. 22.9.1688, K.A. 1343, ff. 746-764vo; Wouter Schouten, *Oost-Indische Reys-Beschrijving* (Amsterdam, 1676), Book III, p. 119; J. Stevenson, "On the Manufacture of Saltpetre as Practiced by the Natives of Tirhut," *Journal and Proceedings of the Asiatic Society of Bengal*, 2 (1833), 23-27.

total output for export to areas outside the region. During 1685-1690, the average annual procurement by the Company was 38,500 maunds, accounting for slightly over 30 percent of the total output of refined saltpetre.[13]

Textiles

In addition to raw silk, opium, and saltpetre, Bengal was a major supplier of cotton and silk textiles. Indeed, by the early years of the eighteenth century, textiles were the biggest single item in the Company's export bill from Bengal. The region provided more textiles to the European companies than the rest of Asia put together. Some of the textiles bought in Bengal by the Dutch were destined for markets within Asia—Japan, Persia, Ceylon, and the Indonesian archipelago. But the bulk of the procurement was for Europe, partly for sale within Holland and partly to be reexported. These textiles were used as wearing apparel, bed furnishings, table covers, curtains, wall hangings, and linings. Muslins and silk piece goods, particularly those brocaded or embroidered or with gold borders, seem to have been reexported in fair quantities to Eastern Europe, the Baltic ports, Russia, and Norway.[14] France was another important reexport market for Bengal silk piece goods.[15] Bengal textiles also figured in the Dutch trade with southern Europe and the Levant. In 1675, for example, cotton *rumals* procured in Pipli in Orissa were reported to be very "useful" in the trade with Spain and Turkey. But in the reexport trade in coarse cotton textiles carried on from Holland with the Guinea coast and the American colonies, the role of Bengal textiles seems to have been quite insignificant.[16]

The comparative advantage of Bengal in relation to the other textile-producing regions of India consisted in the manufacture of fine cotton and silk textiles. In terms of quality, the cotton grown in the vicinity of Dacca

[13] Instructions by van Ommen and van Heck, dated June 30, 1688.

[14] H. Brugmans, "Handel en Nijverheid" in H. Brugmans and others, *Amsterdam in de Zeventiende Eeuw* (The Hague, 1901-1904), part II, pp. 69-74. The French traveller Tavernier wrote, "But for the cloths which are ordered for Poland and Muscovie, it is necessary to have this gold and silver in the Indian style, because the Poles and Russians will have nothing to do with the cloths if they have not gott the threads of gold and silver" (Tavernier, *Travels in India*, II, 28-29).

[15] In 1697, for example, Bengal silk *jamawars* were reported to be doing very well in France. Orders list, March 1697, K.A. 261; Bengal's explanation of why the orders were not supplied in full, 1699, K.A. 1516, f. 77.

[16] It was only toward the end of the seventeenth century that the Dutch had begun procuring the so-called Guinea cloth in Bengal. Even then, the volume of trade in this item continued to be very small. Thus in 1706-1707, the number of pieces exported was only 640 against an order for 20,000 pieces "or as many more as Bengal can supply." Orders list sent by the Board of Directors to Batavia dated March 2, 1705, K.A. 263.

did not have a rival in the entire subcontinent. The quantity grown, however, was rather small, and the bulk of the cotton used in the region had to be imported from areas such as Gujarat. In raw silk, on the other hand, the region was not only self-sufficient but, in fact, supplied large quantities to other areas. More importantly, there was a long tradition of highly skilled craftsmanship in the region.

The Company procured cotton, silk, and mixed cotton and silk textiles in Bengal. Among the cotton textiles, the principal division was between the muslins and the calicoes. Of the two, muslins were more loosely woven and, on an average, were made of finer yarn. The best quality muslins were produced in the district of Dacca, where a particularly well-known centre of production was Sonargaon, situated at a distance of about fifteen miles east of the city of Dacca. The other important manufacturing centres were the Malda district and Santipur in Nadia district. Comparatively less fine varieties were also produced in Patna in Bihar and Balasore in Orissa. The output of the finest Dacca varieties, which have since become almost legendary, was extremely limited and their price so high as to be within the reach of only the very wealthy. Since it would almost certainly have been commercially disastrous for the European companies to trade in these extremely expensive varieties, they restricted their procurement to the commonly manufactured ones which, nevertheless, were the best quality cotton textiles procured by them anywhere in the East.[17]

The principal types procured by the Dutch (in descending order of fineness, workmanship, and cost) were *tanzeb*, *terrindam*, *khasa*, *malmal*, *resta*, and *rehing*.[18] The staple varieties were *khasa* and *malmal*, both plain muslins of good quality. However, quite a few of the pieces procured by the Company in both these varieties were brocaded in gold, silver, or silk threads, usually in floral patterns. Less frequently they were instead embroidered in coloured silks in chain-stitch, in gold and silver threads or

[17] The names of some of the Dacca muslins were *shab-nam* (evening dew), *ab-i-rawan* (running water), and *bakt-hawa* (webs of woven wind). According to Tavernier, muslins "are made so fine, *you can hardly feel them in your hand*, and the thread, when spun, is *scarce discernible*." Quoted in E. Baines, *History of the Cotton Manufacture in Great Britain* (London, 1835), p. 57. James Taylor has recorded a verbal tradition according to which the finest muslins made in Dacca in the early seventeenth century cost as much as Rs. 400 per piece. The best varieties procured by the Dutch hardly ever cost more than Rs. 20 per piece. James Taylor, *A Sketch of the Topography and Statistics of Dacca* (Calcutta, 1840), p. 172.

[18] The other varieties of muslins procured by the Company were *achibany*, *adathy*, *asisbegi*, *chanderbani*, *cottobani*, *dotani*, *ektani*, *ganga-lahari*, *gerberry*, *kabulkhani*, *kamarband*, *kamkhani*, *maypoost*, *milmil*, *mobessabani*, *mohanbani*, *regati*, *rajibegi*, *rudarbani*. The Dutch documentary and other references that form the basis of the description of the different varieties of textiles over the next few paragraphs are far too numerous to be quoted in full. Only the particularly relevant ones have, therefore, been included in the notes.

in cotton itself, which is what probably later came to be known as "chikan" embroidery.[19] Many of the pieces also had their borders woven in gold threads. The *tanzeb* was a superior version of *khasa* involving the use of better quality yarn, larger amount of embroidery work, and better workmanship in general. Amsterdam often reminded the Bengal factors that unless the quality of the *tanzebs* sent by them was up to the mark and the patterns sufficiently "curious," there was a risk that the Dutch merchants would treat them at par with *khasas*. Exactly analogous was the case of *terrindams* and *malmals*.[20] *Resta* was a muslin with stripes produced on the loom, whereas *rehing* had a netlike texture made by passing a single thread of the warp through each division of the reed.[21] In 1701-1702, the average price of a piece of *tanzeb*, *terrindam*, *khasa*, and *malmal* was Rs. 14.25, Rs. 15.00, Rs. 8.50, and Rs. 10.50, respectively. The corresponding prices in the Company's autumn sale in Holland in 1703 were Rs. 25.25, Rs. 25.40, Rs.18.00, and Rs. 15.60, respectively.[22] The rate of gross profit works out at 77.19 percent, 69.33 percent, 111.76 percent, and 48.57 percent, respectively.

The quality differential among different varieties of calicoes was considerably more pronounced than in the case of muslins. The principal centres of production of the finer varieties were the Malda district and the area around Kasimbazar in Murshidabad district; the comparatively coarser varieties were manufactured in Birbhum district, in Patna, and in Pipli and Balasore in Orissa. The principal varieties that the Dutch procured (in a descending order of fineness and cost) were *dorea*, *humhum*, *sologazi*, *chela*, *sanu*, *rumal*, *fota*, *chintz*, Guinea cloth, *garra*, sailcloth, and *dassie*.[23] Some of these, such as *fota*, *garra*, and sailcloth, were plain coarse

---

[19] The *khasas* were used mainly for making gowns, aprons, and petticoats. Petticoats were also made from *tanzebs* and *malmals* and from silks such as *alachas*. John Irwin and P. R. Schwartz, *Studies in Indo-European Textile History* (Ahmedabad, 1966), pp. 46, 49, 57, 67, 72. In the Dutch records, brocading is usually referred to as "woven flowers," and embroidery is usually described as "flowers or patterns created by needle-sewing." Orders lists, March 1714, K.A. 264; March 1715 and March 1716, K.A. 265.

[20] Orders lists, February 1707 (K.A. 263), March 1703 (K.A. 262), March 1705, February 1708, April 1709 (K.A. 263), and March 1716 (K.A. 265); H.B. 15.10.1711, K.A. 1702, ff. 92-94, II Section.

[21] Irwin and Schwartz, *Indo-European Textile History*, p. 70.

[22] The cost price has been calculated from the export invoices of 1701-1702, H.B. 28.9.1701, K.A. 1540; H.XVII. 1.11.1701, K.A. 1537; H.B. 18.12.1701, K.A. 1556, and H.B. 10.4.1702, K.A. 1556. The sale price figures are from K.A. 10228. The rate of conversion between the rupee and the florin at this time was Re. 1 = *f*. 1.5. For a discussion of the limitations of the cost and sale price data, see the Appendix.

[23] The other varieties of calicoes procured by the Company were: (a) fine calicoes: *bafta*, *betilla*, *camelot*, *chela-regatty*, *golmandal*, *lehmenia*, *lungi*, *mistaj*, *nainsukh*, *sekla*, *sjoukoria*, and *taffechela*; (b) ordinary calicoes: *ambertee*, *amirti*, *dariabadi*, *dungaree*, *gasjan*, *lakhori*, *niquania*, *parkal*, *patka*, sailcloth, and *salampuri*.

calicoes with no patterns and were procured unbleached, bleached, or dyed in bright shades. Others such as *humhum* and *sanu* were also plain calicoes but of finer quality. Some of the *humhum* pieces were provided with borders woven in gold threads, others were brocaded in floral patterns. *Dorea* and *chela* were fine calicoes with longitudinal stripes of varying width created on the loom, usually in blue and white yarn in the case of the latter. Occasionally *doreas* were also brocaded in floral patterns. *Dassie* was a coarse calico, usually with red stripes, whereas Guinea cloth was a generic term for a wide range of cheap, brightly coloured, and mostly striped or chequered calicoes. It was a typical Coromandel product, but around the close of the seventeenth century the Dutch succeeded in initiating its production in Kasimbazar in limited quantities.[24] The only important variety of calico manufactured in Bengal for which patterns were created outside the loom was *chintz*—a comparatively coarse variety woven mainly in Patna and to a limited extent in Kasimbazar. In this case, patterns—again usually floral—were probably created by block printing.[25] Cotton painting, that is, the application of the dyes and mordants to the cloth freehand with a brush—a flourishing industry in both Coromandel and Gujarat—was practically unknown in Bengal.[26] In 1701-1702, the average price of a piece of *dorea, humhum, sanu,* and *garra* was reported to be Rs. 9.50, Rs. 5.70, Rs. 3.10, and Rs. 2.35, respectively. The corresponding prices in the Dutch autumn sale of 1703 were Rs.

[24] A similar attempt—motivated by a similar desire to reduce the cost of production given "the abundance of provisions" and consequently a lower cost of living in Bengal—was made in the case of two other typical Coromandel products, *salampuris* and *parcals*, but again with limited success.

[25] Irwin and Schwartz, *Indo-European Textile History*, p. ii. Irwin has suggested (p. 45) that Patna *chintzes* were cotton paintings rather than cotton prints, and has quoted from a letter written in 1700 by the English Court of Directors in London to their factors in Bengal to substantiate this. But the Dutch, who procured this particular variety throughout the period of their trading operations in Bengal, consistently used the word "drukken" (to print) to describe the way the pattern was made. The appropriate word to use to describe the process of painting would have been "schilderen." The unit established for printing *chintzes* within the precincts of the Company's factory at Patna was called the "chitsen-drukkerij" and the workers "drukkers."

[26] Early in the eighteenth century, Amsterdam instructed the Bengal factors to persuade artisans in Patna to manufacture painted *rumals*, used mainly as handkerchiefs. Samples, apparently from Coromandel, were despatched from Amsterdam, but despite strenuous efforts by both the Hugli and the Patna factors, the project proved to be more or less abortive. A small lot of 592 pieces was all that the factors succeeded in sending to Holland once in 1714. The directors found that the cloth used was not of sufficiently good quality, and the standard of painting left a lot to be desired. Attempts to remedy these defects do not appear to have been particularly successful. Orders lists, February 1701 to March 1716, K.A. 262-265. Explanation by Bengal factors of why they were not able to meet all the orders from Holland in full, 1704 (K.A. 1584), 1706 (K.A. 1636), 1707 (K.A. 1653), 1708 (K.A. 1669), 1710 (K.A. 1688), and 1714 (K.A. 1746).

17.40, Rs. 11.50, Rs. 5.10, and Rs. 4.80, suggesting that the gross profit earned was 83.15, 101.75, 64.51, and 104.25 percent, respectively.[27]

Besides cotton textiles, the Company procured substantial quantities of mixed and silk piece goods in Bengal, which was probably the most important producer of these textiles in India. Mixed piece goods were woven by the simultaneous use of cotton and silk yarns, the latter having been derived either from the usual mulberry silk worm or from the silk worm *anthereap aphia*, which produced the wild *tussur* silk.[28] The principal variety in the former group was *jamadani*—described in the Dutch records as flowered *dorea*—a striped fabric brocaded in floral patterns and manufactured mainly in Malda and Kasimbazar. The cotton-*tussur* varieties were manufactured at several centres in Midnapore district, the most important among which was Radhanagar. Limited amounts were also produced in Malda, Hugli, and in Pipli in Orissa. The principal constituents of this group were *alibanee*, multicoloured and striped; *charkhana*, striped or chequered; *gingham*, bright coloured plain or striped; and *nila*, a striped and occasionally brocaded fabric.[29]

The silk textiles procured by the Dutch were exclusively of mulberry silk except in the case of *alachas*, where *tussur* yarn was also used. The principal areas of production were again Malda and Kasimbazar, though limited amounts of particular varieties were also produced in Radhanagar and other centres in Midnapore district. The important varieties procured by the Company were (in a descending order of fineness) *soosy*, *jamawar*, *armosin*, *atlas*, and *alacha*.[30] The staple variety was *armosin*—plain, striped, or chequered fine silk fabric often brocaded or embroidered in coloured silks, silver, or gold threads. Thirty-two and eight-tenths ounces (80 *tolas*) of silk yarn went into an *armosin* 18 yards long, 1½ yards wide and containing a total of 2,400 threads.[31] The shades most in demand in Europe were white, red, blue, yellow, and green, and various combinations thereof. The average price per piece was reported to be Rs. 7.00 in 1698-1699; the corresponding price in the Dutch autumn sale of 1700 was Rs.

---

[27] The cost price has been calculated from the export invoices of 1701-1702, H.B. 28.9.1701, K.A. 1540; H.XVII. 1.11.1701, K.A. 1537; H.B. 18.12.1701, K.A. 1556, and H.B. 10.4.1702, K.A. 1556. The sale price figures are from K.A. 10228.

[28] This silk was erroneously thought by early European traders in India to have been "spun from a herb." Irwin and Schwartz, *Indo-European Textile History*, p. 66.

[29] The other varieties procured by the Company in this group were *charadari*, *chakla*, *cushta*, *mandila*, and *peniscoe*.

[30] The other varieties procured by the Company in this group were *alcatief*, *bandanna*, *butidar*, *dhari*, silk *dorea*, *golga*, *jamawar*, silk *kamarband*, silk *lungi*, *pathola*, *pitambar*, silk *resta*, silk *rumal*, silk *sjoukoria*, silk *taffechela*, *tafta*, and silk *tanzeb*.

[31] Letter from Commissioner van Rheede to Batavia, 6.12.1686, K.A. 1310, ff. 108vo-109vo.

15.00.[32] *Soosy* was a silk fabric with stripes in coloured silks or gold threads; *jamawar* was a silk brocade, and *atlas* was both striped and brocaded. Some *atlas* pieces were also woven in satin weave, and the shades most in demand in Europe were green, blue, and coffee.[33] Finally, an *alacha* was a bright coloured striped silk fabric.

The size of the pieces of textiles procured by the Company was by no means standardized. But the usual dimensions of a piece of muslin were 40 x 2 *covids*, the lower and the upper bounds being 36 x 1 and 48 x 3 *covids*, respectively.[34] Pieces of muslin with a width of 3 *covids*—which could be put to a substantially greater variety of uses—was a specially European-promoted innovation and appears to have been limited to *khasas*, *malmals*, and *adathys* manufactured in Malda district. The dimensions of particular varieties of calicoes such as *dorea* were the same as of muslins, though the usual size in the case of this group was 20-24 x 1½-2¼ *covids*. The ordinary size of both mixed and silk piece goods was 20 x 1-2¼ *covids*, though there were important exceptions such as *charkhana*, with a usual length of 35 *covids*, and *soosy*, with a possible length of as much as 48 *covids*. In any particular variety, the Directors asked for pieces of different sizes in what in their judgment was an optimal mix, though obviously there was no guarantee that the factors would be able to supply them in the same proportion.[35]

THE VALUE OF TRADE: LONG-TERM TRENDS

The data regarding the total value imported by the Company into Bengal, together with its division into treasure and goods, are available only from 1663 onward. These are presented in Table 3.2, which shows the over-whelming role of precious metals in the total import bill. Since Bengal was on a silver standard, the principal form in which these metals were

[32] In 1705, the Directors asked that the *armosins* might be supplied in the following proportions: white (40%), red and blue, red and yellow, and red and green (30%), red (10%), ash gray (10%), brown (5%), and yellow (5%). Orders list, March 1705, K.A. 263; export invoices, H.B. 29.9.1698, K.A. 1500; H.XVII. 6.12.1698, K.A. 1500; H.XVII. 18.12.1698, K.A. 1500; K.A. 10228.

[33] V. Slomann, *Bizarre Designs in Silks* (Copenhagen, 1953), p. 120.

[34] The *covid* was an indigenous measure whose value varied considerably as between different regions. It could be as large as the equivalent of a yard or only half that much. In the orders lists pertaining to Bengal, the terms *covid* and *ell* were used interchangeably by the Directors. The Flemish ell was equal to 27.08 inches. According to Pieter van Dam as well, the equivalent of a *covid* in Bengal was 27 inches. Van Dam, *Beschrijvinge*, II, ɪɪ, 451.

[35] A case in point is the 1714 orders for *khasas*. Of a total of 20,000 pieces, the factors were ordered to supply 3,000 pieces 1½ *covids* wide, 3,500 pieces 2 *covids* wide, 6,500 pieces 2¼ *covids* wide, 4,000 pieces 2⅝ *covids* wide, and 3,000 pieces 3 *covids* wide. Orders list, March 1714, K.A. 264.

TABLE 3.2
Value of Dutch Company's Imports into Bengal, 1663-1717

Year	Treasure (florins)	Goods (florins)	Total (florins)	Proportion of treasure to total value
1663	903,953	165,080	1,069,033	84.55
1664	1,529,904	76,002	1,605,906	95.26
1665	878,327	161,032	1,039,359	84.50
1667	2,085,022	273,001	2,358,023	88.42
1668	1,230,496	146,687	1,377,183	89.34
1669	1,105,204	58,237	1,163,441	94.99
1670	847,286	316,003	1,163,289	72.83
1671	1,812,400	433,683	2,246,083	80.69
1674	1,047,087	476,201	1,523,288	68.73
1675	896,098	206,513	1,102,611	81.27
1678	743,620	281,073	1,024,693	72.57
1679	463,084	194,306	657,390	70.44
1680	1,580,027	274,731	1,854,758	85.18
1681	1,624,607	536,153	2,160,760	75.18
1682	1,242,821	325,459	1,568,280	79.24
1683	1,809,046	412,086	2,221,132	81.44
1684	746,312	45,061	791,373	94.30
1685	478,617	443,954	922,571	51.87
1686	903,745	779,926	1,683,671	53.67
1687	590,773	661,728	1,252,501	47.16
1688	1,300,515	117,912	1,418,427	91.68
1689	1,508,062	219,364	1,727,426	87.30
1690	1,471,805	418,958	1,890,763	77.84
1691	2,687,451	345,974	3,033,425	88.59
1692	1,665,551	405,554	2,071,105	80.41
1693	1,395,515	409,344	1,804,859	77.31
1694	1,756,967	202,061	1,959,028	89.68
1695	1,189,542	284,234	1,473,776	80.71
1696	2,598,987	699,398	3,298,385	78.79
1697	1,624,511	322,006	1,946,517	83.45
1698	2,391,197	340,663	2,731,860	87.52
1699	3,274,672	369,438	3,644,110	89.86
1700	2,617,299	325,564	2,942,863	88.93

TABLE 3.2 (Continued)

Year	Treasure (florins)	Goods (florins)	Total (florins)	Proportion of treasure to total value
1701	2,556,833	120,454	2,677,287	95.50
1702	2,368,480	260,082	2,628,562	90.10
1703	1,953,429	291,876	2,245,305	87.00
1704	1,975,923	140,005	2,115,928	93.38
1705	2,669,255	104,968	2,774,223	96.21
1706	2,931,741	134,830	3,066,571	95.60
1707	3,190,744	112,174	3,302,918	96.60
1708	2,037,654	155,949	2,193,603	92.89
1709	2,048,159	396,437	2,444,596	83.78
1710	3,201,173	198,731	3,399,904	94.15
1711	2,750,890	338,352	3,089,242	89.04
1712	2,765,992	334,826	3,100,818	89.20
1713	2,498,538	81,902	2,580,440	96.82
1714	2,932,746	289,271	3,222,017	91.02
1715	2,585,648	278,200	2,863,848	90.28
1716	3,090,000	127,149	3,217,149	96.04
1717	3,136,000	97,146	3,233,146	96.99

Source: Bengal import invoices in the Dutch records.
Note: Information is not available for the years not included in the table.

imported was silver bullion and coins.[36] The proportion of precious metals to the total value imported varied between a minimum of 47 percent in 1687 to a maximum of 97 percent in 1717. The average for the entire period works out at 87.5 percent. Indeed, the three-year period 1685-1687, when this figure was around only 50 percent, must be treated as an exceptional phase. The temporary ban on the export of gold from Japan during 1685-1686 appears to have obliged Batavia to divert a part of the silver that would ordinarily have gone to Bengal to regions such as the Coromandel coast, where normally only gold was sent. An attempt was

[36] Of the fifty years for which information regarding the value of imports is available over the period 1663-1717, a breakdown for gold and silver is available for forty-two years. Of these forty-two years, silver was the only precious metal imported during thirty-three years. Over the remaining nine years, the proportion of silver to the total of the precious metals imported was as follows: 1668—27.0; 1670—26.0; 1671—33.0; 1674—9.6; 1675—57.6; 1692—68.0; 1698—84.7; 1704—74.8, and 1709—74.8 (invoices of goods imported into Bengal).

67

made to compensate for the shortfall in the supply of silver to Bengal by an increase in the value of the goods sent. The value of the total imports into Bengal, along with the linear trend of these imports, is also presented in Figure 3.1.

The data regarding the value of the Company's export trade from Bengal begin in 1648-1649 and of a total period of 73 years until 1720-1721, information is available for fifty-nine years. These data have been tabulated in Table 3.3: a graphic representation along with a linear trend is to be found in Figure 3.2. As the main function of the imports into Bengal was to finance the procurement of export goods, one would expect a broad similarity in the movements in the two series (Figures 3.1 and 3.2). When such a comparison is made, it is seen that both series are characterized by significant fluctuations that often do not match each other, even after allowance is made for the fact that the coverage and the gaps in the two series are different. But nevertheless, there is a significant upward trend underlying both series. According to the linear trends, imports expanded by $f.$ 38,811 each year and the exports by $f.$ 46,298. The compound rate of growth was 0.85 percent for imports and 1.12 percent for exports. These figures, of course, indicate only a long-term trend that, in effect, was constantly disturbed by all kinds of forces. But one could say that if there was a recession in trade it was followed by recovery, and that the overall direction of trade was upward.

That the import and the export series behaved differently in respect to both the pattern of fluctuations and the compound rate of growth is not altogether surprising. In the first place, the import series starts only in 1663, by which time the total value of trade had become substantially larger than in 1648, when the export series begins. The subsequent rate of growth in the two series would obviously be affected by this. Second, it is important to realise that in any given year, the total purchasing power available to the Company in Bengal would not necessarily match the value of the imports. The imports, including precious metals, would ordinarily fetch a profit, adding to the value imported. Any local borrowings would have a similar result. As against this, the cost of maintenance of the factories in the region would have to be deducted from the total funds available to the factors. And in any case, availability of funds was a necessary but not a sufficient condition for the procurement of the export goods in any given year. This problem was made more complex by the specificity of the Company's demands. It must also be recognized that the export series represents an aggregation of the movements in export values to a number of regions, all of which might not be moving in the same direction. Thus over a given period, the exports to Europe might be rising but those to Japan might be falling. Also, the problems encountered in the procurement of goods from different markets would not necessarily be

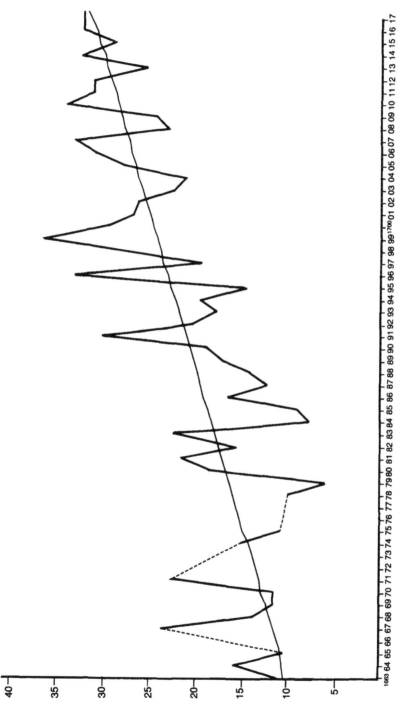

Figure 3.1. Value of Dutch Company's Imports into Bengal, 1663-1717 (in hundred thousand florins)
Note: The broken lines indicate that data are not available for the intervening period.

TABLE 3.3
Value of Dutch Company's Exports from Bengal, 1648-1721

Year	Value (florins)	Year	Value (florins)	Year	Value (florins)
1648-49	150,534	1673-74	1,453,107	1694-95	1,717,362
1649-50	195,431	1674-75	1,313,460	1695-96	2,650,029
1652-53	685,280	1675-76	1,153,769	1696-97	2,031,273
1654-55	752,135	1676-77	1,384,669	1698-99	3,476,371
1655-56	1,266,771	1678-79	1,398,539	1699-1700	2,950,740
1657-58	1,250,863	1679-80	1,088,594	1700-01	4,156,536
1658-59	1,240,527	1680-81	1,996,677	1701-02	3,327,845
1659-60	1,311,805	1681-82	1,923,665	1702-03	2,397,754
1660-61	1,325,002	1682-83	2,209,047	1708-09	2,984,591
1661-62	1,674,982	1683-84	1,894,939	1709-10	4,145,798
1662-63	1,519,572	1684-85	1,776,333	1710-11	3,515,855
1663-64	1,436 548	1685-86	2,266,283	1711-12	3,481,998
1664-65	1,316,516	1686-87	2,141,499	1712-13	2,414,401
1665-66	1,229,360	1687-88	1,308,281	1713-14	3,434,032
1666-67	1,100,536	1688-89	1,613,476	1714-15	3,445,885
1667-68	1,170,807	1689-90	2,025,632	1715-16	3,756,799
1668-69	1,713,016	1690-91	2,345,184	1716-17	3,589,166
1669-70	1,821,839	1691-92	2,510,135	1717-18	4,191,681
1670-71	1,873,971	1692-93	2,935,038	1720-21	4,615,986
1671-72	1,967,870	1693-94	2,641,071		

Source: Bengal import invoices in the Dutch records.
Note: Information is not available for the years not included in the table.

similar, and this would introduce yet another destabilizing factor. Thus it would be futile to look for anything more than a very rough correspondence between the import and the export series.

A scrutiny of the export series suggests that after a comparatively humble beginning in the 1640s, when the value of the annual exports was under f. 0.2 million, the Company made rapid progress, and by the early 1660s reached a level of over f. 1.5 million. The following few decades were characterised by significant ups and downs in the overall context of an upward trend. By the end of the seventeenth century, the value of trade from Bengal had assumed significant proportions, and in 1720-1721, when this study comes to a close, the value of exports exceeded f. 4.5 million.[37]

[37] The rupee equivalent of this would be Rs. 3 million.

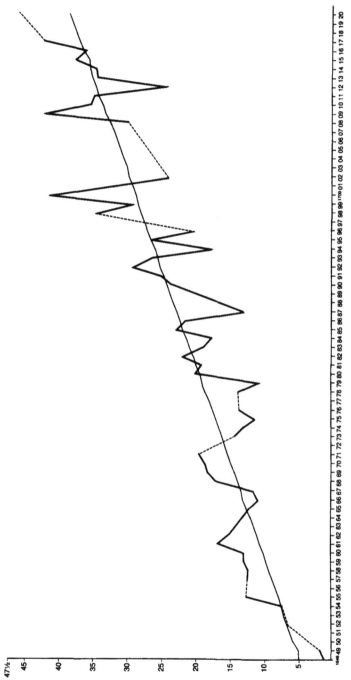

Figure 3.2.   Value of Dutch Company's Exports from Bengal, 1648-1720 (in hundred thousand florins)
Note: the broken lines indicate that data are not available for the intervening period.

Composition of Trade

The growth in the value of the Dutch trade from Bengal was, of course, accompanied by a change in both the composition and the direction of this trade. Unfortunately, the data available to us do not permit construction of time series by value for each of the major export items individually—a necessary prerequisite to a detailed analysis of the changing composition of export trade. As pointed out in the Appendix, the data on the Company's exports have been compiled from the invoices of individual shipments from Bengal. A copy of these invoices used to be provided by the factors at the end of the letter accompanying the relevant shipment. Many of these invoices contained an analysis of the value of the cargo by commodity. But there are only three years for which a *complete* analysis is available of the total value carried for each individual commodity for each of the invoices: 1675-1676, 1701-1702, and 1702-1703. Fortunately, the first of these three years is sufficiently spaced out from the other two (which together could be analyzed as a unit) to allow some perspective on the changing composition of the Company's trade (Table 3.4). It will be seen that the most striking change was the enormously larger role played by textiles at the end of the period.

Direction of Trade

The changing composition of trade was, in fact, a necessary corollary of the changing direction of the Company's trade from the region. Since the export invoices ordinarily did analyse by region the total value of the cargo despatched, much more data are available on the direction of the Company's trade than on its composition. The most outstanding feature was the reversal of the relative role of the trade with the rest of Asia and that with Europe over the last quarter of the seventeenth century. The

TABLE 3.4
Composition of Total Dutch Exports from Bengal (percent)

	1675-1676	1701-1703
Textiles	21.93	54.19
Raw silk	39.57	29.44
Saltpetre	12.11	5 79
Opium	6.64	7.08
Miscellaneous	19.75	3.50
Total	100.00	100.00

Source: Bengal export invoices in the Dutch records.

ratio of the total exports to these two regions changed dramatically over this period from approximately 80:20 to approximately 20:80. This was the combined outcome of a declining role of intra-Asian trade in the overall pattern of the Company's trading activities, and the emergence of textiles and raw silk as major items of export to Europe. Within the intra-Asian branch of trade, the relative role of the exports to Japan, the Indonesian archipelago (Batavia), and the rest of Asia (consisting of Coromandel, Ceylon, Malabar, Persia, Mocha, and some other minor ports) is depicted in Figure 3.3. There was a striking decline in the relative role of the Japan trade from the early years of the last quarter of the seventeenth century onward. This reflected both a decline in the relative role of the Company's intra-Asian trade as a whole and a long-term downward trend in the absolute value of the exports to Japan (Table 3.5). According to the linear trend, between 1660 and 1720 the exports to Japan declined each year by f. 8,392. The compound negative rate of growth was 0.84 percent per annum. The peak of the total exports to Japan was achieved in 1671-1672, just before the introduction of the so-called system of appraised trade in 1672.[38] Until about 1680, Bengal goods accounted for nearly half of the total value of the cargo shipped to Nagasaki. In the 1690s, this figure registered a sharp decline, reaching a low of 18 percent in 1699-1700 (Table 3.6). This probably had something to do with the "limited trade system" introduced in 1685. Under this system, not only was an upper limit imposed on the value of the annual imports into Nagasaki but their composition was also regulated in a manner that considerably reduced the proportion of raw silk in the total cargo.

The counterpart of the decline in the relative importance of intra-Asian trade from Bengal was, of course, the enormous increase in the exports to Europe, which eventually emerged as the principal trading partner of Bengal. According to the linear trend, between 1665 and 1720 the exports to Europe increased each year by f. 50,118. The compound rate of growth was 1.87 percent per annum. The phenomenal increase in this trade was, of course, related to the growing proportion of textiles and raw silk in the Company's total exports to Europe. As Kristof Glamann has shown, the proportion of textiles, silk, and cotton in the total exports increased from 14.16 percent in 1648-1650 to 54.73 percent in 1698-1700. He has also shown that textiles procured in Bengal accounted for 55.13 percent of the total value of textiles exported to Holland in 1697.[39] Bengal's share in raw silk, the other major constituent of this group, was even higher. Bengal silk constituted 83 percent of the total Asian raw silk sold in

[38] For details, see Chapter 5.
[39] Glamann, *Dutch-Asiatic Trade*, pp. 13, 144.

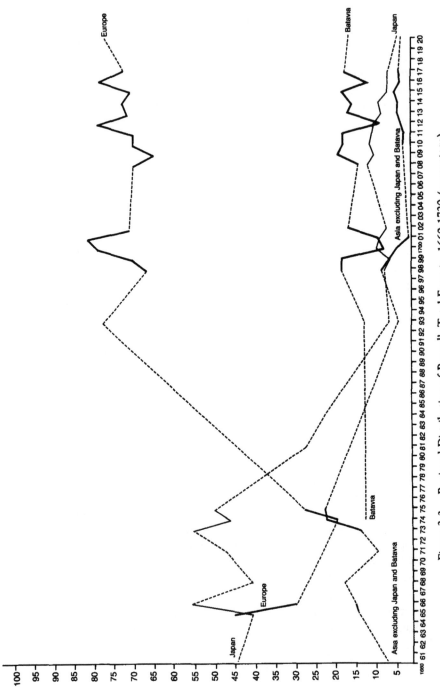

Figure 3.3. Regional Distribution of Bengal's Total Exports, 1660-1720 (percentage)
Note: the broken lines indicate that data are not available for the intervening period.

Amsterdam between 1697 and 1718.[40] The result was that at the turn of the eighteenth century, Bengal emerged as the most important supplier of goods for Europe. The proportion of Bengal goods in the total value exported to Europe (which itself grew at a rapid rate) increased from less than 11 percent in 1666-1667 to as much as 48.4 percent in 1700-1701 (Table 3.6). Over the following two decades, there was a substantial yearly fluctuation in this figure, but the average for the period was 39.33 percent.

THE ENGLISH EAST INDIA COMPANY AS A RIVAL IN TRADE

All through our period, the Dutch Company was by far the most important European trading body operating in Bengal. After their expulsion from Hugli in 1632, the Portuguese presence in the region had been reduced to a small amount of intra-Asian trade carried on by individual merchants. The Danes' involvement in the Bengal trade had never been more than marginal, whereas the Ostenders came in only toward the close of our period. The French had arrived in Bengal around 1690, but over the following thirty years or so, their trade appears to have been on a limited scale.

The story of the English, however, was quite different. They had come to Bengal about the same time as the Dutch, and by 1651 had established a factory at Hugli. Thereafter, their trade had grown at a rapid rate. Table 3.7 presents a comparative picture of the value of trade carried on by the Dutch and the English East India companies over the period 1662-1720. At the end of the period, the Dutch were still way ahead in total value of trade, but in the procurement for Europe alone (which in the case of the English equalled their total procurement), the English were in fact marginally ahead of the Dutch. This latter comparison is not entirely pointless insofar as it draws attention to certain basic problems the Dutch faced in their procurement for the European market. The English had started out in Bengal with a distinct advantage over all their European rivals: the exemption from customs and transit duties that they had been able to obtain from the Mughal authorities subject to an annual tribute of a mere Rs. 3,000.[41] In contrast, over the decade of 1711-1720, for

---

[40] Calculated from "General statement of the goods sold, outstanding debts and the unsold goods in the various chambers," K.A. 10236-10241. The data are in value terms. The ratio has been rounded off to the nearest integer.

[41] The important links in a long and tortuous chain of events were the following. In 1651, by misrepresentation of facts pertaining to the *farman* granted by Emperor Shahjahan in 1650, the Hugli factors had succeeded in obtaining from the *subahdar*, Prince Shah Shuja, a *nishan* exempting them from the payment of customs and transit duties in Bengal. From 1656 onward, however, the factors were obliged to pay to the port authorities at Hugli an

TABLE 3 5

Regional Distribution of the Exports from Bengal, 1660-1721

Year	Europe		Japan		Batavia		Coromandel	
	Value (florins)	% of total	Value (florins)	% of total	Value (florins)	% of total	Value (florins)	% of total
1660-61	N.A.		595,000	44.90	N.A.		5,572	0.42
1665-66	555,597	45.19	500,704[a]	40.72	N.A.		6,686	0.54
1666-67	324,319	29.46	611,349[a]	55.55	N.A.		32,736	2.97
1668-69	N.A.		689,639	40.25	N.A.		11,034	0.64
1671-72	N.A.		925,000	47.00	N.A.		10,411	0.52
1672-73	N.A.		724,000	N.A.	N.A.		N.A.	
1673-74	N.A.		796,000	54.77	N.A.		–	
1674-75	255,490	19.45	603,400	45.93	165,926	12 63	3,945	0.30
1675-76	318,039	27.56	574,759[a]	49.81	N.A.		8,760	0.75
1681-82	N.A.		530,700	27.58	N.A.		–	
1693-94	2,041,061	77.28	167,737	6.35	325,826	12.33	15,401	0.58
1698-99	2,317,994	66.67	263,660	7.58	619,318	17.81	2,291	0.06
1699-1700	2,055,640	69.66	186,885	6.33	523,772	17.75	10,933	0.37
1700-01	3,255,662	78.32	388,904	9.35	317,226	7.63	38,250	0.92
1701-02	2,691,133	80.86	285,345	8.57	302,372	9.08	–	
1702-03	1,693,040	70.60	166,933	6.96	388,638	16.20	N.A.	

Year							
1708-09	2,081,037	69.72	342,436	11.47	413,546	13.85	—	
1709-10	2,675,840	64.54	409,435	9.87	787,977	19 00	N.A.	
1710-11	2,435,872	69.28	382,407	10.87	614,540	17 47	3,693	0.10
1711-12	2,412,611	69.28	373,732	10.73	608,347	17.47	606	0.01
1712-13	1,898,169	78.61	236,907	9.81	207,740	8.60	4,947	0.20
1713-14	2,444,923	71.19	274,394	7 99	569,483	16.58	13,652	0.39
1714-15	2,486,823	72.16	286,661	8.31	527,824	15.31	3,647	0.10
1715-16	2,640,997	70.29	264,149	7.03	672,026	17.88	4,875	0.12
1716-17	2,795,976	77.90	225,636	6.28	416,103	11.59	1,895	0.05
1717-18	3,016,445	71.96	270,502	6.45	736,084	17.56	—	
1720-21	3,508,911	76.01	201,756	4.37	761,890	16.50	9,339	0.20

TABLE 3.5 (Continued)

Year	Ceylon Value (florins)	% of total	Malabar Value (florins)	% of total	Persia Value (florins)	% of total	Rest of Asia Value (florins)	% of total
1660-61	32,721	2.46	—		40,432	3.05	6,430	0.48
1665-66	61,458	4.99	—		102,748	8.35	2,167	0.17
1666-67	80,874	7.34	—		49,036	4.45	2,222	0.20
1668-69	241,602	14.10	—		39,265	2.29	6,289	0.36
1671-72	26,939	1.36	40,113	2.03	92,202	4.68	21,468	1.09
1672-73	N.A.		N.A.		N.A.		N.A.	
1673-74	102,143	7.02	—		96,693	6.65	8,081	0.55
1674-75	122,555	9.33	68,834	5.24	93,310	7.10	—	
1675-76	111,702	9.68	17,370	1.50	97,175	8.42	25,964	2.25
1681-82	60,865	3.16	56,726	2.94	131,541	6.83	N.A.	
1693-94	49,171	1.86	—		40,664	1.53	1,211	0.04
1698-99	110,275	3.17	9,898	0.28	141,071	4.05	11,864	0.34
1699-1700	32,822	1.11	10,848	0.36	126,977	4.30	2,863	0.09
1700-01	19,675	0.47	1,663	0.04	104,094	2.50	31,062	0.74
1701-02	10,758	0.32	—		31,997	0.96	6,240	0.18
1702-03	N.A.		N.A.		70,481	2.93	26,255	1.09

1708-09	2,985	0.10	N.A.		113,432	3.80	31,155	1.04
1709-10	N.A.		4,494	0.10	245,399	5.91	19,918	0.48
1710-11	15,441	0.43	22,540	0.64	41,362	1.17	–	
1711-12	7,439	0.21	13,964	0.40	63,750	1.83	1,549	0.04
1712-13	33,549	1.38	360	0.01	26,083	1.08	6,646	0.27
1713-14	11,988	0.34	9,125	0.26	104,088	3.03	6,379	0.18
1714-15	11,259	0.32	–		98,681	2.86	30,990	0.89
1715-16	31,946	0.85	–		112,787	3.00	30,019	0.79
1716-17	13,924	0.38	10,077	0.28	103,741	2.89	21,814	0.52
1717-18	18,056	0.43	22,734	0.54	99,017	2.36	28,843	0.68
1720-21	34,624	0.75	4,205	0.09	62,198	1.34	33,063	0.71

Source: Bengal export invoices in the Dutch records.
   The regional distribution is available only for the years covered by the Table. For the value of total Dutch exports from Bengal, see
   Table 3.3. For Japan, the following sources were also used.
   1660-61 – *Batavia Dagh-Register.*
   1668-69 – Statement of goods received in Japan, K.A. 1160, f. 533 vo.
   1671-72 to 1673-74, 1681-82 – Bengal goods imported into Japan (Nagasaki records).

aThese figures represent a total of the goods destined for Japan and Batavia.

TABLE 3.6
Share of Bengal Goods in Total Dutch Exports to Europe and Japan

	Europe		Japan	
Year	Total exports (florins)	Proportion of Bengal goods to total exports	Total exports (florins)	Proportion of Bengal goods to total exports
1660-61	N.A.		1,236,854	48.10
1666-67	3,141,643	10.32	N.A.	
1668-69	N.A		1,403,768	49.12
1671-72	N.A.		1,948,008	47.48
1672-73	N.A.		1,469,170	49 27
1673-74	N.A.		1,491,461	53.37
1674-75	4,127,657	6.18	1,147,155	52.59
1675-76	3,577,483	8.89	N.A	
1681-82	N.A.		1,058,134	50.15
1693-94	3,532,244	57.78	449,226	37 33
1698-99	6,569,773	35.28	780,000	33 80
1699-1700	N.A.		1,059,239	17.64
1700-01	6,726,036	48.40		
1701-02	5,685,361	47.33		
1702-03	5,704,842	29.67		
1703-04	4,772,729	23.08		
1704-05	4,712,986	43.70		
1706-07	4,499,477	31.04		
1707-08	5,689,887	34.43		
1708-09	5,732,998	36.29		
1709-10	4,895,801	54.65		
1710-11	6,111,822	39.85		
1711-12	4,401,431	54.81		
1712-13	5,260,128	36.08		
1713-14	7,788,838	31.39		
1714-15	6,825,296	36.43		
1715-16	6,986,624	37.80		
1716-17	6,776,766	41.25		
1717-18	8,281,807	36.42		
1720-21	7,344,993	47 77		

TABLE 3.6 (Continued)

Source· The figures of total exports to Europe are based, with a two year lag, on Reus, *Niederländisch-Ostindischen Compagnie*, Appendix V. The proportion of Bengal goods to the total exports to Europe has been worked out by using these figures in conjunction with the Europe figures in Table 3.5.

    The figures of total exports to Japan are based on Nachod, *Niederlandischen Ostindischen Kompagnie*, pp. ccii-cciv. This information is available only until 1700. The proportion of Bengal goods to the total exports to Japan has been worked out by using these figures in conjunction with the Japan figures in Table 3.5.

Note: The years 1703-1704 to 1707-1708 are included here and not in Table 3.3 because although the figures for exports to Europe are firm, those for total exports from Bengal are not, insofar as the value of exports to some regions is not known.

    Information is not available for the years not included in the table.

example, the average annual liability of the Dutch on account of the customs duties would have worked out at approximately Rs. 120,000.[42] It is true that by under-invoicing the cargo, the Dutch almost always managed to evade part of the customs duties due from them. But however large the evasion might have been—and this was not without risk[43]—there is no question that the Dutch had to pay much more by way of customs duties than their English counterparts. The higher costs would obviously have affected the competitive strength of the Dutch.

Quite apart from this consideration, the growing English trade in the

---

annual tribute of Rs. 3,000 as the price for continued exemption from the customs duty. A royal *farman* issued in 1680 was interpreted by state officials to imply a liability on the part of the English to pay a customs duty of 3.5 percent throughout the Mughal empire, whereas the Company's interpretation limited this liability to the port of Surat. This led to an armed conflict between the Company and the Mughal authorities lasting nearly five years. A *hasb-ul-hukm* issued in February 1691 under the seal of Wazir Asad Khan formalized the duty-exempt status of the Company subject to an annual tribute of Rs. 3,000. This privilege received royal sanction in the form of Farrukhsiyar's well-known *farman* of 1717. *English Factories in India*, 1655-1660, p. 415.; Hugli Diary, 3.8.1678, F.R. Hugli, vol. 1, ff. 71-72; *English Factories in India*, 1665-1667, pp. 258-259; W. Foster, "Gabriel Boughton and the Trading Privileges in Bengal," *Indian Antiquary*, 40 (1911), 247-257; O.C. 5702, vol. 48, Sutanati-Dacca 5.9.1690, F.R. Calcutta, vol. 5, ff. 26-28; Sutanati Diary, 18.12.1690, F.R. Calcutta, vol. 5, p. 8; Sutanati Diary and Consultation Book, May 1691, F.R. Calcutta, vol. 1, ff. 65-66; Sutanati Dairy 7.5.1691, F.R. Calcutta, vol. 1, f. 61; Sutanati-Dacca 5.5.1691, F.R. Calcutta, vol. 5, f. 79; Sutanati Diary 7.8.1691, F.R. Calcutta, vol. 1, ff. 93-94; Home Misc. Series, vol. 69, ff. 130-131; Home Misc. Series, vol. 629, ff. 205-225.

[42] The customs duty payable by the Dutch at this time was 2.5 % of the value of imports and exports. The Dutch were, in principle, exempt from the payment of transit duties.

[43] In this context, one has only to recall that in 1672, when the authorities had detected evasion of customs duties by the Company, it had been obliged to pay a fine of Rs. 150,000 (for details, see Chapter 2).

TABLE 3.7
Average Annual Value of the Exports by the English and the
Dutch East India Company from Bengal, 1662-1720
(in florins)

Period	English East India Company Average annual value of exports to Europe = total exports[a]	Dutch East India Company Average annual value of exports to Europe[b]	Average annual value of total exports (Europe and other parts of Asia)[c]
1662-1670	251,904	439,958	1,464,685
1671-1680	769,356	286,764	1,469,585
1681-1690	892,260	N.A.	1,950,434
1691-1700	1,512,602	2,417,589	2,785,373
1701-1710	1,382,595	2,315,384	3,274,369
1711-1720	2,666,764	2,650,607	3,616,243

[a]Calculated with a two-year lag from Chaudhuri, *The Trading World of Asia*, pp. 508-509. The rate of conversion used is £1 = f.12.

[b]Based on Table 3.5.

[c]Based on Table 3.3.

region posed severe problems of rising prices, indifferent quality, and insufficient availability of goods for the European market. The most intense competition was in the procurement of textiles. An examination of the Bengal factors' annual "explanation of why the orders were not met in full" from 1691 onward suggests that by far the most important reason why the Dutch were unable to procure the various varieties of textiles in the required quantity and the requisite quality was the tough competition by the English. The Bengal-Europe trade in textiles was essentially a luxury trade in which exclusiveness and novelty in designs and patterns mattered a great deal. This, coupled with the intense competition among the Europeans for limited supplies, put a large premium on quick decisions by the European factors. Such a decision might pertain to the purchase of a textile with a new pattern or a textile whose quality or size specification was substantially different from that stated in the relevant orders list. It seems that in the absence of control from a coordinating authority in Asia such as the Council of the Indies at Batavia, the English factors in Bengal were in a much better position than their Dutch counterparts to take such decisions (as of 1700, the Bengal factories were made independent even of the governor at Fort St. George). The value of this advantage increased with time as the volume of trade grew. There is little doubt that by the close of the period, the English Company's trade had become a major stumbling block in the way of the Dutch in Bengal. All that the Dutch factors could do was to make self-righteous statements occasionally about the English activities, such as "Time will show that the English find themselves in the graves they are digging for us."[44]

DISHONEST PRACTICES BY THE COMPANY'S EMPLOYEES

The problems of the Company were not confined to the competition provided by the English. Dishonest conduct by its own employees also contributed significantly to the growing financial and other problems faced from about 1670 onward. "On arrival in Bengal," wrote the well-informed author of a report submitted anonymously to the 17 Gentlemen in 1684, "the first thing the director does is to look around for channels of his private gain."[45] These existed mainly in the disposal of the Company's goods, the procurement of export goods, and illegal private trade.

For the first of these, the mechanism in the 1670s and the early 1680s was as follows. The director entered into a conspiracy with three merchants of Hugli—Sundar Das, Deep Chand Shah, and Jai Biswas—whose financial standing was much too poor for the Company to deal with them in the ordinary course. At a private session prior to the meeting of the Hugli council called to arrange for the sale of the Company's goods, the director and the three merchants worked out a price for each of the commodities that would make it possible for the trio to pay a 20-30 percent commission to the director. At the council meeting, the director introduced Sundar Das and Deep Chand Shah as merchants interested in buying the goods and Jai Biswas as a broker. After a preliminary discussion, the director mentioned the prices the group had already worked out as the minimum the Company would accept. The "broker" then pretended to discuss these prices with the "merchants" and after a while conveyed their acceptance of the deal to the council. The agreement was then ratified by individual members of the council who, for various reasons, dared not incur the displeasure of the director. Offers of substantially higher prices received from other merchants were rejected.[46] Only a minimal number of goods were sent to the subordinate factories, and there were even cases in which the director dictated the name of the merchants to whom the goods sent

[44] H.B. 20.8.1706, K.A. 1612, f. 80.

[45] K.A. 4464 W48, f. 1.

[46] One such case occurred in 1682, when the Company refused to sell *shankhs* (sea shells) to Captain Jan Brengman, a free Dutch merchant, at a price 25 to 30 percent higher than what the three merchants had agreed to pay (K.A. 4464 W48 f. 1d.).

to these factories were to be sold, along with the terms to be offered to them.[47]

The Company was defrauded on a large scale in the procurement of return cargo as well. It was estimated that in many cases the Company paid 8 to 10 percent more than the actual price of the goods procured.[48] There were even cases in which the actual quantity of goods procured was substantially less than that shown in the books.[49]

Even more damaging from the point of view of the Company was the large-scale private trade the factors carried on throughout Asia. In the context of the extremely meagre salaries the Company paid its employees, it was only the possibility of making a quick fortune through private trade that brought most of them to the East. Given its own substantial stakes in intra-Asian trade, the Company did not allow its employees to engage in this trade on their individual accounts. But that did not mean that the servants refrained from doing so. A rough idea of the wide participation in this trade could probably be formed from a statement made by Governor-General Pieter Both in 1612 that if he strictly enforced the provision about the deportation of everyone found participating in private trade, he was afraid that not many of the Company's servants would be left in the East Indies.[50] In the course of time, the Bengal-Batavia branch became probably the most notorious for private trade. The main reason behind this was opium, a high-value, low-bulk, and therefore ideal item for contraband trade, though other Bengal goods such as raw silk and silk textiles also figured in this trade. Pieter van Dam has suggested that at one stage, the volume of illegal private trade from Bengal was nearly as large as that on the Company's account.[51] The anonymous report referred to earlier contained a detailed description of the organisational structure of this trade at the Bengal end. In the year 1679, Director Jacob Verburg founded

[47] For example, Director Constantijn Ranst was accused of withholding from the Hugli council lists of goods asked for by the Kasimbazar council for disposal at their factory. In January 1670, Ranst was reported to have instructed the factors at Kasimbazar to cancel a deal involving the proposed sale of Japanese copper to a certain merchant at Rs. 40 per maund. The factors were directed to sell the copper instead to a merchant named by Ranst at Rs. 36 per maund. Private letter by J. Verburg and H. Fentzel to Batavia 14.12.1673, K.A. 1194, ff. 8-57.

[48] K.A. 4464 W48, f. 2.

[49] The Kasimbazar factors, for example, while receiving raw silk from the suppliers, usually used a scale that brought in only 65 ponds for each maund against the regular 72.5 ponds. Private letter by J. Verburg and H. Fentzel to Batavia, 14.12.1673, K.A. 1194, ff. 8-57.

[50] J. C. Baud, "Proeve van eene Geschiedenis van den Handel en het Verbruik van Opium in Nederlandsch Indie," *Bijdragen tot de Taal-, Land- en Volkenkunde van Nederlandsch Indie*, 1 (1853), 97-98.

[51] B.P. 7.8.1651, K.A. 778, f. 284; instructions to Sterthemius 23.8.1655, K.A. 782, f. 575. H. Terpstra, *De Nederlanders in Voor-Indie* (Amsterdam, 1947), p. 156.

in the name of his wife a "small company" with the specific purpose of carrying on private trade. To facilitate its operations, two of the share-holders in the "company"—both nephews of Verburg's wife—were appointed to the key posts of the directorate's *fiscaal* (the law-enforcement officer) and the Hugli factory's warehouse officer, respectively. In order to enable him to discharge his "duties" properly, the *fiscaal* was provided with a staff large enough to keep an eye on all Dutch ships entering or leaving the port of Hugli. As soon as a ship approached the port, the warehouse officer went aboard and offered to buy whatever private cargo might be on board. The prices offered were obviously considerably below the market, but usually the deals went through because everyone knew that in the event of an unsuccessful negotiation, the *fiscaal* would be promptly informed and the goods confiscated on behalf of the Company. The goods obtained by the warehouse officer in this manner were then sold in the open market at substantially higher prices on the account of the "small company." As far as goods procured in Bengal were concerned, the procedure was to buy them in the name of a nonexistent Bengali merchant. This was done before procurement was begun on the account of the Company, so that the "small company" was ensured of getting the best quality goods at the lowest possible prices. These goods were then loaded on the Company's ships along with the regular cargo.[52] Sometime before the ships were due into the harbour at Batavia, the contraband goods were taken out in small boats. The watch and ward staff at Batavia at times managed to seize part of the smuggled goods, but that made only a very minor dent into the total profit from the operation.[53] The fortunes collected in this manner were often remitted home through bills drawn on the Court of Directors of the English East India Company at London.[54] From the Company's point of view, the factors' private trade involved, in

[52] K.A. 4464 W48, ff. 2b-2d; Valentijn, *Oud en Nieuwe Oost-Indie*, V, 1, p. 176; XVII.B. 25.10.1686, K.A. 460, ff. 366vo-367.

[53] A rough idea of the magnitude of the profit earned could probably be formed by the fact that at Verburg's death in 1681, his wife carried with her to Holland a fortune running to *f*. 600,000. Even the warehouse officer had managed to save a sum of *f*. 150,000 over a period of 3½ to 4 years (K.A. 4464 W48, ff. 2b-2d.).

In 1688, apparently in pursuance of orders from Batavia, Director Arnoldus Muykens wrote to the *faujdar* of Hugli suggesting that since the extensive private trade carried on by the Company's servants deprived the government of a considerble amount of customs revenue, instructions be issued to local merchants to have no dealings whatever with individual Dutch factors. The result was a *sanad* to this effect issued by Nawab Hokultash Khan the following year (B.M. Addl. Ms. 29095, f. 55). But since the *sanad* provided for no machinery of enforcement, this document, like most others of its type, made no difference whatever to the actual situation.

[54] K. N. Chaudhuri, "Treasure and Trade Balances: The East India Company's Export Trade, 1660-1720," *Economic History Review*, Second Series, 21 (1968), 492-493.

addition to the misuse of shipping space, the emergence of yet another rival agency of trade, with serious implications for the Company's own trade. Since this group operated clandestinely, it was ordinarily willing to pay a price above the market and accept a price below it. In the process both the buying and the selling markets were spoiled for the Company.[55]

The Company tried a variety of measures to deal with the problem of dishonest practices by its employees, but with little success. In 1670, Amsterdam instructed Batavia to depute Willem Volger as a special commissioner to investigate into irregularities and dishonest practices at the factories at Malacca, Bengal, and Surat. The commissioner reached Hugli in August 1671, but it seems that he was won over by Director Constantyn Ranst, one of the most corrupt and unscrupulous chiefs Hugli had ever had.[56] In the report Volger submitted to the Batavia Council in January 1672, Ranst and his colleagues were cleared of any suspicion of illegal or dishonest practices.[57] No further steps were taken in this direction until 1677, when the Directors instructed the Batavia Council to issue a proclamation reiterating the clause providing for dismissal from service and deportation to Holland for anyone found engaged in private trade. The proclamation was issued on February 18, 1678, followed by another on January 22, 1680.[58]

In 1681, Batavia sent Nicolaas Baukes to Bengal in the dual capacity of a commissioner and the director. A similar experiment was made at Coromandel and Malabar. The idea was to send people of recognized integrity to head these factories, with the powers of a commissioner. But within two years, Batavia reported a failure of the experiment at all the three factories. In May 1683, yet another proclamation from Batavia prescribed the death penalty for all those found guilty of participation in private trade.[59]

In the meantime, the Directors had been planning to send a high-

---

[55] Some of these issues are discussed at greater length in Chapter 6.

[56] The ship that carried Ranst to Batavia in December 1673 also carried a private letter addressed to the Batavia Council by Jacob Verburg and Herman Fentzel, both senior factors who had provisionally been appointed joint chiefs of the directorate pending the arrival at Hugli of the new director of Bengal, François de Haze. The letter was a list of charges against Ranst including, among others, extortion of funds from the Company's factors as well as from Indian merchants and money-changers. Private letter by J. Verburg and H. Fentzel to the Batavia Council dated 14.12.1673, K.A. 1194, ff. 8-57.

[57] Enclosure to H.B. 19.4.1674, K.A. 1192, f. 349vo.

[58] Instructions by van Ommen and van Heck to Patna factors dated 30 June 1688. Enclosure to H.B. 22.9.1688, K.A. 1343, ff. 770-772.

[59] Van Dam, *Beschrijvinge*, II, ii, 43-44; III, 131. Instructions by van Ommen and van Heck to Patna factors dated June 30, 1688; Baud, "Handel en het Verbruik van Opium," p. 98.

powered commissioner to Bengal, Coromandel, and Surat to suggest measures to curb dishonest practices at these factories. But since a person of sufficiently high rank to be invested with powers wide enough to make the mission effective was not immediately available, Amsterdam had to be content with deputing one Abraham Lense on a fact-finding mission to Bengal. Lense reached Hugli in July 1683, and soon reported several cases of irregularities by the director, by other factors, and by Indian merchants doing business with the Company. One member of the last-mentioned group, whom Lense picked out for special attention was "broker" Jai Biswas (referred to in the anonymous report cited earlier). Lense prepared a long charge-sheet against this man (including the accusation that Biswas had offered him a bribe of Rs. 3,000 for keeping quiet), and pleaded that the director be instructed to stop immediately dealings with or through this man.[60]

Even as Abraham Lense was busy collecting information in Bengal, the Directors wrote to Batavia in November 1683 suggesting the appointment of Isaack Soleman as special commissioner for Bengal, Surat, Persia, and any other factory that needed attention. Soleman reached Bengal late in 1684, and soon thereafter reported gross irregularities in the directorate. He recommended, among other measures, an increase in the number of merchants the Company did business with.[61] But the report he submitted never received any attention.

In 1684, the 17 Gentlemen finally found the man they had been seeking: Hendrick Adriaan van Rheede tot Drakesteyn, heer van Mydrecht, who had served the Company a long time. He had been an extraordinary member of the Batavia Council and was currently a member of the knighthood of Utrecht. Van Rheede was authorized to preside over the council meetings in all the factories he visited, and was invested with extraordinary powers of investigation and punishment, including deportation of anyone found guilty of any irregularity.[62] The commissioner reached Bengal in January 1686 and took a whole year to complete his investigations. He estimated that between 1678 and 1686, the successive directors at Hugli had collected from the three "merchants" to whom alone the Company's

[60] Van Dam, Beschrijvinge, III, 133. Charge-sheet by Abraham Lense against Jai Biswas, enclosure to H.B. 11.1.1684, K.A. 1292, ff. 499-501.

[61] Van Dam, Beschrijvinge, III, 133. Letter from Commissioner Soleman at Hugli to the Board of Directors dated 16.12.1684, K.A. 1286, ff. 310-325; XVII.B. 25.10.1686, K.A. 1460, ff. 363-366; memorandum submitted by Director Huysman to the Batavia Council dated 14.9.1684, enclosure to B.XVII. 9.2.1685, K.A. 1291, ff. 228-233vo; H.B. 6.11.1684, K.A. 1286, f. 68.

[62] Instructions by the Board of Directors to Commissioner-Designate van Rheede, December 1684, K.A. 459, ff. 243vo-255; van Dam, Beschrijvinge, III, 133-134.

goods were sold a total sum of *f.* 230,000. The corresponding amount collected by the successive chiefs of the factory at Kasimbazar from their respective protégés was *f.* 112,000.[63] Gross irregularities were also detected in the procurement of the return cargo.[64] A number of factors, including Director Nicolaas Schagen (who had arrived in Bengal only a few months before van Rheede), *fiscaal* Pieter Mesdag, and warehouse officer van Helsdingen were also found guilty of participation in private trade. The commissioner recommended the recall of Schagen to Batavia, and ordered the deportation of a number of factors, including Mesdag and van Helsdingen. Van Rheede estimated that over the period 1678-1686, the dishonest practices (including private trade) indulged in by the Company's servants in Bengal had resulted in a total loss to the Company of as much as *f.* 3.8 million.[65]

At the time of his departure from Hugli in February 1687, van Rheede left behind a comprehensive set of instructions for the future guidance of the factors in Bengal. These instructions covered all subjects of interest to the Company, from the maintenance of the factory buildings to the procedures to be adopted in the sale and purchase of goods. The latter were designed to divest the director of the nearly absolute authority he had hitherto exercised and delegate a large amount of authority to the Hugli council.[66] The instructions were far-reaching, and though some of them were quite impractical, the core, if implemented faithfully, might well have resulted in a considerable improvement of the overall situation. But the interests that stood to lose by the adoption of the new procedures were evidently strong enough to succeed in resisting their introduction. The result, as van Dam has pointed out, was that "as soon as van Rheede left Bengal, everything returned to the old footing."[67] Not long thereafter, the Batavia Council went so far as formally to rescind some of the pro-

---

[63] Secret letter by van Rheede to Batavia, 16.11.1686, K.A. 1318, ff. 982-983. Although Deep Chand Shah and Jai Biswas were mentioned in both the anonymous report of 1684 and van Rheede's report, the third merchant listed in the former was Sundar Das, whereas in the latter it was Kalyan Das.

[64] Raw silk purchased in Kasimbazar, for example, was found to have been grossly overpaid, in return, of course, for a commission for the chief of the factory. Van Rheede wrote, "On investigation, I have reached the conclusion that these practices . . . are not the result of the lack of knowledge regarding better methods. They instead represent an attempt at trying out new methods of cheating the *Heeren XVII* and trying to become rich by unreasonable means" (van Rheede's instructions to the Bengal factors, 21.2.1687, K.A. 1324, ff. 128-210).

[65] Terpstra, *De Nederlanders in Voor Indie*, pp. 157-158; van Dam, *Beschrijvinge*, II, ii, 25, 27; III, 134; van Rheede's instructions to Bengal factors, 21.2.1687, K.A. 1324, f. 169.

[66] Van Rheede's instructions to Bengal factors, 21.2.1687, K.A. 1324, ff. 128-210. Very similar procedures were to be followed in each of the subordinate factories.

[67] Van Dam, *Beschrijvinge*, III, 134.

cedures that van Rheede had prescribed.[68] The nearly total failure of the van Rheede mission dissuaded the Directors from appointing any more commissions of enquiry over the rest of our period.

At the close of our period in 1720, the Dutch East India Company was beset with the twin problems of severe and growing competition from the English and dishonest practices of various kinds by its employees, whose intensity was probably increasing with time. But the Company was still the most important foreign trading body in Bengal, and the volume of trade it carried on was still growing. It would be several decades before the English would decisively forge ahead of the Dutch. In that process, they would be helped in no small measure by the political and military authority wrested from the Mughals.

---

[68] To take only one example, van Rheede had laid down that a merchant buying the Company's goods was not to be permitted to remove them from the warehouse until such time as he had made the payment in full. But in 1688, the Batavia Council recommended that merchants be permitted to take out, against a down payment of 10 percent, as much as 75 percent of any lot bought by them. The factors were to permit the removal of the remaining 25 percent of the goods as soon as payment for the earlier 75 percent had been completed (H.B. 22.9.1688, K.A. 1343, ff. 732-733vo).

· 4 ·

THE COMMERCIAL ORGANISATION

Because of the large amount of trade carried on with other parts of the subcontinent as well as with a number of countries around the Indian Ocean for centuries, a sophisticated organisational framework catering to this trade had grown in Bengal. This framework included, among other things, a highly organised credit structure, arrangements for hiring space on vessels, and merchants and agents who would organise the procurement and disposal of goods on behalf of their clients, both Indian and foreign. For example, it was usual for merchants in northern India and Persia engaged in trade with Bengal to have permanent factors in a town such as Malda, which was a major centre for the manufacture of particular varieties of textiles that were in great demand in these markets.[1] The existence of this framework was clearly an advantage for the Dutch Company, though it was often frustrated by not being able to modify it in points of detail to meet its special requirements. Most of the time, it was obliged to accept the system as given and adjust its own procedures and practices accordingly.

THE PROVISION OF PURCHASING POWER

Since the Company's primary interest in the Bengal trade was the procurement of export goods for the various Asian and European markets, the first stage in its trading strategy was acquisition of the necessary amount of purchasing power in the local currency. This was done by converting the precious metals as well as the goods imported into the region into silver rupees. In periods of acute shortage of liquid funds, due either to a locking up of the bullion at an imperial mint or an unusual delay in the arrival of the ships from Batavia, the Company borrowed small amounts in the local money market at rates of interest varying between 12 and 18 percent per annum.

Precious Metals

The treasure imported by the Company into Bengal consisted of silver bullion as well as a large and motley supply of both silver and gold coins. All these had to be converted into the local currency before they could

[1] Report by Hendrick Cansius on Malda, 7.9.1670. K.A. 1168, f. 2174.

be used. The basic structure of Mughal coinage is well known,[2] but it might nevertheless be useful to recapitulate some of its important characteristics. The standard coin was the silver rupee, with an alloy content of under 4 percent and weighing about 178 grains. The *sicca* rupee, coined during the current year or possibly the one preceding that, commanded a variable *batta* or premium over the "current" rupee coined in the preceding years of the same reign. The gold coin was the *muhr*—again almost entirely of pure gold with a minimum of alloy; the copper coin was called the *dam*. The Mughals followed a system of "free" mintage under which imperial mints all over the empire minted coins at a small charge for anyone bringing bullion. The charge would include the seigniorage as well as the expenses of coinage; the authorities maintained a high standard of metallic purity in the coins. A corollary of this was the broad correspondence between the stated value of a coin and the intrinsic value of the metal it contained. The parity between the gold *muhr* and the silver rupee was, therefore, not fixed but was determined by the market. The absence of the equivalent of modern monetary management also implied that the accretions to the supply of standardized money (not taking into account uncoined mediums of exchange such as *cauris*) over any period of time was determined not by the government but by the public itself within, of course, the ceiling prescribed by the volume of metals available in the system and the capacity of the imperial mints.

The factors had a choice between sending the bullion and coins to one of the imperial mints in the region to be minted into rupees and getting them exchanged against rupees through professional dealers in money known as *sarrafs*.[3] Each course had advantages and disadvantages, and the factors were always trying to achieve an optimal mix of the two alternatives. The available evidence would seem to suggest that, on an average, it was more profitable for the Company to go to a mint, partly because the *siccas* obtained in the process commanded a *batta* over the current rupees.[4] But a range of possible problems in minting often persuaded the

---

[2] See, for example, Irfan Habib, "The Currency System of the Mughal Empire 1556-1707," *Medieval India Quarterly*, 4 (1961), 1-21.

[3] The royal mints in the Bengal region were at Rajmahal (transferred in the early years of the eighteenth century to Murshidabad), Dacca, Balasore (later Cuttack), and Patna.

[4] For example, the additional profit earned by the Company when it sent its silver to the imperial mint at Rajmahal rather than selling it to a *sarraf* at Hugli or Kasimbazar was 1.57% in 1657, 3.33% in 1660, 7.37% in 1661, 8.23% in 1664, 9.50% in 1665, 2.90% in 1679, and 4.75% in 1691. In the case of gold *koban*, this figure was reported to be 3.87% in 1671. B.H. 19.7.1657, K.A. 784, f. 308; H.B. 29.11.1660, K.A. 1126, ff. 53-54; H.XVII. 13.8.1661, K.A. 1124, f. 537vo; memorandum by outgoing director, van den Broecke, to his successor, van Hyningen, 14.2.1664, K.A. 1137, ff. 458-460; report by van Hyningen, 26.3.1665, K.A. 1142, ff. 1237-1238; H.B. 3.7.1671, K.A. 1174, f. 1859; B.H. 28.7.1691, K.A. 825, f. 364; H.B. 10.4.1680, K.A. 1249, f. 1400vo.

Company to deal instead with the *sarrafs*. For one thing, there was always the risk of unauthorized transit tolls (*rahdari*) being charged on the metals as they were being transported to a mint, even if the Company disregarded as quite remote the risk of plunder on the way.[5] Even after the metal had been deposited at the mint, there was the risk of fraud at the hands of the mint's employees. This was done by declaring the Company's metal to be less pure than it actually was, thus reducing the number of coins admissible against a given amount of metal.[6]

There was also the possibility of an occasional unauthorized cess being imposed by the mint authorities. Thus in 1681, the master of the Rajmahal mint asked for an additional 0.62 percent on top of the usual imperial seigniorage of 3.5 percent. An appeal to the imperial *diwan*, Haji Safi Khan, did result in the grant of a *parwana* instructing the mint master not to impose this additional charge. But the master ignored the *parwana*, saying that a charge once instituted could not be withdrawn.[7] It is not clear how long this additional cess continued, but there is evidence that another similar cess was imposed in 1711.[8] There were even instances when minting privileges were altogether denied to the Company for temporary periods.[9] All these irritants were undoubtedly instrumental in pushing the Company away from the mints, but the principal consideration that often took the Company to the *sarrafs* was the time taken at the

[5] For example, in 1699, the master of the Rajmahal mint wrote to the *subahdar* that the lack of safety to and from the mint as well as recent increases in the unauthorized duties charged on the Europeans' bullion had led to a decline in the total amount brought to his mint by the companies. Since this involved a decline in the imperial income from the mint, the *subahdar* instructed the toll officials to desist from this practice but, it would seem, with little effect (H.B. 1.11.1699, K.A. 1516, ff. 36-37).

[6] Memorandum by the outgoing director, van den Broecke, to his successor, van Hyningen, 14.2.1664, K.A. 1137, ff. 458vo-460. At times, this happened with the active connivance of the Company's broker at the mint. In 1662, for example, the Hugli factors discovered that in the course of the minting of 355 cases of Japanese bar silver (worth approximately Rs. 880,000) they had been defrauded to the tune of Rs. 8,864. A fine of Rs. 10,000 was imposed on broker Ghanshyam and he was dismissed from the service of the Company (H.XVIII. 26.12.1662, K.A. 1128, ff. 176-177). In 1636, the English factors at Surat had written to the Court of Directors in London, "Concerning the coyneing of your gould and silver into the species of this countrey, [it] is free for us, though not safe. Wee should have to doe with such dangerous people in the mint that wee dare not adventure; nor will the most cunning merchants of these parts upon any occasion, but sell all to the sharoffes." *The English Factories in India*, 1634-1636, p. 225.

[7] H.B. 30.11.1681, K.A. 1253, f. 200; H.B. 7.1.1681, K.A. 1267, f. 1292vo; H.B. 11.11.1682, K.A. 1267, f. 1363.

[8] H.B. 15.10.1711, K.A. 1702, ff. 48-49.

[9] Thus in 1666, when the Company refused to sell 20,000 *tolas* of silver to the nawab of Rajmahal, he had the minting of the Company's silver stopped (H.B. 1.4.1666, K.A. 1149, ff. 2238-2239).

mints. The delivery date for even relatively moderate sums of money could be weeks or even months, obliging the Company to borrow in the market and incur an interest cost.[10] The *sarrafs* ordinarily made an on-the-spot payment, though on occasions they asked for time up to two months or an arrangement involving payment in two installments.[11] In such cases, if the Company was not in a position to wait, it had no option but to accept a somewhat lower price from another *sarraf* willing to make an immediate full payment.[12]

In order to draw more custom to themselves, the *sarrafs* were known to try to create artificially adverse conditions for the Europeans at the mint. In 1663, for example, a group of Hugli *sarrafs* approached the master of the Rajmahal mint with the offer of a handsome sum if he would delay the delivery of the rupees coined against the silver deposited by the Dutch. Another such case relates to 1701, when some Hugli *sarrafs* told Subahdar Azim-us-Shan that if he instructed the master of the Rajmahal mint to delay the delivery of the rupees to the European companies, they (the *sarrafs*) would not only get additional business but would also be able to reduce the market price of silver by 5 percent. They offered 60 percent of their anticipated additional profit to the *subahdar* and 20 percent to his *diwan* if the needful were done. Unfortunately, the outcome of these efforts is not recorded.[13] In spite of the problems faced at the mints, of course, the Company used them extensively.

Goods

The goods the Company imported into Bengal were almost entirely of Asian origin. The two principal groups of import items were nonprecious metals such as copper, tin, spelter, and zinc, and spices such as pepper, cloves, nutmeg, mace, and cinnamon. As we have seen, in order to

[10] Instructions by the Governor-General and the Council of the Indies at Batavia to the Director-Designate of Bengal, Pieter Sterthemius, 23.5.1655, K.A. 782, f. 591vo; H.B. 20.5.1680, K.A. 1249, f. 1409.

[11] H.B. 10.2.1678, K.A. 1237, f. 1087vo.

[12] For example, in 1681, a *sarraf* at Kasimbazar offered to buy seventeen cases of bar silver at 95 rupees per 100 *sicca* rupee weight of silver, provided he was allowed to make the payment after two months. The Company tried to reach a compromise by asking him to pay Rs. 160,000 immediately and the balance after a month. The *sarraf*, however, was willing to accommodate the Company only to the extent of paying Rs. 50,000 within ten days. This was not acceptable to the Company, and the whole lot was disposed of to another *sarraf*, Deep Chand, at a price of Rs. 94.75 per 100 *sicca* rupee weight of silver against immediate payment in full (H.B. 9.4.1681, K.A. 1258, ff. 1273vo-1274).

[13] Memorandum by the outgoing director, van den Broecke, to his successor, van Hyningen, 14.2.1664, K.A. 1137, ff. 458-460; H.B. 18.12.1701, K.A. 1556, ff. 12-14.

minimize the imports of the precious metals, the Company tried to maximize the total sales of these goods, even if that involved reducing the price to a point of zero net profit. Indeed, when there was an acute shortage of liquidity or an intense competition in the sale of a particular commodity with a rival body such as the English East India Company, the Company was not averse to selling below cost (defined to include transport and allied costs).[14] In order to ensure that supplies of these goods, many of which were also exported to Europe, were available to Bengal and other Asian factories on a regular basis, Amsterdam had issued standing instructions to Batavia to attach priority to the needs of these factories over those of Holland.[15]

Within this general framework, it is useful to distinguish between goods such as nonprecious metals and pepper on the one hand and the rest of the spices on the other. In the case of the first set of goods, the Company was only one of the sellers in the market, though by far the most important one because of its special position in both Japan and the Indonesian archipelago, where these goods were procured. But in the case of spices such as nutmeg and mace, it had enjoyed monopsony privileges ever since the conquest of Banda in 1621. The problem of smuggling in cloves had also been solved with the conquest of Macassar in 1667. Following the conquest of a part of Ceylon in 1658, monopsony privileges had also been acquired in cinnamon. The pricing policy followed for the two groups of commodities, therefore, differed in important respects.

In the case of the nonprecious metals and pepper, Batavia only insisted that under normal circumstances at least the cost (including the cost of transport and handling) should be recovered. In order to facilitate the implementation of this rule, a minimum sale price was often prescribed for these goods.[16] This was often done for the monopoly spices, as well, but for a different reason. The Company was concerned that the Asian price of these spices should not be allowed to fall to a level that would make it worth their while for the English and others to buy spices in India or elsewhere in Asia and take them to Europe, thus compromising the crucial European monopoly of the Company.[17] While the minimum sale

---

[14] For example, this was done for spelter in 1693 for reasons of liquidity, and for copper in 1705 because of the competition with the English. B.H. 10.5.1693, K.A. 824, f. 753; H.B. 10.10.1705, K.A. 1604, ff. 8-9.

[15] XVII.B. 29.8.1671, K.A. 457; XVII.B. 5.4.1672, K.A. 457; volume not foliated.

[16] The following cases may be noted for Bengal: copper, H.B. 6.11.1684, K.A. 1286, f. 37; B.H. 19.8.1690, K.A. 820, ff. 574-575; tin, B.H. 31.5.1685, K.A. 815, f. 363; spelter, H.B. 18.9.1689, K.A. 1352, f. 43; H.B. 6.9.1692, K.A. 1397, f. 94vo; H.B. 31.1.1693, K.A. 1435, f. 40vo; quicksilver, H.B. 22.9.1691, K.A. 1388, f. 696vo; XVII.B. 21.7.1707. K.A. 462, section on Bengal, volume not foliated; pepper, resolution adopted by the Batavia Council, 7.7.1684, K.A. 599, f. 310.

[17] This was by no means an imaginary fear. In 1680, for example, several English captains

price was being fixed, the Company might as well bear in mind the inelastic demand for these spices and maximize the monopoly revenue by keeping the price at a relatively high level.

The identification of the optimal minimum price for Asia necessarily involved a process of trial and error. As an example of this process, we shall examine the period 1687-1702 in some detail. On the strength of a large annual sale of spices in Surat—the premier spice market in Asia— in the 1670s and the 1680s at prices that were sometimes higher than the prices in Europe, the Directors fixed minimum prices for Asia in 1687 at levels only marginally lower than the prices in Europe. Things proceeded smoothly until 1692, when the annual sale of cloves—by far the most important spice—in Surat was reported to have fallen from an average of 50,000-100,000 ponds to a mere 12,000 ponds. On enquiry, it was established that this was not because the effect of the minimum prices had now begun to be felt, but because van Helsdingen—one of the two acting governors of the Dutch factory at Surat—had rejected offers of prices higher than the minimum in the belief that the merchants could be forced to pay still higher prices. Van Helsdingen was dismissed from the service of the Company, and a new set of minimum prices was announced by Batavia in 1696. The price of cloves was maintained at the 1687 level, but those of the other spices were increased. In the meantime, van Helsdingen had succeeded in convincing the Directors that the 1687 prices were far too low, and that the sales would not suffer if the minimum prices for Asia were revised upward. A new set of minimum prices was, therefore, announced by the Directors in 1697. The new price of cloves was about 6.7 percent higher than the European price. But this happened to be considerably higher than the current market price in a number of Asian factories, with the result that the total sales suffered. The factors in Bengal, among other places, sought Batavia's permission to ignore the new minimum prices. Doubts were also expressed in Holland regarding the wisdom of fixing the Asian minimum prices at a level higher than the current European prices. A commission was, therefore, appointed late in 1702 to go into the question. Those in favour of maintaining the Asian prices at a high level carried the day, and the commission recommended no reduction in prices.[18]

Whereas the Directors or the Batavia Council fixed only the minimum sale prices in the case of specific commodities, the local factors, at times,

---

had bought spices sold by the Dutch at Surat. They were reported to have sold them in England at a profit of more than 100 percent. The English Directors advised their factors at Hugli to follow a similar course of action. English Court of Directors to factors in Hugli, 30.12.1681, L.B. 6, f. 437. Also see Glamann, *Dutch-Asiatic Trade*, pp. 104-108.

[18] H.B. 19.9.1697, K.A. 1484, f. 94; Glamann, *Dutch-Asiatic Trade*, pp. 104-108 and Appendices C and F.

fixed the actual sale prices in accordance with the demand and supply conditions at a particular time. This was often done in Bengal for Japanese bar copper, other nonprecious metals, and pepper.[19] When a minimum price had earlier been prescribed for the given commodity, the price fixed by the local factors obviously could not be lower.

The factors could dispose of the goods in a variety of ways. On a limited scale, they sold through indigenous commission agents who charged between 1 and 1.5 percent of the value of the goods sold.[20] Somewhat more common was the system of public auction of goods whose actual sale price had not already been determined by the factors. In view of the comparatively limited financial standing of most of the merchants participating in such auctions, the Company had to permit the successful bidders to make the payment and collect the goods in installments. But what often happened was that the merchant who had offered the highest bid found himself unable to go through with the deal after he had collected one or more installments of goods, and the Company was left with unsold stocks in its hands.[21]

The procedure followed most often, therefore, was to enter into contracts with local merchants. The financial standing and dependability of these merchants was investigated by the Company's salaried broker (*dalal*) who also collected information about the current market prices of the various goods. Those merchants who were willing to deal with the Company were invited to a meeting of the Hugli council and the terms regarding price and quantity of each of the goods (quantity alone in the case of the fixed-price goods) were mutually agreed upon.[22] In order to be able to enjoy monopoly revenue until their stocks were sold out, merchants buying the monopoly spices often insisted that the Company sell no more of the items in question to anyone else for a specified period of time.[23] Ordinarily,

---

[19] Copper, H.B. 29.10.1684, K.A. 1435, f. 380vo; H.B. 10.10.1705, K.A. 1604, ff. 8-9; H.B. 16.10.1709, K.A. 1669, ff. 41-42; H.B. 20.3.1715, K.A. 1760, f. 7, I Section; H.B. 29.10.1715, K.A. 1760, f. 95, II Section; H.B. 7.6.1717, K.A. 1798, ff. 140-141; H.B. 5.11.1717, K.A. 1783, f. 55vo; tin, H.B. 22.9.1691, K.A. 1388, f. 696vo; H.B. 30.1.1693, K.A. 1435, f. 40vo; pepper, H.B. 22.9.1691, K.A. 1388, f. 696; H.B. 6.9.1692, K.A. 1397, ff. 95-vo; cinnamon, B.H. 27.9.1660, K.A. 1126, ff. 542-543.

[20] Report submitted by Hendrick Cansius to Director de Haze regarding his trip to Malda 30.11.1675, K.A. 1209, ff. 518-vo; H.B. 22.9.1688, K.A. 1343, ff. 732-733vo.

[21] H.B. 31.12.1674, K.A. 1202, ff. 4vo-5vo; H.B. 6.11.1684, K.A. 1286, f. 68; memorandum submitted by Director Huysman to Batavia, 14.9.1684, enclosure to B.XVII. 9.2.1685, K.A. 1291, ff. 228-233vo.

[22] A similar procedure was followed at the subordinate factories at Kasimbazar, Malda, Dacca, Patna, Pipli, and Balasore.

[23] This period varied from a few months to as much as two years (H.B. 28.9.1678, K.A. 1222, f. 527).

the merchants were permitted to make the payment and collect the goods in installments.[24] Quite often, the same merchants would also be providing export goods to the Company. In that case, the goods sold to them were treated as a part of the advance payment admissible to them. The merchants were also provided with the Company's *dastaks* entitling them to an exemption from the transit duties if the goods were taken out of Hugli. This was clearly a malpractice—the goods no longer belonged to the Company and did not qualify for the exemption. But except in the case of goods sold by public auction, it was impossible for the authorities to establish a change in the ownership of the goods. In fact, this was one of the reasons why the Company preferred the contract system to that of public auction.

The Export Trade: The System of Production and Procurement

The Organisation of Production

The principal commodities the Company procured in Bengal were textiles, raw silk, opium, and saltpetre. With the available information, the organisation of production for the market and the system of procurement by the Dutch and other European companies can best be analysed with respect to textiles, which constituted by far the most important segment of the manufacturing industry in Mughal Bengal. Robert Orme's remarks in 1805 that "on the coast of Coromandel, and in the province of Bengal, when at some distance from the high road, or a principal town, it is difficult to find a village in which every man, woman, and child is not employed in making a piece of cloth," may well have applied to our period too.[25]

Weaving, which was partly a caste-based occupation, was carried on both as a full-time occupation and as a subsidiary occupation to agriculture. The greater part of the production for the market, however, appears to have been provided by artisans working full time. Because of an extensive and comparatively inexpensive water transport system in the region, even production for the market was fairly decentralized and spread over a wide

[24] Usually the period over which a particular deal had to be completed ranged from four to eight months. H.B. 20.2.1679, K.A. 1237, f. 1080; H.B. 6.11.1684, K.A. 1286, f. 68; Commissioner Soleman at Hugli to the Directors, 16.12.1684, K.A. 1286, ff. 310-325; H.B. 21.9.1686, K.A. 1318, ff. 930vo, 939.

[25] Robert Orme, *Historical Fragments of the Mogul Empire* (London, 1805), p. 409. Orme concludes the chapter with the statement: "I should perhaps, with my reader, have thought this detail of so simple a subject unnecessary, had I not considered, that the progress of the linen manufacture includes no less than a description of the lives of half the inhabitants of Indostan" (p. 413).

area. But as the proportion of marketed to total output grew over time with an increase in domestic and foreign trade, the so-called *aurungs*—localized centres of manufacturing production for purposes of trade—proliferated, accounting for an ever-rising proportion of total manufacturing output.

Working on the basis of the cotton yarn procured from the spinner (and raw silk from the silk reeler), the basic unit of production in the manufacture of textiles was the weaver operating as an independent artisan. He ordinarily owned the hut where the loom, which also he owned, was installed. To a certain extent, the production of standardized varieties of textiles for traditional markets was carried on on the basis of the weavers' own resources and at their own risk. These goods were then transported to urban centres and sold to merchants. Some of these merchants might themselves be engaged in trade in these goods, while others bought them on inventory for sale to other merchants. There is evidence, for example, that several varieties of comparatively coarse cloth were produced on this basis in the district of Malda for eventual sale to merchants engaged in trade with Pegu, north India (Hindustan), and Persia, which had traditionally been important markets for these varieties.[26]

It seems, however, that only a small proportion of the total marketed output was produced in this manner. The bulk of the production was organised on the basis of agreements between merchants and weavers specifying details such as the quantity to be produced, the price, and the date of delivery. A part—often a substantial part—of the final value of the contract was given in advance to enable the weaver to buy the necessary raw materials as well as sustain himself and his family during the period of production. Clearly, the three key elements in this system were the weavers' need of finance, their relative lack of access to the market, and a desire on their part to avoid risks arising out of their inability to forecast correctly the behaviour of the demand for a given variety of textiles. With the proliferation of the *aurungs* and the emergence of new markets where the traditional varieties with standard sizes and well-defined patterns, designs, and colour combinations would not do, the need to operate through the system of contracts increased considerably. If finance alone were needed, the weavers could have borrowed from professional moneylenders by pledging the final product to them. But the merchant was the only agency that simultaneously provided the credit and guaranteed the purchase of the product.

This organisation, which could be described as the contract system, has

[26] Report by Hendrick Cansius on Malda dated 7.9.1670, K.A. 1168, ff. 2173vo-2174; Peachy at Malda to Job Charnock and Council at Calcutta, 23.10.1690, F.R. Calcutta, vol. 9, f. 100; Calcutta to Malda, 30.10.1690, F.R. Calcutta, vol. 5, f. 81.

sometimes been equated with the standard European putting-out system. But there were important differences between the two. Most often the European producer was provided with the necessary raw materials, and the money payment made to him was only an advance on his wages. At all stages of production, the output belonged to the merchant. The Indian artisan, on the other hand, retained his status as an independent worker, buying his own raw material and exercising formal control over his output until it changed hands. He was still a "price worker" and not yet reduced to the status of a "wage worker." Of course, the merchant who had given the advance had first claim on the output, and debt obligations often rendered the artisans subject to coercive control by the merchants. Nevertheless, the Indian artisan was more independent than his European counterpart.

A long tradition of sophisticated skills coupled with comparatively low labour costs made the textile manufactures of Bengal highly competitive in the world market. The manufacturing in the *aurungs* was organised on a specialised basis.[27] An official report on Malda in 1670 (that is, before significant penetration of the district by the European companies) states that textiles worth Rs. 0.8 to Rs. 1 million were sold in the district annually for export to places such as Pegu, Agra, Surat, and Persia.[28] Table 4.1 summarises the information about the *aurungs* where these textiles were produced (the hinterland of these *aurungs* extended over as many as 350 villages). Services such as bleaching were available in Malda town at fixed prices. Comparatively coarse textiles for traditional markets could be bought against cash. If these were bought directly from producers who brought them into Malda rather than from the merchants, the cost advantage would be between 12 and 15 percent. The mark-up by the merchant would, of course, be substantially greater under the contract system to compensate him for the additional risks borne. These risks were not inconsiderable. For example, a sudden rise in the cost of living in the wake of a famine, or the appointment of a particularly tyrannical official in a given area, might lead to a mass migration of the poor weavers to a more convenient location, to the great discomfiture of the merchants who had entered into contracts with them and given them advances.[29]

The evidence on the weavers' costs and the merchants' mark-up is so

---

[27] For example, in the district of Pipli in Orissa, the *aurung* of Mohanpur specialised in the production of *humhums* (fine calico), *garras* (ordinary calico), *sologazis* (fine calico), and *adathis* (fine muslin); that of Danton in *doreas* (fine calico) and *soosies* (silk); that of Olmara in *seklas*, *rumals* (both fine calicoes), and *alachas* (silk); whereas the *aurung* of Casuri produced only super-fine cotton textiles. Instructions by Director de Haze to van den Hemel, the new chief factor at Balasore and Pipli, 1.2.1675, K.A. 1202, f. 78vo.

[28] Report by Hendrick Cansius on Malda dated 7.9.1670, K.A. 1168, f. 2174.

[29] H.XVII. 22.12.1691, K.A. 1388, ff. 745vo-749.

TABLE 4.1
Manufacturing of Textiles in Malda District, 1670

Name of the aurang(s)	Distance in terms of travelling time from Sadullapur in police station English Bazar	Varieties manufactured	Value of annual output (in rupees)
Douanhadt	1/2 day	alachas, saris	100,000
Dandepur, Salgabaspur, Serot	N.A.	malmals	100,000
Alua, Kailgam	1½ days	coarse and fine khasas	150,000
Lagon, Dapot	3 days	coarse khasas	80,000
Malikpur	2 days	dupattas, mandils and odhnis	120,000
Sialgam, Sripur, Saishat, Haripur, Basepur, Daudpur	3-5 days	several varieties	200,000
Total			750,000

Source: Report by Hendrik Cansius on Malda dated 7.9.1670, K.A. 1168, ff. 2173-2173vo.

Note: It has not been possible to identify the aurangs. Places such as Sadullapur were easily identified in the village directory in the district handbook for Malda issued as part of the West Bengal census publications for 1951, but most others were not. This was partly because names such as Sripur, Haripur, and Daudpur were rather common and occur repeatedly under different police stations.

meagre that it is hazardous to draw any general conclusions from it. But one might look at the data provided by Commissioner van Rheede in 1686-1687 for three grades of *khasas*, a staple variety of muslins. About two-thirds of the price obtained by the weaver covered the costs of the raw material, and the remainder was the reward for his labour.[30] The mark-up by the merchant (calculated on the basis of the price agreed upon at the time of the contract between the Dutch Company and the merchant) was 35 percent in the case of grade I, 55 percent in grade II, and as much as 142 percent in grade III. The Dutch factors maintained that the quality differential among the three grades was much greater than what had been stipulated at the time of the contract. This was particularly so for grade III. It is not clear whether the Company paid the originally agreed-upon

[30] The precise figures were 65 percent for grade I, 66 percent for grade II, and 68 percent for grade III. Instructions by Commissioner van Rheede to the Bengal factors, 21.2.1687, K.A. 1324.

price for all the three grades, or insisted on reducing it for the second and particularly the third grades.[31]

The structure of textile production was flexible enough to respond to changes in demand for its output. Thus the phenomenal increase in the European companies' demand for Bengal textiles in the latter half of the seventeenth and the first half of the eighteenth centuries was accompanied by a rise in the output of the varieties demanded, though there were obviously frustrating time lags and shortages of particular varieties. The increase in output seems to have been achieved primarily through an increase in the proportion of full-time artisans to total artisans. The Dutch factors also noted widespread mobility among the artisans.[32]

Again, the sizes of the textiles as well as their texture, pattern, designs, and colour combinations were adjusted to meet changes in demand. The European companies, for example, normally asked for textiles in sizes considerably larger than was usual in Bengal, and this necessitated resetting the loom and using new matrices. The patterns and designs that would sell in Europe were also often quite different. Initial resistance to the adoption of such innovations was usually overcome by the offer of higher prices and an assured purchase of the entire output produced according to the new specifications.[33] Since the Europeans' general impression of the Indian artisans was that they were good imitators rather than good inventors, the companies brought in expert weavers and dyers from Europe to prepare new samples.[34] The Dutch even started a unit within the precincts of their factory at Hugli where experiments in new designs, patterns, and colour schemes were carried out. Not all the innovations

[31] Needless to say, any reduction in the price actually paid by the Company would correspondingly bring down the mark-up by the merchants. Instructions by Commissioner van Rheede to the Bengal factors, 21.2.1687, K.A. 1324.

[32] For example, in 1675, Director de Haze made the following observation: "We understand that for some years now, many weavers are coming to Balasore from the uplands to settle down there. They make very good *malmals, khasas,* and *sanus* of which the merchants have shown us some samples." Instructions by Director de Haze to the newly appointed chief of Balasore and Pipli, van den Hemel, 1.2.1675, K.A. 1202, f. 80.

[33] Bengal's explanation of why the textile orders could not be supplied in full, 1699, K.A. 1516, ff. 68-69. Instructions to Hendrick Cansius deputed to purchase textiles at Malda, 10.4.1675, K.A. 1202, ff. 145-149vo; B.H. 27.5.1686, K.A. 816, f. 224; letter from Commissioner van Rheede to Batavia, 6.12.1686, K.A. 1310, ff. 108vo-109vo.

[34] For example, the Dutch brought in a weaver and a dyer in 1669, another dyer in 1680, and yet another in 1689. The usual salary for a dyer was Rs. 120 per annum (H.XVII. 8.11.1669, K.A. 1160, f. 243; B.H. 25.10.1689, K.A. 819, f. 977). The English Court of Directors sent a dyer to Bengal in 1668. Another two were sent in 1679 at a salary of £50 (Rs. 400) each per annum plus the provision of a bonus of £20 per native dyer trained well enough to take over as a master dyer. English Court of Directors to Bengal, 20.11.1668, L.B. 4, f. 202; Court of Directors to Bengal, 31.12.1679, L.B. 6, ff. 130, 146.

resulting from these experiments were adopted, of course. There were occasions when the cost of the new product turned out to be prohibitive, and others when the Indian artisans were simply unable to imitate the samples.[35] Given the comparatively lower cost of living (and, therefore, of production) in Bengal, the companies even tried to have certain varieties of textiles traditionally produced in Gujarat and Coromandel manufactured in Bengal. These attempts, however, did not succeed because of the unwillingness of the Gujarati and other craftsmen to share their skills with artisans in Bengal.[36]

The Mode of Procurement

The Company procured textiles for Europe as well as for Japan and other Asian markets. Many of these markets were new for Bengal textiles, and the varieties in demand there were not manufactured on inventory. It was, therefore, necessary to put out contracts to the weavers, and since the Company was not ordinarily able to do this itself, it was obliged to operate through the local merchants. The merchants exploited the situation by charging the Company, for comparable qualities, a higher price than what they asked for from their fellow merchants engaged in foreign trade. In order to facilitate such price discrimination, the varieties manufactured for the Europeans were sometimes labelled *angrezi* (English) as opposed to the rest, which were designated *desawari* (indigenous).[37]

The Company's procurement organisation at Hugli and the subordinate factories was put in motion soon after the receipt of the order lists from Europe and the East Indies, both coming through Batavia. An important functionary in this organization was the *dalal* (broker), a native employee with an intimate knowledge of both the local market and the merchants. He was ordinarily a salaried employee, and his duties included collecting

---

[35] H.B. 22.9.1691, K.A. 1388, f. 690; H.XVII. 22.12.1691, K.A. 1388, ff. 750-vo; B.H. 15.10.1718, K.A. 872, f. 1313. The following cases in which the cost became excessive may be noted. In 1689 the cost of production of a new type of *armosin*—a silk textile—was found to be prohibitive (Hugli to Commissioner van Rheede at Coromandel, 4.8.1689, K.A. 1348, ff. 762-763). In 1669, plans to get the pattern of *jamawars*—also a silk textile—modified to meet the requirements of the French market had to be shelved for the same reason (explanation by Dutch factors at Bengal, 1699, K.A. 1516, f. 77). A disproportionate increase in cost also prevented the Company in 1701 from going ahead with the proposed changes in *dassies*—an ordinary calico (explanation by Dutch factors, 1701, K.A. 1556, ff. 86-89).

[36] H.B. 16.10.1709, K.A. 1669, ff. 53-54; B.H. 10.5.1710, K.A. 858, f. 349; B.H. 23.5.1711, K.A. 857, ff. 421-422; Directors of the new English Company to their factors in Hugli, 7.9.1700, L.B. 11, f. 223.

[37] English factors at Dacca to Calcutta, 17.10.1690, F.R. Calcutta, vol. 9, ff. 105-106.

information about the market price of various goods as well as identifying merchants with a good reputation for honouring contractual obligations.[38] These merchants were brought by the *dalal* to a meeting of the Hugli council, where the Company's requirements were placed before them.[39] Written agreements were entered into between the Company and each of the merchants willing to supply at terms agreed upon in the meeting. The agreement specified the quantity to be supplied, the period of delivery, and the price per piece of each of the different varieties contracted for. The risk of any fluctuations in the price between the date of the agreement and that of delivery had to be borne entirely by the merchants. The merchants were also provided with samples as a guide to what the Company needed by way of quality, texture, pattern, and design. The Company reserved the right to reject pieces that deviated significantly from the relevant sample. In the case of pieces where such deviation was marginal, the price was subject to a suitable adjustment.

The merchants had the goods manufactured mainly on the basis of the contract system which, as we have seen, obliged them to give a part of the value of the contract to the producers in advance. The merchants, therefore, insisted that the Company similarly give them an advance. The argument the factors normally gave to their superiors in justifying their agreement to this demand was that the bulk of the merchants were men of comparatively modest finances and were not in a position to give advances to the producers on their own. Although this certainly was true of some merchants, the more important reason was the wish of all of them to minimize the amount of their own funds risked with the producers. The Company also had reason to believe that the provision of an advance reduced, though it did not eliminate, the possibility that the merchants would supply the goods intended for it to another buyer in consideration of a higher price. But whatever the rationale, advance payment was an essential feature of the arrangement between the Company and the merchants, which might thus be termed the "cash-advance system." The precise proportion of the cash advance to the value of the contract was obviously a matter for negotiation, but the norm appears to have been between 50 and 65 percent. There were, however, occasions on which this figure was as high as 100 percent, and others when it was as little as

---

[38] In the 1690s, the two *dalals* at the chief factory at Hugli were Sattu and Gauri Kant. The latter was paid a salary of Rs. 20 per month, which was later increased to Rs. 32. In the second decade of the eighteenth century, both Sattu and Gauri Kant were succeeded by their respective sons. H.B. 28.2.1695, K.A. 1459, ff. 39-40; B.H. 15.8.1695, K.A. 829, f. 1499; H.B. 9.3.1716, K.A. 1776, ff. 226-227.

[39] A similar procedure was followed at each of the subordinate factories.

25 percent.[40] A part of the advance was sometimes given in goods imported by the Company, but this usually proved counterproductive, since the merchants had to convert the goods into cash before they gave out the contracts to the producers, and so found it difficult to keep to the contracted time schedule.[41] In order to minimize the competition among the merchants for supplies, the Company tried to persuade them to operate as far as possible in different segments of the market.[42] Often, as we have seen, the merchants were provided with the Company's *dastaks*, enabling them to transport goods to be supplied to the Company without paying the *rahdari* duties.[43]

The merchants who did business with the Company were described as *paikars* or *gomashtas*. It was an extremely heterogeneous group. At one end, it included merchants such as Khem Chand Shah, who engaged in large-scale domestic and overseas trade and who owned several ships. At the other end, there were marginal merchants who genuinely depended heavily on the advances received from the Company. Commissioner van Rheede's instructions to the Bengal factors in 1687 contain some useful details. Textile contracts worth a total of Rs. 326,928 were allotted in 1686 to nine merchants. The largest of these, accounting for 28 percent of the total value, went to an important merchant, Kalyan Das, whereas the smallest, accounting for only 2 percent, went to one Dayal Das. The respective share of the other seven merchants was 17, 15, 13, 10, 8, 4, and 3 percent. Half the value of the contract was given to each of the merchants in advance. All nine merchants were Hindus. The dominant group was that of the *banias*, many of whom had migrated from Gujarat and other places. Van Rheede has left a picturesque account of the trading acumen of the Bengal merchants:

> The merchants . . . are exceptionally quick and experienced. When they are still very young and in the laps of their parents and hardly able to walk, they already begin to be trained as merchants. They are made to pretend to engage in trade while playing, first buying *cauris*, followed by silver and gold. In this training as moneychangers, they acquire the capability of engaging in large-scale trade. They are always sober, modest, thrifty, and cunning in identifying the source of their profit, which they are always at pains to maximize. They

---

[40] An example of 100 percent advance was the agreement for the supply of some varieties of textiles at Pipli in 1670. During the Sobha Singh rebellion in the late 1690s, on the other hand, the Company gave an advance of only 25 percent. H.B. 16.11.1670, K.A. 1164, f. 501vo; H.B. 19.9.1697, K.A. 1484, ff. 80-85.

[41] H.B. 4.11.1680, K.A. 1244, ff. 313vo-319.

[42] H.B. 28.8.1678, K.A. 1222, f. 525vo.

[43] This was done, for example, in 1709 in the case of merchant Ram Kishan. H.B. 16.2.1709, K.A. 1669, ff. 27-29.

have an exceptional capability of discovering the humour of those who are in a position to help or hurt them. They flatter those they know they need to be in the good books of. In case of loss, they console themselves easily and can hide their sorrow wonderfully. . . . In general, they are a people with whom one could get along well so long as one is on one's guard.[44]

Many of the merchants operated on an individual basis, although partnerships were also quite common. Whatever the arrangement, the liabilities of a deceased merchant were almost invariably taken over by his heirs, imparting a certain measure of stability and continuity to the system.[45]

Once the goods were delivered into the Company's warehouses, the extent of deviation from the samples was worked out by a committee of the members of the factory's council assisted by the *dalals* and any Dutch experts in the commodity that might currently be available in the factory.[46] The price the Company was willing to pay was then communicated to the merchant. There was room for negotiation in this, and the two parties normally did manage to find a common meeting ground, but that did not always happen and the merchant then had no option but to take his goods back. The Company tried to avoid such breakdowns in negotiations, since the growing competition among the Europeans was increasingly creating a sellers' market.[47] Sometimes the Company even agreed to have particular

[44] Instructions by Commissioner van Rheede to the Bengal factors, 21.2.1687, K.A. 1324, ff. 132vo-133, 150vo-152vo.

[45] The following are some of the cases available in the Company's papers. In 1667, the father and brother of merchant Goreyn Das, recently deceased, informed the Company of their intention to fully honour his obligations to the Company (H.B. 23.8.1667, K.A. 1156, f. 86vo). In 1683, when Sundar Das died, his partner Kalyan Das settled the firm's liability of Rs. 35,000 toward the Company. He also made the son of the deceased, Hari Ballabh Das, his new partner (H.B. 11.1.1684, K.A. 1292, ff. 497vo). In 1690, merchant Dharni Dhar's heir, Jugal Kishore, undertook to meet all his obligations (H.B. 1.2.1690, K.A. 1376, f. 11vo).

[46] It was rarely that the Company found the product supplied to be in perfect conformity with the sample. Thus, of the large variety of textiles supplied at Hugli in 1690, it was only in the case of the Handiaal *adathis* that the sample was found to have been properly reproduced (K.A. 1384, f. 842). There were even cases when the deviation from the sample was so large as to merit a final price no more than 60 percent of that originally stipulated (K.A. 1348, f. 853vo). In the 1680s and the 1690s, the services of Gerrit Klink were used at Hugli in the evaluation of the textiles supplied by the merchants. At Patna, the Company used the services of an opium expert who was paid Re. 1 per case of 145 ponds examined. Instructions by Commissioner van Rheede to the Bengal factors, 21.2.1687, K.A. 1324, f. 154.

[47] To take only one case, in 1689, against the originally stipulated price of Rs. 10 per piece of *khasas*, the Company decided to offer Rs. 9.50 per piece for the grade I pieces in the lot supplied by a particular merchant, Rs. 8.62 per piece for the grade II pieces, and

lots of textiles reevaluated by a committee that included neutral local merchants, whose recommendations were binding on both the parties.[48] In 1687, Commissioner van Rheede made a general recommendation that in textiles valued at more than Rs. 10 per piece, a deviation from the sample of up to Re. 0.37 was to be ignored.[49]

There were sometimes deviations from this structure of procurement by the Company. At places such as Dacca and Pipli the Company also used the services of commission agents (also called *dalals*) to procure export goods. The agent was given a certain amount of money, which he invested among the weavers on behalf of the Company and at the Company's risk. After the goods had been delivered, the agent was entitled to a 2 percent commission (*arhat*) on the total value of the transaction.[50] The Company's *paikars/gomashtas* resented this intruder, and often worked hard to put him out of business.[51] From the point of view of the Company, the commission agent was usually a cheaper intermediary but was used much less extensively than the *paikar*.[52]

The *paikars* sometimes gave subcontracts for part of the goods they had undertaken to supply to the Company. This was particularly true in the case of raw silk, where the capacity of the reeling unit organised by a particular merchant put an upper limit on the amount of raw silk he could hope to supply on his own. Subcontracts were, therefore, given to mer-

---

Rs. 7.72 per piece for the grade III pieces. After negotiations, a mutually acceptable price of Rs. 10 per piece for grade I, Rs. 9.12 per piece for grade II, and Rs. 8.00 per piece for grade III was worked out, and the deal went through (H.XVII. 22.12.1691, K.A. 1388, ff. 745vo-749).

An instance of the breakdown of negotiations was recorded in 1689. In a lot supplied by one Ram Narain against the originally stipulated price of Rs. 21.75 per piece of *tanzebs*, the Company evaluated 50 pieces out of the total lot of 200 pieces at Rs. 14.50 per piece, and the remaining 150 pieces at Rs. 12.50 per piece. In spite of protracted negotiations, the two parties could not agree upon a mutually acceptable price, and Ram Narain had to withdraw the lot (H.XVII. 22.12.1691, K.A. 1388, ff. 745vo-749).

[48] This was done, for example, in 1688 in the case of textiles supplied by merchants Kanu Ram and Ram Narain, and an additional payment of Rs. 600 was made to them (H.B. 22.9.1688, K.A. 1343, ff. 726-727vo).

[49] Instructions by Commissioner van Rheede to the Bengal factors, 21.2.1687, K.A. 1324, f. 154vo.

[50] H.B. 28.2.1672, K.A. 1178, f. 22.

[51] Thus in Pipli, two Muslim *paikars* of the Company, Sheikh Sikandar and Salim Khan, were reported to be constantly at work to oust two Hindu commission agents, Parshu Ram and Kishan Das Brahmin, working for the Company. Parshu Ram was particularly useful to the Company, since he was a brother of the *zamindar* of Mohanpur and Danton and so exercised a certain amount of authority over the artisans in these two *aurangs*, ensuring comparatively more regular supplies. Instructions by de Haze to van den Hemel, newly appointed chief of Balasore and Pipli, 1.2.1675, K.A. 1202, f. 79.

[52] H.B. 26.9.1675, K.A. 1203, f. 69vo.

chants who would not ordinarily get contracts directly from the Company. The subcontractor was given a part of his costs in advance. His own share in the total transaction varied between Rs. 5 and Rs. 10 per bale supplied by him.[53]

An interesting functionary one comes across in the Company's papers is the head weaver (*hoofd-wever*). His precise status is not clear, but he acted as an intermediary between the weavers and the buyers of their produce. He appears to have exercised some authority over the members of his community, ensuring a certain amount of regularity in the supplies. His services were often utilized by the *paikars*, who would enter into a contract with him and give him an advance. On the limited occasions on which it was able to do so, the Company dealt directly with the head weavers and saved on the margin of the *paikars*. Thus, in 1670, a head weaver of Hugli agreed to supply *fotas*—an ordinary calico—at Rs. 70 per twenty pieces, whereas the merchants were asking for a price of Rs. 90. The corresponding figures in the case of sailcloth were Rs. 36 and Rs. 43, respectively. Such deals, however, had to be made very discreetly because the *paikars* were always on the lookout to sabotage them.[54]

Finally, mention might be made of the Company's efforts to short-circuit all the intermediary groups and reach the weavers directly. The Malda Diary suggests that such dealings were fairly extensive in the case of the English Company. The English factors approached the weavers through *dalals*, who together with the weavers were made jointly and severally responsible for the contracts.[55] The evidence relating to direct dealings between the weavers and the Dutch Company is meagre, however, and suggests that for them this was at best a marginal phenomenon.[56] The major hurdle seems to have been the strong opposition of the *paikars* to this arrangement. Many of the weavers were indebted to one or the other of the *paikars* and dared not incur their displeasure by offering to deal directly with the Company.[57]

---

[53] H.B. 11.1.1684, K.A. 1273, ff. 440-444.

[54] Instructions by Commissioner van Rheede to the Bengal factors, 21.2.1687, K.A. 1324, ff. 152vo-153; H.B. 9.2.1686, K.A. 1318, f. 914; H.B. 20.8.1670, K.A. 1167, ff. 1439vo-1441.

[55] W. K. Firminger, ed., "The Malda Diary and Consultations 1680-1682," *Journal and Proceedings of the Asiatic Society of Bengal*, N.S. 14 (1918); Malda Consultations, 29.4.1680, F.R. Hugli, vol. 2, ff. 60-61.

[56] Hugli to van Rheede in Ceylon, 20.2.1690, K.A. 1360, ff. 320vo-321.

[57] For example, in 1675-1676, at Balasore only one weaver, Bharat, who was not indebted to any of the merchants, came forward to deal directly with the Dutch factors. Instructions by Director de Haze to factors van den Hemel and Jasper van Collen at Balasore, 3.2.1676, K.A. 1209, ff. 551vo-552.

The Problems in Procurement

The overwhelming dependence on the cash-advance system created a range of problems for the Company. By far the most serious was the large number of bad debts. For one thing, the *paikars* ordinarily supplied less than they had undertaken either because the producers had not fully honoured their obligations toward them or because they themselves had chosen to supply a part of the goods procured to a third party at better terms. Second, of the goods received by the Company, a part was usually found unacceptable. Finally, even in the case of goods accepted, the final price paid to the merchants was ordinarily lower than that originally agreed upon. The result was that often the value of the goods accepted by the Company from a particular merchant was less than the sum of money given to him in advance. The balance constituted a bad debt. That this was a serious problem would be evident from the fact that in 1674, for example, the cumulative bad debts outstanding against the saltpetre suppliers alone amounted to f. 203,673. This figure was a little over 1.5 times the value of the average annual procurement of this item at this time.[58]

Preventive measures taken by the Company included a closer investigation into the credentials of the *paikars* before contracts were given out to them, and a denial of fresh contracts to *paikars* who owed money to it. But since the Company did not want to lose the bulk of its suppliers to its rivals, the latter measure was invoked only in the case of habitual offenders. The others were simply required to clear at least a part of their earlier obligations simultaneously with the new ones.[59]

In the 1680s, Commissioner van Rheede suggested that the Company ought to try and persuade the *paikars* to accept, in the first instance, only a quarter of the total advances due to them with the assurance that the next installment of another quarter would follow as soon as the obligations corresponding to the first had been met. The merchants, however, refused to accept the arrangement on the ground that it would not be practical for them to contact the artisans several times in a season for small lots at a time. In the case of textiles, it was also pointed out that getting small lots washed and dyed cost more per unit than if this job were organised on a bigger scale.[60] Yet another measure tried by the Company was to

---

[58] H.XVII. 10.12.1674, K.A. 1189, ff. 600-vo; in 1688, the bad debts in saltpetre were reported to be f. 188,838. Instructions by van Ommen and van Heck, June 30, 1688, enclosure to H.B. 22.9.1688, K.A. 1343, f. 754. Average annual procurement estimated from the invoices of the Dutch exports from Bengal.

[59] H.B. 25.3.1682, K.A. 1267, f. 1321vo; H.B. 9.2.1686, K.A. 1318, f. 914; B.H. 3.8.1686, K.A. 816, f. 392.

[60] Hugli to Commissioner van Rheede in Ceylon, 4.8.1690, K.A. 1360, ff. 343-345; H.B. 29.9.1698, K.A. 1500, ff. 85-87.

persuade the merchants to borrow the equivalent of the advances in the local money market and charge the Company for the cost of interest. But since this would have shifted the incidence of a possible default by the producers on to the shoulders of the merchants, they refused to accept this arrangement, either.[61]

Measures adopted by the Company to prevent bad debts from arising included taking a pledge from the *paikars* that they would not do business with a rival European company. If the undertaking were violated, the punishment was to be determined by the chief of the Dutch factory. In the case of saltpetre, where the problem of bad debts was particularly severe, each supplier was obliged to post a security of Rs. 1,000, which was subject to forfeiture if the supplier was found dealing with a third party. Occasionally, the Company even deputed foot soldiers at the houses of the *paikars* and the artisans to ensure that the goods intended for it were not siphoned elsewhere.[62] But with a growing competition among the European buyers for supplies that were not always increasing at a correspondingly fast rate, none of these measures turned out to be particularly workable and the problem of bad debts continued.[63]

In 1675, a number of leading saltpetre merchants of Patna told the Company that if it undertook to procure all the saltpetre it required exclusively through them and arranged to seize and hand over to them the refineries of the saltpetre merchants under debt to it, they would be willing to assume responsibility for all the bad debts on saltpetre accounts in Patna. They admitted that what they were aiming at was an oligoposony vis-à-vis the producers ordinarily producing for the Dutch. But since they would simultaneously have constituted an oligopoly vis-à-vis the Company, and it was in any case not possible to seize the refineries of the indebted suppliers, the offer was turned down.[64]

---

[61] H.B. 10.10.1705, K.A. 1604, f. 25.

[62] Enclosure to H.B. 29.10.1714, K.A. 1746, ff. 95-96, I Section; B.H. 20.8.1669, K.A. 796, f. 591; H.B. 7.6.1717, K.A. 1788, ff. 117-119, I Section; B.H. 19.10.1677, K.A. 804, f. 525; instructions by Director Nicolaas Baukes to the chief factor at Malda, May 1682, enclosure to H.B. 11.11.1682, K.A. 1267, ff. 1392-1394; H.B. 16.3.1710, K.A. 1688, f. 44, I Section; B.H. 25.10.1710, K.A. 856, ff. 1382-1383.

[63] For example, there is only one case in which the Company actually managed to impose a penalty on the erring suppliers. This happened in 1714, when three textile merchants of Hugli were found supplying goods to the French East India Company. The money advanced to them was recovered in full together with interest and a fine of Rs. 10,000. Their names were removed from the list of the Company's merchants and they were expelled from the Company's village of Chinsura. H.B. 30.1.1715, K.A. 1760, ff. 6-7, I Section; H.B. 29.10.1715, K.A. 1760, ff. 42-43, II Section; H.B. 9.3.1716, K.A. 1776, f. 225, I Section.

[64] Report by the chief factor at Patna, van Oosterwijk, 14.11.1675, K.A. 1202, ff. 70-71.

The royal *farman* of 1662 had instructed the Mughal officials not to hinder the Dutch in their efforts to recover debts from native merchants and others. The Dutch interpreted this to imply that they could arrest the defaulting merchants and detain them in their factory till they agreed to clear their obligations. That was often done, in fact, but the results were not very encouraging.[65] In November 1674, the council at Hugli adopted a resolution to refer the cases of some saltpetre merchants indebted to the Company to the court of law at Patna, and simultaneously threaten the provincial administration that if justice was not done, the Company would consider abandoning its factory there.[66] This resolution, however, does not seem to have been put into effect.

Another serious problem the Company often had to face was the receipt of goods from the *paikars* much later than the date mutually agreed upon. Part of the explanation lay in nonadherence to the schedule by the artisans, but this delay in some cases at least was deliberate.[67] The delivery of goods only a few days prior to the scheduled departure of the ships from Hugli left very little time for the factors to examine carefully the goods received, thereby increasing the chances not only that substandard items would be accepted but also that they would be evaluated at the same price as the others. The measures available to the Company to deal with this problem were first, evaluating the goods received late at a price lower than that at which they would normally have been evaluated, second, charging interest for the period between the stipulated and the actual dates of delivery, and third, obtaining undertakings from the merchants that if they did not supply the goods on time, they would be liable to any punishment deemed fit by the director at Hugli.[68] But for fear of losing the merchants to the rival companies, these measures were rarely put into effect.

Finally, the fact that the quality of the goods received was usually poorer

---

[65] *Corpus-Diplomaticum*, II, 217-220; H.B. 9.2.1686, K.A. 1318, ff. 913vo-914; H.B. 21.9.1686, K.A. 1318, f. 930vo.

[66] Resolution adopted by the Hugli Council, 27.11.1674, K.A. 1189, ff. 620-625.

[67] A case in point is that of textile merchant Ram Kishan, who had earlier been removed from the list of the Company's merchants for having had dealings with the English. In 1708 he advised some of the merchants supplying to the Dutch to follow this course of action. Statement by ten merchants supplying textiles to the Company, 15.12.1708, enclosure to H.B. 16.2.1709, K.A. 1669, ff. 194-195.

[68] H.XVII. 15.9.1676, K.A. 1204, f. 592; B.H. 17.6.1681, K.A. 809, f. 241; instructions by Director de Haze to van den Hemel, the new chief factor at Balasore and Pipli, 1.2.1675, K.A. 1202, ff. 79-81vo; H.XVII. 8.12.1686, K.A. 1327, ff. 914vo-915; contract between the Company and a Hugli merchant in 1686, enclosure to van Rheede's instructions to Bengal factors, 21.2.1687, K.A. 1324; H.B. 8.3.1689, K.A. 1352, ff. 19-vo; B.H. 21.6.1689, K.A. 819, ff. 268-269; enclosure to H.B. 16.10.1709, K.A. 1669, ff. 200-201.

than that of the samples given to the *paikars* had important ramifications other than contributing to the emergence of bad debts. The Company, no doubt, paid a lower price for the inferior goods, but this was not an acceptable solution. Given the structure of demand in most of the markets supplied with Bengal goods by the Company, the loss in total revenue consequent upon a deterioration in the quality offered was usually much greater than the saving in total cost. With a view to solving this problem in the case of textiles, Commissioner van Rheede recommended a weekly inspection of the looms belonging to artisans producing textiles for the merchants who had undertaken to supply to the Company. He suggested that if at any stage it was discovered that poor quality raw material was being used or that the specifications were not being precisely followed, the piece under production be cut and destroyed at no charge to the Company.[69] But it is doubtful if such a drastic step was in fact ever taken. In the case of opium, the merchants went so far as to declare that if the factors were not willing to accept between 10 and 13 percent lower grade opium, they would not be in a position to accept new contracts.[70]

The commodity for which the problem of poor quality occurred in its most intense form, however, was raw silk. Various qualities of unreeled silk were mixed together before they were reeled. In addition, the reeling itself was often very defective, with threads running into each other.[71] In the early 1660s, the Company appointed one Jai Biswas for the specific purpose of detecting artisans who used poor quality unreeled silk. He was authorised to confiscate the poor quality lots he so discovered, and was permitted to retain 25 percent of these in addition to his regular salary of Rs. 300 per annum.[72] In a contract given by the Company to a number of merchants a little later, each of them was persuaded to agree to a fine of Rs. 1,000 in case the raw silk he supplied was found to contain inferior quality unreeled raw silk.[73] But these measures at best succeeded in touching only the fringes of the problem. The Company's attempt to impose a special fine of Rs. 25 per bale not properly reeled or containing poor quality raw material did not succeed because of the strong opposition of the merchants.[74] With a view to improving the quality of reeling, the

[69] Instructions by Commissioner van Rheede to Bengal factors, 21.2.1687, K.A.1324, f. 153.

[70] H.B. 5.11.1717, K.A. 1783, ff. 42-44.

[71] Most of the annual order lists sent by *Heeren XVII* to Batavia contain this complaint about the raw silk received from Bengal.

[72] Memorandum by the outgoing director, van den Broecke, to his successor, van Hyningen, 14.2.1664, K.A. 1137, ff. 438-443.

[73] See, for example, the contract given to merchants Prahlad Das and Radha Ballabh, K.A. 1167, f. 1454.

[74] H.XVII. 28.10.1699, K.A. 1516, ff. 14-15.

Company persuaded a number of *paikars* in 1684 to arrange for the reeling of the silk on their own and not leave it to be done on contract. The factors agreed to procure enough raw silk from each of these merchants every year to ensure that the reelers employed by them did not have to sit idle.[75] This arrangement, however, seems to have collapsed soon after it was made. The quality of the raw silk supplied by the merchants, therefore, continued to be unsatisfactory.

THE COMPANY AS A MANUFACTURER

A distinctive feature of the trading operations of the Company in Bengal was its direct, though limited, participation in manufacturing activity organised within the precincts of its factories. The reasons for this participation varied from commodity to commodity. In the case of saltpetre, it was the desire to minimize the cost; in textiles, and especially in raw silk, the principal consideration was to try and solve the problem of the poor quality of the final product supplied by the merchants.

Saltpetre

In the initial stages of the trade with Bengal, the Directors asked only for refined (*kalmi* or *dobara-cabessa*) saltpetre. But the variety mostly available in Bihar was the semirefined one called *dobara*, and anyone insisting on the *kalmi* variety had to pay a disproportionately higher price. In 1655, for example, when the price of *dobara* was reported to be between Re. 0.75 and Re. 1, the refined saltpetre could be had only at Rs. 2.5 per maund. From the very beginning, therefore, the factors procured semirefined saltpetre in Patna and sent it to Coromandel, where the Company had a refining unit of its own. In order to save cost and time, a refining unit was established at Pipli in Orissa in 1641. In the mid-1650s, the annual refining capacity of this unit was reported to be 800,000 lbs., with provision for expansion to 1.2 million lbs. It is not clear why the unit was established at Pipli rather than at Patna. At any rate, another unit was established at Patna in 1656, and the Pipli unit was allowed to fall into disuse.[76] The capacity of the Patna unit was increased rapidly, but not fast enough to keep pace with the growth in demand.[77] The factors could have supplied the shortfall by buying *kalmi* saltpetre through the *paikars*. But as an experimental measure, it was decided to try the *dobara* variety in the Dutch market. As it happened, it did so well that in 1661

[75] Enclosure to H.B. 6.11.1684, K.A. 1296, ff. 3175-3176.
[76] K.B. 30.5.1656, K.A. 1104, ff. 451-vo.
[77] H.B. 29.11.1660, K.A. 1126, ff. 57-58.

the Directors asked for 50 percent of their order to be supplied in this variety. In 1669, the orders were entirely for *dobara* saltpetre.[78] Since there was no point in maintaining the refining unit any longer, the equipment was sold to the local merchants. Some refining kettles were retained by the Company for possible future use, however, and these were occasionally rented out at a charge of Rs. 20 per annum for a big kettle and Rs. 12 for a smaller one.

Textiles

With a view to improving the quality of printing, a unit for the printing of *chintz* (an ordinary calico) was established at Patna sometime in the second half of the seventeenth century, and another at Kasimbazar at the beginning of the eighteenth.[79] In 1717, the Patna unit was reported to be employing two hundred printers. In the 1680s, a small weaving and dyeing unit was also established at Kasimbazar to enable the expert weavers and dyers sent by the Directors to Bengal to conduct the necessary experiments in designs, patterns, and colour combinations.[80]

Raw Silk

The most ambitious of the Company's manufacturing projects was the unit for reeling raw silk established at Kasimbazar—the principal silk emporium in Mughal Bengal—in 1653. This was a measure designed to solve the twin problems of the use of inferior grades of unreeled silk and the poor quality of the reeling of raw silk supplied by the merchants. The Kasimbazar unit had an extraordinarily chequered life, at times reeling nearly all the raw silk exported by the Company, and at others, practically none. When operating at full capacity, it could reel about 1,500 bales (227,625 ponds) of raw silk per annum, and employed over 3,000 men. At the other extreme, the minimum number employed could be less than 100, and the output confined to the production of samples on the basis of which contracts were given to the merchants. Various problems were encountered at different stages, and the scale on which the unit operated at a particular point depended largely on the degree of success achieved in overcoming those problems.

[78] See the Directors' annual order lists sent to Batavia.
[79] Resolution adopted by the Batavia Council, 22.4.1700, K.A. 615, f. 201; H.B. 9.3.1701, K.A. 1540, ff. 20-21; B.H. 9.7.1701, K.A. 839, ff. 579-580.
[80] B.H. 25.5.1717, K.A. 869, ff. 270-272; H.B. 19.5.1687, K.A. 1327, f. 1023; H.B. 13.12.1687, K.A. 1329, f. 2374vo; B.H. 4.11.1688, K.A. 818, f. 1011; B.H. 27.6.1689, K.A. 879, f. 260; XVII.B. 3.11.1690, K.A. 460, f. 588vo.

Initially, the unit was organised on the basis of a contract with a so-called "master reeler." This individual was provided with the equipment necessary for reeling raw silk, accommodation for the reelers, and the necessary raw materials. Against a certain amount of unreeled silk supplied to him, he was supposed to provide the Company with a specified amount of properly reeled silk by a certain date. He was paid in advance a sum calculated at the rate of Rs. 5 per maund of reeled silk he had undertaken to supply. In 1662, the rate was increased to Rs. 5.5 per maund.[81] This arrangement worked exceedingly well in the beginning; in 1655 the unit was reported to be reeling around 800 bales (121,400 ponds) of raw silk per annum. In 1660-1661, of the 1,457 bales of raw silk exported from Bengal, as many as 1,427 (98 percent) had been reeled in this unit.[82] The quality of this raw silk was found to be superior to that usually supplied by the merchants, while the cost turned out to be lower by about half a rupee per seer (1⅖ ponds).[83] But soon the factors discovered that the capacity of the unit had probably been increased at too fast a rate. The Company's demand for unreeled silk having increased very fast, the merchants supplying it began asking for higher prices, while the quality gradually deteriorated and the instances of late delivery multiplied. Again, the late receipt of unreeled silk by the master reeler frequently created a situation in which even the small quantity of reeled raw silk that was to serve as a sample for the part that the Company procured through the *paikars* was not ready in time.[84] This delayed giving out of the contracts to the *paikars*. Moreover, the rapid increase in the number of artisans engaged by the master reeler soon made it impossible for the Company to provide accommodation for all within the premises of the factory, and a large number of men had to be asked to work elsewhere. As a result, it became impossible for the master reeler to keep an eye on the performance of individual reelers. This, coupled with the fact that the quality of the input was gradually deteriorating, brought about an inevitable decline in the quality of the raw silk reeled in the unit. The first complaints in this regard were received from the Directors as early as 1659.[85] Faced with the ever-present threat that the contract would be cancelled unless the quality of reeling was improved, the master reeler often resorted to whipping the artisans whose product was found to be substandard. This, however, only induced these reelers to run away from their jobs. Since each artisan was

[81] P.B. 10.11.1653, K.A. 1091, ff. 458vo-460.
[82] Memorandum by Commissioner Verpoorten, 28.10.1655, enclosure to P.B. 16.11.1655, K.A. 1102, ff. 218-219vo; invoices of exports from Bengal.
[83] B.H. 19.7.1657, K.A. 784, ff. 306-307.
[84] H.B. 26.8.1675, K.A. 1202, ff. 124vo-125.
[85] B.H. 27.8.1659, K.A. 786, ff. 588-589.

paid in advance for the amount of raw silk he was assigned to reel over a certain period, each such desertion led to an increase in the bad debts that the Company found it nearly impossible to recover from the master reeler. Toward the close of the very first year of the establishment of the unit at Kasimbazar, the master reeler was under debt to the Company to the extent of Rs. 2,255 for undelivered reeled silk. The promise to meet this debt in installments over a period of time does not seem to have been kept. In 1662, therefore, the Hugli factors asked for Batavia's permission to reduce the capacity of the unit by 50 percent. In view of the fact that for some reason the raw silk reeled in the unit had been sold in Holland that year at a profit lower than that afforded by the lot supplied by the merchants, the permission was readily granted. The actual reduction in capacity seems to have been more than 50 percent, since we find that of the 1,388 bales supplied by Bengal in 1664-1665, only 158 (11 percent) had been reeled in the unit. The corresponding figures for 1668-1669 were 1,653 and 113 bales (7 percent).[86]

In 1670, the Company appointed a new master reeler against a fresh contract, the main provisions of which were as follows: 1. The amount of reeled silk the master reeler was supposed to supply against a given amount of unreeled silk was to be determined on the basis of a sample reeling of three seers of unreeled silk in the presence of the factors. 2. The rate per maund of raw silk reeled was increased to Rs. 5.75, and the master reeler bound himself to pay Rs. 5 per maund to the artisans. He also agreed not to charge *dasturi* (customary charge) from the reelers. 3. The Company undertook to provide foot soldiers to compel the runaway artisans to return to work. The Company also agreed to provide a clerk to the master reeler to assist him in the maintenance of the accounts. 4. The Company undertook to provide adequate unreeled silk to the master reeler to provide year-round employment to the artisans engaged by him. 5. The master reeler in return assumed responsibility to clear the bad debts outstanding in the name of his predecessor. The contract was witnessed and guaranteed on behalf of master reeler Abhay Ram by two leading merchants, Deep Chand and Jai Chand. The new contract, however, only served to increase the cost of maintaining the unit. It was estimated in 1671 that the raw silk reeled in the unit turned out to be Re. 0.12 to 0.19 per seer more expensive than a comparable quality supplied by the merchants. Moreover, not only did the master reeler find himself unable to clear the debts of his predecessor, he was himself reported in August

[86] P.B. 10.11.1653, K.A. 1091, ff. 360-361; H.B. 26.10.1662, K.A. 1130, ff. 1387-1389; H.XVII. 13.12.1663, K.A. 1132, f. 648vo; H.XVII. 18.8.1665, K.A. 1142, ff. 1187-1189; invoices of Dutch exports from Bengal.

1671 to be under debt to the extent of Rs. 1,394, which the Company eventually had to write off.[87]

The basic organisational structure of the unit was changed in 1674, with the Company itself assuming all risks and the master reeler being demoted from the position of contractor to that of manager at a salary of Rs. 200 per annum. Abhay Ram was replaced by the two sons of ex-master reeler Bal Ram as joint managers. The unit was now a full-fledged man-ufacturing enterprise of the Company, though in terms of output, it was probably at its lowest ebb around this time.[88] Commissioner van Rheede tried to revive the unit by recommending various measures: the procure-ment of unreeled silk directly from the producers—a step that he thought would effect a substantial saving; the advance of only limited sums of money at a time to the manager as wages; and the reeling of florette yarn in addition to raw silk.[89] But none of these recommendations was put into effect, and for the rest of the seventeenth century, the Company continued to procure practically the entire amount of raw silk it required from the merchants.

A conspiracy by the leading silk merchants of Kasimbazar in 1700 to raise the price of raw silk from the usual level of under Rs. 5 per seer to Rs. 6 per seer ostensibly revived the Company's interest in the unit. The merchants were threatened that if they continued to ask for the higher price, the Company would arrange to have all the raw silk it required reeled in its own establishment. The threat worked, and the unit continued to produce only samples. Difficulties in the procurement of florette yarn around this time led to the reeling of this variety of silk in the unit as well, but since the total amount of this yarn procured was rather limited, the number of reelers employed continued to be fairly small.[90]

From 1709 onward, the Company again made a major effort to reel its raw silk in its own unit. The arbitrary increase in the price of raw silk by the merchants in 1714 to Rs. 5.37 per seer encouraged the factors to make an all-out attempt to get all the silk they wanted reeled in the unit, and they succeeded. For the years 1714-1718, information about the place of reeling is available for as much as 86 percent of the raw silk exported by

[87] Contract dated 20.5.1670, K.A. 1167, ff. 1457-1458; instructions by Director Ranst to Kasimbazar factors, 20.4.1671, K.A. 1174, ff. 1884-1890; H.B. 28.10.1670, K.A. 1164, ff. 410-vo; H.B. 3.8.1671, K.A. 1174, f. 1861.

[88] H.B. 19.9.1673, K.A. 1185, f. 32vo; H.B. 27.9.1674, K.A. 1193, f. 157; H.B. 29.8.1676, K.A. 1209, f. 605.

[89] Commissioner van Rheede's instructions to the Bengal factors, 21.2.1687, K.A. 1324, ff. 187-188; van Dam, *Beschrijvinge*, II, II, 62-65.

[90] H.B. 9.3.1701, K.A. 1540, ff. 31-32; B.H. 9.7.1701, K.A. 839, ff. 576-577; H.B. 28.9.1701, K.A. 1540, ff. 66-67.

the Company from Bengal. On an average, as much as 83 percent of this amount was reeled in the Company's own unit. This was the first time since the 1650s that it had been possible to get such a large proportion reeled in the unit. Around this time, the Company began thinking of a further expansion in the capacity of the unit, and in 1715, additional working space was constructed so as to make it possible to accommodate as many as 4,000 reelers.[91]

The establishment of the Kasimbazar unit might be regarded as a development of some importance in the emergence of the capitalist mode of production in Mughal Bengal. This was not simply because of the size of the unit, though that certainly was an important element. Manufacturing production on this scale under one roof on a regular wage-employment basis was rare in Mughal India.[92] The imperial and other workshops (karkhanas) were not fully comparable to the Dutch unit for two reasons. First, the goods manufactured in the karkhanas were intended almost exclusively for use by the royalty, the nobility, rich merchants and others, and for the army rather than for sale in the market. Second, at least some of the big karkhanas appear to have been operated on the basis of underpaid drafted labour rather than with free contract labour.[93] Both these factors make the karkhanas quite different from the Dutch silk manufactory as steps in the growth of the capitalist system of production in Mughal Bengal.

[91] Invoices of exports from Bengal; H.B. 29.10.1714, K.A. 1741, ff. 107-108vo; H.B. 20.10.1715, K.A. 1760, ff. 59-60, I Section; H.B. 31.10.1716, K.A. 1769, ff. 73-vo.

[92] It is true that a large number of workers had to be assembled for constructing forts and other big buildings, as well as ocean-going vessels. But in these cases, as W. H. Moreland (*India at the Death of Akbar* [London, 1923], pp. 173-174) has pointed out, the organisation brought into being did not survive the completion of the particular project for which it had been assembled. The royal mints in the various parts of the empire were undoubtedly fairly big units also. But it should be obvious that the implications of the production of coins by individuals employed on a salary basis by the government were somewhat different from those of the production of goods in a manufactory of the type of the Dutch silk-reeling unit at Kasimbazar.

[93] The English factors at Kasimbazar, for example, reported the following in 1681: "The taftas at Maxudabad and Ameenbazar have come in but very slowly these many days occasioned by the king's corconna—his forcing the weavers of all sorts to attend there to work in that manufactory because the Nawab wants a tent to be finished in time. We sent our vakil to Bal Chand several times but he has been able to do nothing about it because he says that till the tent is finished, he cannot release the weavers from working in the manufactory." Diary kept at the Kasimbazar factory of the English East India Company, 1.12.1681, F. R. Kasimbazar, vol. 2. f. 1. There are similar references available in the records of the Dutch Company. See particularly H.B. 11.1.1684, K.A. 1273, f. 427. At a later date, Abbé Raynal had this to say: "It was a misfortune to them [the artisans] to appear too dexterous because they were then forced to work only for the Government which paid them ill and kept them in a sort of captivity" (quoted in B. C. Allen, *District Gazetteer, Dacca* [Allahabad, 1912], p. 106).

· 5 ·

INTRA-ASIAN TRADE (I): JAPAN

Extensive participation in intra-Asian trade (sometimes also referred to as country trade) was probably the most important factor that distinguished the Dutch East India Company from its principal rivals, the English and later the French East India Company. The substantial pecuniary and other benefits derived from such participation also helped the Company dominate the trade with Europe through the greater part of the seventeenth century. The crucial role played by intra-Asian trade in the overall commercial strategy of the Company is evident from the following remarks of the Directors communicated to the Council of the Indies at Batavia in 1648: "The country trade and the profit from it are the soul of the Company which must be looked after carefully because if the soul decays, the entire body would be destroyed."[1] Three years later, the Directors even expressed the hope that at some point it would be possible for Batavia not only to finance the exports to Europe (which in 1650-1651 amounted to f. 2.7 million) wholly out of the profits from intra-Asian trade but also to send to them in addition some Asian precious metals.[2] Although such extravagant hopes were never realised, the fact remains that throughout the seventeenth century, participation in intra-Asian trade was extremely advantageous to the Company.

Bengal played a major role in the overall framework of the Company's intra-Asian trade. Goods procured in the region figured in the cargo sent to a host of factories between Nagasaki at one end and Gombroon at the other, and in some cases, such as Japan and the Indonesian archipelago, Bengal goods accounted for a substantial proportion of the total cargo sent. Indeed, until about 1680 or so, the Bengal factories derived their significance primarily from the role they played in the trade within Asia.

The trade between Batavia and Japan was an important segment of the Company's intra-Asian trade. With the opening of a large number of new gold and silver mines during the last half of the sixteenth and the early seventeenth centuries, Japan had become one of the most important pro-

---

[1] XVII.B.22.9.1648, K.A.455, f. 120vo.

[2] G. C. Klerk de Reus, *Geschichtlicher Ueberblick der Administrativen, Rechtlichen und Finanziellen Entwicklung der Niederländisch-Ostindischen Compagnie* (Batavia, 1894), Appendix V; van Dam, *Beschrijvinge* I, ii, 61 note 6. In 1646, the Directors had limited their hopes to getting an annual cargo of around f. 2 million per annum from the East without having to pay for it. XVII.B. 16.8.1646, K.A. 453, f. 60vo.

ducers of these metals in Asia.[3] The trade with Japan provided significant quantities of precious metals, which usefully supplemented the supplies from Europe, and in addition, the cost of Japanese silver was generally lower than of the lots procured in Europe.[4] Precious metals from Japan were crucial for trade with the various regions of the Indian subcontinent, among other places. The trade with Japan (to which the Dutch were the only Europeans allowed access from 1639 on) became one of the major elements in the Company's domination of the intra-Asian and the Euro-Asian trade through the greater part of the seventeenth century.

But the Japan trade was by no means easy; it had to be carried on in a singularly hostile environment. The Japanese government imposed a variety of procedures and restrictions whose nature and scope changed continually over time, making it impossible for the Company to evolve a long-term commercial strategy.

Following the establishment of a factory at Hirado in 1609, the Dutch trade with Japan had grown rapidly, and by 1627 the value of the Company's annual imports into the country had grown to $f.$ 0.72 million. But in 1628, following a clash between the Japanese crew of a red-seal ship despatched to Taiwan by an influential Nagasaki merchant and the factors of the Dutch factory at Taiwan, the trading privileges of the Dutch were suspended at Hirado. The suspension was revoked in 1632, and once the Dutch trade had been resumed in 1633, it grew at an astonishingly fast rate.[5] The principal constituent of the cargo sent to Japan during these years was Chinese raw silk, of which 239,540 ponds were sent in 1637. By 1640, this figure had gone up to 340,650 ponds.[6] Between 1634 and 1641, the average value of the annual Dutch cargo to Japan worked out at $f.$ 2.55 million. This amount was larger than that sent to any other factory in Asia and, indeed, approximated the value of the annual cargo to Holland around this time.[7]

[3] A. Kobata, "The Production and Uses of Gold and Silver in 16th and 17th Century Japan," *Economic History Review*, Second Series, 18 (August 1965), 254.

[4] For details, see Chapter 1.

[5] Nachod, *Niederländischen Ostindischen Kompagnie*, pp. ccii-cciv, Table A; E. Kato, "The Japanese-Dutch Trade in the Formative Period of the Seclusion Policy," *Acta Asiatica* (Tokyo), 30 (1976), 38, 54.

[6] Calculated from Nachod, *Niederländischen Ostindischen Kompagnie*, pp. ccv-ccvi, Table C. The figures in ponds are equivalent to Nachod's figures of 191,639 and 272,526 *catties*, respectively. E. Kato has suggested the figure of 110,306 *catties* for 1637 ("The Japanese-Dutch Trade," p. 66). The *catty* was a measure of weight introduced by the Chinese into the Indonesian archipelago and was equivalent of 1.25 Dutch ponds.

[7] Nachod, *Niederländischen Ostindischen Kompagnie*, pp. ccii-cciv, Table A; Kato, "The Japanese-Dutch Trade," p. 42. The average annual value of the cargo received in Holland from Batavia in 1639-1640 and 1640-1641 was $f.$ 2.69 million (Reus, *Niederländisch-Ostindischen Compagnie*, Appendix V).

When the "closed country era" began in 1639, the Portuguese were expelled from Japan, though the Dutch, who constituted the only other European community in Japan at this time, were spared this fate. The Shogun and his advisers seem to have realised that the expulsion of the Dutch, by leaving only the Chinese merchants to supply Japan with foreign goods, might well lead to an inadequate supply of these goods.[8] In view of the loss of trade they had suffered as a result of the expulsion of the Portuguese, a group of Nagasaki merchants petitioned the central government to transfer the trade of the Dutch to their city. The Shogun accepted the proposal chiefly because the islet of Deshima off the Nagasaki harbour—built for the Portuguese in 1635—offered an ideal place for the Dutch to be confined and thus cut off from the mainstream of Japanese life. In May 1641, therefore, the Company was ordered to move its factory to Deshima.[9] The number of Japanese allowed access to the Dutch quarters in the island was kept to a minimum, and the purpose of their visit limited to matters of trade. The Japanese were prohibited from learning Dutch and the Hollanders from learning Japanese; communication was permitted only through interpreters in Portuguese.[10] The commercial restrictions imposed on the Company in 1641 included a ban on the export of gold; the prescription of days on which it could offer its goods for sale, until which time they had to be kept in sealed warehouses; and the extension of the *pancado* system to the entire lot of Chinese raw silk it imported into Japan. This system required the Company to sell Chinese raw silk at a price determined arbitrarily by a guild monopsony consisting of a group of merchants from the five imperial cities of Edo (Tokyo), Osaka, Kyoto, Sakai, and Nagasaki.[11]

[8] For a discussion of the "closed country era" issue in the Japanese historiography, see Leonard Blussé, "Japanese Historiography and European Sources" in P. C. Emmer and H. L. Wesseling, eds., *Reappraisals in Overseas History* (Leiden, 1979), pp. 193-221. Also see Ronald P. Toby, "Reopening the Question of Sakoku: Diplomacy in the Legitimation of the Tokugawa Bakufu," *Journal of Japanese Studies*, 3 (Summer 1977), 323-364. From 1635 onward, the Japanese merchants were not allowed to send their ships out of Japan.

[9] C. R. Boxer, "Jan Compagnie in Japan 1672-1674 or Anglo-Dutch Rivalry in Japan and Formosa," *Transactions of the Asiatic Society of Japan*, Second Series, 7 (1930), 146-147; *Corpus-Diplomaticum*, I, 344.

[10] Other restrictions included a limit of one year on the stay of the factory's director in the country, a ban on the importation of military weapons unless asked for by the central government, and a requirement that all Dutch ships leave Japan by the 20th day of the ninth moon (usually falling between late October and early November) each year. François Valentijn, *Beschrijving van 't Nederlandsch Comptoir op de Kust van Malabar en van Onzen Handel in Japan* (Dordrecht/Amsterdam, 1726), pp. 83-85; *Corpus-Diplomaticum*, I, 338-339, 356-358; *Batavia Dagh-Register 1641-1642*, pp. 69-72.

[11] The *pancado* system was made applicable at the same time to the Chinese raw silk imported by the Chinese merchants. This system owed its origin to the difficulties experienced by the Portuguese in disposing of the large quantity of Chinese raw silk they had brought

Humiliating and commercially injurious as these restrictions were, the Dutch meekly accepted them. The Board of Directors, in fact, went so far as to instruct Batavia to maintain the trade, if necessary, "even from the ships." In a report submitted to the Directors in September 1652, Pieter Sterthemius, the chief of the Nagasaki factory during 1650-1651, wrote, "But I seem to hear a whisper in my ear, that some vexations can surely be endured for the sake of Japan's sweet gains, since Japan is the strongest sinew of the Company's inland trade and of the Indian profits; and this (insofar as our self-respect allows us to endure it) is true."[12] The "sweet gains," of course, were the precious metals the trade provided. The Company maintained trade relations with Japan for more than a century after being subjected to these restrictions. This entire period was characterized by the imposition of one set of controls or the other so that Dutch trade with Japan never again approached anything like the level attained during the years 1634-1641. In fact, in the decades that followed the volume of this trade was regulated to a large extent by the nature and the degree of severity of the regulations under which the Company had to operate.

Though items such as silk and other textiles, hides and skins, spices, sugar, tin, and sandalwood regularly formed part of the Dutch cargo to Japan, the staple item in this trade was raw silk. Until about 1640, the raw silk exported to Nagasaki was almost entirely of Chinese origin. But following the extension of the *pancado* to the entire import of this silk in 1641, the varieties procured in Tonkin and Bengal—particularly the latter—became increasingly important. In fact, Bengal soon came to be the most important single source of goods exported to Japan. Given the multilateral character of Dutch trade in Asia, the fact that Bengal factories played an important role in the conduct of the Japan trade did not necessarily imply that the reverse was also true. But in this instance, that was very much the case, at least until about the mid-1670s. Over this period, a substantial part of the precious metals imported by the Company

---

to Japan in 1602 and 1603. At that time, they had willingly accepted the Japanese offer of a guarantee to buy whatever quantity the Portuguese cared to offer for sale, provided the latter were willing to accept a "fair" price. Since then the Chinese raw silk imported by the Portuguese had been subject to the *pancado* arrangement. In 1633, the *pancado* system had been extended to a part of the Chinese raw silk brought in by the Dutch Company as well. Van Dam, *Beschrijvinge*, II, 1, 422, 442, 454, 455, 828; Nachod, *Niederländischen Ostindischen Kompagnie*, pp. 274, 354-356; *Batavia Dagh-Register*, 1641-1642, p. 70; Kato, "The Japanese-Dutch Trade," pp. 60-63.

[12] Nachod, *Niederländischen Ostindischen Kompagnie*, p. 297; François Valentijn, *Handel in Japan*, p. 127. In 1672, the English factors at Balasore in Orissa wrote to the Court of Directors in London, "This Japan trade by the Dutches Confession is the best they have in these parts which make them comply with the Japaners in all their demands." Letter dated 31.12.1672, F.R. Hugli, vol. 4, f. 11.

into Bengal—which, in turn, constituted the bulk of the total imports into the region—originated in Japan. Japanese bar copper was another major item of import into Bengal.

The history of the Dutch trade between Bengal and Japan over the period 1640—when Bengal goods figured for the first time in the cargo sent to Hirado—and 1720 falls into two broad phases. The period until 1672—when the Japanese government altered the whole basis of trade— was marked by a significant growth in the volume and value of this trade, followed by a period of decline. Within each of these two phases, one could identify two subphases, in the latter of which the pace of development and of decline, respectively, was somewhat accelerated. The duration of the subphases was again conditioned by the changing structure of restrictive measures forced upon foreign traders by the Japanese government. The subphases covered the years 1640-1655 and 1656-1672 during the first phase, and 1673-1685 and 1686-1720 during the second.

THE PHASE OF GROWTH: 1640-1672

Steady Growth, 1640-1655

During the years 1642-1655, when the Chinese raw silk the Company imported into Japan was subject to the *pancado* arrangement, the average annual value of Dutch imports into the country was only *f.* 0.93 million as against *f.* 2.55 million during 1634-1641.[13] But from the viewpoint of the import of Bengal goods into Japan, these were undoubtedly years of growth. Bengal raw silk had been included in the Dutch cargo for Japan for the first time in 1640. Since the Japanese were used to the superior quality white Chinese raw silk, the factors at Hirado had a difficult time selling the variety from Bengal. In fact, at the time the ships that had carried this silk to Japan sailed back for Batavia a few months later, most of it was reported to be lying unsold. The gross profit on the limited amount the factors had succeeded in selling was a mere 36 percent.[14] But the 1641 extension of the *pancado* system to the entire lot of Chinese raw silk imported made the Company reduce the import of this variety from

[13] Calculated from Nachod, *Niederländischen Ostindischen Kompagnie*, pp. ccii-cciv, Table A. For evidence that it was only Chinese raw silk that was subject to the *pancado* arrangement during this period, see van Dam, *Beschrijvinge*, II, 1, 361, 371, 386-387, 397, 487; Nachod, *Niederländischen Ostindischen Kompagnie*, p. 366.

[14] The royal order issued earlier in the year that prohibited the wearing of silk textiles by merchants and the servants of the nobility seems to have contributed to the problem. *Batavia Dagh-Register*, 1640-1641, pp. 130-131, 261.

340,650 ponds in 1640 to 60,150 ponds in 1642.[15] The situation was made still more difficult by reports received in 1644 to the effect that if the Company wanted to procure an adequate quantity of Chinese raw silk for Japan, the price paid would have to be increased.[16] As a result, it was decided to send to Japan relatively more of Persian and Bengal raw silk, neither of which was subject to the *pancado* system. The Persian silk, however, does not appear to have fared well, so it was not exported to Nagasaki at all between 1648 and 1667. The Bengal variety, on the other hand, did extremely well after an initial period of poor sales. In 1646, the Board of Directors went so far as to instruct Batavia to give priority to the orders for this item from Japan over those from Holland. By 1647, the amount of Bengal silk exported to Japan exceeded 30,000 ponds, constituting 29 percent of the total.[17] The gross profit earned on this variety was now more than 100 percent. This figure was reported to have gone up to 200 percent two years later, when the fresh annual orders from Japan amounted to 50,000 ponds. In 1650, Batavia decided to send all the raw silk it had received from Bengal for Holland and Japan entirely to the latter factory. The following year, the gross profit on Bengal silk was reported to be 126 percent, the corresponding figures for the Tonkinese and the Chinese varieties being 72 and 25 percent, respectively. This level came down in the years that followed, but in 1654, Bengal raw silk was still at the top with 81 percent whereas the gross profit on Tonkinese silk was 39 percent and on that from China 34 percent.[18]

Under the *pancado* system, the Nagasaki guild was obliged to buy whatever Chinese raw silk the foreigners cared to offer for sale in a year. Since the *pancado* price was announced on the basis of quantities imported into the country up to a certain date, the Chinese merchants—who accounted for the bulk of the trade in this variety—made it a point to import only limited quantities until that time. But once the price had been announced, they flooded the guild with Chinese silk. A situation of crisis was reached in 1655, when the *pancado* price was fixed at a rather high level so that against an average annual import of 100,000 ponds, the Chinese merchants

[15] Calculated from Nachod, *Niederländischen Ostindischen Kompagnie*, pp. ccv-ccvi, Table C. The entire lot imported by the Company into Japan in 1642 has been assumed to be from China.

[16] *Batavia Dagh-Register*, 1643-1644, p. 147.

[17] XVII.B. 16.8.1646, K.A. 455, f. 60vo. For the amount of Bengal raw silk exported to Japan, see Table 5.1. The figure of the total amount of raw silk imported into Japan is from Nachod, *Niederländischen Ostindischen Kompagnie*, pp. ccv-ccvi, Table C.

[18] B.XVII.31.12.1647, K.A. 1064, f. 69vo; B.XVII.20.1.1651, K.A. 1070, ff. 8vo-9; statement of goods sold in Japan in 1651, K.A. 1075, ff. 421-423; statement of goods sold in Japan in 1654, K.A. 1098, f. 774.

imported 164,500 ponds of Chinese raw silk.[19] The guild found itself unable to buy this large quantity, and petitioned the central government to relieve it of the obligation to buy Chinese raw silk imported into the country after the announcement of the *pancado* price. To the great surprise and consternation of the guild, however, the response of the Shogun was to withdraw the *pancado* system altogether.[20]

The only other export from Bengal to Japan during this period was limited quantities of textiles, both of silk and those manufactured from a mixture of silk and cotton yarn. In 1654, Bengal silk *rumals* were reported to have been sold in Nagasaki at a gross profit of 66 percent and *charkhanas* at 122 percent. The following year, the gross profit on Bengal *armosins* was reported to be 65 percent and on *taffechelas ginghams* 257 percent.[21]

As for the import of precious metals into Bengal, only silver, mainly from Japan, appears to have been involved in these years. Most of this silver was sold to the *sarrafs*, though occasionally a part of it was sent to the royal mint at Rajmahal to be minted into *sicca* rupees. Although the principal bullion market in contemporary Bengal was Kasimbazar, limited quantities were also sold in Hugli, Patna, and Balasore. Among the various types of silver the Company sold in Bengal, that from Japan usually afforded the highest profit.[22] Finally, Japanese bar copper was regularly imported into Hugli all through this period except during 1640-1645, when the export of this metal from Japan was banned.

Rapid Growth, 1656-1672

The withdrawal of the *pancado* system for Chinese silk should ordinarily have persuaded the Company to revive the trade in this particular variety. That this was not in fact done was because Bengal silk had in the meantime become so popular and profitable as to make it unnecessary for the Company to try and resume the trade in Chinese silk. Indeed, it was during this period that the trade in Bengal silk reached its peak and Bengal became

[19] The average is for three years, 1650, 1651, and 1654. Statements of goods imported by Chinese merchants into Nagasaki: K.A. 1075, ff. 498-504 (for 1650); ff. 424-428 (for 1651), and K.A. 1098, ff. 793-794 (for 1654). *Generale Missiven*, III, 65. The figure given by Nachod for 1655 is 175,000 ponds (*Niederländischen Ostindischen Kompagnie*, pp. 354-355).

[20] *Generale Missiven*, III, 65; Valentijn, *Handel in Japan*, p. 94; Nachod, *Niederlandischen Ostindischen Kompagnie*, pp. 354-355.

[21] Calculated from the statement of goods sold in Japan in 1654, K.A. 1098, f. 774; in 1655, K.A. 1103, ff. 831-832.

[22] P.B. 8.12.1649, K.A. 1701, ff. 25-30vo; B.XVII.20.1.1651, K.A. 1070, f.80; H.XVII. 19.11.1683, K.A. 1273, f. 470.

by far the most important supplier of the cargo sent to Nagasaki.[23] The average annual value of the Dutch exports to Japan during this period was *f.* 1.35 million, the highest figure ever attained in the post-1641 period. The average share of Bengal goods in this cargo was as much as 48 percent.[24]

The principal constituent of the cargo to Japan continued to be raw silk. In 1669, for example, this item accounted for 67 percent of the total Dutch imports into Nagasaki. Two-thirds of this silk was from Bengal.[25] Over the period 1656-1672, Bengal silk accounted, on an average, for four-fifths of the total amount of raw silk the Company sent to Japan.[26] In 1657, the great fire in Edo gave rise to rumours that the wearing of silk apparel was likely to be banned. As a result, the demand for raw silk registered a sharp decline and the gross profit on the variety from Bengal dropped to 41 percent. But the rumour turned out to be baseless, and in 1658, the gross profit again went up to 110 percent.[27] Over the following few years, the rate of profit continued to be reasonably high, and in 1661 the Nagasaki factors wrote that they were willing to have as much Bengal silk as Batavia cared to send to them.[28] Batavia quickly responded by exporting 256,000 ponds of this silk, constituting 87 percent of the total. But since the receipt of such a large amount led to a reduction in the price, the Nagasaki factors suggested, in 1664, an upper limit of 170,000 ponds on the amount of Bengal silk that Batavia ought to send them per annum. The subsequent reduction in the volume of Bengal silk exported

[23] In 1657, the Board of Directors observed, "The Bengal-Japan silk trade provides us with the largest amount of capital. . . . Bengal and Japan should, therefore, be used as our milch-cows" (XVII.B.9.10.1657, K.A. 455, f. 511).

[24] The average is for three years, 1661, 1669, and 1672. For the value of Bengal goods exported to Japan, see Table 3.5. The figures of total exports to Japan are based on Nachod, *Niederländischen Ostindischen Kompagnie*, pp. ccii-cciv, Table A, except for 1672, when the *Batavia Dagh-Register* has been preferred as a source because Nachod's figure for this year falls short by the value of the cargo of a ship that was lost on the way.

[25] Statement of goods imported into Japan, 1669, K.A. 1160, ff. 533-vo.

[26] This figure is based on a six-year average, for 1656, 1660, 1661, 1662, 1669, and 1672. For the amount of Bengal raw silk exported to Japan, see Table 5.1. The total amount of raw silk the Company exported to Nagasaki during these years is based on Nachod, Table C, except for 1672 (see n. 24 above). It should be noted that the figure of four-fifths is based on physical quantities and not on the value of the various types of raw silk sent to Japan. It seems, however, that the difference between the physical and the value figures was negligible. In 1669, when information on both the physical quantities and value of the various varieties of silk imported into Japan is available, the share of Bengal raw silk in the total was 67 percent in physical terms and 65 percent in terms of value. Statement of goods imported into Japan, 1669, K.A. 1160, ff. 553-vo.

[27] H.B. 10.3.1658, K.A. 1117, ff. 168-vo; van Dam, *Beschrijvinge*, II, 1, 408.

[28] XVII.B. 23.8.1661, K.A. 456, ff. 423-424; H.XVII. 13.8.1661, K.A. 1124, f. 538; XVII.B. 18.9.1662, K.A. 456, f. 537; H.B. 8.3.1662, K.A. 1130, ff. 484-485.

TABLE 5.1
Bengal Raw Silk Exported to Japan, 1647-1718

Year	Quantity (in Dutch ponds)	Year	Quantity (in Dutch ponds)	Year	Quantity (in Dutch ponds)
1647	30,165	1693-94	43,552	1707-08	30,822
1656	161,595	1694-95	13,657	1708-09	11,006
1660	195,898	1698-99	50,381	1709-10	22,953
1661	178,888	1699-1700	33,537	1710-11	42,845
1662	255,858	1700-01	60,700	1711-12	54,142
1669	151,105	1701-02	45,372	1712-13	36,666
1672	219,116	1702-03	20,895	1713-14	53,062
1673	204,400	1703-04	46,259	1714-15	53,181
1674	223,424	1704-05	13,421	1715-16	53,263
1675	179,874	1705-06	24,583	1716-17	42,321
1682	124,470	1706-07	36,250	1717-18	33,806

Source· The figures for 1647 are based on B.XVII. 31.12.1647, K.A. 1064, f. 69vo; for 1656 on B.H. 7.9.1656, K.A. 783, ff. 344-345, for 1660 on B.H. 27.8.1660, K.A. 787, f. 489, for 1661 on H.B. 2.6.1662, K.A. 1130, ff. 1389-1390; for 1662 on XVII. B. 24.8.1663, K.A. 456, f. 624, for 1669 on the statement of goods received in Japan, 1669, K.A. 1160, ff. 533-vo, for 1672-82 on the *Batavia Dagh-Register* of the relevant years and for 1693-1718 on the invoices of goods exported from Bengal.

Note· Until 1698-1699, information is available only for the years included in the table. The figures until 1682 represent the actual amount of Bengal raw silk exported by Batavia to Japan. Figures for the period 1693-1718, on the other hand, relate to the amount of raw silk the Bengal factors exported to Batavia/ Malacca for Japan. The possibility that the actual amount of Bengal raw silk exported to Japan during this period was slightly different from these figures cannot be ruled out.

was reflected in an increase in the gross profit on this variety to 145 percent in 1666.[29] A further sharp reduction in the total amount of raw silk sent to Nagasaki in 1671 helped push the gross profit on Bengal silk to 192 percent.[30]

The textiles the Company sent to Japan continued to be principally of Chinese and Coromandelese origin. Thus out of a total of 44,247 pieces sent in 1669, those originating in Bengal accounted for only 5,074. The

[29] Letter from the Dutch factors at Nagasaki to the Batavia Council dated October 22, 1664, K.A. 1139, ff. 2430-2432; statement of goods sold in Japan, 1666, K.A. 1149, ff. 1874-1879.

[30] H.B. 28.2.1672, K.A. 1178, ff. 20vo-21. The total amount of raw silk exported to Nagasaki declined from 250,000 ponds in 1670 to 133,500 ponds in 1671 (calculated from Nachod, *Niederländischen Ostindischen Kompagnie*, pp. ccv-ccvi, Table C).

corresponding value figures were f. 274,065 and f. 24,256, respectively.[31] Earlier in 1662, the factors at Nagasaki had complained about the poor quality of white silk *armosins* received from Bengal. Two years later, the gross profit on this particular variety was reported to be only 17 percent. Coloured *armosins* sold at the same time actually rendered a loss of 1 percent. The result was that *armosins* were not among the Bengal textiles ordered by the Nagasaki factors for 1665. As in the case of several other Asian markets—particularly those of the Indonesian archipelago—the consumer tastes in Japan were rather inflexible. In 1664, for example, two varieties of Bengal *taffechelas*, exactly alike in all respects including the cost, but differing in the width of the stripe, fetched very different prices. While the gross profit on the variety with narrow stripes was 117 percent, on that with broad stripes it was only 66 percent.[32] The overall situation improved later in the decade, and in 1669 the gross profit on Bengal *armosins*, *ginghams*, and *taffechelas* was reported to be 61, 156, and 170 percent, respectively.[33]

Between 1667 and 1675, Bengal sugar also figured in the trade with Japan. In 1669, about 83 percent of the sugar sent to Nagasaki was from Bengal and 9 percent from Japara, while the point of origin of the remaining 8 percent was not specified.[34] The following year, the gross profit on the Bengal, Japara, and Batavia varieties was reported to be 176 percent, 66 percent, and 72 percent, respectively. The Hugli factors, therefore, suggested that the entire sugar order from Japan be met with Bengal sugar. But because it was necessary to find a market for Java sugar produced at the initiative of the Company, not only was this suggestion rejected but the export of Bengal sugar to Japan stopped altogether after 1675.[35]

The substantial amount of trade carried on by the Dutch and the Chinese at this time caused a good deal of concern to the Japanese authorities.[36] Given the ban on the export of gold imposed in 1641, the foreigners

[31] Calculated from the statement of goods imported into Japan, 1669, K.A. 1160, ff. 533-vo.

[32] H.B. 4.3.1663, K.A. 1133, ff. 307-308; letter from the Dutch factors in Nagasaki to the Batavia Council dated 22.10.1664, K.A. 1139, ff. 2432-2433; enclosure to that letter, K.A. 1139, ff. 2563-2564.

[33] Calculated from the statement of goods sold in Japan in 1669, K.A. 1160, ff. 530-532.

[34] Calculated from the statement of goods imported into Japan, 1669, K.A. 1160, ff. 533-vo. In absolute terms, the amount of Bengal sugar exported was 227 metric tons in 1669, 270 metric tons in 1672, 50 metric tons in 1673, 80 metric tons in 1674, and 49 metric tons in 1675. The figures for 1672-1675 have been calculated from the *Batavia Dagh-Register* of the relevant years.

[35] H.B. 3.8.1671, K.A. 1174, f. 1852; H.XVII.6.11.1671, K.A. 1669, f. 610.

[36] In 1658, for example, Chinese vessels were reported to have brought into Japan 170,000 ponds of raw silk, 50,000 pieces of silk textiles, and 625 metric tons of sugar (calculated from van Dam, *Beschrijvinge*, II, 1, 409).

procured large quantities of silver, which, in the context of falling domestic output, threatened to denude the country of all its silver.[37] In 1662, the Dutch lost Taiwan—an important Asian supplier of gold—to Cheng Cheng-kung (Coxinga). Since gold was indispensable for the Coromandel trade and the proportion of total bullion received in gold from Holland was extremely small, the Company petitioned the government of Japan to lift the ban on the export of this metal. The prevalent exchange rate between silver and gold appears to have been between 5.6 and 5.8 *taels* per *koban*. As an inducement, the Dutch offered to pay 6.4 *taels* per *koban*. This inducement, coupled with the desire to reduce the pressure on silver, persuaded the Japanese to lift the ban in 1664, though the Dutch were asked to pay 6,8 *taels* per *koban*.[38] The Company accepted the new price and began to procure most of the precious metals in the form of gold rather than silver.[39] It seems, however, that the Chinese merchants, who apparently had been offered the same terms as the Dutch, had no particular incentive to buy the unusually expensive gold. They therefore continued to procure mainly silver. The situation became so desperate that in 1668, the Japanese banned altogether the export of the latter metal. But at the same time, probably to ensure that the Chinese traders did not stop coming to Japan altogether, the silver price of gold was reduced to the domestic parity of 5.6 *taels* per *koban*. The entire burden of the foreigners' demand for precious metals was now transferred to gold. It was not long before the authorities realized that, given that the most important commodity the foreign traders wanted was precious metals, the only effective means

[37] The output of both gold and silver had begun declining from around the middle of the seventeenth century (Kobata, "The Production and Uses of Gold and Silver," p. 245). Oskar Nachod's estimates put the average annual export of silver from Japan by the Company during 1642-1667 at *f.* 1.62 million (at the 1666 exchange rate; calculated from *Niederländischen Ostindischen Kompagnie*, pp. ccvii-ccviii, Table E). According to Takekoshi, an enquiry by the Shogunal magistrates in Nagasaki into the metal situation of the country in 1668 revealed that over the preceding twenty years, the country had been losing, on an average, *f.* 10.5 million worth of silver every year (at the 1666 exchange rate). Over the same period the new silver coins minted at the official mint averaged only *f.* 1.05 million worth per annum. Y. Takekoshi, *The Economic Aspects of the History of the Civilization of Japan* (London, 1930), II, 141). But Takekoshi's estimate of the annual loss of silver appears to be exaggerated. Nachod's data, in conjunction with the limited amount of evidence we have regarding the value of the Chinese merchants' trade during this period, would seem to suggest that the annual loss of specie was probably *f.* 3 to 4 million. But even this amount evidently was large enough to cause grave concern to the Japanese authorities.

[38] Takekoshi, *Civilization of Japan*, II, 160; *Batavia Dagh-Register*, 1664, p. 580.

[39] The Dutch export of gold *koban* from Japan increased from 6,099 pieces in 1664 to 29,876 pieces in 1666, and to 44,816 pieces in 1677. At the same time, the export of silver fell from 568,000 *taels* worth in 1665 to 250,050 *taels* worth in 1666. Nachod, *Niederländischen Ostindischen Kompagnie*, pp. ccvi-ccviii, Tables D and E.

of controlling the outflow of these metals without reducing the quantities of the goods imported was to force a deterioration in the foreigners' terms of trade. The first steps in this direction were taken in 1670. The price of the *koban* was increased from 5.6 to 5.8 *taels* per piece, an executive order was addressed to the Japanese merchants to pay lower prices for foreign goods, and a "suggestion" was made to the Dutch and the Chinese that they voluntarily agree to sell their silk and other goods at a lower price.[40] None of these measures, however, proved helpful. In 1672, therefore, the price of the *koban* was further raised to the pre-1668 level of 6.8 *taels* per piece.[41] Even more far-reaching in significance was the introduction the same year of what the Dutch called *taxatie-handel* (appraised trade). In a way, this was but a reintroduction of the *pancado* system, with the difference that this time it was applicable to *all* goods the foreigners imported into the country.[42] If the Dutch factors were not satisfied with the prices fixed by the Nagasaki guild, they were, of course, free not to sell; but in that case, the goods already in the warehouses could not be carried out of Japan. In such a situation, the factors were presumably expected to wait patiently until the next date fixed for the Dutch sale. In case the factors refused to sell at the *pancado* price fixed for the last sale of a season, they were required to wait until the following year, running the risk that the goods might be damaged in the meantime.[43]

During 1656-1672, Japan continued to be the most important source of precious metals, which, incidentally, accounted for 86 percent of the total imports over this period received by Bengal.[44] In 1667—the first year for which we have detailed information on the origin of precious metals imported into Bengal and a year, like all previous years, in which silver was the only precious metal the Company imported into this region—84 percent of the total silver received at Hugli was of Japanese origin, the

[40] Memorandum by the outgoing director of the Nagasaki factory, de Haze, for his successor, Martinus Ceaser, dated November 2, 1670, K.A. 1168, ff. 2004vo-2005; report by the ex-director, de Haze, on his return to Batavia after relinquishing charge, dated December 6, 1670, K.A. 1168, ff. 2013-2014vo; Nachod, *Niederländischen Ostindischen Kompagnie*, p. ccvii, Table D.

[41] Nachod, *Niederländischen Ostindischen Kompagnie*, p. ccvii, Table D.

[42] Van Dam, *Beschrijvinge*, II, 1, 446-447; Nachod, *Niederländischen Ostindischen Kompagnie*, p. 365.

[43] Until the 1680s, there used to be four Dutch sales every year, when their number came down to three. During the eighteenth century, the number of these sales further declined to two. All the sales of a season were usually held in September/October. A separate *pancado* price was announced for each item in each of the sales. See the details of the Dutch sales in 1674 in K.A. 1193, ff. 50-51; van Dam, *Beschrijvinge*, II, 1, 487.

[44] This is an eight-year average. For the total value of goods and precious metals the Company imported into Bengal, see Table 3.2.

remainder having been imported from Holland.[45] The 1668 ban on the export of silver from Japan led to the substitution for the silver of Japanese gold *koban*.[46] As it happened, until 1676 the gold/silver parity was in favour of gold all over India. And between 1668 and 1672, the *koban* were purchased at a comparatively low price. The net result was that these *koban* afforded a profit of as much as 37 percent in 1669 and 1671.[47] On the other hand, the limited quantities of non-Japanese silver that the Batavia Council sent to Bengal during this period had to be disposed of at a loss both because of the generally adverse parity of silver at this time and because the per unit cost of these varieties was considerably higher than the former cost of the Japanese silver.[48]

The 1668 ban on the export of silver from Japan had been followed by a similar prohibition on the export of copper. As a result, the Bengal price, which had fluctuated during 1660-1668 between Rs. 48.5 and 61.75, now shot up to Rs. 73.5 per 100 ponds.[49] Unlike silver, however, the prohibition on the export of copper proved only short-lived, and with the resumption of copper supplies by the Dutch from 1670, the Bengal price again came down. The downward trend was further accelerated in 1671, when a local famine forced people to dispose of their copper vessels, among other things. The average gross profit the Bengal factors earned on copper during this period was 150 percent—a level substantially higher than this metal brought in Holland. As a result, instructions were issued by the Board of Directors in 1671 that priority be attached to copper orders from Bengal over those from Holland.[50]

---

[45] Import invoices contained in the letters from the Governor-General and Council at Batavia to the factors at Hugli.

[46] Thus in 1668, 1670, and 1671, Japan accounted for 84 percent, 75 percent, and 67 percent, respectively, of the total bullion received by the Hugli factors. In view of the fact that the 1668 invoices did not specify the origin of the remaining 16 percent of the bullion imported into Bengal, Japan's share that year might well have been larger than 84 percent. Import invoices contained in the letters from Batavia to the factors at Hugli.

[47] H.XVII. 11.8.1670, K.A. 1167, f. 1459vo; XVII.B. 28.8.1671, K.A. 457; H.B. 3.7.1671, K.A. 1174, f. 1859. It will be recalled that the silver price of a *koban* stood at 6.8 *taels* during 1664-1668, 5.6 *taels* during 1668-1670, 5.8 *taels* during 1670-1672, and again at 6.8 *taels* thereafter.

[48] For example, at the Rajmahal mint in 1670, the percentage gross loss on bar silver of unspecified origin was 9.6 percent, on silver from Pegu 8.8 percent, and on European rix-dollars 36.87 percent. Enclosure to H.XVII. 22.9.1671, K.A. 1174, f. 19vo.

[49] H.B. 28.2.1671, K.A. 1174, ff. 1831-1832. The Bengal prices have been retained in rupees and not converted into florins because the ever-increasing florin value of the rupee during the latter half of the seventeenth century would tend to artificially inflate the equivalent of the rupee figures over time. (1 Re. = 1.2 florins until 1666, 1.4 florins until 1686, and thereafter 1.5 florins.)

[50] H.B. 3.8.1671, K.A. 1174, f. 1857; XVII. B. 29.8.1671, K.A. 457; XVII.B. 5.4.1672, K.A. 457; volume not foliated.

THE PHASE OF DECLINE: 1673-1720

Decline Begins, 1673-1685

In 1675, the Batavia Council wrote to the governor of Nagasaki that although the Company traded with "all corners of the globe," it had "never yet found a single other place where the purchaser fixed the price."[51] The appeal that the "appraised trade" system be rescinded, however, fell on deaf ears. Given the considerably reduced profit per unit of investment under the new arrangement, the response of the Company was to curtail the volume of trade in all goods. Hence the reduction in the average annual exports during 1673-1685 to *f.* 1.02 million.[52] But the share of Bengal goods in fact increased marginally to a little over 51 percent; this proportion was 75 percent for raw silk alone.[53] As the Company had feared, the "appraised trade" system led to a situation in which the gross profit on raw silk was reported to be only 56 percent in 1674 and 54 percent the following year. Bengal raw silk appraised by the guild in 1677 at *f.* 685 was disposed of by it in the Nagasaki market at *f.* 1185 per 100 ponds, depriving the Company of a margin of 72 percent. The corresponding figure in the case of Tonkin raw silk was reported to be 100 percent.[54] As a result, the amount of raw silk the Company exported to Nagasaki was reduced from the peak of 297,000 ponds in 1672 to 230,000 ponds three years later.[55] In 1679, the Batavia Council instructed the Bengal factors to supply raw silk for Japan only if a minimum gross profit of 80 percent had been earned on it in Nagasaki the previous year. In 1682, following an appraisal of the Company's silk by the Nagasaki guild at a particularly low price, the factors simply refused to sell. The strategy worked, and in the following two appraisals of the season, the Company was given a better deal. This technique was repeated in 1683, again with satisfactory results. The factors reported that if they had accepted the original appraisal of the Bengal *cabessa* variety, the gross profit would have

[51] Van Dam, *Beschrijvinge*, II, 1, 454.

[52] Calculated from Nachod, *Niederländischen Ostindischen Kompagnie*, pp. ccii- cciv, Table A.

[53] These estimates are based on a four-year (1673, 1674, 1675, 1682) average. For the value of Bengal goods exported to Japan, see Table 3.5. The total value of goods the Company exported to Nagasaki during these years is based on Nachod, ibid. For the amount of Bengal raw silk exported to Japan, see Table 5.1. The total amount of raw silk the Company exported to Nagasaki during these years is based on the *Batavia Dagh-Register* of the relevant years.

[54] Statement of goods sold in Japan, 1674, K.A. 1193, ff. 50-51; H.B. 20.3.1675, K.A. 1202, ff. 55-vo; statement of goods sold in Japan, 1675, K.A. 1203, ff. 34vo-35; van Dam, *Beschrijvinge*, II, 1, 460.

[55] Calculated from the *Batavia Dagh-Register* of 1672 and 1675.

been only 68 percent. The refusal to sell at that price led to a rise in the gross profit to 83 percent in the second appraisal and to 89 percent in the third.[56]

The system of "appraised trade" naturally made a big dent in the rate of profit on Bengal textiles, as well. Silk *alachas*, for example, were reported to have been sold in 1675 at a gross profit of only 54 percent. The only Bengal textile that did reasonably well through this period was *gingham*, both the *taffechelas* and the plain varieties. In 1675, the former were sold at a gross profit of 122 percent and the latter at 153 percent. As a result, these *ginghams* constituted practically the whole of Bengal textile cargo—which continued to be rather small—sent to Japan in the first half of the 1680s.[57]

We had noted earlier that notwithstanding the 1668 ban on the export of silver, Japan continued to be the principal supplier of precious metals for Bengal. In fact, in 1674, 90 percent of the total value the Batavia Council sent to Hugli consisted of Japanese gold *koban*. But the large inflow of these coins into Bengal, where their demand for coinage was comparatively limited, led to a decline in their price between 1669 and 1675 from Rs. 20 per piece to Rs. 18 per piece. Given the fact that in 1672 the Japanese had restored the pre-1668 price of the *koban*, the import of these coins into Bengal now became less attractive. The proportion of *koban* to the total value of precious metals imported into Bengal was, therefore, reduced to 42 percent in 1676. The same year, they were sold in Balasore at a gross profit of 7.37 percent and in Hugli and Patna at a 6 percent profit.[58] Between 1677 and 1690, no gold *koban* whatever were imported into Hugli. Japan, which had hitherto been the chief source of precious metals for Bengal, thus disappeared from the scene altogether for more than a decade. The precious metals despatched to Bengal now consisted almost entirely of European silver and silver coins which, in the context of a fast-growing Euro-Asian trade and the stoppage of silver supplies from Japan, were reaching Batavia in ever-growing quantities. Also, Bengal trade had now begun to be increasingly important in the complex of Dutch Euro-Asian trade; in 1680-1681 and 1681-1682, Bengal

[56] B.H. 10.8.1679, K.A. 806, f. 833; B.H. 15.8.1681, K.A. 809, f. 643; van Dam, *Beschrijvinge*, II, 1, 475-476, 478-480.

[57] H.B. 3.2.1676, K.A. 1209, ff. 516-vo; B.H. 17.5.1676, K.A. 803, f. 213; orders for Bengal textiles from Japan, 1682-1684, H.B. 25.3.1682, K.A. 1267, f. 1311vo; H.B. 24.3.1683, K.A. 1276, f. 1168; B.H. 1.6.1683, K.A. 812, f. 676.

[58] Import invoices contained in the letters from the Batavia Council to the factors at Hugli; H.B. 26.9.1675, K.A. 1203, f. 72vo; H.B. 17.3.1676, K.A. 1209, f. 530vo; statement of profit and loss in Bengal between July 1, 1676 and June 30, 1677, K.A. 1217, ff. 540vo-544.

received *all* the European silver that Batavia sent out, and over the following three years, Bengal's share in the total was overwhelming.[59] Between 1673 and 1685, European bar silver and silver coins were sold in Bengal at a gross profit that ranged between 10.62 percent and 24.75 percent.[60]

The prohibition on the export of silver, followed by the restoration, in 1672, of the pre-1668 price of gold *koban*, increased the relative importance of copper in the total Dutch import bill from Japan. Most of the Japanese copper was now sold in Asia itself, mainly the Indian subcontinent. Bengal, however, was still one of the smaller markets for this metal.[61] The average amount sold in this factory per annum between 1678 and 1684 was only 296,430 ponds, at an average gross profit ranging between 68 percent and 115 percent (see Table 5.2).

The Chinese response to the imposition of the appraised trade system was to make up for the lower profit per unit by increasing the volume of trade.[62] This process was considerably accelerated in 1684 when, probably under the pressure of a desperate need for Japanese copper, the mainland dynasty legalized the trade with Japan. The Dutch estimated the total value of Chinese imports into Nagasaki that year at the unusually high figure of *f.* 7 million. This development made the Japanese authorities realise that even a forced deterioration in the foreigners' terms of trade was not adequate to ensure that the annual specie loss did not assume

[59] K. Glamann, *Dutch-Asiatic Trade*, pp. 62-63, 69.

[60] Thus in 1676-1677, bar silver was sold in Patna at a gross profit of 24.75 percent, while in the same factory mark rials afforded a gross profit of 17 percent (statement of profit and loss in Bengal between July 1, 1676 and June 30, 1677, K.A. 1217, ff. 540vo-544). Three years later, bar silver fetched a gross profit of 12.62 percent in Kasimbazar; mark rials were sold there at a gross profit of 14.8 percent, while Mexican rials afforded a gross profit of 11.34 percent. The same year, mark rials were sold in Hugli at a gross profit of 13 percent (statement of profit and loss in Bengal between June 1, 1679 and May 31, 1680, K.A. 1250, f. 269). The gross profit rendered by bar silver in Kasimbazar in 1680-1681 and 1682-1683 was 14.50 percent and 14.33 percent, respectively. In the first of these two years, crown dollars were sold in Kasimbazar at a gross profit of 10.62 percent, cross dollars of 12.19 percent, while mark rials had afforded a gross profit of 15.04 percent (statement of profit and loss in Bengal between June 1, 1680 and May 31, 1681, K.A. 1258, f. 1317vo). Finally, in 1682-1683, cross dollars were sold in Kasimbazar at a gross profit of 11.82 percent and mark rials at 16.75 percent (B.H. 1.6.1683, K.A. 812, f. 710).

[61] K. Glamann, "The Dutch East India Company's Trade in Japanese Copper, 1645-1736," *Scandinavian Economic History Review*, 1 (1953), 51-53.

[62] Thus in 1682, the Chinese merchants were reported to have brought into Nagasaki 209,000 ponds of raw silk (statement of goods imported by the Chinese merchants between November 1, 1681 and October 20, 1682, K.A. 1266, ff. 688-689vo). This figure had been 100,000 ponds during 1650-1654, 164,000 ponds in 1655, and 170,000 ponds in 1658. Statement of goods sold in Japan in 1654, K.A. 1098, f. 744; in 1655, K.A. 1103, ff. 831-832. The figure for 1658 is from van Dam, *Beschrijvinge*, II, 1, 409.

TABLE 5.2
Japanese Copper Sold in Bengal, 1678-1717

Year	Quantity sold (in Dutch ponds)	Price (rupees per 100 ponds)	Gross profit (%)
1678-79	162,430	51	115
1679-80	141,667	50	111
1680-81	456,583	48	102
1681-82	274,807	42	75
1682-83	466,741	40	68
1683-84	276,352	43	79
1701-02	291,312	48	93
1702-03	516,256	46	85
1705-06	356,514	N.A.	N.A.
1706-07	297,500	38	N.A.
1707-08	499,664	38	N.A.
1708-09	561,000	38	N.A.
1709-10	635,868	44	N.A.
1710-11	676,098	44	N.A.
1711-12	143	N.A.	N.A.
1712-13	335,920	44	N.A.
1713-14	387,784	44	61
1714-15	547,536	45	68
1715-16	650,934	52	93
1716-17	148,512	48	N.A.

Source: 1678-84: Statement of goods sold in Bengal, 1678-84, enclosure to H.B.
6.11.1684, K.A. 1286, ff. 429-437.
    1701-17: Glamann, "The Dutch East India Company's Trade in Japanese
Copper, 1645-1736," p. 54.

Note· Information is available only for 1678-1684 and 1701-1717. The price figures
during 1678-1684 represent the weighted average of all the six factories in
Bengal. The price data for 1701-1717 refer to the price at Hugli. It has not
been possible to calculate the gross profit for most of the years during the
period 1701-1717 because of lack of data.

disturbing proportions. The very next year, therefore, the system of what
might be called "limited trade" was introduced. Under the new arrangement, the Company was permitted to import annually goods whose total
sales proceeds were not to exceed f. 1.05 million. Further, the amount of
raw silk the Company could sell during the course of a year was henceforth
to be limited to f. 0.35 million sale value. The upper limit on the annual

134

sale proceeds of goods imported by the Chinese merchants was fixed at
f. 2.1 million.[63] Evidently with a view to soften the impact of the blow
inflicted by this new arrangement, the Japanese at the same time withdrew
the appraised trade system in all goods except raw silk of all varieties.[64]
The year 1685 also witnessed the imposition of a fresh ban on the export
of gold from Japan, though it was withdrawn the following year.[65]

Decline Intensified, 1686-1720

The 1685 regulations, by forcing a sharp reduction in the value of the
imports into Japan as well as a change in their composition to the detriment
of the trade in raw silk, seriously eroded the role of Japan in the overall
trading strategy of the Company. This trend was reinforced in 1696, when
the gold content of the *koban* was reduced from 85.69 percent to 56.41
percent without a reduction in its silver price, making it a much less
attractive coin to procure.[66] Two years later, the appraised trade system
was once again extended to embrace all goods. Also, while the ceiling on
the annual turnover of the Company was raised from *f.* 1.05 to *f.* 1.33
million, a ceiling of 25,000 cases was prescribed on the amount of bar
copper the Company could carry out of Japan in a year.[67] The extension
of the appraised trade system to goods other than raw silk was, however,
withdrawn in 1699. In 1715, the appraised trade system was yet again
extended to cover all goods, the ceiling on the annual export of copper
further reduced to 15,000 cases, and the number of Dutch ships that could
call at Nagasaki in a year limited to two. As a result of the last of these
restrictions, the Company often found it difficult to carry even 15,000
cases of copper out of Japan each year. In 1720, the ceiling on the export
of copper was further lowered to 10,000 cases.[68]

The decline of the Japan trade is apparent in the fact that the average

---

[63] Letter from the Nagasaki factors to Batavia dated 16.10.1685, K.A. 1306, ff. 1063-1064.

[64] Another concession provided in 1685 was that goods the Company found itself unable to sell in the course of a season could be carried back to Batavia. Van Dam, *Beschrijvinge*, II, 1, 487-490.

[65] Glamann, *Dutch Asiatic Trade*, p. 63.

[66] J. T. Kussaka, *Das Japanische Geldwezen* (Jena, 1890), p. 22; Nachod, *Niederländischen Ostindischen Kompagnie*, p. ccvii, Table D.

[67] Van Dam, *Beschrijvinge*, II, 1, p. 542; Glamann, "Japanese Copper," p. 48; 1 case of Japanese copper = 120 Dutch ponds.

[68] "Orders of the Japanese Emperor Concerning the Dutch Trade," 1715, K.A. 1775, ff. 160-161; report by the ex-director of the Nagasaki factory, Joan Aouwer, to the Batavia Council on his arrival at Batavia after relinquishing charge, December 12, 1717, K.A. 1787, f. 77; Glamann, "Japanese Copper," p. 48.

annual value of the total exports to Nagasaki between 1686 and 1700 was reduced to f. 0.63 million.[69] Since the proceeds from the sale of raw silk could no longer exceed f. 350,000, the amount of this item imported into Japan came down from 214,000 ponds in 1682 to 61,340 ponds in 1688, and to 37,077 ponds in 1690.[70] Although the bulk of this silk continued to be from Bengal, this region's average share in the total Dutch cargo to Nagasaki during 1686-1700 shrank to 25 percent.[71] In fact, since the Company could not be certain of the precise quantity of raw silk that would fetch the ceiling amount of f. 350,000 in Japan, and because the amount of raw silk exported to Europe was growing at a rapid rate around this time, what often happened was that the amount of raw silk sent to Japan was less than the maximum allowed.[72] The gross profit on Bengal raw silk was reported to be 63 percent, 74 percent, 85 percent, and 68 percent in 1702, 1704, 1715, and 1717, respectively.[73]

By forcing a rapid decline in the Dutch silk trade and at the same time withdrawing the appraised trade system from goods other than raw silk, the 1685 regulations actually promoted the trade in textiles. The first manifestation of this was an increase by 50 percent in the 1686 Nagasaki

[69] Calculated from Nachod, *Niederländischen Ostindischen Kompagnie*, pp. ccii-cciv, Table A.

[70] The figure for 1682 has been calculated from the *Batavia Dagh-Register*, whereas those for 1688 and 1690 are based on Nachod, *Niederländischen Ostindischen Kompagnie*, pp. ccv-ccvi, Table C.

[71] In 1694 and 1695 (corresponding to 1693-1694 and 1694-1695 in Table 5.1), for example, Bengal silk, on an average, constituted 60 percent of the total amount of raw silk sent to Japan. In the first two decades of the eighteenth century, Bengal became virtually the sole supplier of raw silk for Japan. In 1702, for example, the factors in Nagasaki sold a total of 43,968 ponds of Bengal silk as against 468 ponds of Chinese silk. The corresponding figures in 1704 were 27,987 ponds and 892 ponds, respectively. In 1715 and 1717, the whole of the 45,768 ponds and 46,332 ponds of raw silk, respectively, sold in Nagasaki was from Bengal. Calculated from the statement of goods sold in Japan in 1702, K.A.1555, ff. 126-130; in 1704, K.A. 1583, ff. 84-91; in 1715, K.A. 1775, ff. 153-159, and in 1717, K.A. 1787, ff. 70-75.

The estimate of Bengal's share in total value is based on a five-year (1694, 1696, 1697, 1699, 1700) average. The total value of goods the Company exported to Japan during these years is based on Nachod, *Niederländischen Ostindischen Kompagnie*, pp. ccii-cciv, Table A. For the value of Bengal goods exported to Nagasaki, see Table 3.5. It should be noted that the figures for this period in Table 3.5 refer to the value of goods exported from Bengal to Batavia/Malacca for Japan, and might not necessarily coincide with the value of Bengal goods the Nagasaki factors actually received. As a result, this set of figures might not be wholly comparable to the earlier sets, where the value of the Bengal cargo referred to that actually sent to Japan.

[72] This happened, for example, in 1691, 1693, 1694, and 1695 (van Dam, *Beschrijvinge*, II, i, 508, 516, 525, and 526).

[73] Calculated from the statement of goods sold in 1702, K.A. 1555, ff. 126-130; in 1704, K.A. 1583, ff. 84-91; in 1715, K.A. 1775, ff. 153-159; and in 1717, K.A. 1787, ff. 70-75.

orders for most varieties of Bengal textiles.[74] Bengal *armosins* fetched a gross profit of 137 percent in 1702 and of 92 percent two years later. In the early part of the eighteenth century, Bengal cotton textiles became a regular item of export to Japan (Table 5.3). In 1715, whereas Bengal textiles afforded in Nagasaki an average gross profit of 151 percent, those from Coromandel coast fetched only 116 percent, while the few pieces imported from Gujarat had, in fact, to be sold at a loss of 67 percent.[75]

Between 1686 and 1720, Japan's role as a supplier of precious metals for Bengal was at best marginal. It was only in the few years that Batavia did not receive an adequate amount of silver bullion and coins from Holland that it was found necessary to despatch Japanese gold *koban* and European gold *ducats* to Bengal. Even in these years, both these types of coins together usually did not account for more than about a quarter of the total value of precious metals received by the Hugli factors (Table 3.2). In 1691, when the export of Japanese *koban* to Bengal was resumed after an interval of fourteen years, the price these coins fetched was only Rs. 16 apiece, inducing a loss of 20 percent.[76] The 1696 debasement of this coin should ordinarily have increased the percentage of loss considerably. But fortunately for the Company, the local demand for gold suddenly registered a sharp increase around this time. One of the factors accounting for this was the appointment of Prince Azim-us-Shan, a great collector of gold coins, as the *subahdar* of Bengal in 1697. The result was that notwithstanding the big depreciation in its real value, the price of a *koban* went up in 1698 to Rs. 17.25 per piece.[77] It is notable that in a situation when, on an average, the *koban* were being disposed of in the gold-based currency region of Coromandel at a loss of 15 percent, the loss in Bengal was reported to be only 13 percent in 1705 and 1706, and 10 percent in 1710.[78] However, the amount sold in Bengal was substantially smaller than that on the Coromandel coast.

As for European bar silver and silver coins, the overall situation in the latter half of the 1680s was quite satisfactory. Thus in 1688-1689, whereas bar silver was sold in Kasimbazar at a gross profit of 20.43 percent, the gross profit on Spanish rials sold there was 19.4 percent. The mark rials sold in Patna the same year afforded a gross profit of 29.5 percent. But around the turn of the century, things took a turn for the worse. In 1705-

[74] B.H. 27.5.1686, K.A. 816, ff. 211-212.

[75] Statement of goods sold in Japan in 1702, K.A. 1555, ff. 126-130; in 1704, K.A. 1583, ff. 84-91; in 1715, K.A. 1775, ff. 153-159.

[76] H.B. 18.3.1691, K.A. 1388, f. 677; B.H. 21.6.1692, K.A. 822, f. 388; H.B. 6.9.1692, K.A. 1397, f. 122vo.

[77] H.B. 22.12.1698, K.A. 1500, f. 35; H.B. 7.9.1699, K.A. 1516, ff. 160, 180.

[78] Glamann, *Dutch-Asiatic Trade*, p. 68. H.B. 20.8.1706, K.A. 1622, ff. 238-239; H.B. 16.3.1710, K.A. 1688, ff. 18-19, I Section.

TABLE 5.3
Bengal Textiles Exported to Japan, 1669-1718

1	2	3	4	5	6	7	8	9
Year	Fine cotton muslins (pieces)	Fine cotton calicoes (pieces)	Total of fine cotton textiles (cols. 2 + 3) (pieces)	Ordinary calicoes (pieces)	Total of cotton textiles (cols. 4 + 5) (pieces)	Silk piece goods (pieces)	Silk and cotton mixed piece goods (pieces)	Grand total (cols. 6 + 7 + 8) (pieces)
1669	N.A.	N.A.	1,400	–	1,400	1,274	2,400	5,074
1672	–	–	–	–	–	225	–	225
1673	–	–	–	900	900	264	–	1,164
1682	–	–	–	–	–	900	11,800	12,700
1690-91	–	–	–	–	–	6,456	23,125	29,581
1691-92	–	–	–	–	–	5,111	15,493	20,604
1692-93	–	–	–	–	–	5,785	3,012	8,797
1693-94	–	–	–	–	–	4,217	4,003	8,220
1694-95	–	–	–	–	–	5,775	1,037	6,612
1698-99	–	–	–	120	120	3,452	6,100	9,672
1699-1700	–	–	–	180	180	3,782	1,300	5,262
1700-01	–	–	–	–	–	5,375	5,200	10,575
1701-02	N.A.	N.A.	1,100	–	1,100	3,740	4,600	9,440
1702-03	N.A.	N.A.	3,000	–	3,000	3,300	3,200	9,500
1703-04	–	4,200	4,200	2,000	6,200	6,040	4,700	16,940

1704-05	—	—	2,000	2,000	12,620	6,200	20,820
1705-06	—	—	2,000	2,000	2,500	8,300	12,800
1706-07	—	—	1,200	1,200	8,100	14,500	23,800
1707-08	2,380	2,380	3,540	5,920	12,103	11,500	29,523
1708-09	—	—	4,820	4,820	16,804	14,200	35,824
1709-10	90	—	6,760	6,850	17,817	19,000	43,667
1711-12	1,190	80	2,080	3,350	5,535	4,300	13,185
1713-14	90	252	2,540	2,882	3,068	2,300	8,250
1714-15	310	310	800	1,110	3,494	2,300	6,904
1715-16	1,150	1,150	1,050	2,200	1,959	400	4,559
1716-17	—	—	800	800	2,700	1,600	5,100
1717-18	—	—	2,040	2,040	7,614	5,200	14,854

Source: The figures for 1669 are based on the statement of goods received in Japan, 1669, K.A. 1160, ff. 533-vo, for 1672-1682 on the *Batavia Dagh-Register* of the relevant years, and for 1690-1718 on the invoices of goods exported from Bengal.

Note: Until 1690-1691, information is available only for the years included in the table. These figures represent the actual amount of Bengal textiles Batavia exported to Japan. Figures for the period 1690-1718, on the other hand, relate to the amount of textiles the Bengal factors exported to Batavia/Malacca for Japan. The possibility that the actual amount of Bengal textiles exported to Japan during this period was slightly different from these figures cannot be ruled out.

The constituent varieties of the five groups of textiles are as follows:

Fine cotton muslins: *Achibany, adathy, asisbegi, chanderbani, cottobani, dotani, ektani, ganga-lahari, gerberry, kabulkhani, kamarband, kamkhani, khasa, malmal, maypoost, milmil, mobessabani, mohanbani, regati, rajibegi, rehing, resta, rudarbani, tanzeb, terrindam.*

Fine cotton calicoes: *Bafta, betilla, camelot, 'cacatoes stoffen,' chela, chela-regatty, dorea, golmandal, humhum, lehmenia, lungi, mistaj, nainsukh, rumal, sanu, sekla, sjoukoria, sologazi, taffechela.*

Ordinary cotton calicoes: *Ambertee, amirti, chintz, dariabadi, dassie, dungaree, fota, garra, gasjan, Guinea cloth, lakhori, niquania, parkal, patka, sailcloth, salampuri.*

Silk piece goods: *Alcatif, alacha, armosin, altas, bandanna, butidar, dhari, silk dorea, golga, jamawar, silk kamarband, silk lungi, pathola, pitambar, silk resta, silk rumal, silk sjoukoria, silk taffechela, silk tanzeb, soosy, tafta.*

Silk and cotton mixed piece goods: *Alibanee, charadari, charkhana, chukla, cushta, gingam, jamdani, mandila, nila, peniscoe,* and all other textiles specifically mentioned as a mixture of silk and cotton and cotton or tassar and cotton yarn.

1706, bar silver was sold at a profit of only 1 to 2 percent. In 1714, silver *dukatons*—which around this time constituted the bulk of the silver Bengal received from Batavia—were sold at a loss of 1.6 percent.[79] It seems that a major cause was the rapidly increasing import of silver into Bengal—as in other parts of India—by the English East India Company. In 1699, for example, it was reported that as soon as an English ship dropped anchor at Hugli, the market price of silver registered a sharp decline.[80]

In 1689, probably as a result of the strain the costly campaigns in southern India put on the royal treasury, Emperor Aurangzeb ordered a debasement of the copper *dam* without a corresponding reduction in the amount of copper that must be surrendered at a royal mint in exchange for a given number of *dams*. As a result, the market demand on copper for minting into these coins immediately declined, bringing the price down from Rs. 47 to Rs. 43.4 per 100 ponds. In 1690, the Batavia Council prescribed a minimum price of Rs. 44 per 100 ponds for the Bengal factories, forcing the factors to withdraw from the market.[81] It seems that it was only in 1697-1698 that the factors found it possible to resume sales. Early in the eighteenth century, the English imported into Bengal considerable quantities of copper that they had bought from the Chinese, who apparently had bought it in Japan. The result was that in 1703, the price crashed to Rs. 36.75 per 100 ponds. The factors had no choice but to suspend sales again. The Company was out of the market for two years, but that did not help push the price up, and in 1705 Batavia found it necessary to withdraw the minimum price. It seems, however, that after a while the total amount imported by the English declined, which led to a rise in the price in 1709 to Rs. 44 per 100 ponds.[82] It is remarkable that the Bengal factories which in the 1680s had lagged considerably behind those both in Coromandel and Gujarat had by the close of our period become the most important Asian market for Japanese copper.[83]

[79] Statement of profit and loss in Bengal between June 1, 1688 and May 31, 1689, K.A. 1360, ff. 231-232vo; H.B. 28.12.1705, K.A. 1622, f. 11; H.B. 29.10.1714, K.A. 1741, f. 119vo.

[80] According to K. N. Chaudhuri's estimates, the total value of silver exported by the English Company to the subcontinent increased from £46,329 in 1659-1660 to £281,088 in 1679-1680, to £482,219 in 1699-1700, and to £564,243 in 1719-1720. K. N. Chaudhuri, "Treasure and Trade Balances; The East India Company's Export Trade, 1660-1720," *Economic History Review*, Second Series, 21 (December 1968), 497-498; H.B.7.9.1699, K.A. 1516, f. 156.

[81] Letter from the factors at Hugli to Commissioner van Rheede in Coromandel dated August 4, 1689, K.A. 1348, ff. 780-vo; B.H. 19.8.1690, K.A. 820, ff. 574-575.

[82] B.H. 15.7.1705, K.A. 845, ff. 897-898; H.B. 10.10.1705, K.A. 1604, ff. 8-9; H.B. 16.10.1709, K.A. 1669, ff. 41-42.

[83] Over the sixteen years 1701-1702/1716-1717, Bengal accounted for 28.45 percent of

By the close of our period, the Japan trade had lost most of its attraction for the Company. The limited amount of trade carried on with Japan in the first half of the eighteenth century merely reflected the nonavailability of an alternative Asian source of bullion even at the terms that Japan was now offering. But the crucial role played by this trade in promoting the fortunes of the Company in both the intra-Asian and the Euro-Asian trade had ended with the seventeenth century.

---

the total amount of Japanese copper the Company sold in the whole of Asia. The respective shares of the Coromandel and the Gujarat factories were 25.72 percent and 24.72 percent, respectively. Calculated from Glamann, "Japanese Copper," p. 54, Table II.

· 6 ·

INTRA-ASIAN TRADE (II): INDONESIAN ARCHIPELAGO, COASTAL TRADE, AND PERSIA

Beginning with Japan in the extreme northeast of the great arc of Asian trade, the areas in which Bengal goods figured in the Company's trade were the Indonesian archipelago, the Coromandel coast, Ceylon, the Malabar coast, and Persia, at the northwestern end of the arc. In the case of some of these regions, such as the Indonesian archipelago and Persia, Bengal goods formed an important constituent of the total cargo sent by the Company.

THE INDONESIAN ARCHIPELAGO

In Japan, the Dutch were in the unenviable position of the harassed foreigner constantly subject to the caprice and the whims of an arbitrary regime; in the archipelago, the situation was the exact opposite: they had access to exclusive privileges that followed from the political authority wielded by the Company in the region. We have already noted their exclusive rights in the purchase of spices in the region. In course of time, similar rights were also obtained in nonprecious metals produced in the Malay peninsula. Thus by a treaty with the sultan of Kedah in June 1642, the Dutch were granted the right to buy annually half the total amount of tin available in the sultanate at a fixed price against cash or cotton textiles. Three years later, another treaty concluded with the ruler of Bangery conferred upon the Company monopsony rights in tin and monopoly rights in textiles throughout the kingdom. In 1650, the tin trade of Perak was divided equally between the Dutch and the subjects of Achin; this treaty was reconfirmed in 1659. All these privileges were, of course, qualified to a certain extent by the substantial amount of trade that the Asian traders managed to carry on with these parts in spite of Dutch efforts to the contrary.[1]

Although in a number of cases the Company obtained exclusive rights in the sale of Indian textiles as incidental to the privileges granted to it in the purchase of spices and metals, in other cases the privilege consisted primarily in the monopoly in textiles and other goods sold by the Company

[1] Treaties dated June 18, 1642, *Corpus-Diplomaticum*, I, 365-367; January 1, 1645, ibid., pp. 438-439; August 15, 1650, ibid., II, 538-541; June 20, 1659, ibid., pp. 151-155. S. Arasaratnam, "Some Notes on the Dutch in Malacca and the Indo-Malayan Trade, 1641-1670," *Journal of Southeast Asian History*, 10 (December 1969), 486.

in the region. Perhaps the most important example of the latter was the 1677 agreement with the ruler of Mataram in central Java, whereby the Dutch were granted the sole right to import Indian textiles and opium into the kingdom. A similar privilege was extracted from the king of Palembang in 1678 and from the ruler of Cheribon in January 1681.[2]

The Export Trade

The data available suggest that between 1674 and 1720, the exports from Bengal to the Indonesian archipelago grew by f. 10,557 each year. The compound rate of growth was 1.15 percent per annum. The peak in the trade was reached in 1709-1710, when the value of the exports was f. 787,977. The archipelago's share in the total exports from Bengal during this period fluctuated between 8 and 19 percent.

TEXTILES

Long before the European trading companies made their way into Asian trade, Indian textiles had been a major item of commerce in the Indonesian archipelago. Soon after their arrival in the East, the Dutch began procuring these textiles on the Coromandel coast. The special privileges obtained from the petty rulers in the archipelago enabled the Company to earn considerably more than the usual profit on these textiles.[3] The result was that they soon became by far the most important commodity the Dutch offered in exchange for the local spices and nonprecious metals. In fact, in a number of treaties the Company concluded in the archipelago, one of the clauses specified the rate of exchange between the particular commodity in which it had been granted monopsonistic privileges and important varieties of Indian textiles that it proposed to import.[4] Another index of the crucial role of Indian textiles is the unquestioned domination of these textiles in the mix of goods the Indonesian and Malay traders carried out of Batavia, where they had obtained them from the Company in exchange for a variety of goods.[5]

Within the broad category of inexpensive calicoes, the pattern of de-

---

[2] Treaties dated October 19-20, 1677, Corpus-Diplomaticum, III, 74-79; July 3, 1678, ibid., pp. 140-142; January 7, 1681, ibid., pp. 233-240; May 19, 1681, ibid., pp. 267-270.

[3] Meilink-Roelofsz., Asian Trade, pp. 208-209.

[4] Two of these treaties—both relating to pepper—were the 1649 agreement with the Achinese dominions of Tiku, Priaman, and Indrapoera in western Sumatra (Corpus-Diplomaticum, I, 528-531), and the 1660 agreement with the ruler of Padang in the Malay peninsula (van Dam, Beschrijvinge, II, 1, 290).

[5] The proportion of textiles in the total value of the cargo was 83.52% in 1659, 84.21% in 1661, 76.22% in 1670, 60.50% in 1673, 32.87% in 1674, 41.07% in 1675, 42.68% in 1680, 49.98% in 1681 and 44.62% in 1682. Calculated from the end-of-the-month statements in the Batavia Dagh-Register of the relevant years.

mand in different parts of the archipelago was highly specific by region. Moreland has cited an English factor to the effect that he could not sell his stock at Bantam "because it is chera Mallaia (Malay style) and the people here will wear no other fashion than their own, which is chera Java." Indo-China bought chiefly textiles produced on the Coromandel coast, whereas Siam bought calico from both Coromandel and Gujarat. Of the island markets, the Moluccas, Ceram, Banda, and Amboina bought mainly painted goods from the Coromandel coast. Although it was the Coromandel textiles that sold best in Java, northern and western Sumatra were used to consuming mainly textiles produced in Gujarat.[6]

It is, therefore, not surprising that the Company's textile trade between Bengal and the archipelago was extremely limited, at least until about 1690. In neither of the two commercial treaties referred to above (note 4), did a single Bengal variety figure in the list of Indian textiles to be imported. It is also worth noting that of the total of f. 1,262,565 worth of textiles the Batavia Council ordered for the archipelago for 1686 from Coromandel, Surat, and Bengal, the respective shares of the three factories were 93, 4, and 3 percent.[7]

The sudden jump around 1690 in the number of Bengal textiles exported to the archipelago (Table 6.1) can probably be explained by the fact that this was about the time when the number of coarse cotton textiles available on the Coromandel coast had begun to shrink, their cost had begun going up, and their quality had begun to deteriorate. Unfortunately for the Company, similar problems began to appear soon afterwards in Bengal as well, though not with equal intensity. The first major complaint about the quality of Bengal textiles was received from Batavia in 1696. Two years later, the gross profit on Patna chintz was reported to be only 30 percent. At a Batavia auction in 1703, this particular variety barely fetched its cost price. In 1705, the average gross profit on Bengal textiles was reported to be no higher than 35 percent. In 1713, this figure had gone up slightly to 39 percent, but Balasore dassies—an ordinary calico—had to be sold that year at a loss of 8 percent. Two years later, Batavia reported that the quality of the Bengal garras—an ordinary calico—was "so poor that we do not recall an occasion in the past when such bad quality textiles were received from Bengal."[8]

---

[6] W. H. Moreland, "Indian Exports of Cotton Goods in the Seventeenth Century," *Indian Journal of Economics*, 5 (January 1925), 239, 241-242.

[7] Calculated from van Dam, *Beschrijvinge*, II, ii, 79-80 and 220-221; II, iii, 104-105. This is the only comprehensive list of orders available.

[8] B.H. 2.11.1696, K.A. 831, ff. 1414-1415; B.H. 3.8.1698, K.A. 835, f. 652; B.H. 3.7.1703, K.A. 842, ff. 414-416; B.H. 22.10. 1705, K.A. 845, f. 1598; B.H. 19.10.1713, K.A. 862, f. 103; B.H. 24.5.1715, K.A. 865, ff. 521-522.

OPIUM

The principal Bengal commodity the Company sold in the Indonesian archipelago was opium. It was not grown indigenously in the archipelago, and although it was undoubtedly one of the items the Asian merchants and the Portuguese imported into this part of Asia, the total consumption—which, incidentally, was primarily by smoking rather than by eating as in India and Turkey—seems to have been quite small until about the middle of the seventeenth century.[9] In 1600, for example, the annual consumption of this drug in the islands of Java and Madura was reported to be only 4,000 ponds, which works out at 1/750th part of a Dutch pond per capita per annum. Thirteen years later, the Company estimated that the amount of opium it could hope to sell in the course of a year in the Moluccas—which produced the richest products of the region (spices), and where the consumption of opium is believed to have begun—was about 200 ponds. Later in the century, however, mainly as a result of the large quantities imported by the Dutch, the total consumption in the archipelago grew at an incredibly fast rate. By 1678, for example, the annual consumption in Java and Madura was reported to have gone up to 70,000 ponds, which gives us a figure of 1/54th part of a Dutch pond per capita per annum.[10] Part of the opium the Company auctioned at Batavia found its way to China, thus opening that market to the Indian opium for the first time.

The Company began procuring opium in India for the archipelago in 1640. In the initial stages, the procurement was extremely limited in magnitude and confined to the Malwa variety purchased by the Surat factors.[11] But when the price of this variety began to go up at an alarming rate, the Company decided to begin buying Bihar opium at Patna.[12] This

[9] Meilink-Roelofsz., Asian Trade, pp. 64, 69. It is significant that in not one of the numerous dictionaries of Javanese and Malay words compiled by European travellers in the sixteenth century does one come across the word "opium." This suggests that these travellers probably did not notice the consumption of this drug on any significant scale. J. C. Baud, "Proeve van eene Geschiedenis van den Handel en het Verbruik van Opium in Nederlandsch-Indie," Bijdragen tot de Taal-, Land- en Volkenkunde van Nederlandsch Indie, 1 (1853), 86.

[10] Baud, "Opium," pp. 90, 115. The increase in the total population of the two islands has been taken into account.

[11] It was in 1640 that the Batavia Council for the first time placed an order with the Surat factors for a modest amount of 187 ponds of opium (ibid., p. 96). In 1641, the Council received a mere 42½ ponds of Malwa opium from Surat (Batavia Dagh-Register, 1640-1641, p. 307). It has been estimated that between 1640 and 1652, Batavia received, on an average, only 500 ponds of opium per annum from Surat (Baud, "Opium," p. 100). For evidence to show that the variety procured during this period for the archipelago was exclusively that produced in Malwa, see Batavia Dagh-Register, 1642, p. 187, and 1645, p. 308.

[12] In 1642, the cost of Malwa opium was reported to be Rs. 174 per 100 ponds. Two years

TABLE 6.1
Bengal Textiles Exported to the Indonesian Archipelago, 1666-1718

1	2	3	4	5	6	7	8	9
Year	Fine cotton muslins (pieces)	Fine cotton calicoes (pieces)	Total of fine cotton textiles (cols. 2 + 3) (pieces)	Ordinary cotton calicoes (pieces)	Total of cotton textiles (cols. 4 + 5) (pieces)	Silk piece goods (pieces)	Silk and cotton mixed piece goods (pieces)	Grand total (cols. 6 + 7 + 8) (pieces)
1666-67	N.A.	N.A.	1,500	2,980	4,480	1,778	–	6,258
1674-75	N.A.	N.A.	2,900	2,130	5,030	1,728	378	7,136
1676-77	3,949	400	4,349	1,202	5,551	1,582	94	7,227
1678-79	1,700	500	2,200	4,600	6,800	–	3,200	10,000
1690-91	N.A.	N.A.	7,224	10,553	17,773	112	–	17,889
1691-92	N.A.	N.A.	3,960	18,300	22,620	1,713	–	23,973
1692-93	N.A.	N.A.	15,118	29,455	44,573	575	6,410	51,558
1693-94	N.A.	N.A.	5,955	9,046	15,001	700	700	16,401
1694-95	N.A.	N.A.	4,800	26,230	31,030	–	–	31,030
1698-99	2,520	990	3,510	14,276	17,786	300	–	18,086
1699-1700	1,700	200	1,900	34,360	36,260	525	–	36,785
1700-01	N.A.	N.A.	6,880	18,815	25,695	170	–	25,865
1701-02	N.A.	N.A.	2,120	21,155	23,275	–	960	24,235
1702-03	N.A.	N.A.	5,550	31,790	37,340	–	1,040	38,380
1703-04	3,300	400	3,700	25,171	28,871	7	–	28,878

1704-05	2,320	4,500	6,930	38,080	45,010	7	–	45,017
1705-06	1,500	2,300	3,800	6,460	10,260	3,200	–	13,460
1706-07	N.A.	N.A.	8,010	31,269	39,279	7,758	400	47,437
1707-08	3,700	1,100	4,800	38,610	43,410	1,984	–	45,394
1708-09	3,320	5,660	8,980	42,330	51,330	1,500	–	52,810
1709-10	4,300	5,180	9,480	71,510	80,990	100	–	81,090
1710-11	3,080	6,080	9,160	64,290	73,450	1,025	–	74,475
1711-12	1,620	4,240	5,860	40,849	46,709	750	–	47,459
1712-13	300	900	1,200	9,140	10,340	–	–	10,340
1713-14	720	861	1,581	18,320	19,901	80	–	19,981
1714-15	3,820	2,220	6,040	26,370	32,410	100	–	32,510
1715-16	1,400	900	2,300	44,440	46,740	–	–	46,740
1716-17	1,200	805	2,005	15,780	17,785	200	–	17,985
1717-18	3,740	3,400	7,140	39,370	46,510	–	–	46,510

Source: Invoices of goods exported from Bengal.

Note: The constituent varieties of the five groups of textiles are as in Table 5.3. Information is not available for the years not included in the table.

was done in 1648, though the entire lot was sent to the Malabar coast. This pattern continued for another few years, and it was only from 1653 on that Batavia began receiving Bihar opium.[13] In the initial stages Malabar continued to be the more important of the two markets, and the imports into Batavia were quite small until about the close of the 1660s. There were even years during this period when no Bihar opium reached Batavia (Table 6.2). It should, however, be pointed out that once the Company had begun importing Bihar opium into the archipelago, the Malwa variety brought from Surat disappeared from the scene altogether and Bengal became the sole supplier of this highly profitable drug.[14]

The Batavia Council sold opium to the Indonesian, Malay, Chinese, and other merchants at public auctions held in the town. Often the Council stated beforehand the minimum amount to be sold to an individual bidder, besides occasionally specifying the reserve price below which it would not be willing to sell.[15] The Company usually sold at credit, and occasionally it bound itself not to hold the next auction for a specified period of time, apparently to enable the bulk buyers to enjoy oligopoly privileges for the duration of the period they thought they would need to dispose of the lot. The buyers were not permitted to sell the opium in

---

later, the factors wrote that this had gone up by 48 percent (*Batavia Dagh-Register*, 1642, p. 187, and 1645, p. 230). The cost price of the Patna opium around this time is not known, but in 1664 it was reported to be Rs. 90 per 100 ponds.

[13] The quantity received was 6,800 ponds in April 1653 and 5,168 ponds in June 1653. *Batavia Dagh-Register*, 1653, pp. 36, 88.

[14] For the period 1678-1745, Baud has given figures of the Company's total annual import of opium into the archipelago. A comparison of Baud's figures with those in Table 6.2 (pertaining to the amount of opium the Company imported from Bengal) shows that in several of the years common to both sets of figures, such as 1681-1682, 1700-1701, 1701-1702, and 1716-1717, the two sets agree exactly. In most other years, they come very close to each other. For many years, however, the discrepancy between the two sets is substantial— sometimes in one direction, sometimes in the other. A part of this can be explained by the fact that a consignment that, for example, left Bengal in December 1685, and is included in Table 6.2 under 1685-1686 corresponding to 1685 in Baud's set of figures, would not actually reach Batavia until early in 1686 and would, therefore, form part of the 1686 figure in Baud's table. Moreover, it seems that Baud's figures include that part of the opium illegally imported by the Company's servants which the watch and ward staff at Batavia succeeded in apprehending. Table 6.2 would not include these amounts (Baud, "Opium," pp. 101-102). As an additional check on the validity of the statement that from the 1650s on Bengal was the sole supplier of opium to Batavia, the lists of commodities (available in the *Batavia Dagh-Register*) Batavia received from Surat in 1670 and 1671 were examined. Opium did not form part of the Surat cargo in either of these years.

[15] The provision regarding a minimum amount to be sold gave rise to a whole class of middlemen from among the free Dutch citizens of the town, who bought large amounts from the Company and then sold it in small lots to native merchants who were not in a position to buy directly from the Company (Baud, "Opium," p. 112).

retail in the town of Batavia, partly in order to ensure that the substantial slave population of the town did not have access to the drug.[16] The cases of opium sold were sealed with the Company's insignia to enable the buyers to carry them freely to areas in the archipelago where the Company enjoyed monopolistic rights in this drug.[17] Opium was smoked practically all over the archipelago. But if one were to list the various consuming markets in a descending order of importance to the Company, at the top would probably be the island of Java, then Sumatra, the Malay peninsula, the island of Borneo, and the Moluccas. The greater part of the lot the merchants bought from the Company was carried to the Javanese ports of Grise, Japara, and Cheribon. The other major destinations were Palembang in Sumatra and Malacca in the Malay peninsula.[18]

The 1670s witnessed a significant rise in the amount of Bihar opium exported to the archipelago (Table 6.2). Following an increase in the Batavia price to f. 960 per 100 ponds, the orders for 1673-1674 were increased to 50,000 ponds. Though the amount actually exported against this order was less than 28,000 ponds, it was enough to bring the Batavia price down to f. 811, which, in turn, persuaded the Batavia Council to revert to asking for only 25,000 ponds per annum.[19] In 1677, the Company succeeded in getting monopoly rights in opium in Mataram in Java.[20] A similar privilege was obtained in 1678 in Palembang in Sumatra, and in 1681 in Cheribon in Java.[21] The greater part of the crucial Javanese market and a considerable segment of the Sumatran market were now available

[16] Ibid., p. 113. Similarly, in order to ensure that the spice growers of the Moluccas did not become addicted to opium (which might adversely affect the flow of the precious spices), in 1674 the Company prohibited the sale and consumption of this drug in the region. Ibid., p. 111.

[17] Ibid., p. 112.

[18] Based on the end-of-the-month statements in the *Batavia Dagh-Register* of 1671, 1673, 1674, and 1675. In the last-mentioned of these years, the share of Grise was 22.25 percent, of Japara 16.93 percent, of Cheribon 10.6 percent, of Palembang 13.47 percent, and of Malacca 15.90 percent.

[19] B.H. 23.8.1673, K.A. 800, f. 772; B.H. 26.9.1675, K.A. 802, f. 211; H.B. 5.2.1675, K.A. 1202, f. 48; B.H. 17.6.1676, K.A. 803, f. 105; H.B. 29.8.1676, K.A. 1209, f. 597vo; B.H. 13.8.1680, K.A. 807, f. 844.

[20] According to the terms of this agreement, the king's own subjects were henceforth to be permitted to import opium only if they could prove that they had bought it from the Company at Batavia. In the event of a violation of this provision, the cargo was to be seized and confiscated by the government. *Corpus-Diplomaticum*, III, 74-79.

[21] The terms of the agreement with Palembang were broadly similar to those of that with Mataram, except that the lots of opium and textiles, if any, seized from the subjects of Palembang were to be shared equally by the Company and the local ruler. Supplementary agreement dated July 3, 1678; agreement dated May 19, 1683 (ibid., pp. 140-142, 267-270). Agreement with the ruler of Cheribon dated January 7, 1681 (ibid., pp. 233-240).

TABLE 6.2
Bengal Opium Exported to the Indonesian Archipelago, 1659-1718

Year	Quantity ordered (Dutch ponds)	Quantity exported (Dutch ponds)
1659-60	N.A.	1,360
1660-61	N.A.	3,400
1661-62	4,880-6,100	4,760
1662-63	N.A.	–
1663-64	N.A.	–
1664-65	N.A.	–
1665-66	4,000	748
1666-67	N.A.	4,080
1667-68	2,000-3,000	2,346
1668-69	5,000	5,032
1669-70	4,000-5,000	6,528
1670-71	6,000	5,440
1671-72	12,000-15,000	5,600
1672-73	25,000	19,175
1673-74	50,000	27,627
1674-75	25,000	32,103
1675-76	25,000	26,643
1676-77	25,000	15,139
1677-78	25,000	8,837
1678-79	50,000-100,000	61,899
1679-80	N.A.	28,450
1680-81	N.A.	34,687
1681-82	50,000	60,302
1682-83	50,000	52,381
1683-84	N.A.	33,216
1684-85	N.A.	59,885
1685-86	N.A.	159,210
1686-87	–	1,324
1687-88	N.A.	43,229
1688-89	97,000	51,600

TABLE 6.2 (Continued)

Year	Quantity ordered (Dutch ponds)	Quantity exported (Dutch ponds)
1689-90	116,000	45,530
1690-91	–	62,930
1691-92	87,000	87,000
1692-93	87,000	91,495
1693-94	N.A.	65,540
1694-95	87,000	45,161
1695-96	58,000	88,305
1696-97	145,000	95,733
1697-98	145,000	137,025
1698-99	145,000-174,000	190,828
1699-1700	145,000	69,020
1700-01	145,000	69,020
1701-02	N.A.	87,290
1702-03	87,000-145,000	60,538
1703-04	87,000-145,000	120,580
1704-05	87,000	145,170
1705-06	174,000	78,300
1706-07	145,000-174,000	82,505
1707-08	145,000-174,000	39,005
1708-09	145,000-174,000	91,930
1709-10	145,000-174,000	136,495
1710-11	145,000-174,000	98,890
1711-12	145,000-174,000	116,000
1712-13	145,000-174,000	23,345
1713-14	145,000-174,000	158,920
1714-15	145,000-174,000	168,875
1715-16	145,000-174,000	159,935
1716-17	145,000-174,000	97,440
1717-18	145,000-174,000	146,015

Source: Amount asked for: letters from the Batavia Council to the factors at Hugli.
Amount exported: invoices of goods exported from Bengal.
Note: The figures for the amount asked for are shown against the year in which it was to be supplied.

to the Company on an exclusive basis.[22] The amount ordered from Bengal for 1678-1679 was, therefore, again increased to 50,000 ponds, with the provision that if the factors found that continued procurement was not leading to a deterioration in quality or a significant rise in the price, they could send even 100,000 ponds. In 1679, the average auction price at Batavia was reported to be 300 ryx dollars per picul of 122 ponds, which meant a gross profit of 400 percent. The importance the Batavia Council now attached to the opium trade was reflected in the instructions sent to Hugli to give priority to the procurement of this drug over even that of raw silk.[23] As a provider of purchasing power to the Company in the archipelago, opium was now next only to Indian textiles. The Chinese, Indonesian, and Malay traders who brought to Batavia commodities such as Chinese raw silk, tea, tobacco, vermilion, porcelain, tin, ivory, hides, sappanwood, cotton yarn, rice, wheat, sugar, salt, and oil now bought increasing quantities of Bihar opium in exchange for their wares. Thus although in 1659 these merchants had carried no opium whatever out of Batavia, and the share of this drug in their total cargo was only 0.09 percent in 1661, 1.45 percent in 1673, 4.46 percent in 1674, and 11.31 percent in 1675, this figure had gone up to 24.78 percent in 1681 and to 34.07 percent in 1682.[24]

As a result of the large amount of opium imported into Batavia in 1681-1682 and 1682-1683, the average price at the 1683 auctions came down to f. 480 per 100 ponds. At the same time, the Patna price came down in 1685 from the usual level of around Rs. 118 to Rs. 68 per 100 ponds.[25] The Bengal factors did not let a rare opportunity slip by, and sent the unprecedentedly large amount of nearly 160,000 ponds of this drug to Batavia. Following the receipt of this huge amount, Batavia refrained from placing any fresh orders for 1686-1687, which explains why the amount

[22] As a result, notwithstanding the fact that these privileges were qualified to a certain extent by the smuggling trade in opium by both the Asian and the rival European traders, the sales at Batavia immediately registered a substantial increase (end-of-the-month statements in the *Batavia Dagh-Register*, 1680-1682).

[23] H.B. 30.3.1679, K.A. 1237, f. 1100vo; B.H. 10.8.1679, K.A. 806, f. 827.

[24] In absolute terms, the value of the opium carried out of Batavia had increased from f. 279 in 1661 to f. 47,646 in 1675, to f. 144,981 in 1681, and to f. 186,306 in 1682. The proportion of Indian textiles in the total cargo had correspondingly declined from 83.52% in 1659, 84.21% in 1661, and 60.5% in 1673 to 41.07% in 1675, 49.98% in 1681, and 44.62% in 1682. Calculated from the end-of-the-month statements in the *Batavia Dagh-Register* of the relevant years.

[25] B.H. 26.8.1683, K.A. 812, f. 1378. It might be noted that the greater part of the opium produced in Bihar was actually distributed from the Agra market, so that the price at Agra had a determining influence on the price at Patna. Thus the sharp decline in the Patna price in 1685 had actually originated at Agra. The circumstances that caused this decline are not clear.

exported that year was practically nil.[26] The proclamation issued by Emperor Aurangzeb in 1693 temporarily suspending the trading privileges of the European companies forced the factors to try to buy opium, among other goods, in the name of Indian merchants. Although they had a good measure of success in this, the amount exported nevertheless suffered during the two years the prohibition on trade officially lasted. The limited quantities received in Batavia, however, took the local price in 1695 up to $f.$ 1,200 per 100 ponds.[27]

According to J. C. Baud, the annual consumption of opium in Java and Madura had increased from 4,000 ponds at the beginning of the seventeenth century to 70,000 ponds by 1678. By 1707, this figure had gone up to 108,266 ponds, which works out at 1/39th part of a Dutch pond per capita per annum. Earlier in 1683, the Company had estimated the annual demand in the entire archipelago to be around 116,000 ponds.[28] To their mounting dismay, however, the Governor-General and Council discovered that their efforts at monopolizing this highly profitable and growing market were being severely undermined by both Asian and rival European traders engaged in the opium trade. The competitors' trade not only cut deeply into the Company's potential market, but, being characterized by enormous fluctuations in its total volume from year to year, had a destabilizing influence on the average auction prices at Batavia. In fact, the dependence of these prices on the amount the Company itself offered for sale in a given year steadily decreased. Among the Asian traders participating in this trade were Indians, Armenians, Indonesians, Malays, and Chinese, while the Europeans included Danes, Portuguese, and, most important of all, English—both private traders and the East India Company. Until 1682, these traders operated mainly from Bantam. But with the fall of that city to the Dutch in that year, the English East India Company moved to Benkulen in southwest Sumatra. The others moved partly to Achin in northern Sumatra and partly to Malacca in the Malay peninsula. Besides carrying on a large amount of trade in areas where the Dutch had no special privileges, these traders appear to have succeeded in bringing in limited quantities of opium into Mataram, Cheribon, and Palembang, as well, which were officially the exclusive preserves of the Dutch.[29] In 1701, the Patna agents of several Armenian and English traders disclosed that they had orders to procure as much opium as they could,

---

[26] H.XVII. 8.12.1686, K.A. 1327, f. 918vo.

[27] H.B. 18.1.1694, K.A. 1435, f. 287vo; B.H. 28.6.1694, K.A. 826, ff. 939-942; B.H. (secret letter) 25.8.1695, K.A. 829, ff. 1496-1498.

[28] Baud, "Opium," p. 115; B.H. 26.8.1683, K.A. 812, f. 1378.

[29] B.H. 27.7.1695, K.A. 829, ff. 1163-1164; B.H. 27.7.1709, K.A. 854, ff. 445-446; Baud, "Opium," pp. 103-109, 114.

irrespective of the price they had to pay. The following year, some English traders bought a substantial amount of opium at Patna that the Dutch had earlier rejected for being of too poor a quality. In 1706, the Hugli factors reported that, *as usual*, a number of English traders had sent to the archipelago that year a total of 58,000 ponds of opium procured at Patna and an unspecified amount procured at Hugli.[30] As for the English East India Company, it seems that after being driven out of Bantam in 1682 it did not conduct any significant amount of trade in opium until 1707, when the Court of Directors in London instructed the factors at Fort William to send 1,200 ponds of opium to the factory at Benkulen. In 1712, the Dutch factors reported that the English company had sent a considerable amount of opium to their factory at Benkulen.[31]

To the great irritation of the authorities at Batavia, by far the greatest competition to the Company in the opium trade was probably provided by its own servants engaged in a clandestine trade in this drug. Being a high-value, low-bulk item, opium was ideally suited for this trade. In an unusually bountiful year such as 1676, these servants managed to smuggle in as much as 140,000 ponds, several times the amount imported on the account of the Company.[32] Further, given that these servants were un-derstandably in a great hurry to dispose of the smuggled opium, the decline in the sale price at Batavia was greater than would have been the case if the same amount had been brought in by legitimate rival traders.[33]

At one level, there was nothing the Batavia Council could do about the competition by Asian and rival European traders except to be more vigilant and try to minimize the extent of smuggling into areas where it enjoyed monopolistic rights. As for its own servants, the Company pre-scribed from time to time deterrent penalties for those apprehended by the watch and ward staff. Such proclamations were made in 1678, 1680, and 1683. The last of these went as far as to prescribe punishment by

[30] H.B. 28.9.1701, K.A. 1540, ff. 32-34; H.B. 11.12.1702, K.A. 1556, ff. 132-133; XVII.B. 23.8.1708, K.A. 462; volume not foliated.

[31] Letter from the Court of Directors in London to the factors of the United Company at Calcutta, 7.2.1707, L.B. 13, ff. 99-100; H.B. 25.3.1712, K.A. 1720, f. 112, I Section.

[32] XVII.B. 18.10.1677, K.A. 458; volume not foliated. In the correspondence between Bengal and Batavia, one comes across innumerable references to the illegal opium trade by the Company's servants. The Company regarded this as the main reason why its own sales were not larger. See, for example, secret letter B.H. 9.8.1678, K.A. 805, f. 741; resolution adopted by the Batavia Council dated August 5, 1678, K.A. 593, f. 222; B.H. 1.6.1683, K.A. 812, ff. 729-730; B.H. 26.8.1683, K.A. 812, f. 1378; B.H. 27.7.1695 (secret letter), K.A. 829, ff. 1163-1164; B.H. 2.6.1700, K.A. 838, f. 467.

[33] Resolution adopted by the Batavia Council dated August 5, 1678, K.A. 593, f. 222; B.H. 9.8.1678, K.A. 805, f. 741.

death, but apparently it had little effect on the total volume of this illegal trade.[34]

With a view to facing the challenge posed by the competitors (including their own servants) at a more general level, the Governor-General and Council took a number of steps that included instructions to the Bengal factors to keep the cost of the drug as low as possible by confining their procurement to Patna, and to be extremely particular about the quality of the opium they sent to Batavia.[35] In 1695, the Batavia Council decided that the only effective way to squeeze the competitors out of business was to undersell them for as long as necessary. The amount ordered from Bengal for 1696-1697 was, therefore, increased substantially (Table 6.2).[36] The amount actually exported by the Hugli factors also went up, although from 1699 successive poor crops in Bihar necessitated a reduction in exports. In 1698, the Council observed that it had succeeded in bringing down the price of opium throughout Java. The Batavia price also came down in August 1699 to $f.$ 500 per 100 ponds.[37] The Company held on in the hope that its rivals—particularly its own servants—would soon feel the strain and begin to pull out. But these hopes were belied when it was discovered in 1700 that the rivals' volume of trade at both Achin and Malacca had in fact been growing. What the Council had apparently not taken into account was the fact that its competitors usually succeeded in procuring opium at Patna at a lower price than its own factors did, and that in view of their considerably lower overhead costs (except, of course,

[34] Instructions by van Ommen and van Heck to Patna factors dated June 20, 1688, enclosure to H.B. 22.9.1688, K.A. 1347, ff. 770vo-772; Baud, "Opium," p. 98.

[35] In 1697, the Batavia Council wrote to the factors at Hugli that if the Council received any substandard opium, it would send it back to them. Three years later, it was pointed out that comparatively inferior-quality opium fetched $f.$ 40 to $f.$ 60 per 100 ponds less than standard-quality opium. In 1709, instructions were sent to Hugli to send only first-quality opium, even if that necessitated leaving part of the orders unfulfilled. H.B. 13.9.1690, K.A. 1360, f. 368vo; B.H. 3.5.1697, K.A. 832, f. 463; B.H. 20.8.1699, K.A. 836, f. 500; B.H. 2.6.1700, K.A. 838, ff. 492-493; B.H. 8.5.1701, K.A. 839, f. 392; B.H. 27.7.1709, K.A. 854, ff. 424-425; B.H. 10.5.1710, K.A. 856, ff. 357-359; B.H. 8.8.1710, K.A. 856, f. 796; H.B. 8.11.1710, K.A. 1688, ff. 102-103; B.H. 7.8.1711, K.A. 857, ff. 737-738.

[36] This decision was conveyed to Bengal in a secret missive addressed to the director at Hugli. In order to ensure that the substantial increase in the amount the Company intended to procure at Patna did not result in a sharp rise in the price there, the director was instructed to ask the Patna factors in the first instance to procure only the usual 8,000-9,000 ponds. Once a substantial lot had been procured, the Patna factors were to be informed of the true extent of the amount ordered by Batavia. B.H. (secret letter) 27.7.1695, K.A. 829, ff. 1163-1164.

[37] H.B. 1.11.1699, K.A. 1516, ff. 38-39; H.B. 28.9.1700, K.A. 1530, f. 109; H.B. 28.9.1701, K.A. 1540, ff. 32-34; B.H. 9.8.1698, K.A. 835, f. 546; B.H. 20.8.1699, K.A. 836, f. 500.

in the case of the English East India Company), they could afford to operate at low rates of profit per unit of investment. In fact, it was the Company more than anyone else who felt the strain of the reduced price of opium most severely. Early in 1700, the Council reported that at the current price, the Company was running a net loss on the opium bought at Hugli.[38] The percentage of loss increased substantially later in the year, when the Batavia price touched an all-time low of f. 320 per 100 ponds.[39] The Council was forced to admit that its strategy had been a miserable failure. The amount of opium ordered from Bengal was, therefore, reduced again, and the usual practice of selling at the highest possible price restored. In 1703, the gross profit on the lot bought at Patna was reported to be 255 percent; the lot bought at Hugli had afforded a gross profit of 100 percent.[40] Two years later, the total profit from the sale of Bengal opium during the course of the year was reported to be f. 335,000.[41] The amount ordered was, therefore, increased again (Table 6.2). The actual amount exported from Hugli had increased in the meantime from an average of 77,000 ponds during the years 1688-1689 to 1697-1698 to 94,000 ponds during the years 1698-1699 to 1707-1708. Over the decade 1707-1708 to 1717-1718, this figure went up further to 120,000 ponds. The volume of the competitors' trade seems to have gone up as well during this period, and although the overall situation was reported to be satisfactory in 1711 and 1713, the gross profit earned on opium in 1712 was only 46 percent.[42]

PROVISIONS

Besides textiles and opium, the Company imported Bengal rice, wheat, butter, and bacon into Batavia and Malacca. The greater part of the total requirement of rice and wheat in the Dutch-controlled territories in the archipelago was met by the Indonesian and Malay traders calling at Batavia.[43] The Company also procured considerable quantities of rice in Mataram and Macassar in Java. It was, in fact, only in years when supplies from the usual sources within the archipelago failed that the Governor-General and Council looked to the Coromandel coast, Kanara on the west coast of India, and, above all, to Bengal—the granary of seventeenth-

[38] B.H. 2.6.1700, K.A. 838, ff. 467, 492-493. The Hugli price was usually considerably higher than the Patna price.

[39] B.H. 24.11.1700, K.A. 838, ff. 1265-1266.

[40] B.H. 3.7.1703, K.A. 842, ff. 414-416.

[41] In the same year, the total profit on Bengal textiles was only f. 7,281. B.H. 22.10.1705, K.A. 845, f. 1598.

[42] H.B. 7.4.1711, K.A. 1702, ff. 129-130; H.B. 6.3.1713, K.A. 1734, f. 28, I Section; B.H. 27.7.1712, K.A. 860, ff. 589-592.

[43] Based on the end-of-the-month statements in the Batavia Dagh-Register.

century India—for rice. Thus the Company procured substantial quantities of this grain in Bengal in 1652-1653, 1656-1657 and 1660-1662, when the ruler of Mataram imposed an embargo on the Company's export of rice from his kingdom.[44] In the mid-1670s, the Batavia Council again faced difficulties in procuring rice in the archipelago; hence the renewed dependence on Bengal during this period. Bengal wheat was exported to Batavia more often, but the volume of trade in this grain was substantially less than that in rice. It might also be noted that Bengal was one of the chief Asian sources for the butter and bacon the Governor-General and Council required for their establishments at Batavia and elsewhere in the archipelago.

The Import Trade

SPICES

Among the items the Company imported from the archipelago into Bengal must first be mentioned spices—cloves, nutmeg (both the whole kernels called "noten" and the broken ones called "rompen"), and mace. By virtue of the monopsonistic privileges the Company enjoyed in the Spice islands, these spices were procured at throwaway prices. On the other hand, the price realised in Bengal was very high. The local demand for spices was inelastic over a broad price range, even though they were essentially an item of luxury consumption. While the rich Muslim aristocracy, as well as some other sections, were willing to pay extremely high prices for the coveted spices, most other sections of the community found them beyond their reach even if there was to be a fairly sharp decline in the price. This, together with the fact that the Company also had a virtual monopoly in these spices in Bengal and elsewhere in India, prompted it to keep the price pegged at a high level, ensuring the maximum monopoly revenue.[45] The result was a staggeringly high rate of profit. For example, cloves were sold in Bengal in the 1670s and the early 1680s at an average gross profit of 837 percent; by the second decade of the eighteenth century, this figure had gone up to 1,306 percent. The corresponding figures in the

[44] B.P. 28.8.1652, K.A. 779, ff. 602-603; B.P. 21.10.1653, K.A. 780, f. 439; B.P. 28.8.1654, K.A. 781, f. 370; B.P. 7.9.1656, K.A. 783, ff. 353-354; B.H. 19.9.1657, K.A. 784, f. 315; resolution adopted by the Batavia Council dated 16.7.1657, K.A. 577 (volume not foliated); B.H. 1.9.1657, K.A. 784, f. 406; B.H. 27.8.1660, K.A. 787, ff. 496-498; H.B. 29.11.1660, K.A. 1126, f. 48; B.H. 10.9.1661, K.A. 788, f. 501.

[45] H.B. 6.11.1684, K.A. 1286, f. 46; H.XVIII. 8.12.1686, K.A. 1327, ff. 917-918; XVII.B. 25.10.1686, K.A. 460, ff. 368-vo; H.B. 29.3.1692, K.A. 1397, ff. 59vo-62vo; B.H. 21.6.1692, K.A. 822, ff. 385-386; H.XVII. 24.11.1695, K.A. 1471, ff. 28-29.

case of nutmeg were 1,940 and 4,289 percent, respectively, while in the case of mace, the respective percentages were 694 and 1,216.[46]

In order to discourage rival European traders from buying up spices in India and importing them into Europe, thus compromising the Company's monopoly there, the Directors prescribed minimum sale prices for Asia for each of the major spices. This was done for the first time in 1653, when the minimum price of cloves was fixed at Rs. 200 per 100 ponds, of nutmeg Rs. 119, and of mace Rs. 292.[47] As it happened, the actual prices in Bengal around this time were higher than these, so that they were unaffected.[48] During 1678-1684, the Bengal factors sold on the average 5,573 ponds of cloves, 4,475 ponds of nutmeg, and 955 ponds of mace per annum.[49]

An unusually large annual sale of spices in Surat—the premier spice market in Asia—in the 1670s and the early 1680s, at prices that were sometimes even higher than those in Amsterdam, led the Board of Directors to believe that an increase in the minimum Asian prices would not have an adverse effect on the total amount sold. In 1687, therefore, these prices were revised upward. The new prices were Rs. 290 per 100 ponds for cloves, Rs. 167 for nutmeg, and Rs. 317 for mace.[50] Although

[46] Information regarding goods sold in Bengal is available for the years 1673-1674 to 1683-1684, 1711-1712 and 1713-1714 to 1716-1717. The information for the period 1673-1684 is available in the statement of goods sold in Bengal, 1673-1684, enclosure to H.B. 6.11.1684, K.A. 1286, ff. 429-437. The information for the years 1711-1717 is based on reports of goods sold in Bengal: H.B. 25.3.1712, K.A. 1720, f. 103, I Section; H.B. 6.3.1713, K.A. 1734, ff. 21-22; H.B. 26.2.1714, K.A. 1746, ff. 73-74, I Section; H.B. 29.10.1714, K.A. 1741, ff. 149vo; H.B. 30.1.1715, K.A. 1760, ff. 4-5, I Section; H.B. 20.3.1715, K.A. 1760, f. 91, I Section; H.B. 29.10.1715, K.A. 1760, ff. 95-96, II Section; H.B. 9.3.1716, K.A. 1776, ff. 216-217, I Section; H.B. 31.10.1716, K.A. 1769, ff. 178vo-179; H.B. 28.2.1717, K.A. 1788, ff. 96-97; H.B. 5.11.1717, K.A. 1783, ff. 55vo-56.

[47] The prices were actually prescribed in stuivers per pond at 48 for cloves, 33 for "noten," 24 for "rompen," and 70 for mace; van Dam, Beschrijvinge, II, III, 118, 125. The sales and price information regarding the nutmeg the Company sold in Bengal is usually not available separately for the "noten" and the "rompen" varieties. The minimum price given in the text is, therefore, the average of the minimum prices fixed for the two varieties. In 1687, when the Asian minimum prices were redefined, the Board of Directors fixed the price only of the "rompen" variety. This has been assumed to be the representative price for both types. The minimum prices fixed in 1697 are for "noten," the only variety sold in Bengal at that time.

[48] Cloves were reported to be selling in 1650 at Rs. 220, nutmeg in 1662 at Rs. 125, and mace in 1654 at Rs. 309 per 100 ponds. P.B. 1.11.1650, K.A. 1070, f. 561vo; H.B. 15.11.1662, K.A. 1130, f. 1487; P.B. 12.3.1654, K.A. 1094, f. 627vo.

[49] See note 46. The sales information for the years 1673-1678 is not available for all subordinate factories and has, therefore, not been used.

[50] The prices were actually fixed in terms of "light" stuivers per pond at 87 for cloves, 50 for "rompen," and 95 for mace. The rate of exchange between the rupee and the florin from 1687 was Re. 1 = f. 1.5 (van Dam, Beschrijvinge, II, III, 125).

the prevalent Bengal prices of cloves and mace were higher than the new minimum prices, that was not true of nutmeg, whose local price now had to be revised upward. The Board revised the minimum prices for Asia for the second time in 1696 and for the third time in 1697.[51] After the latest revision, the price of cloves stood at Rs. 333, of nutmeg at Rs. 240, and of mace at Rs. 533 per 100 ponds. In view of the ban on the Dutch trade in Bengal between 1693 and 1695, followed immediately by the rebellion of Zamindar Sobha Singh that lasted until 1697, the sale and prices of these spices in the region had been particularly low during the few years preceding the price revision of 1697.[52] In this context, the new minimum prices were found to be too high and the Hugli factors wrote to Batavia asking for their permission to ignore them. Although the Batavia Council acceded to this request with respect to cloves, it did not do so for nutmeg and mace, where the differential between the current Hugli prices and the new Asian minimum prices was very large. As a result, the Bengal factors found themselves unable to sell either of these two spices.[53] This, however, was true only for a short time. The repeated contention of the Hugli factors that the demand for spices was highly inelastic was borne out by an early resumption of sales at the new prices. The Maratha incursions into Gujarat in the early years of the eighteenth century were reported to have helped Bengal factors capture a part of the crucial north Indian market for spices, at least temporarily, bringing about a further increase in the sale of spices in Bengal. By 1712, matters had come to such a pass that the Hugli factors regretted that the Batavia Council had not approved of their suggestion to let them further increase the prices of all the three spices, an action that the factors thought would have had no injurious effect whatever on the total amount sold. In fact, spices were doing quite well in Bengal around this time. The average amount sold per annum during 1711-1717 was 8,533 ponds of cloves, 4,205 ponds of nutmeg, and 335 ponds of mace.[54] In comparison to Gujarat and the Coromandel coast, of course, Bengal was still a very small market for spices.[55]

[51] H.B. 19.9.1697, K.A. 1484, f. 94; van Dam, Beschrijvinge, II, III, 125; B.H. (secret letter), 23.4.1699, K.A. 836, ff. 212-213. For details see Chapter 4.

[52] The Hugli price of cloves, for example, had come down from Rs. 338 in the early 1680s to Rs. 309 per 100 ponds by 1697. Statement of goods sold in Bengal, 1697-1698, K.A. 1516, ff. 24-31.

[53] H.B. 19.9.1697, K.A. 1484, f. 94; H.B. 31.1.1699, K.A. 1516, f. 15; B.H. (secret letter), 23.4.1699, K.A. 836, ff. 212-213; H.B. 9.3.1701, K.A. 1540, f. 23.

[54] H.XVII. 4.11.1706, K.A. 1622, ff. 45-46; H.B. 24.12.1706, K.A. 1636, ff. 5-6; H.B. 17.8.1712, K.A. 1710, f. 82; and see note 46.

[55] For example, during the three-year period, 1714-1715 to 1716-1717, for which comparable information is available regarding the amount of spices sold in the other three Dutch factories in India, one finds that the amount of cloves sold in Bengal accounted for only

Pepper was the other major constituent of the group of spices the Company imported into Bengal. It was brought in from both the archipelago and the Malabar coast. Bengal was an important market for pepper, but the Company had to face a stiff and growing competition in this item from both the Asian merchants and the English East India Company.[56] It was to this competition that the Bengal factors ascribed the fall in the market price from Rs. 29 in 1661 to Rs. 23 per 100 ponds in 1667, bringing the gross profit down from 218 percent to 133 percent.[57] In the years that followed, the situation became even more difficult. Thus during 1678-1684, although the Bengal factors managed to sell, on an average, 472,806 ponds of pepper per annum, the price declined almost continuously, so that the average gross profit earned was only 50 percent.[58] The decline in the Hugli price of pepper in 1682-1683 to Rs. 14 per 100 ponds created a situation of great concern at Batavia. The Governor-General and Council were aware that large quantities of Asian pepper regularly reached Europe through the English East India Company. But they did not want to aggravate this problem further by selling pepper so cheaply in Asia as to encourage the English to buy it up and carry it to Europe. A floor price of Rs. 18 per 100 ponds was, therefore, prescribed for Bengal. However, by the time this communication reached Hugli, things had improved considerably because of the virtual cessation of English trade in Bengal between 1685 and 1690 in the context of their troubles with the provincial government. The factors quickly increased the price to Rs. 19.5 in 1685 and to Rs. 22 per 100 ponds in 1688. Once the English resumed their trade in 1690, the situation again became rather difficult. It seems that sometime in the 1690s, Batavia had lowered or withdrawn the minimum

---

9.28 percent of the total amount sold in India. The share of Surat, Coromandel, and Malabar was 58.05, 30.44, and 2.21 percent, respectively. In the case of nutmeg, the share of the four factories was 7.32, 46.92, 42.84, and 2.90 percent, respectively. The corresponding figures in the case of mace were 5.13, 22.54, 55.93, and 16.38 percent, respectively. For the information base for Bengal, see note 46. The figures for the other three factories are from Indira Anand, "India's Overseas Trade, 1715-1725" (Ph.D. dissertation, University of Delhi, 1970), pp. 125-127.

[56] Since the sales and price data do not distinguish between the varieties imported from these two regions, it is necessary that the entire amount of pepper imported be treated together. Since the greater part of the supplies appear to have originated in the archipelago, the import of pepper is discussed in the present section rather than in the Malabar section. It might be noted that over the three-year period 1714-1715 to 1716-1717, for which comparable information for regions other than Bengal is available to us, the sales in Bengal accounted, on an average, for 45.35 percent of the total amount sold in India. The share of Surat and the Coromandel coast was 38.29 percent and 16.34 percent, respectively. For figures for Bengal see note 46. The figures for Surat and Coromandel are from Anand, "India's Overseas Trade," pp. 125-127.

[57] H.XVII, 8.12.1661, K.A. 1124, f. 185; H.XVII. 5.9.1667, K.A. 1156, f. 871.

[58] See note 46.

sale price for Bengal fixed in 1689 at Rs. 22 per 100 ponds: in 1697-1698, we find the Hugli factors selling a considerable quantity of pepper at Rs. 17 per 100 ponds. In 1707, the factors themselves fixed the sale price at Rs. 19, and since the market price was considerably lower, failed to sell any pepper. Between 1711 and 1717, the Company managed to sell, on an average, 483,149 ponds of pepper per annum at an average gross profit of 81 percent.[59]

NONPRECIOUS METALS

The other major group of commodities the Dutch imported into Bengal from the archipelago was nonprecious metals—tin, spelter, lead, mercury, and vermilion.[60] The greater part of tin was purchased in the Malay peninsula, though limited quantities were also purchased from the Indonesian, Malay, and Chinese merchants calling at Batavia. These merchants also supplied spelter, mercury, and vermilion. Some mercury and vermilion and the greater part of lead, however, appears to have been brought in from Holland. Until about the early 1670s, the Company had no difficulty in selling these metals in Bengal in reasonably large quantities at a good profit. Thus in 1670-1671, the gross profit on tin was reported to be 90 percent, on lead 108 percent, on spelter 75 percent, on mercury 44 percent, and on vermilion 38 percent. But later in the 1670s and the early 1680s, the situation became somewhat more difficult, at least in the case of tin and lead. Between 1673 and 1684, for example, the average gross profit on tin came down to 40 percent and on lead to 77 percent, though for spelter, it went up to 88 percent, for mercury to 56 percent, and for vermilion to 81 percent.[61] The Dutch factors ascribed this to growing competition mainly by the English East India Company, who were importing ever larger quantities of tin and lead into Bengal. In 1685, Batavia prescribed a floor price of Rs. 44 per 100 ponds for tin to be sold in Bengal. Since this was considerably in excess of the actual market price, the factors had no alternative but to suspend sales. Five years later, the Batavia Council withdrew the minimum price, and in 1697-1698, the Hugli factors were reported to have sold tin at the unprecedentedly low price of Rs. 21 per 100 ponds.[62] In the case of spelter, the Batavia Council

[59] Resolution adopted by the Batavia Council dated 7.7.1684, K.A. 599, f. 310; B.H. 31.5.1685, K.A. 815, ff. 361-362; H.B. 11.11.1688, K.A. 1343, f. 799; B.H. 20.8.1689, K.A. 819, f. 568; statement of goods sold in Bengal in 1697-1698, K.A. 1516, ff. 24-31; H.B. 18.3.1707, K.A. 1636, ff. 85-86; and see note 46.

[60] In order to present a connected account, this group of commodities is discussed in its entirety in the present section.

[61] H.B. 8.10.1671, K.A. 1174, ff. 1881-vo; and see note 46.

[62] B.H. 31.5.1685, K.A. 815, f. 363; statement of goods sold in Bengal, 1697-1698, K.A. 1516, ff. 24-31.

laid down in 1689 a minimum price of Rs. 23 per 100 ponds. In 1693, however, the minimum price was withdrawn, and four years later, the Hugli factors sold spelter at Rs. 18 per 100 ponds, earning a gross profit of 11 percent. As a result of an extraordinarily large amount imported by the English, the market price of lead fell in 1691 to Rs. 8.5 per 100 ponds, and the Dutch factors decided to withdraw from the market. That same year, Batavia prescribed a minimum price of Rs. 220 for mercury, forcing the Bengal factors to suspend the sale of this metal.[63]

In 1705, the Batavia Council informed the Bengal factors that although they could sell spelter at cost price, they must ensure that a minimum of 15-20 percent gross profit was earned on lead. The figure of minimum gross profit suggested in the case of tin was 25 percent.[64] Over the period 1711-1717, the factors managed to sell, on an average, 94,080 ponds of spelter per annum, compared with 88,928 ponds during 1678-1684. The corresponding figures in the case of lead were 139,509 and 36,565 ponds. But the average annual amount of tin sold declined from 57,911 ponds during 1678-1684 to 33,082 ponds during 1711-1717. Both mercury and vermilion had practically disappeared from the list of goods the Company sold in Bengal in the second decade of the eighteenth century.[65]

In addition to spices and metals, Batavia sent sandalwood—procured mainly in the Timor group of islands—to Bengal. But the quantities sold were insignificant and there were years when the Bengal factors failed to sell any sandalwood whatever. As in the case of nonprecious metals, the long-term trend in the price of sandalwood was downward, though there were considerable fluctuations from year to year.

COASTAL TRADE

The role of Bengal goods in the Company's trade with the rest of the Indian coast (which may be deemed to include Ceylon, though strictly speaking that would not be correct) was quite small. The Company carried

[63] H.B. 18.9.1689, K.A. 1352, f. 43; H.B. 6.9.1692, K.A. 1347, f. 94vo; H.B. 30.1.1693, K.A. 1435, f. 40vo; statement of goods sold in Bengal, 1697-1698, K.A. 1516, ff. 24-31; H.B. 22.9.1691, K.A. 1388, f. 696vo.

[64] B.H. 15.7.1705, K.A. 845, ff. 898-900.

[65] See note 46. It might, however, be pointed out that between 1714-1715 and 1716-1717, Bengal on an average still accounted for 37.22 percent of the total amount of tin the Company sold in India. The respective shares of Surat, Coromandel, and Malabar were 27.68, 21.15, and 13.93 percent. The share of Bengal was still higher in the case of spelter (66.04 percent) with Surat, Coromandel, and Malabar, respectively, accounting for 25.41, 0.73, and 7.81 percent of the total amount sold. For figures for Bengal see note 46. The figures for Surat, Coromandel, and Malabar are from Anand, "India's Overseas Trade." pp. 120-122.

on virtually no trade between Bengal and Gujarat. There were also areas such as the Coromandel coast from which the Company imported nothing whatever into Bengal.

The Coromandel Coast

The export of Bengal goods to Coromandel was very limited in value. The goods exported included textiles, raw silk, sugar, long pepper, rice, wheat, and butter. Among textiles, it was only the varieties manufactured with fine cotton and silk that entered this trade. The volume of trade was insignificant except during 1688-1692, when there was a sudden but temporary rise in the gross profit on Bengal silk textiles.[66] Again, it was only during this brief phase that Bengal raw silk was sent to Coromandel in any quantity (Table 6.3). The trade in sugar, too, was limited in magnitude except during 1683-1684 and 1685-1686. The trade in long pepper had begun in 1664, when a trial consignment of 100 ponds was sent to Coromandel. Initially, the Coromandel factors were very enthusiastic about this item, but after a while they reported a decline in the rate of profit. In 1692, they went so far as to request Batavia not to send them any more Bengal long pepper, since they were finding it very difficult to earn a profit on it.[67] The amount of Bengal rice, wheat, and butter sent to Coromandel was negligible throughout our period.

Ceylon

The principal Bengal commodities exported to Ceylon were rice, wheat, sugar, butter, long pepper, raw silk, and textiles. Over the forty-year period 1661-1700, the annual rice orders from Ceylon ranged between 1.5 and 3 million ponds (750 and 1,500 metric tons), depending partly upon the amount imported by the Indian traders in the previous season and partly upon that expected in the current season on the Company's own account from Kanara on the west coast of India. Due to the limitations of tonnage, however, the Hugli factors were never in a position to meet these orders in full. In fact, it was but rarely that the amount exported exceeded a million ponds (500 metric tons). A major crop failure in Bengal in 1668, resulting in a ban on the movement of this grain out of the province, forced the Hugli factors to suspend temporarily the export of rice to Ceylon,

[66] Letter from the factors at Hugli to Commissioner van Rheede in Coromandel dated 4.8.1689, K.A. 1348, ff. 763-vo; H.B. 18.9.1689, K.A. 1352, f. 44; B.H. 22.11.1689, K.A. 1348, ff. 1126-1127.

[67] B.H. 12.11.1694, K.A. 827, f. 2412; H.B. 28.2.1695, K.A. 1459, ff. 22-23.

TABLE 6.3
Bengal Raw Silk Exported to Coromandel, Ceylon, and Malabar,
1661-1718

Year	Coromandel (Dutch ponds)	Ceylon (Dutch ponds)	Malabar (Dutch ponds)
1661-62	N.A.	1,728	N.A.
1662-63	N.A.	2,880	N.A.
1663-64	N.A.	–	N.A.
1664-65	1,440	N.A.	3,168
1665-66	N.A.	9,504	–
1666-67	–	6,480	–
1667-68	–	6,048	–
1668-69	–	–	–
1669-70	–	19,440	7,056
1670-71	–	–	–
1671-72	–	–	N.A.
1672-73	–	–	–
1673-74	–	4,320	–
1674-75	–	2,880	–
1675-76	–	–	–
1676-77	304	–	N.A.
1677-78	–	N.A.	N.A.
1678-79	–	N.A.	N.A.
1679-80	N.A.	N.A.	N.A.
1680-81	N.A.	303	N.A.
1681-82	–	–	–
1682-83	–	607	–
1683-84	–	607	3,338
1684-85	N.A.	N.A.	–
1685-86	–	N.A.	N.A.
1686-87	–	2,428	–
1687-88	N.A.	N.A.	–
1688-89	9,864	910	–
1689-90	31,109	607	–
1690-91	21,245	152	–
1691-92	–	607	–
1692-93	N.A.	N.A.	–
1693-94	–	–	–

TABLE 6.3 (Continued)

Year	Coromandel (Dutch ponds)	Ceylon (Dutch ponds)	Malabar (Dutch ponds)
1694-95	N.A.	–	–
1695-96	N.A.	–	–
1696-97	–	–	–
1697-98	–	–	–
1698-99	–	4,856	1,821
1699-1700	–	–	–
1700-01	910	–	–
1701-02	–	–	–
1702-03	N.A.	N.A.	–
1703-04	–	N.A.	–
1704-05	–	–	–
1705-06	–	–	–
1706-07	N.A.	–	–
1707-08	–	–	–
1708-09	–	–	–
1709-10	–	–	–
1710-11	–	–	2,448
1711-12	–	–	–
1712-13	–	–	–
1713-14	–	–	–
1714-15	–	–	–
1715-16	–	4,097	–
1716-17	–	–	1,858
1717-18	–	–	2,076

Source: Invoices of goods exported from Bengal.

among other places.[68] Around the same time, the Dutch government of Ceylon took steps to increase the domestic output of this grain with a view to reduce, if not eliminate, the island's dependence on foreign rice.[69] It is not clear how successful these efforts were, but we do know that the Dutch rice trade between Bengal and Ceylon practically came to an end

[68] H.B. 7.4.1668, K.A. 1158, f. 907vo; H.B. 29.12.1668, K.A. 1163, f. 1695vo.

[69] Report on Ceylon by Rykloff van Goens dated November 7, 1676, K.A. 1204, ff. 307-308; S. Arasaratnam, Dutch Power in Ceylon, 1658-1687 (Amsterdam, 1958), p. 151.

around the turn of the century.[70] This might have been the result either of the attainment of self-sufficiency by Ceylon or of a proportionately larger dependence on alternative sources of supply such as Kanara. The volume of trade in provisions other than rice and in raw silk and textiles was very limited throughout our period (Tables 6.3 and 6.4).

Among the goods imported from Ceylon were cinnamon, areca nuts, large sea shells (shankhs), and elephants. Ceylonese cinnamon growers belonging to the Chalia caste were obliged to deliver to the Company— the ruler of a large part of the island since 1658—a certain minimum amount of cinnamon per annum free of cost. A nominal payment was stipulated for deliveries in excess of the minimum obligatory amount. The transportation of the cinnamon to the coast was also the responsibility of the Chalia kulis. Coupled with the monopoly enjoyed by the Company in Bengal, this involved an extremely high profit on this item, which was comparable with that on Indonesian cloves and mace.[71] Between 1678 and 1684, the Bengal factors sold, on the average, 1,830 ponds of cinnamon per annum at an average gross profit of 846 percent. When the Board of Directors increased the Asian minimum price of cinnamon to Rs. 187-200 in 1697, the price in Hugli was only Rs. 162 per 100 ponds. As in the case of other spices, Hugli wrote to the Batavia Council asking for permission to ignore the new minimum price for cinnamon. In a secret missive to the director at Hugli, the Batavia Council acceded to the request. During the remainder of our period, Hugli continued to sell cinnamon at Rs. 162 per 100 ponds. The average amount sold per annum during 1711-1717 was 1,644 ponds at an average gross profit of 677 percent.[72]

Areca nuts were consumed with betel leaves in large quantities all over Bengal, but about 80 percent of the total demand was met by nuts produced

[70] From then on, it was only in emergencies occasioned by local crop failures, such as in 1709, that Ceylon asked for rice from Bengal. H.B. 16.10.1709, K.A. 1669, ff. 147, 151.

[71] By a series of treaties with a number of rulers on the Malabar coast, where an inferior variety of cinnamon known as "cassia ligna" was grown, the Company succeeded in virtually destroying the Indian merchants' trade in Malabar cinnamon (Asasaratnam, *Dutch Power in Ceylon*, pp. 185-186, 190-191). It is true that until 1696, the Company permitted Bengal merchants going to Ceylon to bring back cinnamon, but the quantities so imported were insignificant.

[72] See note 46; B.H. (secret letter), 23.4.1699, K.A. 836, ff. 121-213. As in the case of the Indonesian spices, Bengal was a much smaller market for cinnamon than Surat. For example, over the three years 1714-1715 to 1716-1717, one finds that the total amount sold in Bengal was only 6,300 ponds as against 11,180 ponds sold in Surat. The sales in Coromandel and Malabar were very much smaller than in Bengal. Information on the amount sold in Surat, Coromandel, and Malabar is from Anand, "India's Overseas Trade," pp. 125-127.

around Dacca itself. Between 1678 and 1684, the Bengal factors sold, on an average, 582,724 ponds (291 metric tons) of these nuts per annum at an average gross profit of 100 percent.[73]

The *shankhs* imported from Ceylon were dug up from the sea bed in the straits between Ceylon and India and were used in Bengal and other parts of the country for religious ceremonies, for making ornaments, and as drinking vessels. The price in Bengal (and consequently the gross profit earned) depended to a considerable degree on the amount imported by the Indian traders in a given year. Thus the average price of these *shankhs* came down from Rs. 7 in 1661-1662 to Rs. 4 per 100 pieces in 1666-1667, when a large amount was imported by the Indian merchants. This pulled the gross profit down from 108 percent to 25 percent.[74] With the decline in the volume of the Bengal merchants' trade with Ceylon around the 1680s, the price and the sales of the Company's *shankhs* went up considerably.

Finally, as far as trade in elephants was concerned, problems such as the large rate of mortality on the way, the heavy cost of maintenance in the interval between the arrival of the elephants at Hugli and their sale, and, most important of all, the frequent troubles the Company had with the local state officials, including the *subahdar* (who provided the bulk of the market), with regard to the price and the recovery of the amount once the deal had been finalized, prevented it from becoming quantitatively significant. In 1674, the director and council at Hugli wrote to their counterparts in Ceylon that the elephant trade "brings us more troubles than profits."[75] Around the turn of the century, the Company stopped importing Ceylonese elephants into Bengal.

Malabar

The major item the Company procured in Malabar was pepper.[76] The goods exported to this area included Japanese bar copper and Indonesian

---

[73] See note 46.

[74] H.B. 8.12.1661, K.A. 1124, f. 185; H.XVII. 5.9.1667, K.A. 1156, f. 871.

[75] Princes Shah Shuja and Azim-us-Shan, who were *subahdars* of Bengal between 1639-1659 (with an interruption during 1647-1649) and 1697-1703, respectively, reserved the first right to buy the elephants the Company imported, usually at prices arbitrarily determined by themselves. Prince Azim-us-Shan occasionally also asked for one or more elephants as a gift. P.B. 10.3.1655, K.A. 1100, f. 385vo; B.P. 19.9.1656, K.A. 783, f. 351; H.B. 4.11.1698, K.A. 1500, f. 17; H.B. 29.9.1698, K.A. 1500, f. 115; H.B. 31.1.1699, K.A. 1516, ff. 13-14; memorandum by Governor Ryklof van Goens of Ceylon for the Ceylon factors dated April 12, 1675, K.A. 1202, ff. 270vo-271.

[76] Part of the pepper the Company imported into Bengal was from Malabar. For a discussion of the import of pepper, see the section on the Indonesian archipelago.

TABLE 6.4
Bengal Textiles Exported to Coromandel, Ceylon, and Malabar,
1657-1718

Year	Coromandel	Ceylon	Malabar
1657-58	N.A.	6,880	N.A.
1661-62	N.A.	2,673	N.A.
1662-63	N.A.	6,500	N.A.
1663-64	280	7,603	N.A.
1664-65	116	N.A.	N.A.
1666-67	4,221	6,590	N.A.
1667-68	−	4,807	N.A.
1668-69	−	3,180	N.A.
1669-70	−	2,268	N.A.
1670-71	−	10,295	N.A.
1671-72	−	−	N.A.
1672-73	−	−	N.A.
1673-74	−	4,978	N.A.
1674-75	50	1,659	2,169
1675-76	1,946	1,873	3,242
1676-77	737	310	2,900
1677-78	−	N.A.	N.A.
1678-79	−	N.A.	N.A.
1679-80	N.A.	N.A.	N.A.
1680-81	N.A.	530	N.A.
1681-82	−	1,280	3,227
1682-83	733	414	2,509
1683-84	1,672	3,902	886
1685-86	416	N.A.	N.A.
1686-87	504	732	1,591
1687-88	N.A.	N.A.	1,480
1688-89	15,233	1,614	16,132
1689-90	42,084	3,272	8,285
1690-91	39,168	4,268	17,995
1691-92	35,682	7,051	38,726
1692-93	N.A.	N.A.	N.A.
1693-94	840	1,652	−
1694-95	N.A.	−	N.A.

168

TABLE 6.4 (Continued)

Year	Coromandel	Ceylon	Malabar
1695-96	N.A.	–	–
1696-97	–	–	–
1697-98	–	–	–
1698-99	–	2,900	675
1699-1700	–	1,130	3,400
1700-01	8,780	1,350	400
1701-02	–	–	N.A.
1702-03	N.A.	N.A.	1,780
1703-04	–	N.A.	–
1704-05	–	1,600	–
1705-06	–	–	1,000
1706-07	–	–	N.A.
1707-08	–	1,305	1,868
1708-09	–	1,120	–
1709-10	–	763	2,735
1710-11	–	1,488	1,443
1711-12	–	1,485	1,850
1712-13	–	N.A.	93
1713-14	1,225	1,585	1,020
1714-15	400	1,730	–
1715-16	200	3,718	–
1716-17	497	2,400	200
1717-18	–	4,350	3,520

Source: Invoices of goods exported from Bengal.
Note: Information is not available for the years not included in the table.

spices, besides cotton textiles, and opium procured in different parts of India. The trade in opium began sometime in the 1640s. In the initial stages, it was only the variety produced in Malwa in central India that was sent to Malabar from Surat. An increase in the cost price of the Malwa opium around 1645 persuaded the Company to try the Bihar variety. Procurement in Patna began in 1648, and the Bihar opium soon replaced the Malwa variety. In 1651-1652, 7,000 ponds of Bihar opium was exported to Malabar. But in 1653, the market was reported to be rather slack and Batavia advised Bengal not to send opium to Malabar for a while.[77] Between 1663 and 1672, the Company succeeded in wresting from the local rulers in Malabar exclusive trading rights in both pepper and opium.[78] Even though these rights were qualified to a certain extent by the large-scale smuggling carried on by Indian merchants, the amount of opium sold in Malabar registered a substantial increase.[79] In 1664, the outgoing director of the Bengal factories, van den Broecke, recommended to his successsor, van Hyningen, that 12,000 to 16,000 ponds of opium be sent to Malabar per annum. Later in the same year, the Dutch commander at Cochin expressed the hope that he would be able to sell 16,000 ponds of opium per annum at a gross profit of f. 100,000.[80]

After the conquest of Cochin in 1663, the Company had fixed the price of opium at the relatively high level of 100 ponds of pepper against 1 pond of opium. But in order to promote sales as well as discourage smuggling, the price was successively lowered in 1664 to 75, 60, and finally to 50 ponds of pepper per pond of opium. Five years later, the pepper/opium ratio was further lowered to 40/1.[81] Between 1673 and 1677, the amount of opium the Bengal factors exported to Malabar was at a fairly high level, except in 1675-1676, when an illegal detention of the Company's opium boats by the nawab of Patna forced the Hugli factors to reduce the amount exported (Table 6.5).[82]

In the meantime, the Bengal factors had also been sending to Malabar small quantities of raw silk since 1664-1665 and of textiles of all varieties

[77] Generale Missiven, II, 507; B.P. 21.10.1653, K.A. 780, f. 438.

[78] See, for example, the treaty with the king of Cochin dated May 20, 1663; with the king of Marta dated February 7, 1664; with the representative of the king of Kolattiri dated July 1664; with the raja of Bekkenkur dated March 12, 1665; with the king of Travancore dated April 25, 1665, and with the zamorin of Calicut dated February 6, 1672. Corpus-Diplomaticum, II, 244, 262, 264-265, 279, 299, 318-320, 325, 456.

[79] In May 1664, after a tour of inspection of the Dutch factories in Malabar, Governor Hutstard of Ceylon reported a rampant smuggling trade in both pepper and opium, possibly with the connivance of the local princes (Batavia Dagh-Register, 1664, p. 171; see also pp. 355, 574). In April 1678, two Indian agents of the Company informed the Batavia Council that considerable quantities of opium were being smuggled into Malabar (ibid., 1678, pp. 242-243).

In their letter dated January 1, 1666, the English factors in Malabar reported to the Court of Directors in London: "the natives of those parts not being able to live without ophium which now they cannot have but from the Dutch . . . they have all the pepper which is the growth of those parts in truck for it." W. Foster, ed., The English Factories in India, 1665-1667, p. 101.

[80] Memorandum dated 24.2.1664, K.A. 1137, f. 450; Batavia Dagh-Register, 1664, p. 574.

[81] Batavia Dagh-Register, 1664, pp. 188, 327, 410, 574; ibid., 1665, p. 260; resolution adopted by the Batavia Council dated 25.8.1665, K.A. 580, ff. 264-265; Generale Missiven, III, 699.

[82] H.B. 15.11.1676, K.A. 1209, ff. 503vo-504.

TABLE 6.5

Bengal Opium Exported to the Malabar Coast, 1657-1718

Year	Quantity exported (Dutch ponds)	Year	Quantity exported (Dutch ponds)	Year	Quantity exported (Dutch ponds)
1657-58	6,238	1672-73	–	1691-92	59,046
1658-59	N.A.	1673-74	22,713	1692-93	50,025
1659-60	–	1674-75	27,985	1693-94 to 1704-05	–
1660-61	4,760	1675-76	8,555	1705 06	2,900
1661-62	6,800	1676-77	28,235	1706-07 to 1709-10	–
1662-63	N.A.				
1663-64	16,048	1677-78 to 1680-81	N.A.	1710-11	2,610
1664-65	10,200	1681-82	22,910	1711-12	–
1665-66	N.A.	1682-83	26,390	1712-13	N.A.
1666-67	11,152	1683-84	8,421	1713-14	1,450
1667-68	11,560	1684-85 to 1687-88	N.A.	1714-15 to 1717-18	–
1668-69	14,284				
1669-70	11,844	1688-89	3,280		
1670-71	28,577	1689-90	23,635		
1671-72	N.A.	1690-91	17,835		

Source: Invoices of goods exported from Bengal.

since 1674-1675 (Tables 6.3 and 6.4). Bengal opium and silk textiles did unusually well in Malabar in 1690, so that the orders for both these items were increased substantially. Hence the comparatively large amounts exported in 1691-1692 and 1692-1693 in the case of opium and in 1691-1692 in that of silk textiles. It was, however, found impossible to sell such large quantities in Malabar, and the greater part of both items had to be sent on to Batavia.[83] About this time, the general profitability of intra-Asian trade was declining, while trade with Europe—particularly in Bengal goods—was becoming increasingly more important. It was therefore decided to divert the limited capital resources available to the Company away from branches such as the Bengal-Malabar trade to the Bengal-Europe trade. As a result, the Dutch Bengal-Malabar trade practically came to an end before the century closed.

Persia

The principal commodities the Company imported into Persia were Indonesian spices and pepper; Ceylonese cinnamon; Japanese copper; Indian, Taiwanese, and Indonesian sugar; and Indian textiles. The principal item procured in return was raw silk, though after a while the Company also began participating in a thriving smuggling trade in Persian silver *abassis*. These coins found their way to several of the Dutch factories in Asia, including Bengal. The volume of the trade with Persia, begun in 1623, was rather limited until 1652, when the Company entered into an agreement with Shah Abbas II. According to this agreement, the Company was exempted from the payment of tolls on imports into and exports from Persia up to a maximum of f. 800,000 per annum. In return, the Dutch factors were obliged to purchase annually 600 bales of raw silk from the Crown at a fixed price of f. 1,000 per bale.[84] The factors at Gombroon estimated that in addition to the f. 600,000 required for the purchase of raw silk, they would need annually another f. 40,000, partly for the purchase of minor commodities such as rosewater, and partly to defray the necessary establishment costs. They also estimated that they could hope to sell annually goods costing f. 876,000, on which they could reasonably expect to earn a gross profit of f. 620,000. The deficit of f. 20,000, the factors argued, could be made up by carrying Asian merchants' goods on freight to and from Persia. Of the total of f. 876,000 worth of goods that the factors hoped to sell in Persia over the course of a year, Bengal goods

---

[83] H.B. 22.9.1691, K.A. 1388, f. 699vo; H.B. 11.1.1693, K.A. 1435, ff. 136-vo; H.B. 28.6.1694, K.A. 826, ff. 943-944; B.H. 23.8.1694, K.A. 827, f. 1791.

[84] A copy of this agreement is available in K.A. 1212, f. 665.

were to account for *f.* 100,000.[85] Although the average gross profit on the entire lot of goods sold was expected to be 71 percent, Bengal goods were expected to yield 80 percent.[86] The actual rate of growth of the volume of trade, however, was considerably lower than had been anticipated.[87] In 1655, for example, the actual value of imports into Persia was only *f.* 512,295; the Bengal cargo, consisting of sugar and textiles, accounted for no more than *f.* 41,944.[88] Usually, Bengal sent its cargo directly to Persia via Coromandel or Surat, but occasionally it was sent to Batavia, which arranged for its transportation to Gombroon.

SUGAR

Persia was one of the major Asian markets for sugar. In 1644, the Company had estimated that it could hope to sell 1.8 million ponds (900 metric tons) of sugar annually from its Persian factories. But the actual amount it imported into Persia that year was only 700,000 ponds, all of which had been purchased in Taiwan.[89] In 1647 the Persian factors asked for the first time for a small amount, 150,000 ponds, of Bengal sugar. By 1650, both the amount asked for and that actually exported from Bengal had gone up to 450,000 ponds (Table 6.6). The Company procured in Bengal the so-called "powder" sugar, though limited quantities of "candy" sugar were also purchased. The principal areas where sugar was procured were Sripur near Sonargaon in Dacca district, Chandrakona in Bardwan district (now in Midnapore district), and the districts of Birbhum and Hugli. The variety purchased in Sripur was the most expensive, but also the one that afforded the highest profit in the Persian market.[90] Though

[85] The estimated share of goods from the various regions of Asia was: Surat and Mocha, *f.* 330,000 (37.67 percent); Indonesian archipelago and Ceylon, *f.* 270,000 (30.82 percent); Coromandel coast, *f.* 100,000 (11.41 percent); Bengal, *f.* 100,000 (11.41 percent); Sind, *f.* 60,000 (6.84 percent); and Malabar coast, *f.* 16,000 (1.82 percent). Estimate dated May 25, 1652, K.A. 1079, ff. 349vo-350.

[86] The estimated rate of gross profit on goods from the various Asian regions was: Indonesian archipelago and Ceylon, 115 percent; Bengal, 80 percent; Coromandel coast, 75 percent; Sind, 75 percent; Malabar coast, 62 percent, and Surat and Mocha, 30 percent. Ibid.

[87] The Company was not interested in buying raw silk worth *f.* 600,000 in Persia, and had agreed to do so only under duress. The fact that the actual rate of growth of the trade was smaller than had been anticipated made such a large procurement of silk impossible in any case. The Company, therefore, tried and succeeded in bypassing the clause relating to the procurement of 600 bales of silk by gratifying the right officials at various levels.

[88] The share of the various regions in the total imports was: Taiwan, Surat, and Ceylon, *f.* 320,526 (62.56 percent); Indonesian archipelago, *f.* 96,563 (18.84 percent); Sind, *f.* 53,263 (10.39 percent); and Bengal, *f.* 41,944 (8.18 percent). Statement of goods received in Persia, 1655, K.A. 1099, ff. 526-527.

[89] Glamann, *Dutch-Asiatic Trade*, p. 158; B.P. 8.7.1645, K.A. 772, f. 320.

[90] In 1670, the cost of the four varieties per 100 ponds was reported to be: Sripur, Rs. 6;

TABLE 6.6
Bengal Sugar Exported to Persia, 1650-1718

Year	Quantity ordered (Dutch ponds)	Quantity exported (Dutch ponds)
1650-51	450,000	450,000
1651-52	N.A.	–
1652-53	N.A.	N.A.
1653-54	N.A.	N.A.
1654-55	N.A.	–
1655-56	250,000	229,955
1656-57	300,000	421,728
1657-58	N.A.	455,704
1658-59	N.A.	–
1659-60	N.A.	466,563
1660-61	N.A.	488,470
1661-62	N.A.	403,460
1662-63	unlimited	1,174,539
1663-64	1,000,000	1,044,886
1664-65	700,000	762,548
1665-66	N.A.	827,314
1666-67	N.A.	694,973
1667-68	N.A.	496,761
1668-69	N.A.	516,800
1669-70	700,000-1,000,000	519,763
1670-71	N.A.	985,470
1671-72	N.A.	629,121
1672-73	N.A.	N.A.
1673-74	N.A.	874,062
1674-75	1,000,000	1,011,905
1675-76	1,000,000	702,386
1676-77	600,000-650,000	442,343
1677-78	N.A.	566,790
1678-79	N.A.	N.A.
1679-80	N.A.	N.A.
1680-81	N.A.	1,461,920
1681-82	N.A.	953,008
1682-83	N.A.	1,012,508

174

TABLE 6.6 (Continued)

Year	Quantity ordered (Dutch ponds)	Quantity exported (Dutch ponds)
1683-84	N.A.	863,386
1684-85	1,000,000	968,251
1685-86	800,000	424,458
1686-87 to 1705-06	N.A.	N.A.
1706-07	N.A.	176,256
1707-08	N.A.	339,456
1708-09 to 1717-18	N.A.	–

Source: Quantity ordered: The correspondence between Hugli, Persia, and Batavia.
Quantity exported: Invoices of goods exported from Bengal.

the amount asked for by the Gombroon factors declined from the mid-1650s, the actual amount exported from Bengal was usually in excess of 400,000 ponds. In 1658, the gross profit on Bengal sugar was 194 percent.[91]

The troubles in Taiwan that led to its loss in 1662 prompted Batavia to ask Bengal in 1661 to send as much sugar to Persia as it could. As a result, the amount exported in 1662-1663 jumped to 1.17 million ponds. The amount of Java sugar Batavia sent to Persia that year was only 90,000 ponds. The gross profit on the two varieties was reported to be 172 percent and 159 percent respectively. But intense competition by private English merchants as well as by Indian and other Asian traders led to a decline in the gross profit on the Bengal variety to 96 percent in 1664, and to 86 percent two years later. The Hugli factors tried to deal with this situation by measures such as increasing their own procurement to ensure that not enough was left in the market for the competitors to buy and sending their ships early in the season so that they reached Persia before the rivals' ships, but with little success.[92] In 1672, the factors at Gombroon adopted another strategy. Since a substantial proportion of the goods the English brought to Gombroon were bought by merchants from Isfahan, the factors decided to discourage these merchants from dealing with the English by

Chandrakona, Rs. 4.40; Birbhum, Rs. 5; and Hugli, Rs. 4.33 (H.B. 4.4.1670, K.A. 1167, ff. 1398vo-1399; P.B. 27.10.1654, K.A. 1094, f. 665vo).

[91] B.H. 13.9.1658, K.A. 785, f. 446.

[92] B.H. 26.8.1661, K.A. 788, f. 457; statement of goods sold in Persia, 1663, K.A. 1129, ff. 1683-1684; H.B. 31.10.1663, K.A. 1135, ff. 2233vo-2234vo; H.XVII. 19.12.1664, K.A. 1136, f. 588; H.B. 15.11.1666, K.A. 1147, ff. 641-642; H.B. 14.4.1670, K.A. 1167, f. 1429; H.B. 19.11.1674, K.A. 1193, ff. 207vo-208.

underselling them at Isfahan by a substantial margin. That this policy was reasonably effective is borne out by a report received in 1675 that a number of Isfahan merchants had refused to buy sugar from English ships that had reached Persia before the Dutch ships. Although the rigour of English competition was lessened as a result, it by no means came to an end; in fact, in the 1680s, the English East India Company itself carried on trade with Persia in Bengal sugar.[93]

The Hugli factors exported to Persia a record amount of 1.46 million ponds of sugar in 1680-1681, on which the Gombroon factors made a gross profit of 186 percent.[94] But this was also the time when the Batavia Council was trying to find a market for the Javanese sugar produced under its own auspices. As a result, even though all through the 1680s the sugar from Bengal consistently afforded a higher gross profit than the variety from Java, the Council instructed the Bengal factors to progressively reduce the amount of sugar they exported to Persia.[95] In 1691, Bengal was asked not to send any sugar whatever to Gombroon. But the fact that it was found necessary to repeat this instruction in 1696 suggests that Hugli probably continued to send limited quantities for a while.[96] It seems that it was only around 1700 that the Bengal-Persia sugar trade finally came to an end. The small quantities exported in 1706-1707 and 1707-1708 were intended simply to serve as ballast on the ships going to Persia.

TEXTILES

The only other item exported from Bengal to Persia was textiles. The gross profit the Company earned on these textiles was hardly ever in excess of 50 percent; usually it was much less. In net terms, the profit was often negligible, and instances in which the Company incurred a net loss, though rare, were not unknown. The principal reason behind this poor performance was the cut-throat competition the Company had to face from the Indian and Armenian traders. These traders knew both the Bengal and the Persian markets more intimately, and were subject to considerably smaller overhead costs, enabling them to operate on a smaller profit per

[93] Memorandum by Director François de Haze for his successor, Frederick Benth, May 6, 1674, K.A. 1193, ff. 497-vo; H.B. 26.8.1675, K.A. 1202, ff. 109-110; letter from the Court of Directors in London to their factors at Hugli dated 23.12.1681, L.B. 6, f. 436; consultation dated September 1, 1682, F.R. Hugli, vol. 3., f. 100; Directors to Bengal, 15.11.1682, L.B. 7, f. 107; Directors to Bengal, 3.10.1684, L.B. 7, f. 380; Directors to Bengal, 27.8.1688, L.B. 8, f. 575.

[94] H.B. 9.4.1681, K.A. 1258, f. 1277vo.

[95] The respective gross profit on the two varieties was 171 and 121 percent in 1681, 178 and 137 percent in 1686, and 161 and 147 percent in 1688 (Glamann, *Dutch-Asiatic Trade*, p. 160, Table 30).

[96] B.H. 25.6.1691, K.A. 821, f. 221; B.H. 22.5.1696, K.A. 830, f. 510.

unit. The reason why the Company participated in this trade at all was that earning a net profit, although obviously very welcome, was not a precondition to trade with areas providing profitable return cargo—in this case, raw silk and especially the silver *abassies*.

The principal varieties of Indian textiles in demand in Persia were those manufactured from inferior-grade cotton and consumed by the masses. These varieties were imported almost entirely from the Coromandel coast and Gujarat, both of which had a distinct advantage over Bengal in these particular types of textiles. The market for the finer varieties imported from Bengal was rather limited, even though Turkish merchants also came to Persia to buy these textiles.[97] The principal market for Bengal textiles was the imperial capital of Isfahan. The first time the Company exported Bengal textiles to Persia was in 1655-1656. The quantity was very small (Table 6.7), but even this was found to be an excess, and the factors at Gombroon asked their counterparts at Hugli not to send any textiles for a while. It was only in 1658, when these textiles were reported to have afforded an average gross profit of 60 percent that the trade was resumed.[98] The volume continued to be limited, however, the gross profit poor, and the varieties entering the trade practically confined to those manufactured from fine cotton.[99] In order to minimize the chances of net loss, the Batavia Council laid down in 1665 a minimum of 40 percent gross profit on a particular variety in a given year as a precondition to the export of that variety the following year.[100]

The volume of the Bengal-Persia textile trade began to pick up from 1673, partly as a result of the special efforts (such as trying out new varieties) made by François de Haze, the new director of the Persian factories. In 1676, the gross profit on Malda *khasas* was reported to have gone up to 54 percent and on *malmals* to 94 percent.[101] As a result, 1677-

---

[97] Memorandum by Director François de Haze of Persia for his successor, Frederick Benth, dated May 6, 1674, K.A. 1193, ff. 493-505. Turkey was also supplied by the Company with textiles from Bengal and other parts of India via Holland.

[98] Memorandum by Director de Haze, May 6, 1674, K.A. 1193, ff. 493-505; P.B. 10.3.1655, K.A. 1100, ff. 373vo-374; P.B. 16.11.1655, K.A. 1102, ff. 196-vo; B.XVII. 14.12.1658, K.A. 1115, f. 81.

[99] For example, *malmals* were sold at a gross profit of 40 percent in 1662 and 35 percent in 1663, *charkhanas* at 29 percent in 1663, *ambertees* at 39 percent in 1663, while *garras* sold the same year rendered a loss of 23 percent (H.B. 26.10.1662, K.A. 1130, f. 1377vo; H.B. 31.10.1663; K.A. 1135, ff. 2234vo-2235; statement in K.A. 1160, ff. 1683-1684). In 1666, the average gross profit on Bengal textiles was reported to be so poor that the factors at Gombroon refrained from placing fresh orders (H.B. 15.12.1666, K.A. 1147, ff. 641-642).

[100] B.H. 1.7.1665, K.A. 792, f. 394.

[101] Report by ex-Director Benth of Persia on his return to Batavia after relinquishing charge, November 25, 1679, K.A. 1238, ff. 1707-1719.

TABLE 6.7
Bengal Textiles Exported to Persia, 1655-1718

1	2	3	4	5	6	7	8	9
Year	Fine cotton muslins (pieces)	Fine cotton calicoes (pieces)	Total of fine cotton textiles (cols. 2+3) (pieces)	Ordinary cotton calicoes (pieces)	Total of cotton textiles (cols. 4+5) (pieces)	Silk piece goods (pieces)	Silk and cotton mixed piece goods (pieces)	Grand total (cols. 6+7+8) (pieces)
1655-56	N.A.	N.A.	1,514	—	1,514	—	1,050	2,564
1662-63	N.A.	N.A.	1,200	—	1,200	—	—	1,200
1663-64	N.A.	N.A.	138	—	138	—	—	138
1664-65	N.A.	N.A.	1,100	—	1,100	500	—	1,600
1665-66	N.A.	N.A.	3,000	—	3,000	—	—	3,000
1666-67	—	—	—	—	—	—	—	—
1667-68	—	—	—	—	—	—	—	—
1668-69	—	—	100	—	100	—	—	100
1669-70	—	—	1,184	—	1,184	—	500	1,684
1670-71	N.A.	N.A.	N.A.	N.A.	N.A.	N.A.	N.A.	1,649
1671-72	—	2,850	2,850	—	2,850	—	—	2,850
1672-73	—	—	—	—	—	—	—	—
1673-74	N.A.	N.A.	8,525	—	8,525	—	—	8,525
1674-75	N.A.	N.A.	2,180	—	2,180	—	—	2,180
1675-76	N.A.	N.A.	8,663	—	8,663	—	—	8,663

1676-77	2,895	6,460	9,355	795	10,150	100	400	10,650
1677-78	14,805	2,800	17,605	–	17,605	11,264	400	29,269
1680-81	N.A.	N.A.	33,760	–	33,760	6,139	3,434	43,333
1681-82	N.A.	N.A.	5,870	–	5,870	14,975	–	20,845
1682-83	N.A.	N.A.	5,849	–	5,849	17,169	–	23,018
1683-84	N.A.	N.A.	9,026	–	9,026	8,385	–	17,411
1684-85	N.A.	N.A.	22,406	2,300	24,706	–	1,700	26,406
1685-86	N.A.	N.A.	26,405	–	26,405	940	2,700	30,045
1686-87	N.A.	N.A.	1,047	–	1,047	–	390	1,437
1687-88	–	–	–	–	–	–	–	–
1688-89	N.A.	N.A.	9,100	1,700	10,800	–	4,200	15,000
1689-90	–	–	–	–	–	–	–	–
1690-91	N.A.	N.A.	22,495	2,880	25,375	4,000	1,240	30,615
1691-92	N.A.	N.A.	5,268	–	5,268	–	1,326	6,594
1693-94	N.A.	N.A.	4,387	1,750	6,137	–	–	6,137
1694-95	N.A.	N.A.	6,398	500	6,898	1,082	100	8,080
1696-97	N.A.	N.A.	1,378	6,630	8,008	–	2,050	10,058
1697-98	4,780	6,200	10,980	10,818	21,798	–	700	22,498
1698-99	5,210	9,984	15,194	9,040	24,234	2,720	1,761	28,715
1699-1700	4,550	3,830	8,380	18,934	27,314	4,220	2,710	34,244
1700-01	6,220	1,553	7,773	19,340	27,113	1,600	200	28,913

TABLE 6.7 (Continued)

Year	Fine cotton muslins (pieces)	Fine cotton calicoes (pieces)	Total of fine cotton textiles (cols. 2+3) (pieces)	Ordinary cotton calicoes (pieces)	Total of cotton textiles (cols. 4+5) (pieces)	Silk piece goods (pieces)	Silk and cotton mixed piece goods (pieces)	Grand total (cols. 6+7+8) (pieces)
	2	3	4	5	6	7	8	9
1701-02	N.A.	N.A.	6,765	3,700	10,465	–	800	11,265
1702-03	N.A.	N.A.	3,600	1,500	5,100	800	5,040	10,940
1703-04	7,657	2,500	10,157	17,443	27,600	–	900	28,500
1704-05	16,177	2,500	18,677	25,743	44,420	–	900	45,320
1708-09	–	4,450	4,450	16,000	20,450	2,580	–	23,030
1709-10	25,580	9,200	34,780	44,179	78,959	2,000	–	80,959
1710-11	4,500	1,600	6,100	2,360	8,460	–	–	8,460
1711-12	10,710	900	11,610	6,874	18,484	–	–	18,484
1712-13	240	1,100	1,340	800	2,140	–	–	2,140
1713-14	8,680	1,400	10,080	11,278	21,358	–	–	21,358
1714-15	7,920	3,443	11,363	6,550	17,913	443	–	18,356
1715-16	6,852	6,926	13,778	7,504	21,282	2,676	–	23,958
1716-17	11,413	6,433	17,846	4,326	22,172	1,660	–	23,832
1717-18	5,296	2,000	7,296	5,431	12,727	4,218	–	16,945

Source: Invoices of goods exported from Bengal.
Note: The constituent varieties of the five groups of textiles are as in Table 5.3. Information is not available for the years not included in the table.

1678 witnessed a considerable increase in the number of fine cotton textiles exported to Gombroon, and was also the year in which both silk and mixed textiles began to be exported to Persia fairly regularly. But in 1681, the gross profit on *khasas* was again reported to be poor, while *malmals* had actually to be sold at a loss. The explanation given by the factors at Gombroon was that over the preceding few years, the domestic output of textiles (including those of silk) had gone up considerably, leading to a fall in the demand for imported textiles, which, on an average, were more expensive for comparable qualities.[102] Domestic troubles in Persia between 1686 and 1689 led to a virtual stoppage of sales and, therefore, of exports during this period. The amount exported recovered in 1690-1691, but slumped again following orders from the Batavia Council to the Hugli factors to send textiles to Gombroon only if the available capital resources permitted this after orders from Holland, Japan, the Indonesian archipelago, and Ceylon had been met in full. Though this stipulation was withdrawn in 1694, it was only from 1697-1698 that the exports to Persia again increased. In 1698, Bengal textiles were reported to have afforded, on an average, a gross profit of only 45 percent.[103] In view of this and of the fact that the Bengal-Persia sugar trade had practically come to an end by this time, in 1700 the Batavia Council reduced to $f.$ 150,000 the upper limit on the value of Bengal goods that could be exported to Persia per annum (fixed initially in 1695 at $f.$ 200,000 and subsequently raised in 1698 to $f.$ 250,000).[104] The value of actual exports in the subsequent period was, in fact, usually very much smaller than even this limit. On the advice of Director Hoogkamer of Persia, in 1703 Bengal sent a number of new varieties of textiles to Gombroon for a trial. But these did no better than the others, with the result that the following year, the Batavia Council went to the extent of suggesting a possible termination of the Bengal-Persia textile trade.[105] Although that was not done, the situation continued to be precarious and the volume of trade small. In 1710, the profit level was reported to be so poor that the Batavia Council found it necessary to reduce to 25 percent the minimum gross profit in a given

[102] H.B. 20.9.1681, K.A. 1258, f. 1300; report by the Dutch resident at Isfahan dated February 27, 1680, K.A. 1232, ff. 602-603; memorandum by ex-Director Casembroot of Persia on his return to Batavia after relinquishing charge, November 25, 1682, K.A. 1268, f. 2726vo.

[103] H.XVII. 6.12.1687, K.A. 1327, f. 920vo; B.H. 25.6.1691, K.A. 821, f. 221; B.H. 26.8.1694, K.A. 826, ff. 952-953; B.H. 19.5.1699, K.A. 836, f. 331.

[104] B.H. 12.5.1695, K.A. 828, f. 608; B.H. 9.8.1698, K.A. 835, f. 544; B.H. 26.9.1700, K.A. 838, f. 576; B.H. 9.7.1701, K.A. 839, ff. 578-579.

[105] B.H. 4.7.1704, K.A. 844, ff. 374-375.

year to qualify a variety of textile for export in the following year; this is a level that would probably have entailed a net loss.[106]

An analysis of the Company's extensive participation in intra-Asian trade underscores the crucial role of its "privileged status" in ensuring the profitability of its operations in a given region. The Indonesian archipelago, Ceylon, and, to a smaller extent, the Malabar coast are examples of this. The case of Japan was somewhat more complex. In that it was the only European trading agency allowed there, the Company certainly had a privileged status in Japan. But the value of this status was compromised by the range of commercial restrictions and procedures that the Company was subjected to. For a variety of reasons, the Company's participation in intra-Asian trade began to shrink as of the last quarter of the seventeenth century. From the vantage point of Bengal, the rising trade at this time was with Europe, to which we now turn.

[106] B.H. 25.10.1710, K.A. 856, ff. 1387-1388.

· 7 ·

THE TRADE WITH EUROPE

The contribution of the Bengal factories to the Company's trade with Europe consisted of textiles, raw silk, and saltpetre. The Company had begun to procure these goods for Europe soon after the establishment of trade relations with the region in the 1630s, though it was not until the last quarter of the seventeenth century that Bengal became a major supplier to the European market. Indeed, the period between 1636—when the Directors first asked for small amounts of Bengal textiles and raw silk— and 1720 can conveniently be viewed as consisting of two distinct phases. The first phase, lasting until about 1678, was one of consolidation, whereas the following decades were characterised by a significant growth in the value of Bengal-Holland trade. Within each of these two phases, one could identify fairly clear-cut subphases. These covered the years 1636-1654 and 1655-1678 during the first phase, and 1679-1692 and 1693-1720 during the second. The gaps in the statistical data are much more marked during the first phase than during the second.

The Phase of Consolidation: 1636-1678

For a variety of reasons, the trade between Bengal and Holland was at a rather low level throughout this period. For one thing, given the composition of exports to Holland during this period, with only a limited role for goods such as raw silk and textiles, it was inevitable that Bengal would account for only a small proportion of the total exports. And even this limited potential was not fully realised because of the priority given to the requirements of intra-Asian trade. Thus we find that the Directors' orders for Bengal raw silk for Holland during this period were almost invariably accompanied by the qualification that such orders were to be supplied only after the raw silk requirements of the bullion-providing Japan trade had been met in full. Apart from limiting the growth of the trade between Bengal and Holland, such a policy also implied that fluctuations in supply affected chiefly the supplies to Europe. Hence the frequent wide gaps between orders for and supplies of Bengal raw silk to Holland over this period.

The Early Years: 1636-1654

As evidenced by the Directors' orders lists, the volume of trade in Bengal textiles was extremely limited during these years. Initially, the orders were exclusively for muslins—*khasas* and *malmals*—used as wearing apparel. Other varieties of fine cotton textiles, used both as wearing apparel and as furnishings, appeared in the orders lists a few years later. Cotton and silk mixed piece goods—*ginghams*—were included in the orders lists in 1643, whereas ordinary calicoes—bleached *garras*—were first asked for in 1648. Silk textiles procured during these years were those made in China and to a limited extent in Japan. Bengal fine cotton and mixed piece goods would seem to have served a small and exclusive market, which explains both the Directors' continued insistence on high quality and the high profit earned on these textiles.[1]

The Bengal factories were more important during this period for the raw silk procured there. In the initial stages of the Company's trade in Asia, it was exclusively the Chinese raw silk procured from the Chinese junks off Batavia and in other parts of the archipelago that had been sent to Holland.[2] But with the growth of the Japan trade, the Company was obliged to send most of the Chinese raw silk it was able to obtain to Japan, where it was the item most in demand in exchange for precious metals. The establishment of trade relations with Persia in 1623 opened up a new and substantial source of raw silk. By 1631, the amount of Chinese raw silk ordered for Holland was only 12 percent of that from Persia. A rise in cost price, accompanied by a simultaneous fall in the sale price in the subsequent period, however, reduced the gross profit on Persian silk to as low as 25 percent in 1637.[3] Things became worse still in the 1640s, a time marked by constant troubles between the Company and the Shah of Persia. The differences were finally resolved in 1652, but only after the Company had agreed to buy a minimum of 600 bales (120,000 ponds) of raw silk annually at a fixed price. In the meantime, immediately after the opening of direct trade with Bengal, the Directors had begun placing

---

[1] Orders lists, 1638, 1639, 1640, 1642 (all K.A. 250) and 1649 (K.A. 251). In the orders list of 1642, the cost price of a Bengal *khasa* was estimated to be between f. 6.30 and f. 7.87. In 1635, this particular variety had been sold in Amsterdam (small quantities of Bengal goods used to reach Amsterdam via Coromandel before direct trade with Bengal had begun) at f. 33.07 per piece. Even assuming the 1633 cost price to be as high as f. 8.00 per piece, the 1635 price afforded a gross profit of more than 300 percent (orders list, September 1642, K.A. 250; resolution of the *Heeren XVII* dated September 3, 1635, ibid).

[2] This silk was reported to have afforded in Holland a gross profit of 320 percent in 1621 and of 325 percent the following year. Glamann, *Dutch-Asiatic Trade*, p. 114.

[3] Persian silk was not found suitable for the Japanese market and could, therefore, be spared for Holland. Glamann, *Dutch-Asiatic Trade*, p. 116.

orders for the raw silk produced there. The principal attraction of Bengal silk was that although it was substantially cheaper than both the Chinese and Persian varieties, it fetched a price only slightly lower than the former and about the same as the latter.[4] The orders for Bengal raw silk, which were extremely modest in the beginning, picked up fast, reaching the figure of 50,000 ponds in 1650 and of 80,000 ponds two years later. The actual supplies, however, seem to have been considerably smaller, mainly because of the priority attached to the orders from Japan, where Bengal raw silk had already become a major item of trade. There were even years, such as 1650-1651, when Batavia was not in a position to send any Bengal raw silk whatever to Holland. As a result, the principal variety sold in Holland around this time was that from Persia.[5] The gross profit on the limited quantities of Bengal silk that reached Holland was, however, very handsome.[6] Encouraged by the high profit, the Directors increased the orders for Bengal raw silk in January 1654 to 200,000 ponds (or more, subject to a maximum total cost of f. 1 million). Although the actual amount exported from Bengal in 1655-1656 does not seem to have been anywhere near this figure, the increase in the total amount exported from Bengal for the various Asian factories and Europe from 178,000 ponds in 1654-1655 to 251,000 ponds in 1655-1656 is probably explicable largely in terms of an increased amount exported to Holland.

The only other item of any significance procured in Bengal for the Dutch market was saltpetre. In the early part of the seventeenth century, it was procured mainly on the Coromandel coast and to a limited extent in Gujarat. From the late 1630s, however, Bengal increasingly replaced

[4] In 1631, the Chinese and the Persian varieties were estimated to have cost f. 3.5 and f. 4.00 per pond, respectively. The cost of Bengal silk in this year is not known, but eleven years later, the Directors estimated its cost at f. 2.25 per pond. In September 1636, the sale price of the three varieties was reported to be f. 10.2, f. 9.0, and f. 9.3 per pond, respectively. Ibid., pp. 116-121; resolution adopted by the *Heeren XVII* dated 18.9.1636, K.A. 250; volume not foliated.

[5] B.XVIII [G.M.]. 20.1.1651, K.A. 1070, ff. 8vo-9. In 1653-1654—the first year for which detailed information regarding Asian silk sold at the Amsterdam Chamber is available—out of a total of 76,463 ponds of raw silk sold, the share of the Bengal variety was only 6.04 percent (7.00 percent in terms of value), the remainder being divided between Persian (93.19 percent in physical terms and 91.84 percent in terms of value) and Tonkin raw silk (0.77 percent and 1.16 percent). K.A. 10234; volume not foliated.

[6] In 1649, Bengal raw silk was reported to be affording an "incomparably" larger profit than the Persian silk (XVII.B. 23.9.1649, K.A. 455, f. 147vo). In 1653-1654, the gross profit was around 200 percent. The sale price that year was f. 8.92 per pond. The exact figure of the cost price in 1651-1652, when this lot was purchased, is not available, but it seems that it was around the same level as in 1648-1649, that is, f. 2.83 per pond (the sale price figure is from K.A. 10234; the cost figure is from B.XVII [G.M.]. 18.1.1649, K.A. 1066, f. 91vo).

both these sources. This was a period marked by one war or another in Europe and the demand was extremely high.[7] Between 1649-1650, the first year for which sales information is available, and 1653-1654, the annual amount sold in Amsterdam went up from 105,000 ponds to 303,000 ponds.[8] Over the same period, the price increased from *f.* 37 to *f.* 66 per 100 ponds. The gross profit in 1653-1654 was as high as approximately 1,000 percent, a level rarely achieved even in the case of the monopoly spices.[9]

The Years of Ups and Downs: 1655-1678

The two and a half decades or so following the reorganisation of the Bengal factories into an independent directorate in 1655 were marked by significant fluctuations in the volume of trade between Bengal and Europe. This was also the period when the English East India Company emerged as a rival in this trade.

There was a gradual increase in the European demand for Indian textiles during this period, for use as wearing apparel as well as furnishings. The procurement of silk piece goods was begun in Bengal in 1658. In 1660, the average gross profit on Bengal textiles was reported to be 200 percent, which was considerably higher than that earned on the textiles from Coromandel.[10] Hence the increase in the orders for Bengal textiles despatched in August 1660 (Table 7.1). But the information relating to the rates of profit earned in Holland on Bengal textiles in the middle and late 1660s does not indicate a satisfactory return.[11] Indeed, in 1665 the orders for Bengal textiles were sharply slashed and several varieties, particularly in the fine cotton group, were dropped altogether. The situation was equally bad with regard to the silk piece goods. Between 1668 and 1674, it was only once (in 1670) that orders were placed for silk *armosins*—the principal variety of silk textiles procured in Bengal. In 1671, the total

[7] The Thirty Years' War ended only in 1648. Even after that, the conflict between Spain and France continued until the Treaty of the Pyrenees marked its settlement in 1659. Among the other wars in the early 1650s, one might make a special mention of the First Anglo-Dutch War (1652-1654).

[8] The Amsterdam sales represented on an average about 50 percent of the total sales in all six chambers put together.

[9] K.A. 10234; B.P. 28.8.1654, K.A. 781, f. 366. The sales figures have been rounded to the nearest thousand.

[10] H.XVII. 7.8.1662, K.A. 1129, f.1232vo.

[11] In 1664, the gross profit on *armosins* was reported to be only 37 percent. Three years later, although the gross profit on *garras* was 176 percent, that on *malmals* was 92 percent, on *khasas* 84 percent, on *adathys* and *humhums* 57 percent each, and on *sanus* only 36 percent (XVII.B. 14.5.1667, K.A. 457; volume not foliated; H.B. 7.4.1668, K.A. 1150, f. 908vo).

orders for Bengal textiles were increased somewhat, and the Directors decided that if the price situation so warranted, they would hold back part of the goods received.[12]

The data on the actual export of textiles from Bengal for Holland during this period are extremely limited (Table 7.2). But these would seem to suggest that the amounts exported usually fell far short of the amounts ordered, besides fluctuating far more violently than the orders did. The explanation given by the Bengal factors for this was the frequent shortage of liquid capital as well as the growing competition by the English East India Company. The supply of textiles procured by the two companies was rising more slowly than the demand for them, leading to insufficient availability and rising prices.[13] It was pointed out that in comparison with the Dutch, the English were willing to pay substantially higher prices. They also reportedly accepted pieces of whatever quality and size the merchants chose to offer them, including pieces rejected by the Dutch. The more aggressive procurement policy of the English was reflected in a complaint the Dutch Board of Directors made in 1676 that many Dutch merchants were in fact buying Indian textiles in London.[14]

The imposition toward the end of the 1660s of a 3.75 percent additional duty on textiles manufactured at Dacca induced the Dutch factors to try and procure comparable varieties produced at Malda. Efforts were also made to save on the margin of the merchants by dealing at Malda directly with the weavers as far as possible. The Directors expressed the hope that this might constitute a turning point in the Bengal textile trade. But the Company's efforts in this behalf met with only marginal success, and the cost of the textiles continued to be high. In a moment of exasperation, the Directors went so far as to write to Batavia in 1676 that if the cost of the Bengal textiles could not be kept in check, they would seriously consider stopping further imports.[15]

As far as raw silk was concerned, the Amsterdam price declined from f. 8.34 in 1654-1655 to f. 5.38 per pond in 1658-1659.[16] The Directors ascribed this to a fall in demand because of the many wars raging in Europe

---

[12] Resolution dated 12.10.1671, K.A. 256 (not foliated).

[13] The documents consistently speak of a rise in cost price due to the competition by the English, but specific cases are not cited. A negative piece of information is, however, available for 1665, when it was reported that in view of the temporary suspension of procurement by the English, the price of a silk *armosin* (ordinarily f. 8.4-9.8) had come down by f. 1.4 (H.XVII. 18.8.1665, K.A. 1142, f. 1163; H.XVII. 12.11.1665, K.A. 1142, f. 1132).

[14] XVII.B. 21.10.1676, K.A. 458; XVII.B. 11.5.1677, K.A. 458; volume not foliated.

[15] XVII.B. 14.5.1672, K.A. 457; XVII.B. 16.5.1676, K.A. 458; the volumes are not foliated.

[16] This is the average price of Chinese, Persian, and Bengal raw silk sold in Amsterdam. Prices for individual varieties are not available for these years. K.A. 10234 (not foliated).

TABLE 7.1

Bengal Textiles Ordered from Holland, 1636-1716

Orders dispatched in	Fine cotton muslins (pieces)	Fine cotton calicoes (pieces)	Total of fine cotton textiles (cols. 2+3) (pieces)	Ordinary cotton calicoes (pieces)	Total of cotton textiles (cols. 4+5) (pieces)	Silk piece goods (pieces)	Silk and cotton mixed piece goods (pieces)	Grand total (cols. 6+7+8) (pieces)
1	2	3	4	5	6	7	8	9
September 1636	200	–	200	–	200	–	–	200
September 1638	1,000-1,400	–	1,000-1,400	–	1,000-1,400	–	–	1,000-1,400
September 1639	1,000-1,500	–	1,000-1,500	–	1,000 1,500	–	–	1,000-1,500
September 1640	1,000-1,500	–	1,000-1,500	–	1,000-1,500	–	–	1,000-1,500
September 1641	–	500	500	–	500	–	–	500
September 1642	1,000-1,500	1,000	2,000-2,500	–	2,000-2,500	–	–	2,000-2,500
August 1643	3,500	1,000	4,500	500	5,000	–	1,000	6,000
September 1644	1,200	400	1,600	200	1,800	–	400	2,200
September 1645	1,200	400	1,600	200	1,800	–	400	2,200
August 1646	1,200	400	1,600	200	1,800	–	1,000	2,800
November 1647	2,000	400	2,400	200	2,600	–	2,000	4,600
September 1648	2,000	400	2,400	1,400	3,800	–	2,000	5,800
September 1649	6,600	1,000	7,600	2,000	9,600	–	2,000	11,600
September 1650	13,000	3,000	16,000	7,000	23,000	–	4,000	27,000
September 1651	13,000	3,000	16,000	7,000	23,000	–	4,000	27,000

Date							
September 1652	13,000	3,000	16,000	5,000	21,000	—	4,000	25,000
January 1654	9,000	2,000	11,000	4,000	15,000	—	3,000	18,000
November 1655	11,000	2,000	13,000	7,500	20,500	—	4,000	24,500
October 1656	10,500	2,500	13,000	14,000	27,000	—	6,000	33,000
October 1657	13,500	2,500	16,000	15,000	31,000	—	9,000	40,000
August 1658	8,500	1,000	9,500	14,000	23,500	2,000	7,000	32,500
September 1659	12,200	2,500	14,700	14,000	28,700	2,000	5,000	35,700
August 1660	12,700	2,500	15,200	18,000	33,200	2,000	8,000	43,200
September 1661	13,000	2,500	15,500	8,500	24,000	—	5,000	29,000
September 1662	12,200	2,500	14,700	7,000	21,700	—	4,000	25,700
August 1663	11,500	3,000	14,500	12,000	26,500	—	4,000	30,500
October 1664	14,000	4,000	18,000	10,500	28,500	2,500	5,000	36,000
November 1665	8,000	1,000	9,000	7,000	16,000	1,400	5,000	22,400
October 1666	5,200	—	5,200	6,500	11,700	1,600	5,000	18,300
November 1667	5,000	400	5,400	9,500	14,900	1,800	5,000	21,700
August 1668	5,000	2,000	7,000	10,500	17,500	—	6,000	23,500
August 1669	6,000	2,000	8,000	10,000	18,000	—	4,000	22,000
September 1670	8,000	2,400	10,400	12,000	22,400	1,500	4,000	27,900
August 1671	11,000	4,400	15,400	11,000	26,400	—	6,000	32,400
September 1672	13,000	6,000	19,000	25,000	44,000	—	6,000	50,000
November 1673	7,500	2,000	9,500	16,000	25,500	—	9,500	35,000

TABLE 7.1 (Continued)

1	2	3	4	5	6	7	8	9
Orders dispatched in	Fine cotton muslins (pieces)	Fine cotton calicoes (pieces)	Total of fine cotton textiles (cols. 2+3) (pieces)	Ordinary cotton calicoes (pieces)	Total of cotton textiles (cols. 4+5) (pieces)	Silk piece goods (pieces)	Silk and cotton mixed piece goods (pieces)	Grand total (cols. 6+7+8) (pieces)
November 1674	7,000	6,000	13,000	24,000	37,000	9,000	–	46,000
September 1675	12,000	3,000	15,000	32,000	47,000	10,000	11,000	68,000
October 1676	14,700	4,500	19,200	45,200	64,400	10,000	10,000	84,400
October 1677	14,200	12,000	26,200	27,000	53,200	15,000	16,000	84,200
October 1678	14,000	5,000	19,000	26,900	45,900	15,000	8,000	68,900
November 1679	12,400	7,000	19,400	28,600	48,000	4,000	6,000	58,000
October 1680	15,000	8,000	23,000	18,600	41,600	8,000	1,000	50,600
November 1681	13,000	9,000	22,000	22,000	44,000	10,000	8,200	62,200
December 1682	10,000	11,000	21,000	16,500	37,500	5,000	8,200	50,700
December 1684	16,000	15,500	31,500	28,000	59,500	25,500	16,000	100,500
October 1685	11,500-13,500	11,000	22,500-24,500	27,500	50,000-52,000	19,100	14,500	83,600-85,600
October 1686	9,500	6,800	16,300	23,000	39,300	12,500	24,000	75,800
November 1687	11,000	6,800	17,800	24,000	41,800	28,500	25,000	95,300-95,800
November 1688	14,500	9,300	23,800	65,000-75,000	88,800-98,800	14,800	26,800	130,400-140,000

Date							
December 1689	14,000	2,800	16,800	59,000-69,000	75,800-85,800	28,000-28,100	15,500	118,800-128,900
December 1690	13,500-13,600	6,800	20,300-20,400	87,000	107,300-107,400	25,700-27,000	43,000	176,000-177,400
December 1691	17,500	18,000	35,500	116,000-122,000	157,500	39,000-39,300	48,000-49,000	238,500-245,800
December 1692	19,200-19,300	17,300-17,400	36,500-36,700	107,000-115,000	143,500-151,700	35,900-36,000	45,000-45,500	224,400-233,200
March 1694	23,500	20,800	44,300	59,000-67,000	103,300-111,300	36,700	45,000	185,000-193,000
March 1695	26,000	21,000-21,100	47,000-47,100	109,000-117,000	156,000-164,100	39,400-44,600	43,000	238,400-251,700
December 1695	28,000	16,800-16,900	44,800-44,900	100,000-118,000	154,800-162,900	32,100	49,000	235,900-244,000
March 1697	27,400	14,000	41,400	116,000-117,000	157,400-158,400	28,000-28,300	46,000-47,500	231,400-234,200
July 1698	30,400	13,000-14,000	43,400-44,400	127,000	170,400-171,400	33,400-33,700	49,200-50,300	253,000-255,400
March 1699	29,300-29,800	14,700	44,000-44,500	138,000-139,000	182,000-183,500	32,000-32,200	54,400	268,400-270,100
February 1700	35,300	12,700	48,000	127,000-128,000	175,000-176,000	39,500-39,700	58,500	273,000-274,200
February 1701	39,900-40,100	26,200	66,100-66,300	168,000-172,000	234,100-238,300	39,200-39,400	46,800-48,800	320,100-326,500
November 1701	39,300	35,300	74,600	170,000-171,000	244,600-245,600	39,900	39,600-40,100	324,100-325,600

TABLE 7.1 (Continued)

1	2	3	4	5	6	7	8	9
Orders dispatched in	Fine cotton muslins (pieces)	Fine cotton calicoes (pieces)	Total of fine cotton textiles (cols. 2+3) (pieces)	Ordinary cotton calicoes (pieces)	Total of cotton textiles (cols. 4+5) (pieces)	Silk piece goods (pieces)	Silk and cotton mixed piece goods (pieces)	Grand total (cols. 6+7+8) (pieces)
March 1703	37,900	29,500-30,500	67,400-68,400	167,000-170,000	234,400-238,400	41,800	42,000-42,500	318,200-322,700
March 1704	36,700	25,000	61,700	172,000-177,000	233,700-238,700	38,900	28,600-29,100	301,200-306,700
March 1705	37,200-39,200	27,000	64,200-66,200	167,500-170,500	231,700-236,700	41,000-41,200	28,100	300,800-306,000
March 1706	45,200	29,000	74,200	168,500-171,500	242,700-245,700	39,200-39,400	18,500	300,400-303,600
February 1707	45,700	27,900-29,900	73,600-75,600	168,500-172,000	242,100-247,600	37,200	19,500	298,800-304,300
February 1708	49,000	29,900-31,900	78,900-80,900	152,000-155,000	230,900-235,900	37,200-37,500	19,000-20,200	287,100-293,600
April 1709	49,400	30,100-32,100	79,500-81,500	159,000-164,000	238,500-245,500	31,900-32,200	19,000-20,200	289,400-297,900
March 1710	47,400-47,900	31,600-33,700	79,000-81,600	170,000-173,000	249,000-254,600	29,400-32,800	19,200-20,500	297,600-307,900
March 1711	47,300-47,900	30,100-32,100	77,400-80,000	158,000-162,000	235,400-242,000	29,900-32,900	16,500-17,700	281,800-292,600

March	1712	46,900-47,000	31,900-34,000	78,800-81,000	154,000-160,000	232,800-241,000	24,800-27,000	10,500-10,800	268,100-278,800
March	1713	47,200-47,300	30,900-32,900	78,100-80,200	156,000	234,100-236,200	24,800-27,000	8,500-9,000	267,400-272,200
March	1714	N.A.	N.A.	N.A.	N.A.	219,100-221,200	19,200-21,400	9,500-11,000	247,800-252,600
March	1715	N.A.	N.A.	N.A.	N.A.	245,400-250,600	26,200-28,300	10,600-10,800	282,200-289,700
March	1716	N.A.	N.A.	N.A.	N.A.	245,400-250,600	27,300-29,300	10,600-10,800	283,300-290,700

Source: Annual orders lists sent by the Board of Directors in Amsterdam to the Governor-General and Council at Batavia, K.A. 250-265.

Note: For the constituent varieties of the five groups of textiles, see Table 5.3.

TABLE 7.2
Bengal Textiles Exported to Holland, 1665-1718

1	2	3	4	5	6	7	8	9
Year	Fine cotton muslins (pieces)	Fine cotton calicoes (pieces)	Total of fine cotton textiles (cols. 2+3) (pieces)	Ordinary cotton calicoes (pieces)	Total of cotton textiles (cols. 4+5) (pieces)	Silk piece goods (pieces)	Silk and cotton mixed piece goods (pieces)	Grand total (cols. 6+7+8) (pieces)
1665-66	N.A.	N.A.	N.A.	N.A.	24,640	2,000	–	26,640
1666-67	N.A.	N.A.	N.A.	N.A.	12,680	1,900	–	14,580
1674-75	N.A.	N.A.	N.A.	N.A.	8,110	301	–	8,411
1675-76	N.A.	N.A.	N.A.	N.A.	14,153	1,177	3,600	18,930
1678-79	6,462	1,579	8,041	1,732	9,773	2,000	–	11,773
1679-80	7,839	12,096	19,935	9,857	29,810	5,661	9,100	44,553
1690-91	N.A.	N.A.	N.A.	N.A.	57,498	21,653	5,300	84,451
1691-92	N.A.	N.A.	N.A.	N.A.	76,084	19,830	10,814	106,728
1692-93	N.A.	N.A.	N.A.	N.A.	105,857	18,577	13,309	137,743
1693-94	N.A.	N.A.	N.A.	N.A.	126,393	35,068	23,589	185,050
1694-95	N.A.	N.A.	N.A.	N.A.	90,159	15,660	16,650	122,469
1698-99	N.A.	N.A.	N.A.	N.A.	205,412	24,549	18,900	248,861
1699-1700	28,220	23,045	51,265	36,003	87,268	15,778	16,848	119,894
1700-01	57,334	28,420	85,754	134,389	220,143	24,639	23,000	267,782
1701-02	N.A.	N.A.	N.A.	N.A.	119,920	22,395	32,160	174,475
1702-03	N.A.	N.A.	N.A.	N.A.	134,226	2,435	50,520	187,181

Year							
1703-04	10,950	9,160	20,110	62,857	82,967	1,700	23,600	108,267
1704-05	28,980	13,830	42,810	88,890	131,700	26,518	10,740	168,958
1705-06	30,490	16,100	46,590	67,680	114,270	12,650	15,600	142,520
1706-07	N.A.	N.A.	N.A.	N.A.	101,120	13,741	14,340	129,201
1707-08	25,860	18,180	44,040	74,288	118,328	23,070	16,300	157,698
1708-09	23,898	25,240	49,138	88,960	138,098	31,037	9,860	178,995
1709-10	46,428	27,065	73,493	169,755	243,248	14,503	19,040	276,791
1710-11	34,550	23,056	57,606	110,040	167,646	24,875	19,080	211,601
1711-12	31,492	14,072	45,567	95,803	141,370	24,432	17,300	183,102
1712-13	29,002	19,898	48,900	99,025	147,925	24,911	10,500	183,336
1713-14	48,445	26,060	74,505	61,569	136,074	21,668	10,214	167,956
1714-15	42,132	22,613	64,745	119,137	183,882	20,660	8,406	212,948
1715-16	38,155	26,705	64,860	129,729	194,589	25,220	8,550	228,359
1716-17	41,603	40,221	81,824	115,768	197,592	25,492	9,750	232,834
1717-18	44,166	40,574	84,740	131,505	216,245	23,580	11,288	251,113

Source: Invoices of goods exported from Bengal.

Notes: The constituent varieties of the five groups of textiles are as in Table 5.3. In the few cases where the amount of textiles exported is stated in terms of packets rather than pieces, the rate of conversion adopted is 1 packet = 100 pieces. This is the rate in practically all invoices that specify the quantities in terms of both pieces and packets. A few invoices contain bland categories such as "textiles" or "Malda piece goods," etc. These have been distributed over the five groups *pro rata*. Information is not available for the years not included in the table.

at the time.[17] The gross profit on Bengal raw silk in 1658 was only 59 percent.[18] As a result, the amount of this raw silk ordered in August 1658 was only half of that ordered in November 1655, which was again only half the amount that had been asked for in January 1654 (Table 7.3). Fortunately for the Company, the war of succession for the Mughal throne broke out in 1657, and the land route between Kasimbazar and Agra became unsafe for commercial traffic. The resulting cessation of the procurement of raw silk by the Agra merchants led to a decline in the Kasimbazar price from Rs. 5.00 in 1656 to Rs. 3.25 per seer in 1657. The gross profit on the lot bought in 1657-1658 and sold in 1660, therefore, went up to 140 percent, followed by an increase in the orders to 80,000 ponds.[19] But once the war was over in 1659, the pressure of the pent-up demand of the Agra merchants, coupled with a decreased total output, forced the price up to Rs. 5.25-5.75 per seer in 1659-1660.[20] By about this time, the English had also begun to procure raw silk in Bengal, and, as in the case of textiles, did not hesitate to accept lots that had been rejected by the Dutch.

The substantial increase in the total European procurement also led to a decline in quality.[21] The raw silk supplied to the Company was often found to have been reeled from inferior grade cocoons, and the quality of reeling also left much to be desired; the Directors often complained that threads were running into each other. The silk reeling unit established within the precincts of the Company's factory at Kasimbazar was designed to solve this problem, but the degree of success was limited. Around this time, the demand in Holland was not very great, either. The average Amsterdam price of Asian silk in 1663-1664, for example, was only f. 6.65 per pond. The gross profit on Bengal silk during this year was only

[17] The conflicts specially mentioned by the Directors were the Swedish invasions of Poland (1655-1657) and Denmark (1657-1658). XVII.B. 16.4.1658, K.A. 456, ff. 28-29; B.H. 7.7.1659, K.A. 786, f. 440.

[18] H.XVII. 12.5.1659, K.A. 1119, f. 891.

[19] H.B. 10.3.1658, K.A. 1117, ff. 168vo; H.B. 27.10.1658, K.A. 1117, f. 183vo; H.B. 8.3.1662, K.A. 1130, ff. 487-488; H.XVII. 1.8.1662, K.A. 1129, f. 1232vo.

[20] H.B. 18.3.1660, K.A. 1123, f. 752. During the war of succession, a large number of mulberry fields had been transferred to rice. This process was, no doubt, reversed after the war was over. Yet even in 1661, the total output of raw silk was estimated at only two-thirds of the prewar level. Memorandum by outgoing Director van den Broecke for his successor, van Hyningen, dated February 14, 1664, K.A. 1137, ff. 438-443; H.XVII. 13.8.1661, K.A. 1124, f. 537vo.

[21] P.B. 10.3.1655, K.A. 1100, ff. 381vo-383; P.B. 16.11.1655, K.A. 1102, ff. 191vo-192vo. Between 1652-1653 and 1661-1662, the total amount of raw silk exported by the Dutch from Bengal increased from 132,000 ponds to 388,000 ponds (export invoices). Practically all orders lists from 1661 on contained complaints about the quality of the raw silk received from Bengal.

196

TABLE 7.3
Bengal Raw Silk Ordered from Holland, 1636-1716

Orders dispatched in	Tanna-banna (Dutch ponds)	Tanny (Dutch ponds)	Total (Dutch ponds)
September 1636	2,440-3,660	–	2,440-3,660
September 1637	N.A.	N.A.	N.A.
September 1638	2,440-3,660	–	2,440-3,660
September 1639	2,440-3,660	–	2,440-3,660
September 1640	2,440-3,660	–	2,440-3,660
September 1641	3,660-4,880	–	3,660-4,880
September 1642	10,000	–	10,000
August 1643	20,000-30,000	–	20,000-30,000
September 1644	10,000	–	10,000
September 1645	20,000-25,000	–	20,000-25,000
August 1646	15,000	–	15,000
November 1647	20,000	–	20,000
September 1648	20,000	–	20,000
September 1649	40,000-50,000	–	40,000-50,000
September 1650	50,000	–	50,000
September 1651	50,000	–	50,000
September 1652	80,000	–	80,000
January 1654	200,000	–	200,000
November 1655	100,000	–	100,000
October 1656	80,000	–	80,000
October 1657	80,000	–	80,000
August 1658	50,000	–	50,000
September 1659	60,000	–	60,000
August 1660	80,000	–	80,000
September 1661	50,000-60,000	–	50,000-60,000
September 1662	50,000	–	50,000
August 1663	70,000	–	70,000
October 1664	50,000-55,000	–	50,000-55,000
November 1665	40,000	–	40,000
October 1666	50,000	–	50,000
November 1667	50,000	–	50,000
August 1668	80,000	–	80,000
August 1669	80,000	–	80,000

TABLE 7.3 (Continued)

Orders dispatched in	Tanna-banna (Dutch ponds)	Tanny (Dutch ponds)	Total (Dutch ponds)
September 1670	75,000-85,000	–	75,000-85,000
August 1671	75,000-85,000	–	75,000-85,000
September 1672	50,000	–	50,000
November 1673	43,000	–	43,000
November 1674	53,000	–	53,000
September 1675	86,000	–	86,000
October 1676	85,000	10,000	95,000
October 1677	65,000	10,000	75,000
October 1678	55,000	6,000	61,000
November 1679	N.A.	N.A.	80,000
October 1680	80,000	20,000	100,000
November 1681	N.A.	N.A.	80,000
December 1682	20,000	40,000	60,000
November 1683	N.A.	N.A.	60,000-80,000
December 1684	36,000	100,000	136,000
October 1685	12,000	100,000	112,000
October 1686	18,000	120,000	138,000
November 1687		120,000	120,000
November 1688	60,000-70,000	80,000	140,000-150,000
December 1689	70,000-80,000	100,000	170,000-180,000
December 1690	70,000-80,000	140,000	210,000-220,000
December 1691	70,000-80,000	140,000	210,000-220,000
December 1692	60,000	150,000	210,000
March 1694	50,000	180,000	230,000
March 1695	50,000	170,000	220,000
December 1695	50,000	130,000	180,000
March 1697	60,000	140,000	200,000
July 1698	60,000	180,000	240,000
March 1699	60,000	180,000	240,000
February 1700	50,000	205,000	255,000
February 1701	70,000	220,000	290,000
November 1701	60,000	220,000	280,000
March 1703	40,000	200,000	240,000

TABLE 7.3 (Continued)

Orders dispatched in		Tanna-banna (Dutch ponds)	Tanny (Dutch ponds)	Total (Dutch ponds)
March	1704	32,000	200,000	232,000
March	1705	45,000	200,000	245,000
March	1706	30,000	200,000	230,000
February	1707	23,000-24,000	150,000	173,000-174,000
February	1708	30,000	150,000	180,000
April	1709	24,000	120,000	144,000
April	1710	24,000	134,000	158,000
March	1711	24,000	120,000	144,000
March	1712	22,000	120,000	142,000
March	1713	34,000	155,000	189,000
March	1714	35,000	155,000	190,000
March	1715	46,000	175,000	221,000
March	1716	35,000	190,000	225,000

Source: Annual orders lists sent by the Board of Directors in Amsterdam to the Governor-General and Council at Batavia, K.A. 250-265.

95 percent. The amount asked for was, therefore, progressively reduced, the trough being reached in 1665 with orders for only 40,000 ponds. Things improved a little later, with the average Amsterdam price going up to f. 7.84 per pond in 1666-1667. The gross profit on Bengal silk was now 136 percent, and the orders for Bengal silk again went up to 80,000 ponds in 1668.[22] This, however, was only a short-lived phenomenon, and in 1671 the Directors again complained about a poor market. The all-time low was reached in 1672-1673, when the price came down to f. 5.23 per pond. The situation improved somewhat later in the decade.[23] But right until the close of the 1670s, the Asian raw silk that dominated the Dutch market was still that from Persia.[24]

The years under discussion also witnessed the beginning of the trade in

[22] H.XVII. 18.8.1665, K.A. 1142, ff. 1162-1164; H.B. 7.4.1668, K.A. 1158, f. 908vo.

[23] In 1671, the gross profit on the *bariga* variety of Bengal *tanna-banna* silk was reported to be 88 percent; on the *cabessa* variety it was only 45 percent. XVII.B. 29.8.1671, K.A. 457 (not foliated); K.A. 10234 (not foliated); H.B. 31.5.1675, K.A. 1202, f. 100vo; H.B. 17.3.1676, K.A. 1209, f. 534vo; XVII.B. 31.8.1678, K.A. 458 (not foliated).

[24] In 1676-1677, for example, against 81,501 ponds of Persian silk sold in Amsterdam, the amount of Bengal silk sold was only 14,227 ponds. The amount of Chinese silk sold appears to have been even smaller (K.A. 10234, not foliated).

mochta silk (florette yarn) (Table 7.4). The gross profit on this variety was reported to be 108 percent in 1663-1664 and 139 percent three years later.[25]

In the case of saltpetre, the Amsterdam price tended to decline after the conclusion of the First Anglo-Dutch War in 1654. But since salpetre was one of the principal ballast items the Company procured in Asia, the amount ordered was not only maintained at the former level but was increased in 1658 to 2 million ponds, leading to a commensurate rise in the amount exported from Bengal (Table 7.5). The Second Anglo-Dutch War (1665-1667) led to a rise in the Amsterdam price to *f.* 46 per 100 ponds, and the following year the gross profit was reported to be 659 percent. In order to be able to exert a greater influence on the sale price, the Directors declared in 1667 their intention to build up large stocks of saltpetre. In 1669, therefore, the orders were increased to 3 million ponds, even though after the war with England was over, the price had again declined and the gross profit had fallen to 313 percent. The Bihar famine of 1670-1672 led to a sharp reduction in the actual exports during these and the following few years. In 1676, the orders were redefined in terms of the amount required to ballast the homebound ships, which around this time was stated to be between 2.5 and 3 million ponds.[26]

The total value of the goods exported from Bengal for Holland in 1675-1676—the last year for which detailed information is available during the period 1636–1678—was over a little over *f.* 318,000. This constituted about 9 percent of the total Asian cargo exported to Holland that year which reached its destination the following year. A little over 56 percent of the total value of the Bengal cargo for Holland consisted of textiles and raw silk (41.6 percent for textiles and 14.6 percent for raw silk), 38 percent of saltpetre, and the remaining 6 percent of miscellaneous goods such as borax and sea shells. The share of Bengal textiles and raw silk in the total export of these items from Asia by the Company was 13 percent; the proportion in the case of saltpetre was as high as 68 percent.[27]

---

[25] H.XVII. 18.8.1665, K.A. 1142, ff. 1162-1164; H.B. 7.4.1668, K.A. 1158, f. 908vo.

[26] H.B. 7.4. 1668, K.A. 1158, f. 908vo; XVII.B. 20.11.1667, K.A. 457 (not foliated); XVII.B. 26.4.1668, K.A. 457; XVII.B. 25.8.1669, K.A. 457 (not foliated); H.B. 6.1.1672, K.A. 1178, f. 4vo; H.B. 28.2.1672, K.A. 1178, f. 20; H.B. 26.11.1683, K.A. 1329, ff. 2365-vo.

[27] Information regarding the total value of the imports into Holland has been taken from Reus, *Niederländisch-Ostindischen Compagnie*, Appendix V. The proportion that particular Bengal goods formed of the total of those goods exported to Holland has been worked out on the basis of Glamann's data. According to him, "textiles, silk, cotton, etc." accounted for 36.46 percent and 54.73 percent, and saltpetre 5.08 percent and 3.92 percent of the total value of the cargo sent to Holland in 1668-1670 and 1698-1700, respectively (*Dutch-Asiatic Trade*, Table I, p. 13). Since our data relate to 1675-1676, the share of "silk and

The Phase of Growth: 1679-1720

The close of the 1670s marked the beginning of a major shift in the role of Bengal in the structure of Dutch trade in Asia. Over the four decades that followed, Bengal trade derived its significance mainly from the role it played in the Company's Euro-Asian rather than its intra-Asian trade, as had hitherto been the case. This was the result partly of stagnation in the Dutch intra-Asian trade during this period. The Euro-Asian trade, on the other hand, was not only growing steadily but was marked by a structural change in the composition of the exports to Holland, with goods procured in Bengal, among other places, accounting for a growing proportion of the total. The share of pepper and other spices in the total export bill declined from 68 percent in 1648-1650 to 43 percent by 1668-1670 and to 23 percent by the close of the century. The dominant group in the new structure of exports was "textiles and raw silk," whose share in the total over the same period increased from 14 to 36 percent and then to 55 percent.[28] This was the result of an almost revolutionary change in European fashions during the last quarter of the seventeenth century. Indian muslins and calicoes now became extremely popular all over Europe for both male and female dress. In 1681, for example, an English politician, Pollexfen, declared, "As ill weeds grow apace, so these manufactured goods from India met with such a kind reception that from the greatest gallants to the meanest Cook Maids, nothing was thought so fit to adorn their persons as the Fabrick from India."[29] By virtue of their relative cheapness, Indian white cotton fabrics also increasingly replaced Flemish and German

textiles" and saltpetre in the total has been assumed to be 40 percent and 5 percent, respectively. It may be noted here that the fact that Bengal saltpetre constituted only 68 percent of the cargo sent to Holland in 1675-1676 does not *necessarily* mean that any significant quantities of saltpetre were procured in any other part of Asia. In this particular year, the amount received from Bengal may well have been supplemented by stocks built from amounts received in the previous years.

[28] Glamann, *Dutch-Asiatic Trade*, Table I, p. 13. The figures have been rounded. The group also included cotton, but the volume of trade in it was so small that for all practical purposes it may be ignored.

[29] From a speech before the Board of Trade, Commonwealth Relations Office Library Tracts, Vol. 83, p. 50 (quoted in Irwin and Schwartz, *Indo-European Textile History*, p. 13). A similar story was told by an English merchant, John Cary: "It was Scarce thought about twenty Years since that we should ever see *Calicoes*, the Ornaments of our greatest Gallants (for such they are, whether we call them *Muslins*, *Shades*, or any thing else) when they were then rarely used . . . but now few think themselves well drest till they are made up in *Calicoes* both Men and Women, *Calicoe Shirts*, *Neckcloths*, *Cuffs*, *Pocket-Hankerchiefs*, for the former, *Head-Dresses*, *Night-royls*, *Hoods*, *Sleeves*, *Aprons*, *Gowns*, *Petticoats* and what not for the latter, besides *India-Stockings* for both Sexes." John Cary, *A Discourse Concerning the East India Trade* (London, 1699), pp. 4-5.

TABLE 7.4
Bengal *Mochta* Silk (Florette Yarn) Exported to Holland,
1672-1718

Year	Quantity ordered (Dutch ponds)	Quantity exported (Dutch ponds)
1672-73	10,000	N.A.
1673-74	N.A.	N.A.
1674-75	N.A.	N.A.
1675-76	10,000	17,906
1676-77	10,000	N.A.
1677-78	30,000	N.A.
1678-79	30,000	17,451
1679-80	15,000	21,548
1680-81	12,000	N.A.
1681-82	10,000-12,000	N.A.
1682-83	12,000	N.A.
1683-84	25,000	N.A.
1684-85	25,000	N.A.
1685-86	N.A.	N.A.
1686-87	18,000-20,000	N.A.
1687-88	25,000	N.A.
1688-89	25,000	N.A.
1689-90	30,000	N.A.
1690-91	30,000	18,967
1691-92	30,000	26,101
1692-93	30,000	26,708
1693-94	30,000	41,276
1694-95	30,000	12,443
1695-96	30,000	N.A.
1696-97	30,000	N.A.
1697-98	30,000	N.A.
1698-99	30,000	24,280
1699-1700	30,000	5,615
1700-01	30,000	27,618
1701-02	30,000	24,735
1702-03	50,000	–
1703-04	30,000	5,463
1704-05	30,000	35,840

TABLE 7.4 (Continued)

Year	Quantity ordered (Dutch ponds)	Quantity exported (Dutch ponds)
1705-06	30,000	25,698
1706-07	30,000	5,463
1707-08	30,000	3,446
1708-09	30,000	21,848
1709-10	30,000	30,348
1710-11	20,000	15,616
1711-12	20,000	24,777
1712-13	20,000	14,522
1713-14	20,000	21,089
1714-15	20,000	20,028
1715-16	20,000	20,323
1716-17	25,000	25,000
1717-18	24,000	24,006

Source: Quantity ordered: Annual orders lists sent by the Board of Directors in Amsterdam to the Governor-General and Council at Batavia, K.A. 250-265. Quantity exported· Invoices of goods exported from Bengal.

Note: The quantity ordered is based on the orders dispatched two years earlier. Thus the quantity ordered shown against 1672-1673 is based on the orders dispatched in September 1670.

linen for use in undergarments.[30] Traditional homemade woollen stuffs were abandoned on a large scale in favour of silks and finery. Eastern silk textiles were not as fine as those manufactured from the finest Italian and French raw silk, but they had the merit of being substantially cheaper and, therefore, within the reach of a much larger section of the community.

The invasion of Europe by textiles from the East caused a commotion among indigenous producers of linen, silk, and woollen textiles. In England, the manufacturers' opposition to the import of these textiles was sufficiently vocal to lead to the passage of a Parliamentary Act in 1700 prohibiting the import of "all wrought silks, Bengals and stuffs mixed with silk or herba, of the manufacture of Persia, China or the East Indies and all calicoes painted, dyed or printed or stained there."[31] But since this

[30] Slomann, *Bizarre Designs in Silks*, p. 100. Europe's own production of cotton textiles was negligible.

[31] Directors of the "New" English Company to Edward Littleton and Council in Bengal, March 15, 1700, L.B. 11, f. 173, and April 12, 1700, L.B. 11, f. 180; Directors of the

TABLE 7.5
Bengal Saltpetre Exported to Holland, 1653-1718

Year	Quantity ordered (Dutch ponds)	Quantity exported (Dutch ponds)
1653-54	N.A.	151,520
1654-55	N.A.	412,115
1656-57	N.A	613,267
1657-58	1,000,000	1,006,048
1658-59	1,200,000	1,168,364
1659-60	1,200,000-1,500,000	709,852
1660-61	2,000,000	1,799,203
1661-62	2,000,000	1,746,446
1662-63	1,600,000-1,800,000	2,096,780
1663-64	1,600,000-1,800,000	1,886,898
1664-65	1,600,000-1,700,000	1,358,232
1665-66	1,800,000-2,000,000	1,812,200
1666-67	2,600,000	2,628,880
1667-68	2,600,000	2,363,136
1668-69	2,600,000	3,691,440
1669-70	2,600,000	3,327,240
1670-71	2,600,000	1,835,320
1671-72	3,000,000	N.A.
1672-73	3,000,000	N.A.
1673-74	3,000,000	761,600
1674-75	3,000,000	2,925,420
1675-76	3,000,000	2,244,000
1676-77	3,000,000	2,611,200
1677-78	3,000,000	1,041,963
1678-79	Ballast requirement	4,408,304
1679-80	Ballast requirement	3,711,018
1680-81	Ballast requirement	3,824,760
1681-82	Ballast requirement	2,575,024
1682-83	Ballast requirement	2,288,200
1683-84	Ballast requirement	1,428,000
1684-85	Ballast requirement	N.A.
1685-86	N.A.	3,304,005
1686-87	Ballast requirement	2,433,040
1687-88	Ballast requirement	2,142,000

TABLE 7.5 (Continued)

Year	Quantity ordered (Dutch ponds)	Quantity exported (Dutch ponds)
1688-89	Ballast requirement	3,524,495
1689-90	Ballast requirement	1,693,450
1690-91	Ballast requirement	1,116,600
1691-92	3,000,000	3,197,250
1692-93	3,000,000	2,407,000
1693-94	3,000,000	2,583,900
1694-95	3,000,000	2,546,335
1695-96	3,000,000	N.A.
1696-97	3,000,000	4,038,250
1697-98	3,000,000	N.A.
1698-99	3,000,000	3,886,000
1699-1700	3,000,000	3,059,500
1700-01	3,000,000	3,289,680
1701-02	3,000,000	3,290,485
1702-03	3,000,000-3,500,000	1,838,215
1703-04	3,000,000-3,500,000	2,729,335
1704-05	3,000,000-3,500,000	3,466,515
1705-06	3,000,000-3,500,000	2,102,600
1706-07	3,000,000-3,500,000	2,563,165
1707-08	3,000,000-3,500,000	3,808,280
1708-09	3,000,000-3,500,000	3,622,245
1709-10	3,000,000-3,500,000	4,770,500
1710-11	3,000,000-3,500,000	4,640,000
1711-12	3,000,000-3,500,000	3,654,000
1712-13	3,000,000-3,500,000	1,967,070
1713-14	3,000,000-3,500,000	3,277,000
1714-15	3,000,000-3,500,000	4,697,800
1715-16	3,000,000-3,500,000	4,250,705
1716-17	3,000,000-3,500,000	2,929,000
1717-18	3,000,000-3,500,000	3,438,820

Source. Quantity ordered. Annual orders lists sent by the Board of Directors in Amsterdam to the Governor-General and Council at Batavia, K.A. 250-265. Quantity exported· Invoices of goods exported from Bengal.

Note: The quantity ordered is based on the orders dispatched two years earlier. Thus the quantity ordered shown against 1653-1654 is based on the orders dispatched in September 1651.

simply involved an increase in the import of white calicoes and muslins from India, which were then printed in England, another act was passed twenty years later altogether prohibiting the use or wear of printed calicoes in England. Of course, neither of the two acts affected in any way the reexport trade in Eastern textiles. The result was that an ever increasing proportion of these textiles imported by the English East India Company was reexported to, among other places, the various European markets, including Holland. Even though, over the late seventeenth and the early part of the eighteenth centuries, the quantity of Eastern textiles imported by the Dutch East India Company into Holland would probably have been about the same as that imported by the English East India Company into England, and even though Holland had a fairly well-developed linen and silk textile industry, the Dutch Company was not subjected at any stage to the type of restrictions its English counterpart had to operate under. As early as 1643, in the course of the discussions pertaining to the renewal of the charter of the Company, several manufacturers of silk textiles in Amsterdam had informed the States of Holland that as a result of the import of silk textiles from the East Indies, a number of their apprentices had been thrown out of work. These people had been forced to migrate to the southern Netherlands, Germany, or England. Alternatively, they had become soldiers in the service of the Dutch East India Company or had taken up jobs in the fleet to Greenland. They therefore petitioned the States for a total prohibition on the import of silk textiles by the Company. In January 1644, the States of Holland resolved to try and persuade the other provinces in the Union to have the States-General impose a limit of f. 60,000 on the annual import of silk manufactures by the Company. No steps were taken to put this resolution into effect, however, and the document renewing the Company's charter in June 1647 imposed no limit on the volume of its trade in silk or any other textiles.[32] The matter came up again at the time of the renewal of the charter in 1694-1695. At the request of the silk-textile manufacturers and merchants of their province, the representatives of Haarlem in the States-General declared their intention of not voting for the renewal unless a ban was imposed on the Company's imports of cotton textiles, silk textiles, and twisted silk. The Company was also to be required to import each year a certain minimum amount of raw silk. The objection to the import of cotton textiles was later withdrawn on the condition that the Company

---

"Old" Company to factors in Bengal, January 10, 1701, L.B. 10, f. 406, and March 5, 1702, L.B. 10, f. 538; S. Bhattacharya, *The East India Company and the Economy of Bengal from 1704 to 1740* (London, 1954), p. 158.

[32] Leonie van Nierop, "De Zijdenijverheid van Amsterdam, Historisch Geschetst," *Tijdschrift voor Geschiedenis*, 45 (1930), 171-172.

would be asked to import simultaneously as much cotton yarn as possible. Soon thereafter, when the Company pointed out that it no longer imported twisted silk anyway, the objection to the import of this variety of silk was also withdrawn. Regarding the ban on silk textiles and the obligatory import of raw silk, all that the representatives ulitmately achieved was the extraction of a promise from the Company that in future it would "consult" each year the Haarlem silk industry before placing orders for these two items with the Company's factors in the East.[33] The manufacturers' "advice" was not to be binding, and in 1740, a number of "leading manufacturers of gold-, silk-, wool-, and cotton stuffs" informed the States of Holland that the Company had in any case not bothered to carry out the promised consultations. They pointed out that whereas at the turn of the century, the Company used to import 220,000-240,000 ponds of raw silk per annum, the annual amount imported over the decade 1730-1739 was less than one-third of that figure. Replying to this charge, the Company pointed out that the number of silk piece goods imported had also fallen from 38,000 pieces in 1693 to 24,000 pieces in 1739, and that over the decade 1730-1739, the annual import of silk piece goods that directly competed with indigenous products had only been 3,800 pieces. The Company further submitted that even if it stopped importing Eastern textiles, they would still reach Holland because the 3 percent import duty introduced in 1725 was hardly likely to discourage the English and the other Europeans from reexporting these textiles to Holland. Consequently, once again nothing was done and the Company continued to be free to import whatever it wanted and in whatever quantities. In the ultimate analysis, the failure of the manufacturers' efforts can be ascribed partly to the strong position of the Company in national politics and partly to the half-heartedness and overall weakness of the manufacturers' opposition. It is significant that in 1694-1695 the powerful silk-textile manufacturers of Amsterdam refused to back up the Haarlem manufacturing interests. Again in 1740, the manufacturers from Amsterdam and Utrecht declined to sign the petition presented to the States of Holland. The attitude of the Amsterdam silk manufacturers can perhaps be rationalized in terms of the enormous competitive strength they had acquired by the close of the seventeenth century, when the import of the Eastern silk and other textiles became quantitatively significant.[34]

Although the Company procured limited quantities of Japanese and Chinese silk piece goods, the principal source for textiles of all types was the Indian subcontinent. And on the subcontinent, Bengal was the prin-

---

[33] Van Dam, *Beschrijvinge*, I, ii, 112-113; van Nierop, "Zijdenijverheid," 46 (1931), 51.
[34] Van Nierop, "Zijdenijverheid," 46 (1931), 51, 132-133.

cipal supplier of the varieties now most in demand, so that her relative role in the network of the Company's Euro-Asian trade grew rapidly. This role was further bolstered by a rise in the European demand for another of Bengal's major products, raw silk. An increase in the European consumption of silk textiles, among other varieties, led to an increased domestic production of these textiles, which involved an increase in the demand of raw silk, a part of which came from Asia. The practical cessation of supplies from Italy—by far the most important European producer of raw silk—and Turkey during the 1690s increased the dependence of the Dutch silk textile industry on Asian raw silk.[35] Until the 1670s, the Company procured most of the raw silk it imported into Europe in Persia, even though the gross profit on this was the lowest of the three Asian varieties. This apparently paradoxical situation was the result, on the one hand, of the necessity to divert the greater part of the Chinese and the Bengal varieties to Japan, and on the other, of the 1652 agreement with the Shah of Persia. Although the Company managed each year, no doubt with the connivance of state officials, to get away with buying a much smaller amount in Persia than it was officially obliged to, most of what was procured had to be brought to Holland because it could not be sold in Asia.

The situation changed radically during the last two decades of the seventeenth century and, as in the case of textiles, Bengal became the principal supplier of raw silk to Holland. Given the declining importance of the Japan trade, the bulk of the Bengal raw silk procured could now be sent to Holland. The same was true of Chinese raw silk, except that the lower cost of the Bengal variety made it preferable to the former. Moreover, the quality differential between Chinese and Bengal raw silk was considerably reduced by the introduction in Holland in 1680 of the *tanny* variety of Bengal silk, which was much superior in quality to the *tanna-banna* and only slightly more expensive.[36] The share of *tanny* in the total amount of Bengal raw silk ordered went up from a little over 20 percent in 1680 to 73.5 percent in 1684, when the total amount asked for was 136,000 ponds. In 1687, the orders were exclusively for *tanny* silk. As for Chinese raw silk, orders during the greater part of the 1680s fluctuated between 15,000 and 30,000 ponds. The sale price of this variety

[35] The supplies of Italian silk were interrupted due to Italy's involvement in the Nine Years' War, whereas those from Turkey were stopped by the French War.

[36] The Bengal factors had sent a sample of 25 bales (3,794 ponds) of *tanny* raw silk to Europe in 1669, the year in which it was first produced (H.XVII. 6.11.1671, K.A. 1169, f. 611vo). The Directors included this variety in their orders for the first time in 1676. The first consignment containing this variety left Bengal in 1679-1680, reaching Holland in 1680-1681.

came down from *f.* 12.6 per pond in 1684 to *f.* 3.9-4.2 in 1688.[37] The competition by Bengal *tanny* silk may have had a role in this, though no specific evidence is available in this regard. The orders for Chinese raw silk were reduced to 4,000-5,000 ponds in 1688, and no orders whatever were placed over the following two years. There was a short-lived boom in this silk between 1698 and 1703, with the amount ordered reaching a peak of 40,000 ponds in 1701. After 1703, Chinese raw silk ceased to be of any importance in the Euro-Asian trade of the Company.[38] The last two decades of the seventeenth century also witnessed a considerable decline in the total amount of Persian raw silk reaching Holland. The Shah of Persia and his merchants now realised that it was more profitable for them to sell their silk in the Levant rather than to the Dutch and, therefore, became even more lax in enforcing the 1652 agreement.[39] The Persian raw silk and the *bariga* variety of Bengal *tanna-banna* raw silk were close substitutes for specific uses. The orders for *bariga*, therefore, fluctuated wildly in accordance with the actual or expected receipts of the Persian raw silk. This partly explains the considerable fluctuations in orders for Bengal raw silk during this period.[40]

By the end of the seventeenth century, Bengal had indisputably become the most important supplier of textiles and raw silk to Holland. More than 50 percent of the textiles imported into Holland originated in Bengal; over the period 1679-1718, Bengal raw silk accounted for 83 percent of the total Asian raw silk sold in Amsterdam, the respective shares of the lots from Persia and China being 10 and 7 percent.[41] As far as saltpetre was concerned, practically all the supplies came from Bengal. As a result, Bengal came to have the distinction of being by far the most important Dutch factory in Asia, providing on an average approximately two-fifths of the total value of the cargo reaching Holland.

The Years of Steady Growth: 1679-1692

The orders list sent by the Directors in 1677 reflected the first major manifestation of the new pattern of demand for textiles in Europe. The

---

[37] Glamann, *Dutch-Asiatic Trade*, p. 128.

[38] Orders lists, November 1688-March 1704, K.A. 259-262; volumes not foliated.

[39] Glamann, *Dutch-Asiatic Trade*, p. 126.

[40] Thus although in 1689 the orders for *bariga* stood at the huge figure of 60,000-70,000 ponds (subject to the qualification that this amount was to be reduced by the amount of Persian silk, if any, that Batavia might send to Holland), they had come down to 10,000 ponds in 1692. This had followed the reduction in its sale price from *f.* 6 per pond to *f.* 4.5 per pond following the unexpected receipt of a large amount of Persian silk. Orders lists, December 1689-December 1692, K.A. 259-260; volumes not foliated.

[41] In physical terms, the corresponding figures were 78, 15 and 7 percent, respectively. These are rounded figures and have been calculated from K.A. 10236-10241.

orders for fine calicoes, silk, and mixed piece goods were substantially increased whereas those for ordinary calicoes—procured mainly in Coromandel—were reduced.[42] The result was a sharp kink in the export curve in 1679-1680, though given the general shortages, the actual supplies bore little relation to the amounts ordered except in the case of the fine calicoes. The gross profit on Bengal muslins was reported to be substantially higher in 1682 than it was in 1679.[43] Initially, the greater part of the increased demand for muslins and fine calicoes for use as wearing apparel came from the well-to-do sections of the community, so that the Directors asked almost exclusively for the more expensive varieties of these textiles.[44] With the spread of the fashion among consumers who were not so well off, however, it became profitable from the early 1690s on to import comparatively less fine qualities of these textiles as well, which in fact often afforded a higher gross profit.[45] In the procurement of textiles, the Company continued to face a growing competition from the English Company until about 1685, when the English trade was rudely interrupted by the outbreak of hostilities between the English Company and the Mughal authorities.

The increased European demand for Asian raw silk was reflected in a rise in the total amount sold in Amsterdam from 93,000 ponds in 1679-1680 to 117,000 ponds in 1680-1681.[46] Even more striking was the rise in the share of Bengal silk from 23 percent to 40 percent, though Persian silk still sold more. The orders were, therefore, increased in 1680 to 100,000 ponds of Bengal and 15,000 ponds of Chinese raw silk.[47] The following few years were marked by severe fluctuations, but by 1684-1685, the total Amsterdam sales had gone up to 125,000 ponds, with Bengal raw silk accounting for a little over two-thirds of the total (a little over three-fourths in terms of value), the remainder being all Persian silk, as no Chinese silk was sold that year. In 1691, Bengal raw silk accounted

---

[42] Orders list, October 1677, K.A. 257; volume not foliated.

[43] The respective percentage figures for 1682 and 1679 were: 165 and 131 for Dacca *khasas*, 219 and 183 for Malda *khasas*, 160 and 133 for Dacca *malmals*, and 249 and 173 for Malda *malmals*. H.B. 9.4.1681, K.A. 1258, ff. 1277vo; B.H. 17.6.1681, K.A. 809, ff. 251-252; B.H. 26.8.1683, K.A. 812, f. 1372; H.B. 11.1.1684, K.A. 1273, f. 417vo.

[44] All orders lists from November 1679 to December 1689 specifically recommended the procurement of only the more expensive varieties of muslins and calicoes. K.A. 257-259; the volumes are not foliated.

[45] Orders lists, December 1690 and December 1691. K.A. 259-260; volumes not foliated.

[46] K.A. 10236; volume not foliated. The figures have been rounded to the nearest thousand. On an average, the amount sold in Amsterdam represented about 50 percent of the total sold in the six chambers put together.

[47] Raw silk was sold only in the autumn sale, so that the sale of 1680-1681 had been completed before fresh orders were dispatched in October 1680. As far as Persian raw silk was concerned, the practice since 1668 had been to instruct Batavia to send to Europe only the amount that they could not absorb within Asia.

for 95 percent of the total amount sold in Amsterdam, with the result that orders for this variety were increased to 210,000-220,000 ponds. Over the years 1679-1692 as a whole, the average share of Bengal, Persian, and Chinese raw silk in the total turnover at Amsterdam was 64, 28 and 8 percent respectively; the corresponding figures in terms of value were 70, 20, and 10 percent.[48] It is remarkable that notwithstanding the phenomenal rise in the amount of raw silk ordered from Bengal during this period, the actual supplies not only kept pace with but in certain years even exceeded the orders. This seems to have been due in part to the homogeneity of the product, unlike textiles for which specific requirements of length, width, and design somewhat slowed the process of adjusting the output to the growing demand. Of course, the large supplies brought on a fall in the Amsterdam price and gross profit.[49] The slight improvement in price late in the 1680s and the early 1690s might have been associated with the temporary cessation of the reexport from London to Holland of Bengal raw silk, following the English troubles with the Mughal authorities.[50]

The reexport of saltpetre by the English Company to Holland resulted in a decline in the Amsterdam price of this commodity to f. 18 per 100 ponds in 1682-1683 and 1683-1684. The temporary suspension of English trade in Bengal was, therefore, a boon reflected in a rise in the price to f. 33 per 100 ponds in 1689-1690. The considerable increase in the Dutch export of saltpetre from Bengal from 1678-1679 onward was the result of Batavia's efforts to build up large stocks. By the late 1680s, however, the stocks were so large that the Governor-General and Council found it necessary to instruct Bengal to reduce supplies drastically. Hence the limited amounts exported in 1689-1690 and 1690-1691.

The Years of Rapid Growth: 1693-1720

The value of the trade between Bengal and Holland grew at an unprecedentedly rapid rate during the last decade of the seventeenth and the first two decades of the eighteenth centuries. The average annual value of the exports from Bengal to Holland between 1693-1694 and 1720-1721

[48] K.A. 10236-10238; volumes not foliated.

[49] Between 1678-1679 and 1685-1686, the average Amsterdam price of Bengal raw silk registered a decline from f. 6.46 per pond to f 5.54 per pond (K.A. 10236-10237; volumes not foliated). Between 1680 and 1684, the gross profit on the *cabessa* variety of Bengal *tannabanna* raw silk came down from 118 percent to 37 percent. The corresponding figures in the case of the *banga* variety were 236 percent and 52 percent. The *tanny* silk was reported to be doing better, but the precise gross profit figures for this variety are not available (B.H. 17.6.1681, K.A. 809, f. 238; XVII.B. 24.6.1684, K.A. 459, f. 169).

[50] In 1684, the Directors had written that fair quantities of Bengal raw silk were being reexported by the English to Holland (XVII.B. 24.6.1684, K.A. 459, f. 169).

was *f.* 2.49 million.[51] This is to be contrasted with the figure of *f.* 0.36 million between 1665-1666 and 1675-1676.[52] The growth in the average annual value of the total Dutch exports from Bengal to all regions was from *f.* 2 million between 1679-1680 and 1692-1693 to *f.* 3.24 million between 1693-1694 and 1720-1721. In the exports during the latter period, the average share of the goods destined for Europe was as high as 72.5 percent.[53] As for the total Dutch exports from Asia to Holland, the growth in the average annual value over the same two time periods was from *f.* 4.20 million to *f.* 5.94 million.[54] Bengal goods accounted, on an average, for 39.65 percent of the cargoes sent to Europe during the latter period.[55] There can be little doubt that exports from no other single region in Asia would have approached this figure.

There was a substantial expansion in the export of Bengal textiles to Europe during this period. On an average, in terms of value, Bengal now supplied more textiles to Holland than the rest of Asia put together. Out of textiles worth *f.* 2.35 million that reached Holland in 1697, for example, those originating in Bengal accounted for as much as 55 percent, the remainder having been procured on the Coromandel coast, Tuticorin, Gujarat, Tonkin, China, and Japan.[56] A remarkable feature of this period was the emergence of Bengal as a major supplier of ordinary calicoes also to Europe. This was partly the result of the increasing shortage and rising costs in Coromandel, which was an important centre for the production of similar textiles.[57]

[51] This figure is based on information available for 17 out of 28 years covered by this period (see Table 3.5).

[52] This is the only earlier period for which comparable information is available. Even for this period, information is available only for four out of eleven years. The average figure is based on information for these four years (see Table 3.5).

[53] Whereas the figure for the period 1679-1680 to 1692-1693 is based on information available for all fourteen years, that for the period 1693-1694 to 1720-1721 is based on information available for twenty out of the twenty-eight years (see Table 3.3). Of the twenty-eight years in the later period, information for the value of both total exports from Bengal and exports to Europe is available for seventeen years (see Table 3.5). For these seventeen years, the average annual value of the total exports from Bengal was *f.* 3.44 million.

[54] These figures are based on Reus, *Niederländisch-Ostindischen Compagnie*, Appendix V. It has been assumed that the goods recorded as having arrived in Holland during 1681, for example, had left the East Indies during 1679-1680.

[55] This figure is based on information available for twenty out of the twenty-eight years covered by this period. The upper and the lower bounds were 57.78 percent in 1693-1694 and 23.08 percent in 1703-1704.

[56] The respective shares of the various regions were: Bengal 55.13 percent, Coromandel coast 26.64 percent, Tuticorin 4.29 percent, Gujarat 1.85 percent, and Tonkin, China, and Japan together 12.05 percent (calculated from Glamann, *Dutch-Asiatic Trade*, p. 144).

[57] The Directors specifically noted this fact in the orders lists of March 1694 and March 1697 (K.A. 260 and 261). Bengal ordinary calicoes, on an average, did very well in Holland during this period. In 1697 and 1698, Patna *chintz*, for example, was reported to be in good

The expansion in the volume of textile trade during this period was accompanied by a variety of problems including a gap, at times quite wide, between the amounts of particular varieties of textiles ordered and the actual amounts received and also a rising cost price for many of the varieties. In the case of some of these varieties, there was also a marginal deterioration in quality. The latter was reflected in the prices fetched in Amsterdam.[58] The changing profitability of different varieties of textiles was reflected in a modification in the mix of varieties ordered for the following season. The other reaction to a falling rate of profit on particular varieties of textiles was a censure by the Directors of the Bengal factors for alleged carelessness in the procurement.[59] In 1713, the Directors went to the extent of writing that if the continued rise in the cost of Bengal textiles was not arrested, they would have no alternative but to reduce the value of trade. In a letter to Batavia three years later, they reported that the Dutch textile merchants were getting increasingly worried about the rising cost of the Indian textiles. That the situation had indeed become serious was borne out by the fact that in 1716-1717, the average gross profit on Bengal textiles sold in Amsterdam was reported to be no higher than 34.5 percent.[60]

Some of these problems, particularly those related to the inadequacy of supplies, owed their origin to largely extraneous circumstances. The revolt by Zamindar Sobha Singh, which kept the province in a state of grave disorder for nearly two and a half years between the middle of 1695 and the close of 1697, is an example. The factories at Patna and Kasimbazar had to be temporarily abandoned, and were reopened only in December 1697 and March 1698, respectively. At the other factories, it was decided to cut the proportion of advances to the value of contracts given to the merchants to as little as 25 percent. Although this reduced the amount of money risked during a period of great uncertainty, the impact on the amounts procured was, predictably, disastrous. The varieties whose procurement particularly suffered were silk textiles procured in Kasimbazar, mixed *rumals* and striped *ginghams* procured in Radhanagar, and *fotas* and *sanus* procured mainly in Birbhum district.[61] The end of the revolt was

---

demand. In 1697, the gross profit on Bengal sailcloth was reported to be 200 percent (Orders lists, March 1697 and July 1698, K.A. 261; volume not foliated).

[58] Between 1698 and 1700, for example, the price of Bengal *khasas* declined from *f.* 35.5 to *f.* 29 per piece, of *malmals* from *f.* 46.25 to *f.* 30.37 per piece, of *tanzebs* from *f.* 56.75 to *f.* 37.06 per piece, and of *terrindams* from *f.* 58.12 to *f.* 47.50 per piece (K.A. 10228; volume not foliated).

[59] This was indeed done quite frequently; of the four orders lists sent between 1701 and 1704, three carried such a censure.

[60] Orders list, March 1713, K.A. 264 (volume not foliated); resolution of the Heeren XVII dated 9.3.1716, K.A. 198 (volume not foliated); B.H. 24.5.1718, K.A. 871, ff. 261-263.

[61] To cite a few cases, in 1697 the Bengal factors were not able to supply any mixed

reflected in a significant increase in the number of Bengal textiles exported to Batavia for Holland in 1698-1699.[62]

The Company's worries were, however, not altogether over. Prince Azim-us-Shan, the new *subahdar* who had been sent to Bengal to crush the revolt, was known to engage in a substantial amount of trade on his personal account, involving compulsory acquisition of goods from merchants and artisans at prices below the market.[63] Besides, the armed forces that had accompanied the prince stayed on in Bengal for some time. Some of the supplies of ordinary calicoes such as *garras* and *fotas* were diverted to use by the army at terms not sufficiently remunerative to the producers. Both these factors led to some disruption in production and availability, with obvious implications for the Company.[64] The extremely poor cotton crop in 1699 was yet another contributor to the shortage of ordinary calicoes, since cotton accounted for a substantial proportion of their total cost.[65]

The 1701 ban on the Company's trade, though only partially enforced, proved yet another obstacle, particularly in the procurement of varieties ordinarily purchased in Kasimbazar.[66] A temporary closure of the Kasimbazar and the Patna factories between 1704 and 1707 also affected the procurement adversely, even though the Company used the Hugli merchants to procure varieties ordinarily purchased at these factories.[67] The

---

rumals, striped *ginghams*, or *mobessabanys*. The orders for these three varieties were 5,000 pieces, 2,000 pieces and 400 pieces, respectively. Against orders for 5,000 pieces of *sanus*, the factors found it possible to supply only 2,930 pieces. The corresponding figures in the case of *fotas* were 8,000-10,000 pieces and 5,900 pieces. Bengal's explanation of why the orders were not supplied in full, 1697, K.A. 1484, ff. 42-47.

[62] It might be noted that the Bengal factors also cited the 1699 revolt by the *zamindar* of Radhanagar—where the Company procured mainly silk and mixed textiles—as a minor contributor to the shortages faced by the Company in these varieties that year. Bengal's explanation, 1699, K.A. 1516, ff. 58-87, II Section.

[63] Ibid., ff. 66-67. The prince's excesses reached a point at which the emperor was forced not only to administer a strong reprimand to him but also to reduce his *mansab* (rank) by 1,000 horses. Abdul Karim, *Murshid Quli Khan and His Times* (Dacca, 1963), p. 3.

[64] In 1699, the Bengal factors reported that in several *aurungs* all over the province, a number of looms had been lying deserted for many months. Against orders for 8,000 pieces of Handiaal *humhums*, the factors were able to supply only 2,400 pieces. The corresponding figures for *fotas* were 10,000 pieces and 5,100 pieces. In the case of sailcloth, the situation was even worse. Against orders for 14,800 pieces, the factors were able to supply only 1,200 pieces, allegedly because the greater part of the lot produced for the Company had been seized by state officials for use by the army. Bengal's explanation of why the orders were not supplied in full, 1699, K.A. 1516, ff. 61, 66-67, 70-71.

[65] As a result of the poor cotton crop, the price of imported Surat cotton was reported to have gone up from *f.* 13.5 to *f.* 30 per maund. Ibid., ff. 61-71.

[66] Ibid., 1702, K.A. 1556, ff. 184, 191, II Section.

[67] Against the annual requirement of 12,000 pieces of Patna *chintz*, the factors succeeded in procuring only 1,800 pieces in 1705 and none during the following two years. Similarly

procurement in 1712 was disrupted by the rumours of a possible war of succession following the death of Emperor Shah Alam.[68] The supply of ordinary calicoes was also adversly affected by several poor crops of cotton between 1711 and 1716.[69]

In addition to the factors discussed so far, each of which affected the procurement of textiles only during specified periods, there was the crucially important factor of the growing trade carried on in the region by the English East India Company. From the last decade of the seventeenth century onward, the rate of growth of the English trade had been remarkable. Indeed, the average annual exports to England during the decade of 1711-1720 were marginally higher than those by the Dutch Company to Holland, though in terms of the total exports from Bengal to all regions, the Dutch were still way ahead. Given that a higher proportion of English exports from Bengal to Europe consisted of textiles than in the case of the Dutch, it follows that the value of textiles procured by the English for Europe would have been larger than that of the Dutch.[70] This obviously led to cutthroat competition between the two companies for supplies of textiles, which generally increased at a rate somewhat slower than demand. Also, as pointed out earlier, the English displayed a much greater degree of flexibility in their dealings with the merchants than their Dutch counterparts were allowed to do by Batavia. In 1694, for example, the Dutch factors reported, "The English as a rule pay whatever price the weavers [merchants] ask for, so that we too have to pay a relatively high price, while the pieces supplied to us are not of the right quality. If we protest to the merchants about this, they flatly tell us that they are willing to take the goods back because they know that they can easily sell them to others."[71] An observation recorded three years later is even more re-

---

in 1706, the Company failed to procure any silk *rumals*, ordinarily purchased in Kasimbazar. Ibid., 1705, K.A. 1622, ff. 78-111, I Section; 1706, K.A. 1636, ff. 20-58, I Section; and 1707, K.A. 1653, ff. 127-180, I Section.

[68] Ibid., 1712, K.A. 1720, ff. 223-267, II Section.

[69] In 1711, for example, the factors were able to get only 11,217 pieces of sailcloth against contracts for 20,000 pieces. The corresponding figures for *garras* were 23,200 pieces and 35,000 pieces. Two years later, the price of cotton was reported to have gone up by 20-25 percent and a number of merchants simply refused to accept contracts for ordinary calicoes. In the case of *garras*, for example, against an order for 35,000 pieces, the factors were able to supply only 9,200 pieces. Ibid., 1711, K.A. 1720, ff. 168-224, I Section, and 1713, K.A. 1734, ff. 188-219, I Section; B.H. 13.7.1714, K.A. 864, ff. 652-653.

[70] Even though the value of the Bengal-Europe trade carried on by the two companies was roughly equal, the exports of both raw silk and saltpetre—the other two important commodities entering this trade—were much greater in the case of Dutch East India Company. For the Dutch figures of the export of these two commodities, see Tables 7.5 and 7.6. The figures for the English Company are available in K. N. Chaudhuri, *The Trading World of Asia and the English East India Company, 1660-1760* (Cambridge, 1978), Appendix 5.

[71] Bengal's explanation, 1694, K.A. 1435, f. 452.

vealing. According to the Dutch factors, the factors of the "New" English Company "not only accept whatever is offered to them but are also willing to offer prices so high that the merchants are surprised by their conduct in no small measure."[72] The English also displayed greater initiative in introducing new patterns and designs in the European market.[73] This gave them a substantial advantage over their Dutch rivals.

The response of the Dutch Company to the growing English competition was limited to taking such steps as minimizing the rejection rate among the textiles received from suppliers and ensuring that the factors did not have to forego potential supplies because of the shortage of liquid funds. It was in this context that in 1696 special instructions were issued by the Directors to Batavia that Bengal must be kept adequately provided with funds, even if that necessitated a cut in the usual remittances to other factories.[74]

Coming next to raw silk, we find that between 1693 and 1720, Bengal raw silk accounted, on an average, for as much as 88 percent of the total Asian raw silk sold in the Amsterdam market. In terms of value, this figure was 90 percent. The share of Persian raw silk was 6 percent in physical and 4 percent in value terms, whereas Chinese raw silk accounted for 6 percent of the total lot sold in terms of both quantity and value.[75] The Dutch silk textile industry had come to depend a great deal on Bengal for the supply of necessary raw material. The Amsterdam price of Bengal raw silk generally increased from 1693 onward, reaching an all-time peak of ƒ. 12.08 per pond in 1698. The orders for Bengal raw silk, therefore, continued to be at a fairly high level, culminating in a peak of 290,000 ponds in February 1701. But thereafter, the Directors' dissatisfaction with the quality of this silk led to a general reduction in orders. The trough was reached in February 1707, when the orders were for no more than 173,000-174,000 ponds.

[72] Ibid., 1697, K.A. 1484, ff. 46-47.

[73] As early as 1681, the English Court of Directors had written to their factors in Bengal: "Now this for a constant and generall Rule, that in all flowered silks you change ye fashion and flower as much as you can every yeare, for English Ladies and they say ye French and other Europeans will give twice as much for a new thing not seen in Europe before, though worse, than they will give for a better silk for [of] the same fashion worn ye former yeare." Later the same year, they had written: "Of all silk wares, take it for a certain rule that whatever is new, gaudy or unusual will always find a good price at our candle" (quoted in Slomann, *Bizarre Designs in Silks*, p. 114).

[74] See the resolution adopted by the Batavia Council on April 18, 1701, K.A. 616, f. 152. Both in 1693 and 1694 the Bengal factors had cited shortage of funds as one of the reasons why they were not able to supply the orders in full (Bengal's explanation, 1693, K.A. 1435, f. 252; and 1694, K.A. 1435, f. 452); Bengal section of the annual orders list dated November 15, 1696, K.A. 261; volume not foliated.

[75] Calculated from K.A. 10238-10242; volumes not foliated. The percentage figures have been rounded to the nearest integer.

216

The actual supplies from Bengal were rather erratic until about 1706-1707 (Table 7.6). First, there was the dislocation caused by the Sobha Singh revolt in the late 1690s. The Dutch silk textile industry immediately felt the impact of the resulting disruption in supplies. In July 1698, the Directors wrote: "The extremely limited amount of [Bengal raw] silk we received this year has caused very great inconvenience to the manufacturers here. Due to the shortage of raw silk, hundreds of looms are unemployed and the workmen are loitering about idle. In view of the fact that the current price of raw silk here is extremely high, you can well imagine how much we have lost because of the limited amounts received by us." A similar statement was made in 1701 about the Bengal *mochta* silk: "The small amount received has inconvenienced the producers so much that a number of manufacturing units had to stop production. The price of this variety has gone even beyond that of the best grade *tanny* silk."[76]

The reason behind the extremely poor export of raw silk in 1702-1703 and the limited amount in 1703-1704 was the ban imposed on Dutch trade in 1701, which was withdrawn only in November 1702. The ban was enforced much more vigorously in the silk emporium of Kasimbazar than it was in many other parts of the region.[77] The limited amounts exported in 1705-1706 and 1706-1707 were, however, at the instance of Batavia, who planned to supplement the supplies from Bengal with 1,400 bales (212,000 ponds) of raw silk seized from Indian ships recently captured off Surat.[78]

Competition from the English East India Company was of much smaller consequence in raw silk than in textiles. The English trade in this item was still quite limited, and much smaller than that of the Dutch.[79] But

---

[76] Orders list, July 1698, K.A. 261; February 1701, K.A. 262; volumes not foliated.

[77] The Company's efforts to procure raw silk clandestinely through Indian merchants were not particulary successful. In 1702, for example, a Kasimbazar merchant, Golal Chand, agreed to supply raw silk to the Company at Hugli against actual cost plus 9 percent, out of which he estimated that 6 percent would go as tolls and bribes to toll officials on the way. At the last moment, however, he backed out for fear of earning the wrath of the administration in case it was discovered that the silk he was carrying was intended for delivery to the Company (H.B. 30.9.1702, K.A. 1548, ff. 1234-1237).

[78] H.XVII. 4.11.1706, K.A. 1622, f. 43.

[79] The average annual export to Europe of Bengal raw silk by the English East India Company and by the Dutch is as follows:

Years	Exports by the English East India Company (in Dutch ponds)	Exports by the Dutch East India Company (in Dutch ponds)
1691-1700	49,034	182,620
1701-1710	31,321	128,239
1711-1720	51,106	175,656

TABLE 7.6
Bengal Raw Silk Exported to Holland, 1669-1718

Year	Tanna-banna (Dutch ponds)	Tanny (Dutch ponds)	Total (Dutch ponds)
1669-70	80,563	—	80,563
1678-79	128,077	—	128,077
1679-80	N.A.	N.A.	82,703
1690-91	N.A.	N.A.	121,096
1691-92	47,346	89,836	137,182
1692-93	22,307	149,018	171,326
1693-94	49,318	214,271	263,590
1694-95	N.A.	N.A.	109,260
1698-99	—	170,567	170,567
1699-1700	—	198,944	198,944
1700-01	—	227,473	227,473
1701-02	43,097	220,492	263,589
1702-03	2,124	—	2,124
1703-04	27,314	48,559	75,873
1704-05	20,820	164,769	185,589
1705-06	2,839	71,226	74,065
1706-07	5,294	69,507	74,801
1707-08	12,196	109,451	121,647
1708-09	28,535	132,843	161,378
1709-10	24,918	151,290	176,208
1710-11	21,138	125,976	147,114
1711-12	20,834	138,592	159,426
1712-13	18,699	93,609	112,308
1713-14	22,069	120,628	142,967
1714-15	34,154	155,085	189,239
1715-16	26,222	165,826	192,078
1716-17	45,774	175,022	220,796
1717-18	34,142	178,637	212,779

Source· Invoices of goods exported from Bengal.
Note· Information is not available for the years not included in the table.

even so, the English presence in the market helped convert it into a sellers' market. This became evident, for example, in 1699, when the Dutch factors tried to arrest deterioration in the quality of raw silk supplied by the merchants by declaring their intention of imposing a fine of *f*. 35 for each imperfectly reeled bale supplied by the merchants. The Company, however, succeeded in giving out fresh contracts only after the threatened innovation had been withdrawn.[80]

The low price of Bengal raw silk in the Amsterdam market in the early years of the eighteenth century continued to cause concern to the Directors. This was reflected in a general reduction in orders. It was only from 1715 onward that the orders again exceeded 200,000 ponds per annum. As for the actual supplies from 1707-1708 on, there was a remarkable correspondence with the orders—except in 1712-1713, due probably to the dislocation caused by the death of Emperor Shah Alam. It might also be noted here that the increase in the cost price of raw silk to Rs. 5.37 per seer in 1714 prompted the Company to have as much as possible of the raw silk it exported reeled in its own unit in the Kasimbazar factory. We have information regarding the place of reeling for 86 percent of the total raw silk exported by the Company from Bengal to all regions between 1714 and 1718. Of this, as much as 83.25 percent was reeled in the Company's own reelery.[81]

The period under review also witnessed a general expansion in the Company's export of saltpetre from Bengal. From 1701 onward, the annual orders were increased from 3 million ponds to 3-3.5 million ponds or the ballast requirements of the homebound ships, whichever was higher. The actual supplies from Bengal generally kept pace with the orders. Indeed, in keeping with Batavia's desire to build up stocks of saltpetre locally, the Bengal factors often supplied in excess of the orders. The effect of the 1692 ban on the procurement of saltpetre by the European companies was not particularly severe for the Dutch because of the availability of large stocks at Hugli.[82] However, the 1701 ban on Dutch trade and the tem-

---

The difference would be even more marked if one compared the total Dutch exports of raw silk from Bengal per annum with the English figure. The figures for the Dutch Company have been calculated from Table 7.6. Those for the English Company have been calculated with a two-year lag from Chaudhuri, *The Trading World of Asia*, Appendix 5, and converted into Dutch ponds at the rate of 1 Dutch pond = 1.09 pounds avoirdupois.

[80] H.XVII. 28.10.1699, K.A. 1516, ff. 14-15; Bengal's explanation 1699, K.A. 1516, f. 72.

[81] See Chapter 4.

[82] This ban had been imposed by a *hasb-ul-hukm* issued by Wazir Asad Khan. According to the information of the Dutch, the sultan of Turkey had written to Aurangzeb that the gunpowder used by the European powers in their wars against him was made partly from

porary closure of the Patna factory in 1703-1704 affected the volume of exports in 1702-1703 and 1705-1706, respectively.

From the point of view of the Directors, the disturbing element about the saltpetre imports from Bengal was the deterioration in the quality of the lots received.[83] The result was a decline in the gross profit on Bengal saltpetre from as much as 275 percent in 1701 to 102 percent in 1708. The Directors pointed out that if this continued, they would have to reduce the volume of trade in this item.[84] But given the fact that a certain amount of ballast cargo had to be carried in any case, and saltpetre was among the most profitable ballast items available to the Company, the threatened decline in the volume of trade never occurred.

By the close of the period covered by the present study, the Company's trade between Bengal and Holland had attained significant proportions. Indeed, Bengal now supplied more goods for Holland than any other Asian region. Also, the total value of the trade carried on by the Company in the region was still substantially larger than that of its main European rival—the English East India Company. But with respect to the trade between Bengal and Europe, the English Company had indeed become a source of great anxiety to the latter, at least in the matter of the procurement of textiles.

Indian saltpetre, and that the ban on the European companies' trade in this item would be highly appreciated by him. The ban was withdrawn in January 1694 (Patna to Hugli, 8.12.1692, K.A. 1397, ff. 183vo-184).

[83] In July 1698, for example, the Directors pointed out that against a previous average loss of 4 to 5 percent during the course of refining, the lots of *dobara* saltpetre received during the preceding few years had rendered a loss of as much as 12 to 16 percent. Practically all the orders lists from this time onward contained growing complaints regarding the quality of the Bengal saltpetre (Orders lists, July 1698-March 1716, K.A. 261-265).

[84] Orders list, March 1710, K.A. 264; volume not foliated.

· 8 ·

THE COMPANY AND THE ECONOMY

In the preceding chapters, we have outlined the crucial role of the Bengal trade in the Dutch Company's trading network within Asia as well as between Asia and Europe. Continued participation in this trade was obviously of great importance to the Company, and possibly to the national economy of Holland. But how important was the Company's trade (and by implication that of the other European companies and private European traders) for the economy of Bengal during our period? We have seen that within the overall framework of a predominantly agrarian society, the Bengal region was well known for the production of a significant volume of manufacturing output and an impressive involvement in trade—both internal and foreign. The nonavailability of precise data relating to such key elements as the sectoral origin of income and the industrial distribution of the work force, however, makes it impossible to assign definite values to the relative size of the three major sectors in the economy: agriculture, manufacturing, and services including trade. Since we do not know the precise size of the foreign trade sector, it is not possible to work out the relative importance of the Dutch Company's (and other European companies') trade in the sector. It is possible that even at the peak of the Company's trade in the region, when it dominated the region's trade along particular routes and in particular commodities, the overall volume and value of trade handled by the Company was not a very large part of the total trade from the region. Also, the value of the total trade from the region, though quite large in an absolute sense, may have constituted a relatively modest proportion of total economic activity. It is, therefore, important to analyse the role of the Company's trade in the economy of the region in the right perspective and make the necessary allowances for possible biases in the documentation.

It need hardly be stressed that the implications of the European trading companies' activities for the Asian societies they operated in went beyond the realm of economics. In some of these societies, such as parts of the Indonesian archipelago, the Dutch Company managed to assume territorial authority from the very beginning. In such cases, the Europeans' presence affected a variety of spheres—political, social, and religious—in addition to economic. But even in areas such as India where a colonial relationship with a European power did not emerge until after our period, the trading

221

activities of the companies had implications that were more than economic. Also, it was not only the littoral, where the companies largely
concentrated their activities, that was affected by their trade. In a variety
of ways, some of them indirect, the interior was also affected. Even the
Deccan, which had hardly any direct trade links with the Europeans, was
not immune to this process. One of the key elements in this was the
import of large quantities of precious metals by the companies. Richards,
for example, has argued that importing these metals contributed to the
expansion of the Mughal regime.[1] Indeed, the interdependence among
the various dimensions of company activity makes it difficult to fully isolate
the economic dimension from the rest. But for analytical convenience,
we will confine our discussion to the purely economic dimension. Even
within that, we will concentrate on the direct and clearly identifiable
implications of the Europeans' trade. Not taking into account the indirect
and the more obscure implications, however, is not to deny their existence
or importance.

DISPLACEMENT EFFECT OF THE COMPANY'S TRADE

Before one undertakes a systematic analysis of the implications of the
Dutch Company's trade for the economy of Bengal, it is necessary to know
whether it displaced trade by other agencies such as Indian and other
Asian merchants. If it were established that such was indeed the case,
then the volume of trade displaced by the Company would have to be
deducted from its own trade before one could work out its implications
for the economy. But if the Company's trade had no such displacement
effect, its own trade could be regarded as a net contribution to the region's
trade. This would be so even if the net addition to the region's trade over
a specified period of time was smaller than this amount because of a
simultaneous decline in the value of trade carried on by other agencies
for reasons not related to the trade of the Company. The implications for
the economy would, of course, be different in these two sets of
circumstances.

The displacement effect of the Company's trade can be analysed with
reference to each of the major branches of trade from Bengal that the
Company participated in. There can be little doubt that the Company's
trade between Bengal and Europe was for all practical purposes a net
addition to the total trade on this branch. In the period prior to the

---

[1] J. F. Richards, "Mughal State Finance and the Premodern World Economy," *Comparative Studies in Society and History*, 23 (1981), 285-308.

discovery of the all-sea route via the Cape of Good Hope, Bengal goods had figured only marginally in the Indian cargoes that reached Europe. Given Portuguese priorities and the structure of their trade, the situation did not change materially during the sixteenth century. Indeed, even after the arrival of the English and the Dutch East India companies on the scene in the early seventeenth century, the volume of Bengal-Europe trade continued to be small. It was only during the last quarter of the seventeenth century that Europe emerged as a major trading partner of Bengal.

The situation with regard to the possible displacement effect of the Company's trade along a number of branches within Asia is more complicated. In the Bengal-Japan branch, the Company's trade could hardly have had any displacement effect: there is no evidence suggesting direct commercial contacts between the two regions until the Dutch started the process. It is, of course, possible that some of the Bengal wares sold in the Indonesian archipelago had reached Japan through the Chinese or other merchants.[2] In that event, however, the displacement effect would have to be looked for in the trade with the archipelago and not Japan.

The displacement potential of the Company's trade from Bengal with the Indonesian archipelago, Ceylon, and Persia, where the Company competed with the Indian merchants, was quite substantial. One can use the shipping lists in the Dutch records to form a broad idea of the trends in the Indian merchants' coastal and overseas trade from the Bengal ports. Unfortunately, the information in these lists pertaining to the volume of cargo carried is largely unusable because a wide variety of units of measurement were used, and they cannot always be translated into a common unit. One has to rely, therefore, mainly on the number of vessels in operation to ascertain movements in trade. Since the average size and the mix of the Asian vessels engaged in trade from Bengal during this period did not undergo any great change, this procedure is unlikely to bias the results seriously. For this analysis we will ignore ships operated by the European companies, by the factors of these companies engaged in intra-Asian trade on their own, and by private European merchants. (Ships operated by the Armenian merchants will be included in the estimates, however.)

As argued earlier, Bengal's trade with Surat, the Persian Gulf, and the Red Sea was dominated by merchants based at Surat, while that with the

---

[2] See XVII.B. 8.10.1685, K.A. 459, ff. 277vo-278. Das Gupta has suggested that the "Gores" of Tome Pires who bought Bengal textiles at Malacca might have been Japanese or from islands near Japan (Ashin Das Gupta, "Indian Merchants and the Trade in the Indian Ocean," in Tapan Raychaudhuri and Irfan Habib, eds., *Cambridge Economic History of India*, I (Cambridge, 1982), 409.

Malabar and the Coromandel coasts was carried on predominantly by merchants based at the two respective coasts. The broad conclusion suggested by the number of vessels that left Hugli for these areas is that although there was no clearly discernible trend one way or the other in the trade with Surat, the Persian Gulf, the Red Sea, and the Malabar coast, the Coromandel trade was on the increase.[3] The picture is much clearer with regard to the branches of trade controlled by the merchants based in Bengal: Ceylon, the Maldive islands, and the eastward branch including Burma, Siam, Sumatra, the Malay peninsula, and the Philippines. The trade with Ceylon practically dried up and the eastward trade suffered a heavy decline, but the trade with the Maldives increased substantially.[4] The overall position in relation to all the branches of trade from Bengal taken together was, therefore, mixed, with no clear trend in many branches, a clear decline in trade along others, and an increase along two branches.

The displacement effect of the Dutch Company's operations on the trade carried on by the Indian merchants from the Bengal ports can perhaps best be studied in relation to a branch of trade that witnessed a significant decline and was an important branch of trade for both Indian merchants and the Company. One could then hope to capture the effects of the trade rivalry between the two parties. These requirements are met by the eastward trade from Bengal. In addition, this branch was dominated by merchants based in Bengal, thus providing a link between the movements in this trade and developments in the Bengal region.

The eastward trade from Bengal consisted of four sub-branches: the trade with Arakan and Pegu; the trade with Siam, with Tenasserim as the

---

[3] The analysis is confined to the port of Hugli because this port dominated the trade with these regions. The number of ships leaving this port for Surat fluctuated sharply from 5 in 1696-1697 to 15 in 1699-1700, 6 in 1704-1705, down to 1 in 1706-1707, as many as 12 in 1709-1710, 9 in 1711-1712, 5 each in 1712-1713 and 1713-1714, 3 in 1715-1716 and again 5 in 1717-1718. The shipments to Persia never exceeded one a year, whereas it was only in 1696-1697 and 1717-1718 that one ship each was sent to the port of Jedda in the Red Sea. A similar absence of a clear trend is suggested by the departures for Malabar, which numbered 2 in 1696-1697, 1 each in 1699-1700 and 1706-1707, 2 in 1711-1712, and 3 in 1713-1714. The figures for Coromandel are not unambiguous, but would generally seem to suggest an upward trend. Thus in the late 1690s, the number of departures from Hugli was 6 in 1696-1697 and 7 in 1699-1700. The fluctuations were more violent in the early years of the eighteenth century, but a figure of 31 was reached in 1712-1713 and of 20 in the following season. The numbers were 9 in 1715-1716 and 11 in 1717-1718 (Bengal shipping lists).

[4] The trade with Ceylon was conducted mainly from the port of Balasore. The departures from this port for Ceylon came down from an annual average of four in the early 1680s to zero from the late 1690s onward. The evidence for the movements in the eastward trade and the trade with the Maldive islands is discussed in detail later in this chapter.

principal port; the trade with Sumatra and the Malay peninsula, the ports in the area being Achin, Malacca, Perak, Junk-Ceylon, and Kedah; and the trade with Manila in the Philippines.[5] The eastward trade was carried on from both the Hugli and the Balasore ports, though the latter was considerably more important.

The evidence regarding movements in the trade from Bengal before 1671 has been drawn from the *Batavia Dagh-Registers* and from the correspondence between Hugli and Batavia, and thereafter from shipping lists. Prior to 1671 the evidence is fragmentary, and consists only of the number of ships operated or intended for operation along a given route in any particular year or part thereof. The information in the shipping lists of outgoing and incoming vessels at Balasore and Hugli is somewhat more detailed.[6] Similar lists are not available for the other two ports in

[5] The principal items of export to and import from the eastward region were as follows (arranged in a descending order of importance):

Area	Exports	Imports
Arakan and Pegu	textiles, rice, oil, butter, opium	specie, elephants, ivory, tin
Siam	textiles, rice, butter, opium	elephants, spelter, bell-metal
Sumatra and Malay peninsula	textiles, rice, opium, butter, saltpetre, raw silk	tin, gold, pepper, spelter, copper, bell-metal
Philippines	textiles, rice, butter	tin, ivory, copper

This information is based on the Bengal shipping lists and the correspondence between the Dutch factors at Hugli and Batavia.

[6] For the period 1671 to 1718, the available lists of Asian ships that left Balasore for various destinations and those that came into Balasore number thirteen each. For Hugli, the corresponding numbers are eighteen and twenty-two. Since not all these lists pertain to the same period of each sailing season, they are not always fully comparable with one another. Our interest lies primarily in establishing trends in the volume of the eastward trade from Bengal. An analysis of the available lists suggests that the bulk of the outward movement of ships from Balasore to the ports of interest took place between January and March, and that from Hugli between December and the following March. On this basis, we have selected the lists of outgoing vessels for the following seasons, which are broadly comparable:
  Balasore: 1680-1681 to 1683-1684, 1697-1698 to 1701-1702
  Hugli: 1696-1697, 1699-1700, 1704-1705, 1706-1707 to 1709-1710, 1711-1712 to 1713-1714, 1715-1716, 1717-1718
For purposes of illustration, however, two incomplete lists pertaining to vessels that left the port of Hugli in two seasons in the 1680s have also been used. As far as the incoming vessels are concerned, the construction of a comparable series of lists posed certain problems. For example, for the 1698 season, there are two lists of ships coming into Balasore covering the periods February 28, 1698 to August 20, 1698 and September 1, 1698 to February 20, 1699; the beginning and end dates of actual sailings were March 10, 1698 to August 18, 1698 and October 16, 1698 to December 4, 1698 respectively. The other lists available for Balasore pertain roughly to the period covered by the first of these two lists; none pertaining to October-December in other seasons is available. We have, therefore, ignored the list pertaining to October-December 1698. Based on the comparable lists for Balasore, our conclusion is that there was a distinct decline in the volume of Asian merchants' trade between

the Bengal region: Pipli in Orissa and Calcutta in Bengal. This should not significantly affect our broad conclusions, however. Pipli's port went out of operation around 1670, when the river on which it was situated silted up. The port of Calcutta began to be used only after the town was founded in 1690 and the English East India Company's chief factory in Bengal was transferred there. Calcutta does not seem to have been used by Asian merchants to any significant extent for trade between Bengal and Southeast Asia during our period.[7]

In the eastward trade from Bengal, the trade with Arakan-Pegu and the Philippines was comparatively insignificant. The trade with Tenasserim in Siam, on the other hand, was very important. It was reported in 1636 that the amount of textiles imported into Tenasserim that year by four Muslim ships—two of which had come from Bengal—was large enough to cause a glut in the local textile market. In 1642, the Dutch factors ascribed the poor sale of textiles by the Company in Siam to the large imports by Indian merchants from the Coromandel coast and Bengal. We find a similar suggestion made once again nearly twenty years later. In 1672, as many as twelve Indian vessels were reported to be getting ready at the port of Balasore for a voyage to Tenasserim.[8] But soon thereafter trade along this route seems to have declined rather rapidly. Thus, from the shipping lists, one finds that the number of Asian vessels that left Balasore for the port of Tenasserim was only four each in 1680-1681, 1681-1682 and 1682-1683. In the five seasons between 1697-1698 and 1701-1702 for which comparable information is available, not a single Asian ship left Balasore for Tenasserim. According to the list of ships that came

---

Balasore and Southeast Asia between the early 1680s and late 1690s. If this conclusion is to be negated by reference to the possible pattern of shipments in the months of October to December in each season, it would be necessary to presume a contrary and offsetting movement over these two decades in the volume of trade conducted during these months. Since the list for October-December 1698 contains no shipment from Southeast Asia, it appears reasonable to reject such a presumption. For our analysis, we have selected the lists of the incoming ships for the following seasons, which are broadly comparable:

Balasore: 1682, 1683, 1698 (first list only), 1699

Hugli: 1700-1702, 1704, 1706, 1708-1710, 1717, 1718

[7] The available evidence suggests that at the beginning of the eighteenth century, the port of Hugli was still the focal point of the trade from the province of Bengal (as distinct from the Bengal region, which included Bihar and Orissa). Thus Alexander Hamilton, who visited Bengal in 1705-1706, wrote of Hugli, "This Town of *Hughly* drives a great Trade, because all foreign Goods are brought thither for Import, and all Goods of the Product of *Bengal* are brought hither for Exportation. . . . It affords rich Cargoes for fifty or sixty Ships yearly, besides what is carried to neighbouring Countries in small Vessels." Alexander Hamilton, *A New Account of the East Indies*, edited by William Foster (London, 1930), II, 12.

[8] B.XVII. 28.12.1636, K.A. 1029, f. 186; *Batavia Dagh-Register*, 1642, p. 122; 1661, p. 364; H.B. 28.3.1672, K.A. 1178, f. 117.

into Balasore, the number from Tenasserim diminished from eight in 1682 to four in 1683 and one in 1699, the last year for which information is available.[9] Taking individual items of trade, one finds that the amount of tin imported by Asian merchants from Tenasserim into Balasore declined from 1,551 maunds in 1683 to 370 maunds in 1699. Copper imports declined from 1,135 maunds in 1682 to 325 maunds in 1699, whereas the number of elephants imported came down from 122 in 1682 to 10 in 1699.[10] As for the port of Hugli, the information in the shipping lists becomes available only from 1696-1697 onward. By that time the decline in this trade had perhaps already taken place.[11]

Another major eastern port of call for Asian ships from Bengal was Achin on the northern tip of Sumatra. The number of these ships was stated to be at least six in 1643-1644 and at least four in 1664-1665.[12] But the trade with Achin also declined perceptibly over the last two decades of the seventeenth century. Thus, according to the shipping lists, the number of ships that left Balasore for Achin came down from an average of two per annum between 1680-1681 and 1683-1684 to one in 1698-1699 and none at all between 1699-1700 and 1701-1702. Similarly, according to the lists of ships arriving at Balasore, three vessels came in from Achin in 1682 and two in 1683; there are no entries whatever for Achin in 1698 and 1699. As for the port of Hugli, over the twelve seasons for which information is available between 1696-1697 and 1717-1718, the number of ships that left this port for Achin was two in two of these seasons, one in another two and none in the other eight. Similarly, over the ten seasons between 1700 and 1718 for which information is available, only two ships arrived from Achin—one in 1704 and one in 1717.[13]

Finally, as far as the Malay peninsula is concerned, at least four ships from Bengal were reported to have called at Malacca in 1641-1642. In

[9] The lack of correspondence in the shipping lists between the number of outgoing vessels in a given season and those arriving in the immediately following season is partly explained by the fact that a vessel sent out, for example, from Balasore to Tenasserim might have been directed to come back to Surat rather than Balasore. The possibility of this happening frequently was increased by the fact that even in branches of trade dominated by merchants based in Bengal, there were other Asian merchants participating who were not based at the port of destination, either. Thus the chances of the example given above being applicable to a vessel operated by a merchant based at Surat are quite good.

[10] Calculated from the Bengal shipping lists.

[11] The number of Asian ships that left Hugli for Tenasserim was one in 1696-1697, two in 1704-1705, one each in 1706-1707 and 1708-1709, and none in the remaining seasons for which comparable information is available. The number of ships arriving from Tenasserim at Hugli was one in 1701, three in 1710, one in 1718, and none in the remaining seasons (Bengal shipping lists).

[12] *Batavia Dagh-Register*, 1644, pp. 43-44; 1665, p. 48.

[13] Bengal shipping lists.

October 1642, the authorities at Batavia noted that merchants from Bengal and Achin had imported into Perak quantities of textiles large enough to halt the Company's sale of textiles there.[14] In November 1653, Prince Shah Shuja, Faujdar Nawazish Khan of Rajmahal, and Diwan Malik Beg of Orissa were reported to be preparing a ship each to be sent to Kedah.[15] But by the time we reach the period for which information is available in the shipping lists, trade along this route had already declined considerably. Of the Asian vessels leaving Balasore, only one is reported to have gone to Kedah in 1697-1698; of those arriving at Balasore, only one vessel from Malacca is recorded in 1683. As for the port of Hugli, only one ship is reported to have left for Malacca in 1715-1716 and another as having arrived from Malacca in 1706. Regarding the other ports in the peninsula, only one ship is recorded as having left Hugli for Kedah in 1715-1716. No vessel arrived at Hugli from these ports during the years for which information is available.

Considering together all the ports in the eastward trade—including those in Arakan-Pegu and the Philippines—we find that the number of vessels leaving Balasore for these ports came down from an annual average of seven in the early 1680s to three in 1697-1698, two in 1698-1699, one each in 1699-1700 and 1700-1701, and to zero in 1701-1702, the last year for which information is available. As for the ships coming into Balasore, these totalled twenty in 1682 and 1683 together; in the 1690s, there was only one in the years 1698 and 1699. For the port of Hugli, over the twelve comparable seasons between 1696-1697 and 1717-1718, the number of vessels that left this port for the region was four in one season, three in another, two in yet another, one in another five, and none in the remaining four.[16] Similarly, over the ten seasons between 1700 and 1718 for which comparable information is available to us, the number of vessels that came into Hugli from this region was three in one of the seasons, two in another, one in another four, and none in the remaining four.[17] Taking into account all the available data for both

---

[14] *Batavia Dagh-Register*, 1642, pp. 160, 178-179.

[15] P.B. 10.11.1653, K.A. 1091, ff. 468vo-469.

[16] According to the shipping lists, the number of ships in each season was as follows:

1696-1697	3	1707-1708	0	1712-1713	0
1699-1700	1	1708-1709	1	1713-1714	0
1704-1705	4	1709-1710	1	1715-1716	2
1706-1707	1	1711-1712	0	1717-1718	1

[17] According to the shipping lists, the number of ships in each season was as follows:

1700	0	1706	1	1710	3
1701	1	1708	0	1717	1
1702	0	1709	0	1718	2
1704	1				

Balasore and Hugli, it appears that the 'Asian merchants' eastward trade from the ports of Bengal registered a marked decline in the last years of the seventeenth and the early years of the eighteenth centuries.

The outstanding feature of this decline was the changing participation of Mughal state officials. There is evidence to suggest that among the merchants based in Bengal, it was the state officials who dominated the eastward trade through the greater part of the seventeenth century. All six of the Asian vessels reported in November 1653 to be preparing to leave Bengal for the eastward ports belonged to these officials. Two belonged to Prince Shah Shuja, *subahdar* of Bengal (one vessel was scheduled to go to Tenasserim and the other to Kedah), another two to Diwan Malik Beg of Orissa (one bound for Achin and the other for Kedah), and one each to Faujdar Nawazish Khan of Rajmahal (scheduled for Kedah) and Nawab Inoriya Muhammad of Orissa (scheduled for Tenasserim). In fact, even the seventh vessel recorded as being equipped at Balasore (for a voyage to Masulipatam) was also operated by an official, Faujdar Ahmed Beg of Hugli.[18] According to the shipping lists for the early 1680s, the domination of these officials in the eastward trade was continuing. But from at least the late 1690s, when the information in the shipping lists is resumed, state officials virtually disappeared from this trade. Thus, of the total of twenty-six eastward-bound ships—including those to Arakan-Pegu and the Philippines—that left Balasore in the four seasons between 1680-1681 and 1683-1684, thirteen were accounted for by merchants based in Bengal. Of these thirteen vessels, as many as eight were on the account of state officials. In the five seasons between 1697-1698 and 1701-1702, of the seven vessels that left Balasore for the eastward ports on the account of Bengal-based merchants, only three were operated by officials. Similarly, of the total of twenty vessels that arrived at Balasore from the eastern ports during 1682 and 1683, eleven were operated by merchants based in Bengal. Of these eleven vessels, seven were on the account of state officials. The sole vessel that came into Balasore from this region in 1699 was operated by an ordinary merchant. As far as Hugli is concerned, only two incomplete lists of outgoing vessels are available for the 1680s. These lists contain a total of seven eastward-bound vessels, all of them on the account of merchants based in Bengal. Six of these vessels were operated by officials. No information regarding ships that came into Hugli is available for the

---

[18] P.B. 10.11.1653, K.A. 1091, ff. 468vo-469. In 1664-1665, fifteen Asian ships are recorded as having left Balasore for various destinations. Information regarding ownership is available for ten of these vessels. Seven belonged to state officials—two each to Nawab Khan Dauran of Orissa, Diwan Malik Beg of Orissa, and Shahbandar Nasib Khan of Balasore, and one to Nawab Amin Muhammad (H.B. 26.3.1665, K.A. 1143, f. 565). It might be noted that for 1653 and possibly also for 1664-1665, the information does not cover the full sailing season.

1680s. As for the 1690s, 1700s, and 1710s, it is remarkable that the Hugli shipping lists for the period do not contain the name of a single Bengal-based official of the Mughal empire.

This analysis of the merchants engaged in the eastward trade from Bengal suggests that whereas officials virtually stopped participating in this trade from about 1690, there was no particular decline in the volume of the eastward trade carried on by ordinary merchants based in Bengal. This is borne out by the relatively limited role of these merchants in this branch of trade in the period before information in the shipping lists becomes available as well as from a comparison of the total number of ships handled by these merchants in the 1680s with those in the 1690s and the first two decades of the eighteenth century. The decline in this trade would then be attributable to the withdrawal of state officials from participation in it.

To evaluate the role of the Dutch East India Company in bringing about a decline in the Asian merchants' eastward trade from Bengal, we must examine the Company's pass policy for the eastward region. The pass system was a legacy from the Portuguese and was designed to regulate Indian and other Asian merchants' trade.[19] In principle, every Indian vessel was obliged to obtain this document from a company prior to sailing. The request might or might not be acceded to; if granted, the document specified, among other things, the items the vessel was permitted to carry and the ports at which it was allowed to call. As we have seen, soon after its arrival in the archipelago at the beginning of the seventeenth century, the Company acquired through a series of treaties with a number of petty rulers in the region significant trade privileges, including monopsonistic rights in all three major spices—cloves, nutmeg, and mace—grown in the Spice islands. To benefit from these privileges and others that might be obtained later, it was considered essential to regulate the trade of the rival

---

[19] A part of the Bengal-eastward trade was carried on by merchants operating from ports such as Tenasserim and Achin. For example, of the four ships that left Balasore for Tenasserim in 1681-1682, one was on the account of the king of Siam. In the preceding season of 1680-1681, the king had accounted for two of the four vessels that had gone from Balasore to Tenasserim. Similarly, in 1680-1681, of the three ships that had left Balasore for Achin, one was on the account of an Achinese merchant. In the absence of domicile information in all the shipping lists about the merchants engaged in trade, it is not possible to isolate such cases on a systematic basis. For the merchants based in Southeast Asia, the trip from Bengal to their respective ports would be a return trip and, as such, the Company's policy would pertain to passes for Bengal. The fact that the Company by no means neglected this aspect is borne out by its refusal, in 1664, to accede to the request by merchants in Malacca for permission to trade with Bengal (*Batavia Dagh-Register*, 1664, p. 110). In theory, the pass issued by a company rendered the vessel immune from attack by the ships of that company alone, but in practice the companies generally honoured each others' passes.

merchants in the Indonesian archipelago.[20] Nothing very much, however, seems to have been done about evolving a long-term pass policy for Asian shipping in the region until after the conquest of Malacca, the principal seaport in the area, from the Portuguese in 1641. This conquest made the Company an important power in the archipelago. The pass policy announced by the Company in 1641 for Asian vessels trading with the Malay peninsula was meant to restrict direct access for these vessels to the "tin ports" north of Malacca, and get them to carry out all their trade at Malacca itself.[21]

The restrictions imposed on Asian shipping in the Malay peninsula, however, proved largely ineffective as long as these vessels had continuing free access to the port of Achin. Since the Achinese and Malay merchants conducted a good deal of trade between the peninsula—particularly Perak, a vassal state of Achin—and Achin, Asian merchants could get at Achin practically everything they wanted from the peninsula. It was against this background that the Batavia Council adopted a resolution in July 1647 imposing an embargo on all Asian shipping in the "tin ports" and Achin. Asian vessels infringing the the embargo were to be seized and confiscated.[22] Factors all over Asia were provided with instructions about the issue of passes in the new context. However, the embargo on Achin was lifted in 1653, and after 1660 passes seem to have been issued for both Achin and Malacca on a fairly liberal basis. But the Company's policy of refusing to grant passes for the Malay ports of Perak, Kedah, Junk-Ceylon, and Bangery continued.[23] Passes appear to have been issued for Tenasserim throughout the period.[24]

[20] In the 1640s and later, for example, the Company obtained monopsony rights in pepper in Palembang, Indragiri, and Jambi, and in tin in Kedah, Bangery, and Perak. Over the same period, monopoly rights were obtained in textiles and opium in Mataram, Cheribon, and Palembang. Corpus-Diplomaticum, I, 365-367, 380-386, 438-439, 528-531, 538-541; II, 151-155, 209-212, 280-282, 285-287, 291-297; III, 74-79, 136-142, 233-240, 267-270.

[21] A significant contribution dealing with this and related issues is Arasaratnam, "Notes on the Dutch in Malacca."

[22] The seriousness of the situation, from the Company's point of view, would be apparent from the fact that in 1646, for example, the Company found that practically all the tin produced in the peninsula had been bought up by Asian merchants. Similar was the case of pepper produced in Sumatra. See Corpus-Diplomaticum, I, 520-521.

[23] B.P. 21.10.1653, K.A. 780, f. 436; Arasaratnam, "Notes on the Dutch in Malacca," p. 489.

[24] This is suggested by the virtual absence of instructions from the Batavia Council to the factors at Hugli to restrict the issue of passes to Asian merchants for Tenasserim, whereas the correspondence contains numerous instances of such instructions regarding Malay ports such as Kedah, Perak, Junk-Ceylon, and Bangery. However, we do have one instance in which the Board of Directors, fearing that Bengal silk and silk piece goods imported into Siam by Asian merchants might possibly find their way to Japan through the Chinese

231

Was it the competition provided by the Company's growing trade between Bengal and the Indonesian archipelago and its pass policy that
brought about a decline in the total Asian merchants' eastward trade from
Bengal? We have seen that trade conducted by ordinary merchants registered no particular decline. If ordinary merchants could survive the Dutch
competition, it seems unlikely that the officials would have been forced
to move out, particularly when they had available to them extensive
powers to enhance their profit from trade. As regards the Company's pass
policy, we have seen that by the 1660s the only ports in the region for
which the Company refused to issue passes were those in the Malay peninsula other than Malacca. Although the Company undoubtedly had the
power to refuse passes for the banned ports to state officials engaged in
trade, in practice the possibility of retaliatory action by these trader-
officials made the Company hesitant to enforce vigorously its pass policy
vis-à-vis this group.[25] Indeed, the Company even had to tolerate their
violation of its policies and procedures. In 1656, for example, a vessel
sent out by Prince Shah Shuja to Kedah—one of the formally banned
peninsular ports—refused to pay the Malacca toll on its way back. In lieu
thereof, the Dutch factors at Malacca forcibly took out from the vessel
tin worth 1,631 rupees. This incident, coupled with the Hugli factors'
refusal to provide naval assistance to the government for the proposed
campaign against Arakan, caused the prince to threaten to raise the rate
of the customs duty payable by the Dutch at Hugli from the usual 4 percent
to 20 percent except on imported bullion. Intervention by officials friendly
to the Company persuaded the prince to offer to settle the affair for 7,521
rupees, which the prince claimed was the local value of the confiscated
tin. The final settlement was for 4,339 rupees.[26] In view of this situation,

merchants and there compete with the Company, wrote to the Batavia Council to instruct
the factors at Hugli not to issue passes for Tenasserim, among other ports (XVII.B. 8.10.1685,
K.A. 459, ff. 277vo-278).

[25] In 1653, for example, the Company refused to grant passes to the vessels of the *faujdar*
of Hugli, Mirza Jafar, and of Diwan Malik Beg of Orissa. But in both these cases, the
Company had to face unpleasant consequences. Mirza Jafar placed various hurdles before
the Company's trade in the area under his jurisdiction (K.B. 3.2.1653, K.A. 1091, f. 394vo).
Diwan Malik Beg ordered the *faujdar* of Pipli and Balasore to have the Dutch factory in
Pipli burnt down. The order was carried out. The ostensible reason given for the outrage
was a clash earlier in the year between some Dutch factors and a number of Muslims carrying
out the Muharram procession in the town of Pipli, in which one Dutchman and several
Muslims had been killed. P.B. 2.4.1653, K.A. 1091, ff. 415-vo; P.B. 10.11.1653, K.A.
1091, f. 448vo; P.B. 15.12.1653, K.A. 1094, ff. 612-613; B.P. 28.8.1654, K.A. 781, ff.
359-363; letter from Johan Verpoorten to Nawab Shamsudaulla of Orissa, enclosure to P.B.
15.11.1654, K.A. 1094, ff. 675-677vo; H.B. 6.3.1660, K.A. 1123, f. 736vo.

[26] B.H. 19.7.1657, K.A. 784, f. 311; H.XVII.4.12.1657, K.A. 1111, ff. 760-761; B.XVII.
17.12.1657, K.A. 1110, ff. 108vo-110.

the pass policy followed by the Company is unlikely to have imposed any significant hardship on state officials engaging in trade between Bengal and the eastward ports.

Our conclusion must be that the growth in the Company's trade and its pass policies were not responsible for the nearly complete withdrawal of Mughal officials from participation in the Bengal-Southeast Asia trade. This conclusion finds strong support in the history of the Asian merchants' trade between Bengal and the Maldive islands. This trade was dominated by merchants based in Bengal and, unlike the eastward trade, it continued to grow until the close of our period. According to the shipping lists, the number of ships from Balasore to the Maldives increased from an annual average of three in the early 1680s to seven between 1697-1698 and 1701-1702. One also finds that the amount of rice exported to the Maldives from Balasore went up from 27,000 maunds in 1680-1681 to 50,500 maunds in 1697-1698; the amount of ordinary cotton textiles increased from 1,200 pieces in 1680-1681 to 2,600 pieces in 1699-1700; the amount of opium increased from 2.5 maunds in 1682-1683 to 4.5 maunds in 1697-1698.[27] The number of ships from Hugli to the Maldives was three in 1699-1700 and four in 1704-1705, though between 1706-1707 and 1717-1718, this number in any one year was two or less.[28] Considering the ports of Balasore and Hugli together, there is little doubt that the trade between Bengal and the Maldives increased during the closing years of the seventeenth and early years of the eighteenth centuries.

But although the Bengal-Maldives trade grew during this period, the participation of state officials declined markedly. Of the twelve vessels that left Balasore for the Maldives in the four seasons between 1680-1681 and 1683-1684, as many as eight were on the account of state officials. In contrast, in the five seasons between 1697-1698 and 1701-1702, only one of the thirty-seven vessels that left Balasore for the Maldives was on the account of an official. As for the port of Hugli, the only information we have for the 1680s is in two incomplete shipping lists: state officials accounted for three of the six vessels recorded as having left for the Maldives. In the 1690s, 1700s, and 1710s, on the other hand, none of the vessels that left Hugli for the Maldives was on the account of a state official. Thus the state officials practically withdrew from a *growing* trade which, in addition, was characterized by the lack of Company competition and the absence of a restrictive pass policy. It would thus seem that the

[27] Calculated from the Bengal shipping lists.

[28] Over the nine seasons for which information is available between 1706-1707 and 1717-1718, the number of these vessels was two in three of the seasons, one in four of the seasons, and zero in the remaining two.

Dutch East India Company had little to do with the officials' near disappearance from foreign trade.[29]

If the Dutch Company's trade and pass policies failed to displace Indian merchants' trade along a route such as the Bengal-Southeast Asia trade, where the Company had a great deal at stake, it is unlikely that it would have done so along other less fiercely competed branches of trade. One could then perhaps proceed on the assumption that the Company's trade in Bengal constituted a net contribution to the region's coastal and overseas trade. This would coincide with a net addition to the region's trade only if the decline in the Indian merchants' trade along particular branches such as the Bengal-Southeast Asia trade was fully compensated by an increase along others such as the Bengal-Maldives branch. In other words, if there was a net decline in the Indian merchants' trade for whatever reason, the net addition to the region's trade would be smaller than the Company's net contribution to this trade.[30]

TRADE AS AN INSTRUMENT OF GROWTH

We have seen earlier that the growth of the Company's trade in Bengal was remarkably rapid. The Company's total exports from the region increased from a humble $f.$ 150,000 in 1648-1649 (which is the first year for which quantitative data are available) to an impressive $f.$ 4.6 million in 1720-1721. By the latter date, Bengal had become by far the biggest Asian supplier of goods for the European market. The impact of the Company's trade on the economy of Bengal would, therefore, have been greater than on any other region of the Indian subcontinent.

The distinguishing characteristic of the Company's trade in Bengal was the import of large quantities of precious metals, mainly silver bullion and coins, into the region. The proportion of precious metals to the total value imported varied between a minimum of 47.16 in 1687 to a maximum of 96.99 in 1717. The average for the entire period works out to 87.5

---

[29] One would be tempted to relate the rapidity of this withdrawal to the deepening crisis in the Mughal *mansabdari-jagirdari* system, which involved a decline in the flow of incomes of the *mansabdar* officials. But participation in foreign trade depended mainly on the stock of capital available to the officials engaged in trade; this, in turn, was probably not depleted at a rate commensurate with the pace of their withdrawal from trade. The cessation of their foreign trading activities could not, therefore, be a consequence merely of the crisis in the *mansabdari-jagirdari* system. A definitive analysis of this phenomenon must await further research.

[30] To anticipate our analysis, in such an event, a part of the export surplus associated with the Company's trade would be generated by the use of the capacity released by the net decline in the Indian merchants' trade from Bengal.

percent.[31] The import of these metals may be regarded as a medium of settling the accounts in the balance of payments. The commodity exports by the Company were substantially and chronically in excess of its commodity imports into Bengal. This was an outcome of the inability of Europe to supply goods that could be sold in India in reasonably large quantities at competitive terms. Europe at this time had an undoubted overall superiority over Asia in the field of scientific and technological knowledge, but not as yet the distinct cost advantage that came with the Industrial Revolution in the late eighteenth and nineteenth centuries. This put the Indian producers, with their considerably lower labour costs and a much longer history of sophisticated skills in handicrafts of various kinds, in a position of advantage over their European counterparts in the production of a variety of manufactured goods. The resultant export surplus for Bengal had to be settled through the import of precious metals. As it happened, Europe was in a position to export precious metals because of its large imports of these metals—mainly silver—in the sixteenth and the early part of the seventeenth centuries from the Spanish possessions in South America. In the case of the Dutch, the European supplies were supplemented by metals obtained elsewhere in Asia. Alternatively, precious metals may be treated as a commodity in which the Company had a comparative advantage and which it found it optimal to import into India to pay for the goods procured there. The important point is that whether the import of precious metals is treated as a settlement medium or as a commodity import, the implications for the economy and the society of the region receiving the metals would not be different. It might be noted here that, given the structure of asset choice available, there was a considerable premium on liquidity in India. Hence there was almost an unlimited demand for precious metals in the country.

This pattern of trade, involving the generation of a substantial and chronic export surplus, had important consequences for the economy of Bengal. Ordinarily, an increase in foreign trade in an economy leads to an increase in the output of export goods and a decline in the production of goods that are now being imported in a larger quantity.[32] Since, by definition, the economy is relatively more efficient in the production of export goods than in that of import goods, the net result of growing trade is an increase in the value of total output in the economy. But in the case of trade of the kind that took place between India and Europe in the seventeenth century, the gain resulting from an increase in the volume

[31] Calculated from Table 3.2.

[32] This is the simple case. In specific situations, in the event of an increase in consumption in an economy, there need not be a fall in the domestic output of particular import-competing goods.

of trade would be much more substantial. In view of the import mainly of precious metals rather than ordinary trade goods, the decline in the domestic production of import-competing goods would at best be marginal.[33] The increase in exports (and export-surplus) would then ordinarily involve a net increase in output and income. In terms of the national income identity $Y = C + I + (X - M)$, an increase in the export surplus $(X - M)$ could be effected through a decline in consumption (C) or/and investment (I) or/and through an increase in output and income (Y).[34] It is extremely unlikely that an increase in exports would have been achieved at the cost of domestic consumption or investment. After all, the increase in exports took place on an entirely voluntary basis not involving a compulsion or coercion of any kind. A society defeated in war and obliged to pay an indemnity may conceivably have to generate an export surplus through a reduction in current consumption. But this would seem far-fetched in our situation.

Ruling out a systematic decline in consumption and/or investment leaves only an increase in real output and income as the source of the export surplus associated with the Dutch Company's trade. This increase could have been achieved through an increase in productivity per unit of input through technological change, a reallocation of resources in a way that more of the high-value export goods were produced, and/or a fuller utilization of existing productive capacity and an increase in the capacity itself.

Historically, the pressure of export demand on domestic capacity has stimulated technological change. For example, the development in steel of the Bessemer process in 1856 and of the Siemens-Martin process ten years later were the result of export pressure. Kindleberger's review of evidence on Britain's growth in both the late eighteenth and the mid-nineteenth centuries also credits much to technological innovation associated with opportunities to enter foreign markets. But in the case of Mughal Bengal, the evidence in the voluminous Company records does not point toward any significant developments along the technological front in the export or any other sector of the economy. This seems to have been essentially the result of the absence of a strong enough motivation for change, given the structure of factor endowments in the economy. A situation characterized by a relatively abundant labour supply and

---

[33] Since for all practical purposes, precious metals were not produced domestically in Mughal India, this would be so even if the imported precious metals are regarded as a commodity import.

[34] To put it differently, $X - M$ will equal $S - I$, where S is the savings in the system. The question, therefore, is how this excess of savings over investment would arise. This could be through a rise in the rate of savings, given a level of income or given the rate of savings, through a rise in the level of income.

a relatively scarce capital supply did not provide a particularly fertile ground for labour-saving technological change, which historically has been the most important variety of technological change. In the manufacturing of textiles, for example, the principal differential advantages enjoyed by the Indian industry over its European counterpart consisted in the considerably lower labour costs that it had to bear and a high level of sophisticated skills in the production of textiles available to it. These two circumstances together put the superior quality Indian textiles in an almost unchallengeable position in the world market until the Industrial Revolution in Britain in the latter half of the eighteenth century robbed the Indian textile industry of its cost advantage. Until this time, therefore, there was hardly any pressure for technological change.

In the absence of technological change, the increase in the output of export goods would seem to have been achieved in part through a reallocation of resources in favour of the production of these goods. It is instructive to note that the price evidence available in the records of the Dutch East India Company suggests that during the latter half of the seventeenth century, the prices of major export items such as particular varieties of textiles and raw silk did in fact respond to the growing imbalance between the Europeans' demand for these items and their supply. The principal source of information on prices in the Dutch records are the invoices of goods sent from Hugli to Batavia and other places. These invoices often contained, in addition to the usual physical quantities, a breakdown of the value of the consignment by commodity, enabling one to calculate the unit values (or prices) for the relevant years. The correspondence between the Dutch factory at Hugli and the Governor-General in Council at Batavia also occasionally contained information regarding prices. For textiles, over the second half of the seventeenth and the first few years of the eighteenth centuries, a reasonably large number of price observations were available in the records for only four varieties procured by the Company—the *khasas* (fine muslin), *doreas* (fine calico), *garras* (ordinary calico), and *armosins* (silk).[35] Although no price trend emerged in the case of *khasas*, there was an upward trend in the case of the other three varieties. The average annual rate of price increase in *doreas*, *garras*, and *armosins* was 1.88 percent, 0.68 percent, and 1.48 percent, respectively. In raw silk, the *tanny* variety, introduced by the merchants from Agra in 1669, was the principal variety the Europeans procured from the early 1680s onward. Our information on this item for the period 1683 to 1717 shows an upward trend with an average annual rate of price increase of 0.89 percent. In the case of the other variety of

[35] Price observations were available for 16 years during 1658-1702 for *khasas*, 10 during 1674-1702 for *doreas*, 16 during 1658-1710 for *garras*, and 13 during 1658-1701 for *armosins*.

raw silk, *tanna-banna*, a statistically significant trend emerged only on the basis of a second-degree polynominal showing a decline until about 1675 and a rise from about 1683 onward.[36] This overall increase in the prices of textiles and raw silk would have constituted a clear signal for reallocating resources to increase the output of these goods. Bengal was one of the most fertile regions of Mughal India, and was the granary not only for several other parts of the country but also for neighbouring countries such as Ceylon. The availability of a food surplus created a margin within which a relative shift from food to commercial crops in response to changing demand could be effected without generating unduly severe strains.[37]

A fast-growing European demand for Bengal textiles and raw silk would also have induced a fuller utilization of existing capacity and subsequently an expansion thereof. Although direct evidence on this kind of phenomenon is hard to come by, there is some indirect evidence. Preindustrial societies are often characterized by a certain amount of slack in the structure of production which can be picked up following an increase in total demand. As for the creation of new capacity, it is well known that there was a great abundance of land in Mughal India, and the moderate amounts of capital required to manufacture new spindles, wheels, looms, and other equipment was unlikely to have posed a serious problem, particularly when the Company provided advances of cash against orders placed.

The question of labour supply is somewhat more complex. Many of the processes involved in the manufacturing of goods procured by the Company, such as relatively expensive varieties of textiles, called for the use of highly skilled and sometimes caste-based labour. Also, the interdependence among the artisans engaged in the various stages of the manufacturing process sometimes tended to create problems. However, on the whole, the supply of labour, including skilled labour, seems to have been reasonably flexible. Artisans engaged in manufacturing on a part-time basis

[36] Price observations were available for 15 years during 1683-1717 for *tanny* and 17 during 1646-1702 for *tanna-banna*.

[37] An example of the responsiveness of Bengal farmers to changing demand is provided by the following case. In 1706, while urging the imperial authorities to withdraw their order banning the Dutch from trading in Bengal, Murshid Quli Khan, the central *diwan* in the province, wrote to say that following the closure of the Dutch factory at Kasimbazar, the Hollanders' demand for raw silk had registered a considerable decline, leading to a substantial shift of land away from mulberry into rice and pulses. This had had an injurious effect on the exchequer's income from land revenue (it is well known that land revenue accounted for the bulk of the total state revenue in Mughal India), insofar as mulberry lands were assessed at Rs. 3 per *bigha* (in Bengal the *bigha* was one-third of an acre) while the corresponding rates for rice and pulses—being lower-value crops—were only Rs. 0.75 and Rs. 0.37 per *bigha*, respectively. This could be reversed only if the fresh ban on Dutch trade was withdrawn immediately, and the Company persuaded to reopen their factory at Kasimbazar. Enclosure to H.B. 9.10.1706, K.A. 1622, ff. 63-68.

seem to have found it worth their while to become full-time artisans and produce exclusively for the market. The plausibility of this pattern is suggested by the growing size of individual *aurungs*—localized centres of manufacturing production—and the intensification of the process of specialisation among different *aurungs*.[38]

A reasonable flexibility of the supply of labour is suggested by other evidence as well. A case in point is the silk reeling unit established within the precincts of the Dutch factory at Kasimbazar in the 1650s. When operated at its maximum capacity, the unit employed over 3,000 artisans. It is important to note that the Company did not face any particular problem in finding artisans for the unit (which by contemporary standards was a fairly big one) at the prevalent market wage rate. This is all the more remarkable in that the unit represented a marked departure from the usual practice of the artisan working in his cottage, free from discipline and supervision, and keeping his own hours.[39] This is not to suggest that rigidities in the supply of particular kinds of skilled labour would not have had to be faced or that the mobilization of additional labour would never have posed any problems. All that is being suggested is that there is a reasonable possibility that the structure of manufacturing and other production in the economy was flexible enough to allow an expansion in output following an increase in total demand in the market.[40]

The export surplus associated with the Dutch Company's trade can then be regarded as a vehicle for an expansion in the total output and income in the economy. For the period between 1648-1649, when quantitative information on the Company's exports is first available, and 1720-1721, the average annual incremental value of the Dutch Company's export

[38] Thus in the district of Pipli in Orissa, the *aurung* of Mohanpur specialised in the production of *humhums*, *garras* (both ordinary calicoes), *sologazis* (fine calico), and *adathis* (fine muslin); that of Danton in *doreas* (fine calico) and *soosies* (silk); that of Olmara in *chaklas* and *rumals* (both fine calicoes) and *alachas* (silk), whereas the *aurung* of Casuri produced only superfine cotton textiles (instructions by Director de Haze to van den Hemel, the new chief factor at Pipli, 1.2.1675, K.A. 1202, ff. 79-81vo). In Malda, the *aurung* producing *malmals* (fine muslin) was reported to be at a distance of two days' journey on foot from that specialising in the production of *khasas* (fine muslin), whereas the one producing *doreas* (fine calico) was another 1½ days' journey further up (H.B. 11.1.1684, K.A. 1273, ff. 419-420).

[39] For details, see Chapter 4. Professor Irfan Habib has indeed spoken of "the superfluity rather than scarcity of skilled labour" in Mughal India. See his "Potentialities of Capitalistic Development in the Economy of Mughal India," *Journal of Economic History*, 29 (March 1969), 66.

[40] China provides an interesting parallel. According to Atwell, "as the nationwide demand for cotton goods soared in the sixteenth century, more and more people turned to weaving and trading full time." William S. Atwell, "Notes on Silver, Foreign Trade, and the Late Ming Economy," *Ch'ing-shih wen-t'i*, 3:8 (1977), 6.

surplus from Bengal works out at f. 49,616.[41] In the Keynesian framework of analysis, one could, in principle, derive the increase in income and output associated with a given incremental value of the export surplus provided information on variables such as the marginal rate of saving and the capital-output ratio were available. But since such information is not available even with a wide margin of error, and any order of magnitude assumed, however plausible, will necessarily be arbitrary, such an exercise is not attempted. All one can say is that given the special character of the Dutch (and other European companies') trade, an increase in the volume of this trade would have been accompanied by an increase in real output and income in the economy, which was facilitated by the existence of a certain amount of slack in the system. But since the magnitude of this increase cannot be measured, it is not possible to indicate how significant this would have been in relation to the level of total income and output in the economy, even if one knew the value of the latter.

Fortunately, the problems encountered in a crude estimation of the implications of the Company's trade for employment are somewhat less intractable. The employment associated with the Company's trade would be that generated by additional production to meet the export demand minus that caused by a decline in domestic production as a result of import substitution. As we have seen, goods accounted for only a small proportion of the imports by the Company, and many of the imported goods (such as spices like cloves, nutmeg, and mace) had no domestic substitutes. The employment reduction effect of the Company's imports would, therefore, have been quite small. The bulk of the Company's exports from Bengal were textiles and raw silk. These two items together accounted for 61.5 percent of total exports in 1675-1676 and 83.63 percent in 1701-1703.[42] Therefore, if one attempted to estimate the implications for employment of the export of textiles and raw silk alone, one would obtain a reasonable approximation of the net employment effect of the Company's trade. Given the limitations of available data, one can attempt the measurement of only the *direct* additional employment generated by the Company's export of textiles and raw silk, ignoring the linkage effects such as addi-

---

[41] This figure has been calculated on the following basis. If one divided the difference in the value of the Company's exports from Bengal over the two terminal points of 1648-1649 and 1720-1721 by the intervening number of years, one obtains a figure of f. 62,020. This figure was reduced by 20 percent to allow for the facts first, that on an average, 12.5 percent of the total imports were in the form of goods and not precious metals, and second, that since a certain amount of profit was earned on the goods sold in Bengal, the realised value of the commodity imports into Bengal was somewhat higher than the value stated in the import invoices. It is important to realise that what we have estimated here is not the absolute value of the export surplus in any one year but its average annual incremental value over the entire period.

[42] See Table 3.4.

tional opportunities now available to merchants dealing with the Company, and so on.

In Table 8.1, we have attempted a very crude and highly tentative estimation of the number of looms required to produce the average amount of textiles exported by the Dutch Company per annum between 1678 and 1718.[43] The procedures used are explained in the notes to the table, and are admittedly subject to modification as more information becomes available.

According to this table, the average number of looms required to produce textiles for the Dutch Company would have ranged between 5,284 (on the criterion of square yardage handled) and 6,169 (on that of the number of pieces exported). The number of jobs in the textile industry (defined to include spinning, weaving, bleaching, finishing, printing, and embroidering) associated with the employment of these looms would, of course, depend on the assumption one makes regarding the number of workers in the industry per loom. Although definitive evidence on this question is difficult to obtain, what is available suggests that one could probably proceed on the assumption that the full-time jobs per loom amounted to 5 or 6—1.5 to 2 for weaving, 2.5 to 3 for spinning, and 1 for bleaching, finishing, printing, and embroidering.[44] On this basis, the

[43] The nonavailability prior to 1678 of a detailed breakdown of the textiles exported into the various categories listed in the table necessitated confining the analysis to the period 1678-1718.

[44] The Textile Enquiry Committee, 1954, suggested a figure of 1.25 weavers per handloom (India, Ministry of Commerce and Industry, *Report of the Textile Enquiry Committee*, [Delhi, 1954], I, 16-17). The same figure was suggested by the Pakistan Fact-finding Committee on Handlooms, 1956 (Pakistan, Ministry of Industries, *Report of the Fact-finding Committee on Handlooms* [Karachi, 1956], p. 21), though a member of the committee, Dr. A. Sadeque, suggested an alternative estimate of 2.25 weavers per loom (p. 217). But these figures apparently relate to all cotton textiles, whereas the European procurement in Bengal was confined largely to the relatively superior varieties, in which case the weaver-loom ratio seems to have been substantially higher. Thus, discussing the cotton manufactures of India, Edward Baines wrote, "When chequered muslins are wrought, three persons are employed at each loom: the *lungri* pulls the thread to form the pattern, the *dobarah* twists the thread, and the *binkarai* weaves." Edward Baines, *History of the Cotton Manufacture in Great Britain* (London, 1966; first printed in 1835), p. 71. The ninth report of the Select Committee, 1783, also suggested a figure of three weavers to a loom producing Dacca muslins (Appendix 51, summarized in K.N. Chaudhuri, "The Structure of Indian Textile Industry in the Seventeenth and Eighteenth Centuries," *Indian Economic and Social History Review*, 11 [June-September, 1974], 162). And then, of course, there were silk and mixed textiles for which contemporary information is extremely limited. Hossain has suggested that a piece of *jamdani* made by a *tanti* weaver required the services of two weavers to lay the warp, one to weave, two persons to weave the floral design and another to tie the threads of the design. (Hamida Hossain, "The Alienation of Weavers: Impact of the Conflict between the Revenue and the Commercial Interests of the East India Company, 1750-1800," *Indian Economic and Social History Review*, 16 [1979], 325.) Taking all these facts into account, the average figure of

jobs attributable to the Dutch Company's procurement of textiles works out at between 26,420 and 37,014. The corresponding number for raw silk over a broadly comparable period works out at 7,350 (Table 8.2) giving us a total of 33,770 to 44,364 full-time jobs associated with the Dutch Company's procurement of textiles and raw silk in Bengal. It need hardly be emphasized that all these figures are extremely crude and subject to a significant margin of error. They are intended to convey only broad orders of magnitude and not precise estimates.

In order to form a broad idea of the relative significance of the Company's procurement of textiles and raw silk, we have related in Table 8.3 the full-time jobs attributable to the procurement by the Company to the probable total size of the work force in the textile manufacturing sector (defined to include the production of raw silk) in the province of Bengal. For this purpose, the province of Bengal appears to be a more appropriate unit than the Bengal region as a whole, for raw silk was procured exclusively and textiles overwhelmingly in the province. Bihar supplied only small quantities of relatively coarse cotton *chintz* produced at Patna, while the procurement in Orissa was confined to small quantities of mixed piece goods manufactured at Pipli and Balasore. Following the procedure explained in the notes to Table 8.3, we estimate the work force in the textile manufacturing sector at one million. The full-time jobs created by the Dutch Company's trade accounted for between 3.37 percent and 4.43 percent of the total work force in the sector. If the analysis is confined to the early years of the eighteenth century, and the trade carried on by the English East India Company is also taken into account, this figure goes up to between 8.69 percent and 11.11 percent.[45] Needless to say, it would

---

1.5 to 2 weavers to a loom for the varieties procured by the companies would, if anything, appear to be an underestimate.

As for spinners, the ninth report of the Select Committee, 1783, mentioned a figure of 80,000 women spinners for a total of 8,400 looms, giving us an average of 9.5 spinners to a loom. But these figures relate exclusively to Dacca muslins, and the women spinners may have been working only part time. Evidence pertaining to preindustrial Britain, where the textile technology on the whole was not very different from that in seventeenth-century India (see for example, Irfan Habib, "The Technology and Economy of Mughal India," *Indian Economic and Social History Review*, 17 [1980], 1-34), suggests that the number of spinners to a loom ranged between 3 and 6. For example: "Spinning had always been the slowest of the textile processes, and, while the treadle-wheel increased the speed slightly, three to five spinsters were still required to keep one weaver supplied with yarn" (Charles Singer et al., eds., *A History of Technology* [Oxford, 1957], III, 161). Again: "We know that a single loom provided work for five or six spinning wheels" (Paul Mantoux, *The Industrial Revolution in the Eighteenth Century* [New York, 1961], p. 208). In order to ensure that there was no overstatement of the employment implications of the Company's trade, we have assumed a figure of 2.5 to 3 full-time spinning jobs to a loom.

[45] See Om Prakash, "Bullion for Goods: International Trade and the Economy of Early

TABLE 8.1
Number of Looms Required to Produce Textiles Exported by
the Dutch East India Company from Bengal per Annum, 1678-1718

1	2	3	4	5	6	7
Category of textiles exported	Number of pieces	Output of pieces per loom per year	Number of looms required to produce the pieces of textiles exported	Square yardage per piece	Total square yardage	Number of looms required to produce the yardage of textiles exported
Fine muslins	40,802	15	2,720	30	1,224,060	
Fine calicoes	27,565	36	766	15	413,475	
Ordinary calicoes	131,562	80	1,645	9	1,184,058	
Silk piece goods	27,986	45	622	12	335,832	
Silk and cotton mixed piece goods	18,707	45	416	12	224,484	
Total	246,622		6,169		3,381,909	5,284

Sources   The figures in column 2 are calculated from the export invoices for the period in the Dutch records. They represent the average for the only 18 years for which a detailed breakdown by category of the textiles exported was available.

For column 3, the following procedure was adopted. According to Francis Buchanan-Hamilton, in the early years of the nineteenth century, the average annual output per loom of pieces of *tanzebs* and *malmals* (both fine muslins) of dimensions comparable to those exported by the Company during our period was 24 each. The pieces, manufactured in the *aurung* of Maghra in Bihar, were valued at Rs 5.25 and Rs 5 each respectively (*An Account of the Districts of Bihar and Patna in 1811-12*, Bihar and Orissa Research Society, Vol. II, Table 43, p. 775). Buchanan-Hamilton also suggested that there was an inverse relation between the quality of a piece, as indicated by its price, and the average output per loom. (Thus in Table 42, p. 774, the average monthly output per loom of *solegazi seatra* valued at Rs 2.25 is shown to be four pieces while that of a *solegazi* of a comparable size but valued at Rs 3 to be only three pieces.) Another source of information on the average output of pieces of different varieties of muslins per loom is a 1776 estimate of "Dacca Cloth Manufactures for Exportation" contained in the Ninth Report from the Select Committee 1783, Appendix 51 and summarized in K.N. Chaudhuri, "The Structure of Indian Textile Industry in the Seventeenth and Eighteenth Centuries," *The Indian Economic and Social History Review*, Vol. XI, Nos. 2-3, July-September, 1974, pp. 162-163. According to this source, the average output per loom of *cora tanjebs* valued at Rs 10 per piece was 10 per annum and that of fine *mulmuls* valued at Rs 29 per piece, 9.4 per annum. While all this information is clearly inadequate to establish a definitive figure or even a range of annual output per loom, it nevertheless would appear to support an assumption of an output of 15 pieces of muslins of the general quality the Company exported from Bengal per loom per annum.

The corresponding figures for the remaining varieties of cotton textiles, for silk piece goods and for the mixed piece goods have been arrived at on the basis of the average price (assuming a generally inverse relation between price and output) and

TABLE 8.1 (Continued)

the average size of the pieces of these varieties of textiles relatively to that of fine muslins.

The figures in column 5 have been arrived at on the basis of the extensive information available in the records of the Dutch and the English East India companies regarding the sizes of the piece goods procured in Bengal. In the Dutch records, the range is from 27 to 36 yards for the length and ¾ to 2¼ yards for the width of a piece of muslin. The corresponding figures for a piece of calico are 15 to 18 yards for length and 1 to 1½ years for width except for varieties such as *dorea* whose sizes were the same as in the case of muslins and the *dassies* which was an unusually small sized textile – at times only 2 square yards per piece. (The different sizes assumed for the Dutch "fine calicoes" and "ordinary calicoes" follow from the good weightage of *dassies* in the latter category.) For silk and mixed piece goods, the usual length per piece was 15 yards and the width between ¾ and 1½ yards except for varieties such as *soosy* where the length of a piece was usually as much as 24 yards and the *charkhana* where it was 17½ yards. The dimensions found in the English records broadly correspond with these figures. For example, the sizes of the *tanzebs*, *khasas* and *malmals* (all muslins) mentioned in these records were 30 yards for length and between ¾ and 2¼ yards for width.

The Dutch records mention the dimensions in *cobidos* or ells while the English recorded them in *covids*. The *cobido* or *covid* (Portuguese for cubit) was a measure with large local variations. According to Pieter van Dam's *Beschryvinge van de Oost-Indische Compagnie*, Vol. II, Part II. p. 451, the *cobido* was the equivalent of 27 inches which was also the size of the Flemish ell. The Directors used the two terms interchangeably. The *cobido* figures have, therefore, been converted into yards at this rate.

The figure in column 7 has been arrived at on the assumption of an average annual output per loom of 640 square yards of cloth of all varieties exported by the Company. No contemporary estimates of square yardage per loom per annum are available, but according to the *Report of the Fact-finding Committee (Handlooms and Mills)*, 1942, Appendix XXIII, p. 294, the average daily output of cotton *saris* of 80 × 80 to 100 × 100 counts per throw-shuttle loom per day was $2\frac{1}{3}$ square yards. Assuming that this figure of daily output per loom is valid *on the average* for the cloth exported by the Company from Bengal and assuming further a work year of 275 days, we get the per annum per loom output of 642 square yards which has been rounded off to 640 square yards.

go up still further if the trade by the other European companies and by individual Europeans in their private capacity is also taken into consideration.

Our information on the distribution of the gains accruing from a growing foreign trade among the various sections engaged in productive activity is extremely limited. The two major groups directly affected by the growth in the volume of the European trade were the merchants dealing with the Company and the artisans who manufactured the export goods. The intense and growing competition among the various European companies,

Eighteenth Century Bengal," *Indian Economic and Social History Review*, 13 (1976), 159-187.

TABLE 8.2
Full-time Jobs Created by the Dutch East India Company's
Export of Raw Silk from Bengal, 1669-1718

(1) Amount of raw silk exported per annum (in bales) (1 bale = 76 kilograms)[1]	(2) Full-time reeling jobs[3]	(3) Full-time complementary jobs in the raw silk manufacturing sector[4]	(4) Total full-time jobs
1,423[2]	2,940	4,410	7,350

Notes:

1. The figure in this column represents the average for 23 years for which detailed information was available over the 49-year period covered by the table. The figure includes a small quantity of *mochta* silk (florette yarn).

2. The figure of 6,000-7,000 bales (600,000-700,000 lbs. at the rate of conversion indicated) given by Tavernier for the 1670 s was wide off the mark (J. B. Tavernier, *Travels in India*, translated by V. Ball and edited by W. Crooke, London, 1925, Vol. II, p. 2).

3. The figure in this column has been arrived at by multiplying that in column 1 by a factor of 2.066. The Dutch silk-reeling unit at Kasimbazar, when operated at its maximum capacity produced, at the close of the seventeenth century, around 1,500 bales of raw silk per annum and employed over 3,000 reelers (the precise number is not indicated). If one assumed that this number was 3,100, the figure one gets is 2.066 reelers per bale reeled.

4. The figure in this column has been arrived at by multiplying that in column 2 by a factor of 1.5. According to Pieter van Dam, the workers who prepared the raw material (called *pattani*) necessary for a seer (1 seer = 2.057 lbs. avoirdupois) of reeled *tanny* raw silk were paid a wage bill of Rs. 0.40. As against this, the reelers who reeled this raw material into *tanny* raw silk got Rs. 0.37. The corresponding figures in the case of *tanna-banna* raw silk were 0.23 and 0.19 rupees respectively (Pieter van Dam, *Beschrijvinge*, Vol. II, Part II, Appendix IV B, pp. 68-71). If one assumed that the wages of a reeler were somewhat higher than of a worker engaged in a pre-reeling operation, the assumption of full-time complementary labor of 1.5 in the raw silk manufacturing sector seems justified.

particularly the Dutch and the English, for Bengal goods such as textiles and raw silk increasingly turned the market into a sellers' market. This was reflected in the growing bargaining strength of the merchants vis-à-vis the companies. For example, in 1709 a number of textile merchants dealing with the Dutch Company refused to accept fresh contracts unless the Company gave them first an assurance that henceforth in the event of only a limited variation between the quality of the sample given out and of the pieces actually supplied by them there would be no deduction made from the price mutually agreed upon at the time of the contract, and second, a refund on the price deductions made on this count on textiles supplied during the preceding season.

The position is much less clear in relation to the textile weavers and other producing groups supplying the merchants. In principle, one would expect that at least a small part of the gain would have been transmitted

TABLE 8.3
Proportion of Full-time Jobs Attributable to the Dutch East India Company's
Procurement of Textiles and Raw Silk to Total Work Force in the Textile Manufacturing Sector
of the Province of Bengal, 1678-1718

(1)	(2)	(3)	(4)	(5)	(6)
Population in 1801 (in millions)[1]	Population in 1711 (in millions)[2]	Total work force (in millions)[3]	Work force in manufacturing sector (in millions)[4]	Work force in the textile manufacturing sector (in millions)[5]	Proportion of 33,770 to 44,364 full-time jobs to the work force in the textile manufacturing sector
28.055	19.99	10.00	2.00	1.00	3.37-4.43

Sources and Notes:

1. This figure is based on D. P. Bhattacharya, *Population in India, 1801-1961 (Based on 1941 area)* (unpublished), Appendix I.

2. According to the estimates of Bhattacharya, the compound rate of growth of population in the province during the precensus period 1801-1871 works out at 0.37 percent per annum. Assuming that population grew at the same rate in the eighteenth century, the figure one gets for 1711 is 19.99 million. It is recognized that this method of extrapolating population estimates backwards is extremely unsatisfactory, but in the absence of anything better we were obliged to follow this procedure. If firm estimates become available, this figure may need substantial revision. The year 1711 has been selected because of its proximity to the close of our period. At an earlier point in time, the population figure would have been lower.

3. Definitive information on participation rates is available only for the census period. The all-persons participation rate for undivided Bengal in 1911 – which was a normal year, a reasonably efficient census, and the first one in which makers and sellers were adequately differentiated – was 36.1 percent (unpublished estimate prepared by J. Krishnamurty). This ratio was probably somewhat higher two centuries earlier. This is because some industries with a considerable female work force participation (such as hand spinning) had declined in the meantime, probably driving some female workers out of the work force. Moreover, in order to ensure that the employment implications of the Company's trade are not overstated, it is vital that the size of the work force not be understated. We have, therefore, used the relatively high participation rate of 50 percent to obtain the figure in this column.

4. The census evidence for 1911 for undivided Bengal shows that the proportion of the work force in the manufacturing sector (all persons) to total work force was 8.4 percent (unpublished estimate of J. Krishnamurty). It is believed that the nineteenth century was characterized by a fairly marked decline in the proportion of the work force engaged in the manufacturing sector to the total work force (described as the process

of deindustrialization). In order to ensure that there is no underestimation of the work force in the manufacturing sector, we have assumed that in our period the work force in this sector accounted for as much as 20 percent of the total work force.

5. The census evidence for 1911 for undivided Bengal shows that the work force (all persons) engaged in the manufacturing of textiles (excluding jute textiles) accounted for 14.2 percent of the total work force in the manufacturing sector (unpublished estimate of J. Krishnamurty). There is a large body of evidence to indicate that the textile industry was highly developed in Mughal Bengal, catering to a large Indian and foreign market. The nineteenth century witnessed a considerable increase in output of cloth per worker because of the emergence of a large cotton textile mill industry in the country. We have, therefore, assumed that the textile industry in our period accounted for as much as 50 percent of total employment in the manufacturing sector.

to the producers in the form of increased employment and better returns. There is some evidence that this indeed happened. Writing in 1700, for example, the Dutch factors at Hugli made the following observation: "The merchants inform us (and on investigation we find that they are speaking the truth) that because of the large number of buyers in the weaving centres and the large sale of textiles, the weavers can no longer be coerced. They weave what is most profitable for them. If one does not accommodate oneself to this situation, then one is not able to procure very much and the supplies go to one's competitors."[46] But it should be emphasized that a variety of constraints often deprived the producers of their proper share in the gain. Perhaps the most important was the large-scale indebtedness of many of the producers to particular merchants.[47] This tied the artisans to these merchants, making it impossible for them to obtain the normal market value for their services. In such a situation, it would not be surprising if the merchants appropriated most of the gains accruing from growing trade.

The European companies' trade was also instrumental in the development of a number of trading centres in the region—such as Kasimbazar—into major commercial emporia, and the founding of a town which, in course of time, became the largest city in the subcontinent. The English founded Calcutta in 1690 after the conclusion of their conflict with the provincial government; within twenty-five years or so, the new town had become a major centre of production and commerce. Its inhabitants, besides the English, were mainly merchants and artisans who had come there from places as far off as Dacca seeking employment and the protection the English settlement afforded against the excesses of local officials.[48]

The Monetary Aspects of the Company's Trade

We have confined the analysis so far to real variables such as output, income, and employment, which were affected by movements in the Dutch and other European companies' trade in the Bengal region. But there is an equally important monetary counterpart to this analysis. The import of large quantities of precious metals by the European companies into Bengal would have had certain consequences for the economy of the

[46] Explanation by the Dutch factors of why the orders were not supplied in full, 1700, K.A. 1530, ff. 17-19, II Section.

[47] In the mid-1670s, for example, an overwhelming proportion of the textile weavers at Balasore and Pipli were reported to be under debt to one merchant or another (instructions by Director de Haze to van den Hemel and Jasper van Collen at Balasore, 3.2.1676, K.A. 1209, ff. 551vo-552).

[48] Explanation by the Dutch factors, 1710, K.A. 1688, f. 205.

region. The average annual value of the treasure imported by the Dutch Company increased from *f*. 1.28 million in the 1660s (when the quantitative information pertaining to imports first becomes available) to *f*. 2.00 million in the 1690s, *f*. 2.43 million in the 1700s, and *f*. 2.87 million in the 1710s.[49] In addition, there were the substantial bullion imports by the English East India Company, besides the small quantities brought in by the French East India Company.

The imported precious metals performed a vital function in the increasingly monetized economy of Mughal Bengal. Given the negligible domestic production of precious metals, the monetary system was heavily dependent on imported bullion. The gold *muhrs* coined in the imperial mints were used essentially for ceremonial purposes and as a store of value. The standard coin was the silver rupee, with an alloy content of under 4 percent and weighing about 178 grains. The *anna* was a fractional silver coin equivalent to 1/16th of a rupee. The copper *dam* (or *paisa*) was a relatively little-used coin in Bengal during our period. The small transactions were taken care of mainly by *cauris* imported in large quantities from the Maldive islands.[50]

The Dutch Company imported substantial quantities of silver and some gold from Europe and Japan, besides a certain amount of bar copper from Japan. The precious metals, imported in the form of bullion or coins such as the rial of eight, were immediately converted into Mughal coins either through the imperial mints in the region or through the *sarrafs*. There was, therefore, an immediate and corresponding increase in the money supply in the economy. A growing supply of money facilitated an increase in the degree of monetization in the economy. It also facilitated the growing monetization of land revenue demand, as well as the increasing recourse to the system of revenue farming. The rise of banking firms was also related in part to this phenomenon. Thus the precious metals imported in ever-increasing quantities had a variety of implications for the economy and the society of the region. In the parallel case of late Ming China, it has been suggested that "Japanese and Spanish-American silver may well have been the most significant factor in the vigorous economic expansion which occurred in China during the period in question. This is true not only because of its direct impact on the silk and porcelain industries, although this clearly was of great importance, but also because an increase in the country's stock of precious metals upon which economic growth

---

[49] These figures are based on the data in Table 3.2. The figure for the 1660s is based on information available for six years, that for the 1690s and 1700s on information for ten years each, and for the 1710s on information available for eight years.

[50] In the Company documents, although one comes across numerous references to the use of *annas* and *cauris*, the references to the use of copper coins are rare.

and business confidence seem to have depended would have been determined almost entirely by how much silver entered the country through foreign trade."[51]

At a more concrete level, an increase in the money supply is ordinarily associated with a rise in the price level. Thus in the classic case of sixteenth-century Europe, the import of substantial quantities of South American silver is believed to have been causally related to the so-called "Price Revolution."[52] It has been suggested that a similar relationship between the import of precious metals and the price level would not have existed in Asia because, given the Oriental penchant for hoarding gold and silver besides the use of these metals for making ornaments, the imported precious metals would not have added to the supply of money in Asian economies and would therefore have exerted no pressure on prices.[53] But in reality the position was that the trading companies were obliged to convert their *entire* supplies of precious metals into Mughal coins before they could begin their procurement of the export goods. There was, therefore, an automatic and corresponding increase in the money supply. It is, of course, possible that a part of the increased money supply might eventually have been hoarded or withdrawn from active circulation. In the present state of our knowledge, it would probably be futile to surmise how significant or marginal this phenomenon might have been.

As regards the actual movement of prices in Bengal during our period, we have already seen that the prices of export goods such as particular varieties of textiles and raw silk registered a general increase. But such a sectoral price rise might only reflect a failure of the supply of these goods to increase as fast as the demand for them, and may not necessarily indicate a general price rise in the economy. For the latter, one would need to look for movements in the prices of the so-called wage-goods, the most important among which would be staple food items such as rice and wheat. W. H. Moreland believed that for Bengal "there is definite evidence of a large and sudden rise in food prices between the years 1650 and 1660." But unfortunately, quite apart from the fact that in the decade under reference the Dutch and other European companies' trade in the region

[51] Atwell, "Notes on Silver," p. 5.

[52] It is another matter that the validity of this hypothesis as well as of the phenomenon of price revolution itself has been intensely debated; see, for example, P. Vilar, "Problems of the Formation of Capitalism," *Past and Present*, 10 (1956), 15-38; Y. S. Brenner, "The Inflation of Prices in Early Sixteenth-Century England," *Economic History Review*, Second Series, 14 (1961), 225-239.

[53] See for example, Earl J. Hamilton, "American Treasure and the Rise of Capitalism, 1500-1700," *Economica*, 27, November 1929, pp. 338-357; Rudolph C. Blitz, "Mercantilist Policies and the Pattern of World Trade, 1500-1750," *Journal of Economic History*, 27 (March 1967), 39-55.

was still in its infancy and, therefore, incapable of bringing about a significant price rise, the "definite" evidence provided by Moreland is too fragile to bear the weight of a major deduction.[54]

One can reconstruct the broad movements in the prices of provisions in Bengal from evidence found in the records of the Dutch East India Company. The provisions for which such information is available are rice, wheat, sugar, and clarified butter. Of these, only sugar was a trade good for the Company. The other provisions figured in the export invoices because these were procured in large quantities in Bengal mainly for consumption by the Dutch establishments at places such as Batavia and Ceylon. Since the quality of the provisions such as rice, wheat, and butter procured partly for use in the Dutch establishments was unlikely to vary a great deal between one year and another, the unit values or prices obtained from the invoices would appear to be broadly comparable over time. Also, unlike export goods such as textiles, the amount of each of the provisions purchased by the Company was insignificant in relation to the total marketed output, making their prices insensitive to variations in the Company's own purchases. The price data are presented in Table 8.4. What clearly stands out from this table is the extremely erratic behaviour of the prices of all provisions. The range in the case of rice, for example, was between a low of 27 rupees per 100 maunds in 1665-1666 to a high of 160 rupees in 1700-1701. As a result, a statistically significant trend upward or downward did not emerge for any of the four provisions.[55]

---

[54] Moreland, *From Akbar to Aurangzeb*, pp. 178-179. The evidence cited by Moreland was a petition in December 1658 by the English factors stationed at Hugli asking for an increase in the allowance for housekeeping charges on account of an alleged trebling in the prices of provisions over the preceding few years (ibid., p. 179). The desirability of refraining from accepting such casual and possibly motivated pieces of evidence as conclusive is suggested by the following statement of an essentially similar variety. In November 1661, the English factors stationed at Madras wrote, "Neither may you ever expect that the commodity [taffetas] can be made here to be afforded as reasonably as in Bengal, *for all provisions of victual, when at the cheapest is here three times dearer than in Kasimbazar and Hugli,* where these taffetas are made" (spellings modernized and emphasis added; William Foster, ed., *English Factories in India*, 1661-1664, p. 65). This statement might, of course, be totally unreliable, since it too might have been motivated by an attempt on the factors' part to conceal their inefficiency (or corruption) in not being able to procure textiles locally at reasonable prices. But taken at its face value in conjunction with the statement by the factors at Hugli, it suggests the highly unlikely situation of the prices of provisions in Bengal in, say, 1650 being on the average only one-ninth of those in Madras—assuming, of course, that the Madras prices did not rise between 1650 and 1661. The purported rise in the Bengal prices in the 1650s may, indeed, never have taken place. One is then forced to conclude that in order to establish a significant change in the prices of provisions in Bengal in the 1650s, one needs evidence more solid than that provided by Moreland.

[55] The trend lines were fitted on the basis of first- and second-degree polynominals on ordinary and log scale.

TABLE 8.4
Prices of Provisions in Bengal, 1657-1714
(rupees per 100 maunds)

Year	Rice	Wheat	Clarified Butter	Sugar
1657-58				444
1658-59	49		693	
1661-62	48	111	750	457
1662-63	71	113	674	463
1663-64				500
1664-65		63	543	
1665-66	27	51	395	433
1666-67	33	90	690	356
1667-68		76	841	
1668-69		82	725	
1669-70	39	65	650	400
1670-71	66	63	571	310
1671-72		133		
1673-74	48		886	350
1674-75	42	77	835	377
1675-76	42	69	534	398
1683-84	42	59	616	
1684-85		77	616	461
1685-86	44	99	668	481
1686-87	53	73	600	422
1687-88	49	114	460	377
1688-89	43	71	522	
1689-90	33		462	
1690-91			470	
1691-92	72	56	571	443
1692-93			550	
1693-94	39	56	538	
1694-95			579	
1695-96		59	671	
1700-01	160			
1701-02		134	949	
1702-03		100	870	
1706-07			659	

252

TABLE 8.4 (Continued)

Year	Rice	Wheat	Clarified Butter	Sugar
1707-08	48			454
1713-14		85		

Source· Export invoices in the Dutch records.

In the absence of information on trends in total and marketed output, any meaningful analysis of such price behaviour would seem to be out of question. All one can say is that the movements in the prices of these provisions do not provide evidence for the general rise in prices in the economy that one might have expected to follow the import of the precious metals by the Dutch and the other European companies.

How does one account for this? Although it is very difficult to provide a definitive answer, a number of possibilities, which are not mutually exclusive, might be considered. In terms of the elementary equation of the quantity theory of money $MV = PT$, a rise in the quantity of money (M) will result in a rise in prices (P) only if the other variables in the equation, the velocity of circulation (V) and the number of transactions (T) remain unchanged. The velocity of the circulation of money in any economy depends on a variety of circumstances, and changes in it are not always easy to predict. The position, however, would seem to be much clearer with regard to the volume of transactions (T). The number of transactions would obviously have increased with the increase in the value of output and income in the economy along the lines discussed earlier. The precious metals the Dutch and other Europeans brought into Bengal were not a gift, but represented payment for physical goods procured that would now have been produced in larger quantities. It is also important to remember that insofar as the Dutch and the other European companies would have conducted all their business in the monetized sector, a growing foreign trade is likely to have been accompanied by an expansion of the monetized sector at the expense of the barter sector. This would imply that the monetized transactions as a proportion of total transactions in the economy would have gone up. Since the equation $MV = PT$ captures only monetized transactions, the effect of this would be similar to that of a rise in T itself. Finally, over the fairly long period that we are concerned with, natural increases in population would also have necessitated a secular rise in output and transactions if the per capita output and availability were not to go down. All these factors would tend to check a general rise in prices consequent upon an increase in the supply of money caused by an increased inflow of precious metals.

To place this discussion in a proper historical perspective, a brief com-

253

ment on the monetary history of the Bengal region is necessary. If one could estimate, even within a certain margin of error, the total supply of money in the economy, one could work out the relative significance of the additions to the money supply as a consequence of the import of precious metals by the Dutch and other European companies. In the present state of our knowledge, however, this is very difficult. But since the total stock of money at any point in time is the cumulative total of all the issues until that time less the amount surrendered for recoinage, the percentage increase in money supply as a result of Dutch and other European companies' imports would seem to have been quite small. As for the import of precious metals by other agencies, it was pointed out earlier that even prior to the arrival of the northwestern European companies, the region was a net importer of precious metals from places such as Sumatra, the Coromandel coast, Malabar, Gujarat, and the Persian Gulf. The Yunnan/Burma border area also provided silver to Bengal.[56] But the direct contribution of Mocha, the so-called "treasure-chest" of the Mughal empire, to this stream was negligible. This is borne out by the reports and other documents submitted by the exploratory missions the Dutch Company sent to Mocha and the neighbouring areas in the second quarter of the seventeenth century. These documents speak of a flourishing trade between Mocha and the ports on the west coast of India, but there is hardly ever any mention of trade with Bengal. Lists detailing goods that were sold in the Red Sea area hardly ever included Bengal textiles or other goods. To take a specific list of foreign ships that arrived at Mocha in the year 1645, one finds that of the twenty ships listed, as many as twelve were from the Gujarat ports, another four from ports on the Malabar coast, two from the Maldive islands, and one each from Dabhol and Achin. No ship was recorded as having gone from Bengal to this Red Sea port.[57] Whatever Mocha treasure reached Bengal would have been through the latter's trade with Gujarat and the southwest coast both by land and along the coast. Although no information is available regarding the movements in the overland trade between Bengal and these regions during the seventeenth and early eighteenth centuries, the information on the coastal trade, as pointed out earlier, suggests no clearly discernible trend one way or the other. This is also true of trade with the Persian Gulf. The imports from Coromandel may have increased as a part of the general increase in trade with that coast, whereas the imports from Sumatra would appear to

[56] John Deyell, "The China Connection: Problems of Silver Supply in Medieval Bengal," in J. F. Richards, ed., *Precious Metals in the Later Medieval and Early Modern Worlds* (Durham, 1983), pp. 207-227.

[57] An account of the trade at Mocha by Antony Oudermeulen, October 20, 1645, K.A. 1057, ff. 426-429.

have suffered a decline. Although the information is clearly inadequate to warrant a definitive conclusion, one might tentatively argue that there is nothing to suggest a major upheaval in the pattern and the quantity of precious metals imported by means of trade into the Bengal region during the seventeenth and the early eighteenth centuries by agencies other than the European trading companies. This would render the Dutch and other European company imports, however small relative to the total stock of money, a net addition to this stock.

The other aspect of the monetary history of Bengal that calls for comment is the possibility that the period we are concerned with may have seen important changes in the net outflow of coined money from the region. One of the channels of outflow was the remittance of funds to places outside the region by Mughal state officials on temporary assignment in Bengal. A large number of senior *mansabdar* officials were known to have amassed large sums of money and carried it with them on their transfer to Delhi or other parts of the empire. There is evidence that such a net outflow of funds took place from Bengal on an almost continuous basis. On occasions, such collections and remittances were arranged in a blatantly illegal manner. A case in point is a remittance by the *subahdar*, Prince Shah Shuja, in 1658. The prince was desperately in need of funds to conduct his campaign for the throne, and asked several Gujarati merchants of Kasimbazar for a loan of Rs. 400,000. The Dutch factors were similarly asked for a loan of Rs. 100,000. On being turned down by both, the prince ordered the confiscation of the bullion deposited by these parties at the Rajmahal mint to be minted into *sicca* rupees. Arrangements were then made for remittance outside the province of an equivalent sum in coined money.[58] It is true that the period after 1660 witnessed the appointment in Bengal of *subahdars* particularly notorious for abusing authority for private gain—men like Mir Jumla, Shaista Khan, and Azim-us-Shan. As a result, the size of the net outflow on this account may well have increased marginally during this period. It is, however, important to keep the matter in perspective and not overstate the implications of this very limited phenomenon.

A more important constituent of the net outflow of funds from Bengal was the remittance to the central treasury at Delhi of the revenues from the *khalisa* lands in the region. In addition, there might have been a net outflow on the account of the assignees of the *jagirs* posted outside the region. In the Todar Mal settlement of 1582, the *khalisa* revenue of Bengal had been fixed at the figure of Rs. 6.34 million. In the Shah Shuja

[58] H.B. 27.10.1658, K.A. 1117, ff. 178-179; H.XVII. 12.5.1659, K.A. 1119, ff. 891-vo; B.H. 7.7.1659, K.A. 786, ff. 421-422; H.XVII. 25.8.1659, K.A. 1120, ff. 286-vo.

settlement of 1658, this figure was revised upward to Rs. 8.76 million. Together with the *jagir* revenue of Rs. 4.35 million, the total revenue assessed in the 1658 settlement was Rs. 13.11 million. This figure remained unchanged until about 1710, when Murshid Quli Khan initiated the process of yet another revision of the Bengal revenues. The reorganization was completed only in 1722, when the total land revenue was revised upward to Rs. 14.28 million, of which the *khalisa* component was Rs. 10.96 million. The increase in the *khalisa* component was achieved partly through a transfer of some of the *jagir* lands to *khalisa*.[59] The transfer of these sums each year would certainly have constituted a drain on the resources of the region. But the point is that this drain began long before the arrival of the Dutch and the English in the region. Between 1658, when the Dutch (and English) presence in the region was still very small, and in about 1710, the amount of revenue remitted out of Bengal remained unchanged. It was only during the closing years of our period that the amount of the remittance would have increased somewhat as part of the process of reorganization of revenues completed in 1722. It would thus seem that over the second half of the seventeenth and the first two decades of the eighteenth centuries, the increase in the net annual average outflow of funds from Bengal would have been marginal at most. It would, therefore, probably be erroneous to ascribe the absence of a general price rise in Bengal in the face of a continuing and growing import of precious metals to an increase in the net outflow of funds from the region.

In conclusion, one can argue that the Dutch (and English) trade in Bengal was a net contribution to the growth of the trade from the region, and that the implications of this trade for the local economy were generally favourable. There was an increase in the level of output, income, and employment in the economy as a result of this trade. One can, however, attempt a quantification of these only up to a point, and even then the exercise is fraught with possibilities of significant margins of error. The most outstanding feature of the Dutch (and English) trade that contributed to this favourable trend was the fact that the trade involved an exchange of precious metals for goods rather than the usual exchange of one set of goods for another.

[59] W. K. Firminger, ed., *The Fifth Report from the Select Committee of the House of Commons on the Affairs of the East India Company, 1812*, II, Appendix IV, pp. 186, 191.

· 9 ·

CONCLUSION

The growing integration of India into the premodern world economy in the seventeenth century had far-reaching implications for her economy and society. The English East India Company, which was an important vehicle of this integration, managed to assume political authority in Bengal in the latter half of the eighteenth century, and became an instrument of the establishment of a colonial relationship between Britain and India. The present study has been concerned with the Dutch East India Company—the other major European trading company operating in India in the seventeenth and the eighteenth centuries. In terms of the volume of trade handled, the Dutch were considerably ahead of the English throughout the period ending in 1720. And, in contrast to the English or even the French, the Dutch presence in India never acquired a political colour. Until the middle of the eighteenth century, the principal concern of all the European companies was commercial. Each of them competed fiercely for the coveted Indian cargoes—textiles, raw silk, saltpetre, and other goods. Undeniably, even during this period, the interaction between the companies and the host society went beyond the domain of economics. But the present study has been confined to the economic dimension of the Dutch Company's operations in the Bengal region.

Perhaps the most distinguishing feature of the Dutch Company's trading strategy was its extensive participation in intra-Asian trade. It is true that the Portuguese had preceded the Dutch in this, but the sophistication of operation and the volume of trade achieved by the Dutch were quite new. Now, for the first time, a single agency of trade operated along the whole of the great arc of Asian trade stretching from the Red Sea and Persian Gulf to Japan. India occupied a key position in the structure of Asian trade by virtue of her capacity to put large quantities of highly competitive mass-consumption manufactured goods on the market. The most important of these were the coarse cotton textiles produced mainly on the Coromandel coast. It is, therefore, not surprising that the Company arrived on this coast very early in its career. Bengal was reached in the early 1630s, and soon became an important trading station of the Company. Bengal raw silk became the staple export to Japan, which was the principal supplier of precious metals in Asia. In the second half of the seventeenth century, Bengal opium found an ever-growing market in the Indonesian archipelago. The spice monopoly enjoyed by the Company in the archi-

257

pelago, together with the exclusive access to the Japan trade during the "closed-country" era, were important factors in the Company's unqualified success and high profits in the intra-Asian trade.

A decline in the general profitability of the intra-Asian trade toward the close of the seventeenth century would normally have cut into the relative importance of the Bengal factories in the structure of Dutch trade in Asia. But as it happened, fine cotton and other textiles as well as raw silk emerged as dominant items of export to Europe at about the same time. Since Bengal was an important producer of these goods, this region suddenly became a major supplier of goods to Holland. The proportion of the total export cargo procured in Bengal and destined for Europe as against that destined for the rest of Asia went up dramatically from about one-fifth to about four-fifths. More than half of the total textiles (in terms of value) reaching Holland at the end of the seventeenth century originated in Bengal. This proportion exceeded 80 percent in the case of raw silk. Small wonder, then, that at the turn of the century, Bengal supplied as much as 40 percent of the total value the Company imported into Holland, and became by far its most important single trading station in the whole of Asia. The situation was not very different in the case of the English East India Company.

The Mughals regarded an expansion in trade with favour, and the European companies were generally welcome in the empire. Both the Dutch and the English companies were exempted from the payment of transit duties throughout Mughal India. The companies' trade brought in a welcome increase in the imperial revenues from the customs duties. Perhaps an even more important consideration was the import of precious metals by these companies into the empire. The Mughal monetary system depended heavily on imported precious metals, and an accretion to the supply of these metals was highly welcome.

The companies' trade in Bengal involved an expansion in real income and output in the economy. The additional export demand for commodities such as textiles and raw silk led to an expansion in the output of these goods. The existence of a slack in the economy together with the possibility of an expansion in capacity made an increase in output possible. The high fertility in the agricultural sector of the region also contributed to this process. The precious metals imported by the companies were symptomatic of the rise in output. It is immaterial whether the import of these metals is regarded as a commodity import or as a means of settling the accounts in the balance of payments. Unfortunately, in the absence of information pertaining to the value of variables such as the marginal rate of saving and the capital-output ratio, it is not possible to measure the resultant increase in income and output. The precise increase in employment cannot be measured either, but one can attempt crude estimates in this direction.

Indian merchants supplying export goods to the Company seem to have been the principal beneficiaries of the growing opportunities opened up by expanding trade. A variety of institutional rigidities, the most important of which seems to have been the widespread indebtedness of the weavers and other artisan groups to the intermediary merchants, prevented the artisans from receiving their proper share in the rising prices of the textiles and other export goods.

The other group of Bengal merchants likely to be directly affected by the growing trade of the Dutch Company were those engaged in coastal and overseas trade from the region. In principle, the growing competition by the Company along branches of Asian trade frequented by these merchants should have posed problems for them. The Company could contain these merchants' trade along particular routes by competition on the basis of its superior resources or special privileges. It could also use the pass system for this purpose. In practice, however, no such thing seems to have happened on any scale. It is true that the pass system represented an arbitrary and institutionalized check on the freedom of navigation, but its effectiveness was extremely limited. A study of the movements in trade along a branch such as Bengal-Southeast Asia suggests that neither the pass nor the trade policies of the Company were instrumental in bringing about a decline in the Indian merchants' trade along this route. If the Company policies failed to be effective on a branch of trade such as this one, where the Company had a great deal at stake, it is unlikely that the Indian merchants would have been eliminated by competition in other less fiercely contested branches. The strength of the Indian merchant evidently lay in his lower overhead costs and a much more intimate familiarity with the mechanics of the markets both at home and at the ports of destination.

Holden Furber has spoken of the cooperation among Europeans and Asians in a variety of fields throughout the seventeenth and the eighteenth centuries.[1] This cooperation took many forms. In situations where it had been forced, it worked only up to a point. An example of this was the requirement that the companies provide a convoy to the Indian ships operating between Surat and the Red Sea. Essentially similar was the matter of the loan by the companies of European captains, steersmen, and sailors. Given a general shortage of these functionaries, particularly because of desertion, the companies agreed to their loan only sparingly.

[1] Holden Furber, *Rival Empires of Trade in the Orient* (Minneapolis and Oxford, 1976), Chapter VII.

Ordinarily, it was only senior state officials engaged in trade, whose displeasure the companies wished to avoid, that were provided with the loan of these personnel.[2] This was also true of the loan or sale of navigational equipment.[3]

Ordinary commercial cooperation between the companies and the Indian merchants included the hiring of freight space and the chartering of vessels for particular voyages. By far the most important Asian route along which both the Dutch and the English companies carried on a substantial amount of freight traffic was that between India and Persia. Soon after the conclusion of the 1652 agreement with Shah Abbas II, the Dutch factors at Gombroon estimated that the Company could hope to earn 20,000 florins per annum by carrying Indian merchants' freight cargo to and from Persia.[4] English participation in the Indo-Persian freight service went up rather rapidly from about 1680 onward. From the beginning of the eighteenth century, the English even began chartering whole ships to Indian merchants. Striking instances of this practice are the chartering of the *Colchester* in 1702 to one of the leading Armenian merchants of Calcutta, Sarhad Israeli, for Gombroon and Basra and the chartering of the *Hester* to the Company's Hindu broker, Janardhan Seth, in 1707 for Persia.[5] As English participation in the freight traffic between India and Persia developed, freight charges appear to have declined.[6] Occasionally, the companies hired freight space on Indian vessels besides chartering them.[7]

---

[2] The Dutch Company provided in 1654 three steersmen to Prince Shah Shuja, in 1660 one steersman to Emperor Aurangzeb for a voyage to Ceylon, and in 1666 one steersman to Nawab Amin Khan for a voyage to Tenasserim, and another steersman to the *faujdar* of Hugli, Syyad Jalal (P.B. 12.3.1654, K.A. 1094, f. 625vo; H.B. 29.11.1660, K.A. 1126, f. 49; H.B. 1.4.1666, K.A. 1149, ff. 2240-2241). Similarly, the English Company was reported to have loaned several steersmen to Nawab Khan Dauran in 1665 (H.B. 26.3.1665, K.A. 1143, ff. 563-565).

[3] In 1666, for example, the Dutch Company sold some navigational equipment to Nawab Amin Khan (H.B. 1.4.1666, K.A. 1149, ff. 2240-2241). Three years earlier, the English factors at Surat had asked the Court of Directors for "ten or fifteen anchors for the supply of the King's jounks" (Foster, ed., *The English Factories in India*, 1661-1664, p. 211).

[4] Estimate dated May 25, 1652, K.A. 1079, ff. 349vo-350.

[5] Diary of the Old English Company kept at Calcutta, December 29, 1702, F.R. Calcutta, vol. 4, ff. 20-22; letter from the Court of Managers to the United English Company in Calcutta dated April 17, 1708, Letter Book 13, ff. 255-256.

[6] In 1685, for example, the Dutch entered into a contract with a number of Bengal merchants for the transportation of passengers and freight to Persia on the *Walenberg* at a cost of 10,000 rupees. But soon thereafter the English offered substantially better terms. The Dutch answered by reducing their price to as low as 3,570 rupees. The documents are silent regarding the eventual outcome of the price war, but we do know that the price offered by the English in the second round was even lower (B.H. 27.5.1686, K.A. 816, f. 213).

[7] For example, the Dutch Company transported cargo worth f. 89,715 from Bengal to

Individual European and Indian merchants also cooperated with each other in a variety of ways. For one thing, these traders collaborated in financing voyages to and from various Asian ports. In 1661, for example, the Dutch factors reported the arrival at Balasore from Ceylon of a vessel financed jointly by a Muslim merchant and a Dutchman named Jacob. Twenty years later, a Frenchman, Jean de St. Jacqy, is recorded as having financed the *Nossenboor* jointly with a Bengali merchant, Hari Shah, on a voyage from Balasore to Achin.[8] Occasionally, the European merchants used the services of Indian agents for equipping and dispatching ships on their behalf.[9]

The implications of the commercial interaction between Asia and Europe for the latter continent have not been analysed in the present study. But by any reckoning, these were important. The century under review witnessed the beginnings of a process that eventually culminated in the European colonization of a large part of the world. The dependence from the close of the seventeenth century onward of the Dutch silk industry on the raw material obtained in Bengal was perhaps but a portent of the nature of economic relationship that was to emerge between the two continents in the nineteenth century.

Coromandel in 1655 on an Indian vessel (P.B. 10.3.1655, K.A. 1100, ff. 374-375). In 1661, the Company chartered four Indian vessels for the transportation of rice from Bengal to Ceylon (H.B. 20.10.1661, K.A. 1226, f. 723). In the same year, an Indian ship chartered by the English arrived at Surat from Achin (*Batavia Dagh-Register*, 1661, p. 327).

[8] *Batavia Dagh-Register*, 1661, p. 399; list of ships that left Balasore in 1680-1681, enclosure to H.B. 9.4.1681, K.A. 1258, ff. 1285-1291.

[9] Thus the *Fateh Shahi* is recorded as having arrived at Hugli on the account—ostensibly personal—of the director of the French East India Company in Bengal in 1716 from Surat, and the following year from Persia. On both these occasions, the vessel had been equipped by one Sheikh Nasir, who is reported to have himself accompanied it on the latter of these two trips. See list of ships that came to Hugli in 1716, K.A. 1769, ff. 210-212; in 1717, K.A. 1783, ff. 91-92.

APPENDIX

A NOTE ON THE DUTCH SOURCES

This study is based mainly on the unpublished material in the archives of the Dutch East India Company preserved at the *Algemeen Rijksarchief* at The Hague and, to a smaller extent, the papers of the English East India Company at the India Office Records, London. The various series of documents consulted are described in the bibliography.

In a paper entitled "Dutch Source Material on Indian Maritime History in the Early Modern Period—An Evaluation" published in the *Indian Historical Review*, 8 (July 1981-January 1982), I have analysed the nature and the limitations of the information available in the Dutch sources. In the present note, I will briefly discuss the statistical and other materials in the Dutch sources used in the writing of Chapters 3, 5, 6, and 7.

THE IMPORT INVOICES AND THE SALES DATA

The import invoices are available, with occasional gaps, from 1663 onward in the letters the factors at Hugli received from Batavia and other Asian factories. These invoices have been used mainly to work out the total value of the goods and the precious metals received at Hugli. Often, the Batavia invoices indicated the point of origin of the goods and the precious metals sent. Information relating to the volume of goods sold in Bengal, the prices at which they were sold, and the gross profit earned on them is available only for two brief segments of time during our period. The first of these covers the period 1673-1684, for which a comprehensive statement relating to all commodities sold is available in K.A. 1286. The other segment is the years 1711-1717, when the Hugli factors regularly sent to Batavia half-yearly statements of goods sold in Bengal.

THE EXPORT INVOICES

The factors at Hugli regularly sent shipments to Batavia carrying goods for Holland as well as the Asian factories. Shipments were also sent directly to other Asian factories, and occasionally to Holland. In the absence of the "negotie-boeken" for our period, the only way to reconstruct the flow of goods from Bengal is to put together the invoices of these shipments found at the end of the accompanying letters available in the "Letters and papers received" series. The results of this exercise, however, are much less satisfactory than one would wish. In the first place, no invoices are available until 1646 in which the exports from Bengal were distinguished from those from Coromandel. Between 1646 and 1648, the missing invoices far outnumber those available, rendering the latter quite unusable. The information for the period 1648-1665, while reasonably complete, is not of much use as far as the Bengal-Holland trade is concerned, except in the case of saltpetre, where the entire amount exported from Bengal was for Holland. This is because the invoices of the ships sent to Batavia during this period did not specify the breakdown by region of the total of goods intended for Holland, Japan, and the Indonesian archipelago. Over the thirty-three-year period 1665-1698, complete information is available only for nine years in the case of raw silk and eleven in that of textiles. This is partly due to the nonavailability of the invoices of one or more shipments in a given year. But more often, this is the result of the absence of breakdown by region of goods in the invoices of one or more shipments in particular years. In view of the enormous annual fluctuations that characterized the export of the textiles and raw silk to Holland during this period, it seemed inadvisable to try to reconstruct the figures for the "incomplete information" years by the use of the usual statistical techniques. For the rest of our period, it is possible to fully reconstruct the volume of trade between Bengal and Holland. Throughout our period, a number of invoices containing a breakdown by region of the physical quantities of the goods carried do not carry a similar breakdown of the cargo by value, though most of them do indicate the *total* value of the goods carried for each individual region. It is, therefore, necessary that the analysis be carried out purely in terms of physical quantities. This particular limitation is not so serious in the case of commodities such as raw silk and saltpetre, where the volume of trade was expressed in terms of a uniform unit—the Dutch *pond*, equivalent to 1.09 pound avoirdupois—and where the range of variation in quality and price between different units in a given lot was fairly limited. The case of textiles, however, was quite different. The quantities in this case were expressed in terms of number of pieces, which are not always reducible to a uniform square yardage. Besides, the price of two textile pieces of similar dimensions could vary considerably, depending on the quality of the raw material used and the degree of workmanship in a given piece. In theory, therefore, an analysis of the trends of trade in textiles exclusively in terms of the number of pieces might not be particularly meaningful. In actual fact, the problem has largely been taken care of by classifying the textiles into five groups— muslins, fine calicoes, ordinary calicoes, cotton-and-silk mixed textiles, and silk piece goods—depending upon the nature of the raw material used and the quality of the final product. Admittedly, there were considerable quality and price variations within each group. Yet the general impression one gathers from the records is that over time the dimensions of different textiles remained broadly unchanged except in the case of the limited quantities procured at Malda, where during the 1680s the Europeans succeeded in initiating the production of three *covid*-wide muslins; and the mix of pieces of different dimensions and qualities within a group also remained largely the same. As such, the orders and export figures of textiles are usable as indicators of trends in trade. Finally, it may be noted that there always was the possibility of a certain amount of discrepancy between the total amount of a particular commodity that left Bengal for Holland and the amount that finally reached there. This was because most of the cargo was routed via the Batavia Council, who, being the central coordinating agency in Asia, had to take an overall view of the requirements of the Euro-Asian and the intra-Asian trade and, therefore, occasionally found it necessary to modify the original destination pattern of part of the goods received from the various Asian factories for Europe and for other parts of Asia. As far as the exports from Bengal to Japan and other Asian destinations were concerned, the available invoices likewise permit only a partial reconstruction of the flow of trade.

THE ANNUAL ORDERS LISTS

The annual orders lists containing regionwise details of the goods ordered by the Directors from the East were despatched to Batavia every year in autumn (but from 1690s on usually in the spring). On receipt, Batavia sent a copy of the relevant section of the list to the chief factory in each region (for example, Hugli in Bengal). Until 1655, when Bengal factories were reorganized into an independent directorate, the orders for Bengal goods were included in the Coromandel section, usually with the words "from Bengal" after the relevant goods. Each regional section of the list began with a general comment on the performance of the goods received the previous year from the region under reference and any complaints or suggestions the Directors might have had to make in that regard. If comments were found in order regarding a particular item, a note was given immediately after the specification of the quantity ordered of the item in question. These comments—in addition, of course, to the sales price information to be discussed presently—are the most graphic and detailed information we have on the performance of individual Asian goods in Holland over time. In fact, these comments make these lists far more useful than would have been the case if they had only contained information about the amounts ordered. These lists are available in an unbroken series except for 1637, 1654 (the orders of autumn 1653 were in fact not despatched until January 1654; the list of orders despatched in the autumn of 1654 is not available), and 1683. It might be noted that similar lists are not available for orders received from or on behalf of the Asian factories such as Japan except for one year, 1703-1704. Annual orders for opium from the Indonesian archipelago and for sugar from Persia can, however, be reconstructed for a part of our period from the correspondence between Hugli, Batavia, and Persia.

"RESPONSE TO ORDERS"

These were sent as enclosures to letters from Hugli to Batavia and were the counterpart of the orders lists. Besides specifying the actual quantities exported, they contained an item-by-item explanation of why Bengal factors were not able to meet all the orders for a given year in full (or, what happened far less often, why the orders for particular items were oversupplied). Unfortunately, these "explanations" begin only in the 1690s and are not particularly reliable for actual quantities procured and exported. Their principal use lies in the information they contain on the specific factors that hindered procurement in given years.

THE PRICE DATA

The correspondence between Hugli and Batavia frequently contained information on the cost price of the various commodities procured in Bengal. The other source of price information is the export invoices mentioned above. Occasionally, these invoices contained, in addition to the usual physical quantities, the value by commodity of the consignment, enabling the researcher to calculate the unit values for the relevant years.

As for price information in the markets where Bengal goods were sold, there is a large body of information available. Volumes carrying K.A. numbers 10234-10242 and entitled "General account of the goods sold, outstanding debts and the unsold goods in the various chambers" contain statements of the total amount of various Asian goods sold in each chamber during the course of a year and the proceeds therefrom, so that one can work out the actual sale prices. Whereas information for the Amsterdam chamber begins in 1649-1650 and is reasonably complete for the rest of our period, except in the case of Bengal raw silk, where information begins only in the 1670s (with the exception of 1653-1654), that for the other chambers not only does not begin until the 1670s and the 1680s, but is extremely incomplete until 1707-1708. It is, therefore, necessary to treat figures of the Amsterdam chamber which, on an average, accounted for about 50 percent of the amount sold in all the six chambers put together, as representative. Although the sales information is very useful for an analysis of the trends in prices and amounts sold of commodities such as Indonesian spices, Japanese copper, Mocha coffee, and Bengal raw silk, which were comparatively homogeneous products with reference to the value of individual units, the situation in the case of such a heterogeneous commodity as textiles was quite different. In the first place, one often comes across bland categories such as "cotton textiles" and "silk piece-goods," where the information available can hardly be used for anything other than for conveying an idea of the total turnover during the course of the year. Even in cases in which the sales and proceeds information is given with reference to individual types of textiles, the derived price indicated only the average for the entire lot, which might at times be misleading. A much more concise source of information on this subject is K.A. 10228, entitled "Collection of the sales in the respective chambers, 1693-1760." This source has the merit of containing information for all the six chambers. It must be pointed out, however, that the quantities contained in this volume are those offered for sale by the Company and represent only approximations to the actual amounts sold. Similarly, both the average sale prices for individual chambers and the all-chamber average prices in this volume are only approximations—though at times very close—to the actual sale price figures. The detailed printed price lists for the Amsterdam chamber of the type one comes across after 1721 are no longer available for our period. Also, consolidated price data of the Holland variety are not available for any of the Asian markets where Bengal goods were sold. An attempt has, however, been made to convey an idea of the performance of Bengal goods in these regions by reference, on a selective basis, to the Company's records pertaining to these factories.

GLOSSARY

abbasi	A coin found in Persia, worth a little over half a Mughal Indian rupee in the seventeenth century
arhat	Commission
aurung	Localized centres of manufacturing production for trade
bahar	A measure of weight between 460 and 500 Dutch ponds
bakshi	The official in charge of military finance
band	A term used to denote the periodical harvesting of the silk cocoons
banjara	A hereditary group of travelling grain traders found in India
batta	A discount applied to Mughal coins older than the year of mintage or to coins considered nonstandard
bigha	A land measure with regional variations. In Bengal, it was one-third of an acre
catty	A measure of weight introduced by the Chinese into the Indonesian archipelago and equivalent to 1.25 Dutch ponds
cauri	The small white shell *Cypraea moneta* current as money in Bengal and other parts of India
covid	An indigenous measure with considerable regional variations. It could be as large as a yard or only half that much. In Bengal, the equivalent of a *covid* was 27 inches
dalal	A broker
dam	A copper coin used in the Mughal empire. At first its value was a fortieth part of a rupee, and later it rose to a thirtieth part
daroga	A term with a variety of connotations. It was usually used for an officer of law. Mint-masters of Mughal India were generally called *darogas* of *taksal*. A *daroga* could also be an agent of a state official carrying out procurement of goods on his behalf
dastak	A permit, chiefly for the transit of goods
dasturi	A customary commission
diwan	Official in charge of the treasury

farmaish	A provision authorizing state authorities to requisition goods for use by the state
farman	A Mughal imperial decree or edict
faujdar	The Mughal military under-governor of a district
gomashta	A heterogenous group of merchants engaged in the procurement of goods on behalf of the European companies
hasb-ul-hukm	The literal meaning of the words is "according to order." This was usually a letter written by a minister under the emperor's directions and conveying his orders
hundi	A bill of exchange
jazia	Poll tax imposed on subjects who were not Muslim
karkhana	A manufactory
karori	A Mughal revenue official originally in charge of a territory yielding 10 million dams in land revenue per annum
katchari	The name of the fleet stationed at Surat and used to curb local pirates like the Sanganians
kaul	A lease or grant in writing; a safe conduct, amnesty, or in fact any written engagement
khalisa	The term used to denote the lands whose revenue went directly to the central Mughal treasury
khandies	A measure of weight: three *khandies* made one deadweight ton
koban	An oval-shaped Japanese gold coin which until 1695 weighed 4.73 momme (= 17.768 grams) and contained 85.69% gold, 14.25% silver, and 0.06% alloy
kuli	A hired labourer or burden-carrier
mansabdar	A Mughal state official eligible to hold both civil and military offices. Each official held a dual numerical rank—*zat* (personal) and *sawar* (cavalry). The *zat* rank determined the official's status in the hierarchy besides his personal salary per annum, whereas the other rank specified the extent of his military obligations. The *sawar* rank also determined the annual sum of money to be reimbursed to the official against this obligation
maund	A measure of weight. In Bengal the maund was equal to 40 seers = 34.05 kg = 68 Dutch ponds
muchalka	A written obligation or bond

muhr	The gold coin of Mughal India
mutasaddi	A high Mughal official usually described by the Europeans as the local governor
nakhuda	Captain of an Indian vessel
nishan	An order or permit usually issued by a prince of the blood
paikar	A merchant working as agent for the procurement of goods for trade
pancado	A system that required foreign merchants coming to Japan to sell Chinese raw silk at a price determined arbitrarily by a guild monopsony consisting of a group of merchants from the five imperial cities of Edo (Tokyo), Osaka, Kyoto, Sakai, and Nagasaki
pargana	A territorial and administrative unit in a Mughal Indian province
parwana	A letter of authority from an official, usually to his subordinate
pattani	Superior grade unspun silk drawn from cocoons
pond	The Dutch pond was approximately equal to 1.09 lbs. avoirdupois
potti	Inferior grade unspun silk drawn from cocoons
qazi	A Muslim judge
rahdari	Transit duty in Mughal India
rawana	A pass or permit
sanad	A diploma, patent, or deed of grant by the government of office, privilege, or right
sarraf	A money changer who occasionally also acted as a banker
sauda-i-khas	Procurement on the account of the state
sawar	See *mansabdar*
seer	A measure of weight equivalent to one-fortieth of the maund
shahbandar	The harbour-master
sicca	Describes Mughal coins of the current year's mintage
subahdar	The Mughal viceroy of a province
tael	The *tael* was the trading name of the Chinese ounce ($\frac{1}{16}$th of a *catty*), and also of the Chinese money of account, often called "the ounce of silver"

talika   Invoices of goods imported and exported, which were submitted to the customs authorities

wakianavis   The official responsible for keeping the Mughal authorities at the capital informed of important developments in his province

zamorin   The title of the Hindu sovereign of Calicut and the country round

zat   See *mansabdar*

BIBLIOGRAPHY

ARCHIVAL SOURCES

Algemeen Rijksarchief, The Hague

Until recently, the volumes containing the Dutch East India Company's papers carried the Koloniaal Archief (K.A.) numbers. These volumes have now been assigned Verenigde Oost-Indische Compagnie (V.O.C.) numbers. We have retained the K.A. numbers in the footnotes, but in this section, the V.O.C. numbers have also been given in brackets. The following series of papers were consulted:

Overgekomen brieven en papieren (Letters and papers received), 1615-1720, and the *Inkomend briefboek* (Incoming letterbook), 1661-1720. Papers relating to Bengal in K.A. 971-1838 (V.O.C. 1059-1946). These two series of papers are, in fact, merged together and carry consecutive serial numbers. These are the most voluminous as well as the most important series of papers in the Dutch archives. They consist of letters written from Batavia to the Directors together with their enclosures. The enclosures consist of a wide variety of material including letters received from the various Asian factories such as Bengal together with copies of correspondence with the Indian authorities, the minutes of the meetings of the Hugli council, financial statements, and so on. Until 1646, the materials for Bengal are found under Coromandel. It is in K.A. 1064 bis (V.O.C. 1164) that a separate section is first devoted to Bengal. In addition to the Bengal papers, papers relating to factories such as Japan and Persia where Bengali goods were sold have also been examined on a selective basis.

Bataviasch uitgaande briefboek (Batavia's outgoing letterbook), 1621-1720. Letters relating to Bengal in K.A. 753-876 (V.O.C. 849-973). This series contains letters written from Batavia to the various Asian factories. Until the 1640s, the material relating to Bengal is to be found in the letters to Coromandel.

Resolutien van Gouverneur-Generaal en Raden (Resolutions of the Governor-General and Council), 1647-1720. Resolutions relating to Bengal in K.A. 571-636 (V.O.C. 669-736).

Copieboek van brieven, instructies en andere papieren van de XVII en de Kamer Amsterdam aan de regeringen van Indie en de Kaap (Copybook of letters, instructions, and other papers sent by the XVII and the Amsterdam Chamber to the Governments of the Indies and the Cape), 1647-1720. Papers relating to Bengal in K.A. 455-464 (V.O.C. 317-326). This series contains letters from the Board of Directors (the Gentlemen XVII) to Batavia. The relevant extracts were sent on to Hugli.

Resolutien genomen op de ordinaris en extra-ordinaris vergaderingen van Heeren XVII (Resolutions adopted at the ordinary and the extraordinary meetings of the Gentlemen XVII), 1635-1720. K.A. 250-266 (V.O.C. 101-117). These resolutions contain, among other things, the lists of goods the Directors ordered annually from the East along with their comments on the performance of the goods received during the previous year. The relevant extracts were sent on to Hugli.

Anonymous report dealing with private trade in Bengal, entitled " 't Oostindische Sacspiegeltje," K.A. 4464 W48 (V.O.C. 4704).

Byeenbrenging van verkopingen in de respective kamers beginnende Anno 1693 en eindigde Anno 1760 (Collection of the sales in the respective chambers beginning in 1693 and ending in 1760), K.A. 10228 (V.O.C. 6989).

Generale staten van verhandelde goederen, uitstaande schulden en onverkochte goederen van de verschillende kamers (General account of the goods sold, outstanding debts, and unsold goods in the various chambers), K.A. 10234-10242 (V.O.C. 4583-4591).

India Office Records, London

The papers of the English East India Company relating to Bengal usefully supplement the Dutch material. The following series of documents were used:

Factory records
    Balasore, volume 1
    Calcutta (including Sutanati), volumes 1-11
    Dacca, volume 1
    Hugli, volumes 1-11
    Kasimbazar, volumes 1-4
    Malda, volumes 1-2
    Patna, volume 1
    Miscellaneous, volumes 3, 3A, 6, 7, 7A, 9, 26
Letters from India, Original Correspondence. Volumes 21-63. O.C. Nos. 2072-8717
Letters to India, Letter Books. Volumes 1-16
Bengal Public Consultations, 1704-1718. Range 1, volumes 1-3

BIBLIOGRAPHY

Bengal General Journals and Ledgers, 1704-1718. Range 174, volumes 70-99

Home Miscellaneous Series. Volumes 34, 36, 42, 47, 57, 68, 74, 92, 456A, 456F, 628-630

Public Records Office, London

Colonial Correspondence, East India C.O. 77/49

British Museum, London

Committee of Shipping, Ship Book, 1673-1790, East India Company's Records, volume II. MS No. Addl. 38872

Abstract of the Ships and the Value of Cargoes Sent Out by the East India Company. MS No. Addl. 15898

Papers Relating to the East India Company, 1682-1701. Ms No. Addl. 22185

List of the Ships Sent from England to "Coast" and "Bay" between 8.1.1684 and 9.3.1688. Sloane MS No. 3671

Persian Copies with English Translations of Firmans & Sunnuds Granted to the Dutch Company. MS No. Addl. 29095

Notes and Observations of East India. Marshall MS, Harley MS No. 4254

PRINTED RECORDS, SELECTIONS

Colenbrander, H. T., and W. Ph. Coolhaas, eds. *Jan Pietersz. Coen, Bescheiden Omtrent Zijn Bedrijf in Indie.* Vols. 1-6 edited by H. T. Colenbrander, vol. 7 (in 2 parts) edited by W. Ph. Coolhaas. The Hague, 1919-1953.

Coolhaas, W. Ph., ed. *Generale Missiven van Gouverneurs-Generaal en Raden Aan Heren XVII der Verenigde Oost-Indische Compagnie.* 7 vols., 1610-1725. The Hague, 1960-1979.

Fawcett, C., ed. *The English Factories in India (New Series) 1670-1684.* 4 vols. Oxford, 1936-1953.

Firminger, W. K., ed. *The Fifth Report from the Select Committee of the House of Commons on the Affairs of the East India Company, 1812.* 3 vols. Calcutta, 1917-1918.

————. "The Malda Diary and Consultations 1680-1682." *Journal and Proceedings of the Asiatic Society of Bengal,* N.S. 14 (1918), 1-241.

Foster, W., ed. *The English Factories in India, 1618-1669.* 13 vols. Oxford, 1906-1927.

Heeres, J. E., and F. W. Stapel, eds. *Corpus-Diplomaticum Neerlando-*

Indicum. Vols. 1-2 edited by J. E. Heeres, vols. 3-6 edited by F. W. Stapel. The Hague, 1907-1953.

Heeres, J. E., and others, eds. *Dagh-Register gehouden in 't Casteel Batavia, 1624-1682.* 31 vols. The Hague/Batavia, 1887-1931.

Prakash, Om, ed. *The Dutch Factories in India, 1617-1623. A Collection of Dutch East India Company Documents Pertaining to India.* New Delhi, 1984.

Wilson, C. R., ed. *The Early Annals of the English in Bengal.* 3 vols. London, 1895-1917.

CONTEMPORARY WORKS

Bernier, François. *Travels in the Mogul Empire, A.D. 1656-1668.* Edited by A. Constable. Oxford, 1934.

Bowrey, Thomas. *A Geographical Account of Countries Round the Bay of Bengal, 1669 to 1679.* Edited by Richard Temple. Cambridge, 1905.

———. *The Papers of Thomas Bowrey 1669-1713.* Edited by Richard Temple. London, 1927.

Cary, J. *A Discourse Concerning the East India Trade.* London, 1699.

Child, Josiah. *A New Discourse of Trade.* London, 1693.

De Jonge, J.K.J. *De Opkomst van het Nederlandsch Gezag in Oost-Indië, 1595-1844.* 17 volumes in 18 parts and 2 registers. The Hague/Amsterdam, 1862-1909.

Fryer, John. *A New Account of East India and Persia, Being Nine Years' Travels 1672-1681.* Edited by W. Crooke. 3 vols. London, 1909-1915.

Hamilton, Alexander. *A New Account of the East Indies.* Edited by William Foster. 2 vols. London, 1930.

Hedges, William. *The Diary of William Hedges 1681-1687.* Edited by R. Barlow and H. Yule. 3 vols. London, 1887-1889.

Manrique, Sebastien. *Travels of Fray Sebastien Manrique 1629-1643.* Edited by C. E. Luard. 2 vols. Oxford, 1927.

Master, Streynsham. *The Diaries of Streynsham Master 1675-1680.* Edited by Richard Temple. 2 vols. London, 1911.

Orme, Robert. *Historical Fragments of the Mogul Empire.* London, 1805.

Pelsaert, Francisco. *Jahangir's India: The Remonstratie of Francisco Pelsaert.* Edited by W. H. Moreland and P. Geyl. Cambridge, 1925.

———. *De geschriften van Francisco Pelsaert over Mughal Indië, 1627 Kroniek en Remonstratie.* Edited by D.H.A. Kolff and H. W. van Santen. The Hague, 1979.

Roe, Thomas. *The Embassy of Sir Thomas Roe to India 1615-1619.* Edited by W. Foster. London, 1926.

Schouten, Wouter. *Oost-Indische Reys-Beschrijving.* Amsterdam, 1676.

Smith, Adam. *The Wealth of Nations.* Reprinted from the 6th edition. London, 1905.

Tavernier, Jean Baptiste. *Travels in India.* Translated by V. Ball and edited by W. Crooke. 2 vols. London, 1925.

Valentijn, François. *Beschrijvinge van 't Nederlandsch Comptoir op de Kust van Malabar en van Onzen Handel in Japan.* Dordrecht/Amsterdam, 1726.

——. *Oud en Nieuw Oost-Indien.* 5 volumes in 8 parts. Dordrecht/ Amsterdam, 1724-1726.

van Dam, Pieter. *Beschrijvinge van de Oost-Indische Compagnie.* Edited by F. W. Stapel and others. 4 books in 7 parts. The Hague, 1927-1954.

Varthema, Ludovico di. *The Itinerary of Ludovico di Varthema of Bologna from 1502 to 1508.* Edited by Richard Temple. London, 1928.

SECONDARY WORKS

Allen, B. C. *District Gazetteer, Dacca.* Allahabad, 1912.

Anand, Indira. "India's Overseas Trade, 1715-1725." Ph.D. dissertation, University of Delhi, 1970.

Arasaratnam, S. "Weavers, Merchants and the Company: The Handloom Industry in South-Eastern India, 1750-1790." *Indian Economic and Social History Review,* 17 (1980), 257-281.

——. "Some Notes on the Dutch in Malacca and the Indo-Malayan Trade, 1641-1670." *Journal of Southeast Asian History,* 10 (December 1969), 480-490.

——. "The Indian Merchants and Their Trading Methods." *Indian Economic and Social History Review,* 3 (1966), 85-95.

——. *Dutch Power in Ceylon, 1658-1687.* Amsterdam, 1958.

Atwell, William S. "International Bullion Flows and the Chinese Economy, *circa* 1530-1650." *Past and Present,* 95 (1982), 68-90.

——. "Notes on Silver, Foreign Trade, and the Late Ming Economy." *Ch'ing-shih wen-t'i,* 3:8 (1977), 1-33.

Aymard, Maurice, ed. *Dutch Capitalism and World Capitalism.* Cambridge, 1982.

Baines, E. *History of the Cotton Manufacture in Great Britain.* London, 1835. Reprint 1966.

Barbour, Violet. *Capitalism in Amsterdam in the Seventeenth Century.* The Johns Hopkins University Studies in Historical and Political Science Series LXVII, No. 1. Baltimore, 1950.

Bassett, D. K. "The Amboyna Massacre of 1623." *Journal of Southeast Asian History,* 1:2 (1960), 1-19.

275

Baud, J. C. "Proeve van eene Geschiedenis van den Handel en het Verbruik van Opium in Nederlandsch Indie." *Bijdragen tot de Taal-, Land-en Volkenkunde van Nederlandsch Indie*, 1 (1853), 79-220.

Bayly, C. A. "Putting Together the Eighteenth Century in India: Trade, Money, and the 'Pre-Colonial' Political Order." Paper presented to the Second Anglo-Dutch Conference on Comparative Colonial History, Leiden University, 1981.

Bhattacharya, S. *The East India Company and the Economy of Bengal from 1704 to 1740*. London, 1954.

Blitz, Rudolph C. "Mercantilist Policies and the Pattern of World Trade, 1500-1750." *Journal of Economic History*, 27 (March 1967), 39-55.

Boxer, C. R. *The Dutch Seaborne Empire*. New York, 1965.

———. "Jan Compagnie in Japan 1672-1674 or Anglo-Dutch Rivalry in Japan and Formosa." *Transactions of the Asiatic Society of Japan*, Second Series, 7 (1930), 138-203.

———. *The Great Ship of Amacon, Annals of Macao and the Old Japan Trade, 1555-1640*. Lisbon, 1959.

Braudel, Fernand. *The Mediterranean and the Mediterranean World in the Age of Philip II*. Translated by Siân Reynolds. 2 volumes. London, 1972-1973.

Brenner, Y. S. "The Inflation of Prices in Early Sixteenth-Century England." *Economic History Review*, Second Series, 14 (1961), 225-239.

Brennig, Joseph J. "The Textile Trade of Seventeenth Century Northern Coromandel: A Study of Pre-Modern Asian Export Industry." Ph.D. dissertation, University of Wisconsin, 1975.

Brugmans, H., and others. *Amsterdam in de Zeventiende Eeuw*. The Hague, 1901-1904.

Bruijn, J. R.; E. S. van Eyck van Helsinga; F. S. Gaastra; and I. Schöffer. *Dutch-Asiatic Shipping*. 2 volumes. The Hague, 1979.

Calkins, P. B. "The Role of Murshidabad as a Regional and Sub-regional Center in Bengal." In R. L. Park, ed., *Urban Bengal*. East Lansing, Michigan, 1969.

Chandra, Satish. "Commercial Activities of the Mughal Emperors during the Seventeenth Century." *Bengal Past and Present*, 78 (1959), 92-97.

Chatterjee, Anjali. *Bengal in the Reign of Aurangzib, 1658-1707*. Calcutta, 1967.

Chaudhuri, K. N. *The Trading World of Asia and the English East India Company, 1660-1760*. Cambridge, 1978.

———. "The Economic and Monetary Problem of European Trade with Asia during the Seventeenth and the Eighteenth Centuries." *Journal of European Economic History*, 4 (1975), 323-356.

———. "The Structure of Indian Textile Industry in the Seventeenth and Eighteenth Centuries." *Indian Economic and Social History Review*, 11 (June-September 1974), 127-182.

———. "Treasure and Trade Balances: The East India Company's Export Trade, 1660-1720." *Economic History Review*, Second Series, 21 (1968), 480-502.

———. *The East India Company*. London, 1965.

———. "The East India Company and the Export of Treasure in the Early Seventeenth Century." *Economic History Review*, Second Series, 16 (1963), 23-38.

Chaudhuri, S. *Trade and Commercial Organisation in Bengal, 1650-1720*. Calcutta, 1975.

Cipolla, Carlo M., ed. *The Fontana Economic History of Europe: the Sixteenth and Seventeenth Centuries*. Glasgow, 1974.

———. *Guns and Sails in the Early Phase of European Expansion, 1400-1700*. London, 1965.

Das Gupta, Ashin. *Indian Merchants and the Decline of Surat c. 1700-1750*. Wiesbaden, 1979.

Deane, P., and W. A. Cole. *British Economic Growth, 1688-1959*. Cambridge, 1969.

Desai, Ashok. "Population and Standard of Living in Akbar's Time." *Indian Economic and Social History Review*, 9 (1972), 43-62.

Emmer, P. C., and H. L. Wesseling, eds. *Reappraisals in Overseas History*. Leiden, 1979.

Foster, W. "Gabriel Boughton and the Trading Privileges in Bengal." *Indian Antiquary*, 40 (1911), 247-257.

Furber, Holden. *Rival Empires of Trade in the Orient, 1600-1800*. Minneapolis and Oxford, 1976.

———. "Asia and the West as Partners before 'Empire' and After." *Journal of Asian Studies*, 28 (1969), 711-721.

Gaastra, F. S. "Geld Tegen Goederen. Een Structurele Verandering in het Nederlands-Aziatisch Handelsverkeer." *Bijdragen en Mededelingen Betreffende de Geschiedenis der Nederlanden*, 89 (1976), 249-272.

———. *De Geschiedenis van de VOC*. Bussum, 1982.

Glamann, Kristof. *Dutch-Asiatic Trade 1620-1740*. Copenhagen/The Hague, 1958.

———. "The Dutch East India Company's Trade in Japanese Copper, 1645-1736." *Scandinavian Economic History Review*, 1 (1953), 41-79.

Goonewardena, K. W. *The Foundation of Dutch Power in Ceylon, 1638-1658*. Amsterdam, 1958.

Habib, Irfan. "The Technology and Economy of Mughal India." *Indian Economic and Social History Review*, 17 (1980), 1-34.

Habib, Irfan. "Potentialities of Capitalistic Development in the Economy of Mughal India." *Journal of Economic History*, 29 (March 1969), 32-78.

———. *The Agrarian System of Mughal India, 1556-1707*. Bombay, 1963.

———. "The Currency System of the Mughal Empire 1556-1707." *Medieval India Quarterly*, 4 (1961), 1-21.

Hamilton, Earl J. "American Treasure and the Rise of Capitalism, 1500-1700." *Economica*, 27 (November 1929), 338-357.

Hasan, Aziza. "The Silver Currency Output of the Mughal Empire and Prices in India during the Sixteenth and Seventeenth Centuries." *Indian Economic and Social History Review*, 6 (1969), 85-116.

Hill, S. C. "Episodes of Piracy in the Eastern Seas, 1519-1851." *Indian Antiquary*, 49 (1920), 1-21.

Hodenpijl, A.K.A. Gijsberti. "De Handhavig der Neutraliteyt van de Nederlandsche Loge te Houghly, bij de Overrompeling van de Engelsche Kolonie Calcutta in Juni, 1756." *Bijdragen tot the Taal-, Land- en Volkenkunde van Nederlandsch Indie*, 76 (1920), 258-283.

Hossain, Hamida. "The Alienation of Weavers: Impact of the Conflict between the Revenue and the Commercial Interests of the East India Company, 1750-1800." *Indian Economic and Social History Review*, 16 (1979), 323-345.

India, Government of. *Report of the Fact-finding Committee (Handlooms and Mills), 1942*. Delhi, 1942.

———. *Report of the Textile Enquiry Committee, 1954*. Delhi, 1954.

Irwin, John, and P. R. Schwartz. *Studies in Indo-European Textile History*. Ahmedabad, 1966.

Karim, Abdul. *Murshid Quli Khan and His Times*. Dacca, 1963.

Kato, Eiichi. "The Japan-Dutch Trade in the Formative Period of the Seclusion Policy, Particularly on the Raw Silk Trade by the Dutch Factory at Hirado, 1620-1640." *Acta Asiatica: Bulletin of the Institute of Eastern Culture: the Toho Gakkai*, 30 (1976), 34-84.

Kernkamp, J. H. *De Handel op den Vijand, 1572-1609*. Utrecht, 1931.

Kobata, A. "The Production and Uses of Gold and Silver in 16th and 17th Century Japan." *Economic History Review*, Second Series, 18 (August 1965), 245-266.

Kussaka, J. T. *Das Japanische Geldwezen*. Jena, 1890.

Kuznets, S. *Modern Economic Growth: Rate, Structure and Spread*. New Haven, 1966.

Leonard, Karen. "The 'Great Firm' Theory of the Decline of the Mughal Empire." *Comparative Studies in Society and History*, 13 (1979), 151-167.

Lequin, F. *Het Personeel van de Verenigde Oost-Indische Compagnie in Azië in de Achtiende Eeuw, Meer in het Bijzonder in de Vestiging Bengalen.* 2 volumes. Leiden, 1982.

Leupe, P. A. "Rapport van Van Goens (1655)." *Bijdragen tot de Taal-Land- en Volkenkunde van Nederlandsch Indie,* 4 (1856), 141-180.

Little, J. H. "The House of Jagatseth." *Bengal Past and Present,* 20 (1920), 111-200; 22 (1921), 1-119.

MacLeod, N. *De Oost-Indische Compagnie als Zeemogenheid in Azië, 1602-1605.* 2 volumes. Rijswijk, 1927.

Mantoux, Paul. *The Industrial Revolution in the Eighteenth Century.* New York, 1961.

Marshall, P. J. *East Indian Fortunes: The British in Bengal in the Eighteenth Century.* Oxford, 1976.

Masselman, G. *The Cradle of Colonialism.* New Haven, 1963.

Meilink-Roelofsz., M.A.P. *De VOC in Azie.* Bussum, 1976.

———. *Asian Trade and European Influence in the Indonesian Archipelago between 1500 and about 1630.* The Hague, 1962.

Menderhausen, Horst, and Nancy V. Meyer. *The Concept of Hostile Trade, and a Case Study of Seventeenth Century Japan.* Santa Monica, Cal., 1965.

Moreland, W. H. *India at the Death of Akbar.* London, 1923.

———. *From Akbar to Aurangzeb: A Study in Indian Economic History.* London, 1923. Reprint Delhi, 1962.

———. "Indian Exports of Cotton Goods in the Seventeenth Century." *Indian Journal of Economics,* 5 (January 1925), 225-245.

Nachod, Oskar. *Die Beziehungen der Niederländischen Ostindischen Kompagnie zu Japan im Siebzehnten Jahrhundert.* Leipzig, 1897.

O'Malley, L.S.S., and M. Chakravarti. *District Gazetteer, Hooghly.* Calcutta, 1912.

Pakistan, Government of. *Report of the Fact-finding Committee on Hand-looms, 1956.* Karachi, 1956.

Pearson, M. N. *Merchants and Rulers in Gujarat: The Response to the Portuguese in the Sixteenth Century.* Berkeley and Los Angeles, 1976.

Perlin, Frank. "Proto-Industrialization and Pre-Colonial South Asia." *Past and Present,* 98 (1983), 30-95.

———. "Pre-Colonial South Asia and Western Penetration in the Seventeenth to Nineteenth Centuries. A Problem of Epistemological Status." *Review,* 4 (1980), 267-306.

Prakash, Om. "Dutch Source Material on Indian Maritime History in the Early Modern Period—An Evaluation." *Indian Historical Review,* 8 (1981-1982).

———. "Some Aspects of Trade in Mughal India." Presidential address,

Medieval India Section, *Proceedings of the Indian History Congress*, Bodh-Gaya Session, 1981, pp. 173-187.

———. "European Trade and South Asian Economies: Some Regional Contrasts 1600-1800." In L. Blussé and F. S. Gaastra, eds., *Companies and Trade: Essays on Overseas Trading Companies during the Ancien Régime*. The Hague, 1981, pp. 189-205.

———. "Asian Trade and European Impact: A Study of the Trade from Bengal 1630-1720." In Blair B. Kling and M. N. Pearson, eds., *The Age of Partnership, Europeans in Asia Before Dominion*. Honolulu, 1979, pp. 43-70.

———. "Bullion for Goods: International Trade and the Economy of Early Eighteenth Century Bengal." *Indian Economic and Social History Review*, 13 (1976), 159-187.

———. "Bengal Textiles in Seventeenth Century International Trade." In Warren M. Gunderson, ed., *Studies on Bengal*. East Lansing, Michigan, Spring 1976.

———. "The Dutch East India Company in Bengal: Trade Privileges and Problems 1633-1712." *Indian Economic and Social History Review*, 9 (1972), 258-287.

———. "The European Trading Companies and the Merchants of Bengal, 1650-1725." *Indian Economic and Social History Review*, 1 (1964), 37-63.

———, and J. Krishnamurty. "Mughal Silver Currency: A Critique." *Indian Economic and Social History Review*, 7 (1970), 139-150.

Radwan, Ann Bos. *The Dutch in Western India 1601-1632*. Calcutta, 1978.

Ray, Indrani. "The French Company and the Merchants of Bengal, 1680-1730." *Indian Economic and Social History Review*, 8 (1971), 41-55.

Ray, J. C. "Textile Industry in Ancient India." *Journal of the Bihar and Orissa Research Society*, 3 (1917), 180-245.

Raychaudhuri, Tapan. *Jan Company in Coromandel, 1605-1690*. The Hague, 1962.

———, and Irfan Habib, eds. *The Cambridge Economic History of India*. Vol. 1. Cambridge, 1982.

Reus, G. C. Klerk de. *Geschichtlicher Ueberblick der Administrativen, Rechtlichen und Finanziellen Entwickelung der Niederländisch-Ostindischen Compagnie*. Batavia, 1894.

Richards, J. F., ed. *Precious Metals in the Late Medieval and Early Modern Worlds*. Durham, N.C., 1983.

———. "Mughal State Finance and the Premodern World Economy." *Comparative Studies in Society and History*, 23 (1981), 285-308.

Sarkar, Jadunath. *The History of Aurangzeb*. 5 vols. London, 1924.

————. "The Affairs of the English Factory at Surat, 1694-1700." *Indian Historical Records Commission Proceedings*, 5 (1923), 6-13.

————. "The Feringi Pirates of Chatgaon, 1665 A.D." *Journal and Proceedings of the Asiatic Society of Bengal*, 3 (1907), 419-425.

————. "The Conquest of Chatgaon, 1666 A.D." *Journal and Proceedings of the Asiatic Society of Bengal*, 3 (1907), 405-417.

Saxe, Elizabeth Lee. "Fortune's Tangled Web: Trading Networks of English \ Enterprises in Eastern India, 1657-1717." Ph.D. dissertation, Yale University, 1979.

Seiichi, Iwao. "Japanese Foreign Trade in the 16th and 17th Centuries." *Acta Asiatica: Bulletin of the Institute of Eastern Culture: the Toho Gakkai*, 30 (1976), 1-18.

Singer, Charles, and others. *A History of Technology*. Oxford, 1957.

Slomann, V. *Bizarre Designs in Silks*. Copenhagen, 1953.

Steensgaard, Niels. *The Asian Trade Revolution of the Seventeenth Century: The East India Companies and the Decline of Caravan Trade*. Chicago, 1974.

Stevenson, J. "On the Manufacture of Saltpetre as Practiced by the Natives of Tirhut." *Journal and Proceedings of the Asiatic Society of Bengal*, 2 (1833), 23-27.

Takekoshi, Y. *The Economic Aspects of the History of the Civilization of Japan*. London, 1930.

Taylor, James. *A Sketch of the Topography and Statistics of Dacca*. Calcutta, 1840.

Terpstra, H. *De Nederlanders in Voor-Indie*. Amsterdam, 1947.

Toby, Ronald P. "Reopening the Question of Sakoku: Diplomacy in the Legitimation of the Tokugawa Bakufu." *The Journal of Japanese Studies*, 3 (1977), 323-364.

van Dillen, J. G. "Amsterdam als Wereldmarkt der Edele Metalen in de 17de en 18de Eeuw." *De Economist*, 72 (1923), 538-550, 583-598, 717-730.

van Leur, J. C. *Indonesian Trade and Society: Essays in Asian Social and Economic History*. The Hague, 1955.

van Lohuizen, J. *The Dutch East India Company and Mysore*. The Hague, 1961.

van Nierop, Leonie. "De Zijdenijverheid van Amsterdam, Historisch Geschetst." *Tijdschrift voor Geschiedenis*, 45 (1930), 18-40, 152-172; 46 (1931), 28-55, 113-143.

van Santen, H. W. *De Verenigde Oost-Indische Compagnie in Gujarat en Hindustan, 1620-1660*. Leiden, 1982.

Vilar, P. "Problems of the Formation of Capitalism." *Past and Present*, 10 (1956), 15-38.

Villiers, Alan. *The Indian Ocean*. London, 1952.

Wallerstein, Immanuel. *The Modern World System, II: Mercantilism and the Consolidation of the European World-Economy, 1600-1750*. New York/London, 1980.

Wills, John E., Jr. *Pepper, Guns and Parleys: The Dutch East India Company and China, 1662-1681*. Cambridge, Mass., 1974.

INDEX

283

LIBRARY OF CONGRESS CATALOGING IN PUBLICATION DATA

Prakash, Om, 1940-
The Dutch East India Company and the economy of Bengal,
1630-1720.

Bibliography: p.   Includes index.
1. Nederlandsche Oost-Indische Compagnie.   2. Bengal
(India)—Economic conditions.   3. Asia—Commerce—
Europe—History—17th century.   4. Europe—Commerce—
Asia—History—17th century.   I. Title.
HF483.E6P73 1985   382'.095414'00601   84-26484
ISBN 0-691-05447-9 (alk. paper)